The Establishment of Communist Regimes in Eastern Europe, 1944–1949

The Establishment of Communist Regimes in Eastern Europe, 1944–1949

EDITED BY

Norman Naimark and Leonid Gibianskii

WestviewPress
A Division of HarperCollins*Publishers*

Copyright © 1997 by Westview Press, A Division of HarperCollins Publishers, Inc.

Published in 1997 in the United States of America by Westview Press, 5500 Central Avenue, Boulder,
Colorado 80301-2877, and in the United Kingdom by Westview Press, 12 Hid's Copse Road,
Cumnor Hill, Oxford OX2 9JJ

A CIP catalog record for this book is available from the Library of Congress
ISBN 0-8133-8997-6 (hc)

The paper used in this publication meets the requirements of the American National Standard for
Permanence of Paper for Printed Library Materials Z39.48-1984.

10   9   8   7   6   5   4   3   2   1

Contents

Introduction

Norman Naimark and Leonid Gibianskii

This book is the product of a project on "The Establishment of Communist Regimes in Eastern Europe," which joins the efforts of scholars in Russia, the United States, and Europe (East and West) in a reevaluation of the history of postwar Eastern Europe, 1945-1950. The editors are publishing two volumes from the work presented at the project's Moscow conference of March 29-31, 1994. One volume will appear in Russian and will be published in Moscow. The English-language volume, published by Westview, is not identical to the Russian version. Though some of the papers will be published in both volumes, this book highlights the contributions of young American scholars, who have been able to use newly opened archives in Eastern Europe, and Russian East Europeanists, whose work may be unfamiliar to Western readers.

After nearly a half century, the Communist domination of Eastern Europe has come to an end. For five decades, the countries of Yugoslavia, Poland, Albania, Bulgaria, Romania, Hungary, Czecho-slovakia, and the Soviet zone of Germany – together comprising a region stretching from the Baltic to the Mediterranean Sea – were forced to live behind the "Iron Curtain," described in Winston Churchill's famous Fulton, Missouri speech of March 1946. Although these regimes did not last longer than a single generation, they were characterized by such fundamental assaults on individual rights and autonomous social institutions that, in fact, the period of Communist domination constituted an entire epoch for the peoples of Eastern Europe. The effect of the totalitarian system on these countries was so profound that their emergence from behind the "Iron Curtain" has been a wrenching process. But, as the papers in this volume demonstrate, the beginning of this history – the establishment of Communist regimes in the region – was no less difficult or traumatic.

Historiography in the East

For forty-five years the historiography of the emergence of Communist regimes in Eastern Europe was confronted with nearly insuperable obstacles. Researchers from the countries of "real socialism," as well as from all over the world, were denied access to critical documents on the subject from archives in the region and from the Soviet Union. The Kremlin and the East European governments attempted to draw a picture of events according to their own propagandistic needs, systematically withholding relevant documents. This practice persisted even after the death of Stalin. The total inaccessibility of documents – which continued in effect until the collapse of the Communist system – was most pronounced in the Soviet Union and in the more conservative regimes of Eastern Europe. But even in those countries whose regimes had undergone significant liberalization after 1956, like Poland or Hungary, researchers' access to important documents was extremely limited. The practices of censorship by regimes and self-censorship by historians magnified the deficiencies of serious scholarship on the postwar period.

Access to critical materials having to do with the 1940s was, however, made possible in some cases as a result of cataclysmic events in the Communist world. For example, in the wake of the Soviet-Yugoslav conflict that exploded in 1948 and the fierce anti-Tito campaign launched by Stalin and his henchmen as a result, the Yugoslav government began to publish previously secret material about relations between the Kremlin and the Yugoslav Communists; about the genesis of the conflict; and about discrete episodes in the creation of the Cominform.[1] These publications contained a great deal of factual material that provided unusual insights into relations between Moscow and her East European subordinates during the period of the formation of the Soviet bloc. At the same time, the Yugoslav publications were governed by the canons of Communist propaganda: documents were selected in conformance with the political interests of the Yugoslav government.

Another case in which documents became available due to political crisis is that of Czechoslovakia in 1968. During the Soviet intervention, a number of Czechoslovak historians and publicists were able to flee the country, carrying with them copies of important documents from the Communist Party archives. In contrast to the Yugoslav materials, these documents were published as a protest against the Communist authorities, not to bolster them. Czechoslovak scholars in emigration were also free from ideological constraints in their selection and presentation of documents. Nonetheless, the authors of these publications were limited by the amount of material they were able to take out of the country, and therefore they were able to tell only part of the story.[2]

Research on the immediate postwar period was limited in the countries of the Soviet bloc not just by the lack of available documents, but by restrictions placed by the governments on the scholars themselves. Researchers were expected to adhere to the official ideological line of their respective regimes. Of course, the flexibility (or rigidity) of the ideological line varied from country to country and period to period. In the post-Stalin period, conditions for scholarship were in this sense less restrictive in Hungary and Poland than, for example, in Bulgaria and the USSR, and even less so than in Albania and Romania. But in some senses this is a bit like drawing distinctions between the various circles of Hell. As a matter of course, in all the socialist countries historians were forced to honor the ideological pronouncements of the masters. This was particularly the case when researching the establishment of the Communist regimes, since any divergence from the official history had the potential to raise indelicate questions regarding the legitimacy of the regime.

In order to insure that historians conformed to the political needs of the leadership, the regimes introduced broad mechanisms of ideological control and direct censorship of all publications. Censorship occurred simultaneously at different levels: there were special censorship authorities, whose job it was to review all material that was intended for publication; editors and publishers of journals, who were subordinated to these authorities; and the Party organs, to whom editors and publishers sent for approval works that might cause even the smallest bit of political discomfort. At the preliminary stages, the academic institutions, which housed the work, served censorship functions. Finally, there was self-censorship among the authors themselves, who – well aware of their place in the pyramid of censorship – limited themselves according to the"rules of the game" of the time and place.[3]

In special cases, East European historians were allowed access to materials, even secret documents of the Communist leadership, that were closed to most scholars. But even with this improved access to documentation, these historians could not write openly and honestly about Party history.[4] In the historical literature of the socialist countries, the best one could hope for was the analysis of discrete and compartmentalized events in the establishment of Communist regimes. Since the end of the 1950s, Polish and Hungarian historiography has contained a number of works in this tradition, as has Czechoslovak historiography in the brief period of the "Prague Spring" in 1968. To a lesser extent, the 1948 split incited the Yugoslavs to produce a historical literature on the establishment of the regimes. If the Bulgarians and the East Germans wrote very little indeed on the postwar period, Albanian and Romanian historiography on these questions can barely be said to have existed at all. Although in some of these works there was useful archival material and growing scholarly sophistication, on the whole, the historiography in socialist countries on the problems of the establishment of Communist governments to a greater or lesser extent remained derivative of official ideological canons.

Works that openly broke with official ideology were a rarity, and usually these could be published only in the West. For example, in her work on the establishment of the Communist system in Poland, Krystyna Kersten challenged the Polish Party's view of its own past. But the book could be published only in emigration (it later circulated in the Polish underground).[5] If in some cases, such works were published in the country itself as a result of the weakening of the regime or the inattention of the censors, the aroused authorities could act suddenly to withdraw the book from sale, remove it from public libraries, and ban its further distribution. Such was the case of Veselin Djuretić's book on the struggle in Yugoslavia from 1941 to 1945, and the circumstances which facilitated the Communist victory in that country.[6]

The collapse of "real socialism" in Eastern Europe and the Soviet Union has at long last eliminated most of these obstacles to conducting research. Historians in the East European countries and Russia are no longer subject to ideological control over the content of their work. While not all archives have been opened for research, the process of declassification is underway, and more and more materials on the postwar situation are becoming available to scholars from all over the world. The changes that have occurred in Eastern Europe over the past six years have inaugurated a new stage in the scholarship of the establishment of Communist regimes in the post-World War II period. With the availability of newly declassified archival resources, memoirs of participants, and interviews with veterans of the Communist movement, scholars can ask novel questions and offer fresh insights into the processes of Soviet takeover and the Communist "revolution."

To be sure, access to previously classified archival material varies from country to country in the former socialist world, as does its use in scholarly work. For obvious reasons, the study of the history of the German Democratic Republic, including the formation of its Communist regime, has gone the furthest in opening the doors of the past to intense research and critical examination.[7] Because the GDR had ceased to exist as a separate country, its Communist Party, the SED, lost control over its archives and papers, and the new political authority in the east – the Federal Republic of Germany – had a vested interest in exploring every nook and cranny of the East German past.

In some ways, the Czech situation approaches that of the German, to the extent that the earlier Czechoslovak archives remained intact after the fall of the socialist republic. In the cases of Poland and Hungary, like that of Czech Republic, historians have gained substantial access to the archives of the postwar period. In the former Yugoslaviaa, archival access varies from country to country, although in general, historians have been able to explore the postwar period in archival sources. However, some archives of the central organs of the Communist Party located in Belgrade have been more accessible to some historians, than to others.

Romanian and Albanian historians have encountered the most formidable difficulties in their attempts to reconstruct the Communist past. In Albania, many of the difficulties derive from the conditions in the archives themselves, as well as from the shortage of trained archivists. While poor conditions in the archives are also a factor in Romania, the inaccessibility of Central Committee archives can be traced to the Ceauscescu period, when sensitive materials were removed from Bucharest during the 1989 revolution. But historians have also noted that there are disturbing continuities between the new government and the old regime in Romania. So far, the authorities are unwilling to open the Party archives, making a documented analysis of the secret police's role in Romanian society, for example, all but impossible.

Despite periodic delays in the opening of archives and in the declassification of documents throughout the region, new research and writing on the history of the Soviet Bloc is now fostered by genuine scholarly interchange and argument. At the March 1994 conference on which this volume was based, scholars from a dozen different countries presented their work on the postwar period. Historians from Poland, Russia, and the West openly discussed their views about the nature and extent of NKVD repressions of the AK (Armija Krajowa or Home Army) fighters in 1944 and 1945, and they could do so on the bases of newly released documents from Russian and Polish archives. This volume is the fruit of new international cooperation, new research and new publications in the field.

Given the pivotal position of Moscow in the establishment of Communist regimes in Eastern Europe and the formation of the Soviet bloc, Russian archival materials have become central to research on this period. Significant changes have occurred over the past several years in the Russian archival administration, enabling access to previously closed collections, especially in the former Party archives (now the Russian Center for the Preservation and Study of Recent Historical Documents, RTsKhIDNI), the State Archives of the Russian Federation (GARF), and in the Archives of Ministry of Foreign Affairs (Foreign Policy Archive of the Russian Federation, AVPRF). An enormous amount of new material on the situation in postwar Eastern Europe and on Soviet policy in the region has been made available from these archives to both foreign and domestic scholars. However, the process of declassification is sometimes uneven; the scope of available collections is limited; and some of the most important material remains inaccessible to researchers. The archives of the President of the Russian Federation, which hold the papers of the Soviet leadership, are available only to a handful of selected scholars and on a very limited basis. Other archives important for the study of postwar Eastern Europe, like the archives of the Soviet secret services or the most important military archives, are also closed in the main to researchers. Of even greater concern are indications of reversals in relatively liberal archival policies. Increasingly, limitations have been imposed on the delivery of materials; some collections have been closed to use altogether; and other materials which had been declassified have been reclassified.

Despite the difficulties of research in Russia and in some of the countries of Eastern Europe, tremendous strides have been made, not only in access to archival documents elucidating the establishment of Communist regimes in Eastern Europe, but in the publication of these documents for the use of students and scholars all over the world. The publication of materials relevant to the Communist seizure of power is particularly noteworthy in the Czech Republic and Poland. Among these publications are the documents of the leading organs of the Communist parties and the government, the secret police, institutions of ideological control, the ministries of foreign affairs, etc. In the past few years, a number of books which draw on many of these previously classified documents have been published.[8] In other cases, the work proceeds at a more moderate pace. Only a few isolated collections of documents have appeared during the past few years in Yugoslavia and Bulgaria.[9] A great deal of scholarly resources has been devoted to a series of new projects involving Russian archival and academic centers on the one hand, and researchers, academic institutions and publishers from other countries, on the other. Russian document collections which explore the relationship between Moscow and different East European countries,[10] and an extensive treatment of the protocols of the Cominform (a joint project of the Feltrenelli Foundation and RTsKhIDNI[11]) are among the first fruits of these joint ventures.

New historical analyses of the postwar Communist takeover are also beginning to appear in the countries of Eastern Europe based on these newly released documents.[12] Russian scholars are also turning their attention to analyzing the Soviet role in the creation of the socialist bloc within the context of the social-political processes taking place in the entire Eastern European region.[13] Particularly in the case of the Russians, but also in Eastern Europe, arguments about the emergence of the Communist system after World War II are complicated by deeply held stereotypes that are hard for some historians to abandon. Sometimes, historians attempt to combine uncritically the arguments from the literature of the Communist period with new archival documentation.[14] But most historians in the former Communist world, even if sometimes unable to break completely with ideologically conditioned views of the past, have made great strides in developing more veracious and nuanced renditions of the formation of the Communist bloc.

Western Historiography

Western historians of the Communist takeover of Eastern Europe in the 1940s were free of the formal ideological strictures which constrained their colleagues in the socialist world. Nevertheless, they were handicapped by their lack of access to the relevant archival materials. Without the necessary documentation, they could, at best, extrapolate the contours of the system based on second-hand accounts, instead of examining the actual processes by which Communist hegemony was established in Eastern Europe.

At the beginnning of the 1950s, closely following upon the events they described, Hugh Seton-Watson, Francois Fejto, and Adam Ulam established the fundamental lines of Western scholarship on the Soviet bloc.[15] Especially Seton-Watson's *East European Revolution* coined the terms of analysis for the Western understanding of the establishment of Communist governments in Eastern Europe. Although they were unable to use primary resources in the Communist countries themselves, these scholars and their successors attempted to compensate for this lack by scrutinizing every piece of evidence that made its way out of the Soviet bloc. Seton-Watson took advantage of his experiences in the British Foreign Office after the war to collect material and meet with East European leaders.[16] The Communist press served as important sources for these historians, as did the memoirs and articles of East European emigrants who had fled Communist rule.

Almost ten years after the appearance of Seton-Watson's book, the historiography of the Soviet takeover made great strides thanks to the publication of Zbigniew Brzezinski's *The Soviet Bloc*.[17] In contrast to Seton-Watson, Brzezinski was able to use valuable archival documents, including the Yugoslav documents published during the Yugoslav-Soviet split, and Polish documents critical of Stalin published after the 20th Party Congress. Given this new evidence, Brzezinski justifiably placed more emphasis on diversity within the East European experience. But his conclusions were essentially the same: the Communist "takeover" in Eastern Europe was ultimately designed and executed by Moscow for the purpose of extending its sphere of influence in Europe and the world.

In both books, Soviet policy is portrayed as having been finely calibrated to the task of keeping the Western powers from intervening in Eastern Europe. (This was a task that was made much easier by the relative indifference of the West to the fate of Eastern Europe, as has been demonstrated in the subsequent historiography.[18]) Seton-Watson and Brzezinski also underlined the Soviets' successful use of "salami tactics" – of temporarily allying with the left wing of "bourgeois" and social-democratic parties, while increasingly "slicing away" opponents on the right.

The underlying thesis of this historiography was refined, if not changed in the main, by the subsequent work of such influential historians as Charles Gati and Vojtech Mastny. Gati, for example, emphasized the divergent paths of the East European countries in the immediate postwar period, 1944-45 to 1948. Poland's case was "*sui generis*," he notes, while Hungary and Czechoslovakia conceivably could have represented a "third way" in Eastern Europe.[19] According to this view, then, the first meeting of the Cominform at Szklarska Poręba in September 1947 was the beginning of the end. The Czech coup in February 1948 closed off all possibilities of different paths to socialism. But before that, according to this historiography, it was not a foregone conclusion that a uniform model would be imposed on Eastern Europe. Western scholarship on the creation of the German Democratic Republic also supports this contention. In a recent book on Stalin and the GDR, Wilfried Loth opines that alternative paths for the GDR existed all the way until the 1950s.[20]

Mastny added important dimensions to the original Seton-Watson/ Brzezinski argument in his *Russia's Road to Cold War*. First of all, he was able to trace the ways in which the Soviets exploited the international context of the war and immediate postwar period for the purposes of creating "friendly" regimes in the East. Moreover, with a broader document base than his predecessors, especially with regards to East European sources, he was able to factor in the actions and intentions of East European Communists as they coincided with or diverged from those of the Soviet Party.[21] The historiography of the Soviet-Yugoslav split concerned itself with these divergencies from the very beginning.[22] But with the opening of the East European and Russian archives, these arguments – especially between Soviet and Polish, Czechoslovak, Hungarian, and Romanian comrades – certainly will be revisited.

At the same time, historians like R.V. Burks in his classic study, *Dynamics of Communism in Eastern Europe,* and Jan Gross in his earlier works, as well as in his contribution to this volume, rightly insisted that the historiography of the establishment of Communist regimes in Eastern Europe should not be limited to the political history of the Soviet takeover.[23] There can be few doubts that the combination of the presence of the Soviet army, the intrigues of the Soviet secret police, the designs of the Soviet Central Committee, and the instructions of Soviet Ministries played *the* central role in the construction of socialist governments in the region. Brzezinski and Seton-Watson had it right the first time. Nevertheless, one has to understand the societies in which these regimes were established in order to come to terms with the acceptance of, even at times the preference for, socialist solutions to economic and political problems in at least some parts of the region. R. V. Burks touched on these issues, but Gross expands on this analysis by suggesting – as have a number of British and German historians – that the periodization of the Communist takeover should be altered to span the period from before Stalingrad to the end of 1948.[24] The social, political, and demographic changes that occurred in this period did not start or stop with May 1945. In fact, the Communist takeover was accompanied by powerful shifts in the locus of social leadership throughout the area.

As a result, it is not enough to demonstrate that the Soviets effectively seized control of the area. One also has to ask why significant elements within these societies were susceptible to Communist solutions and how the Communist parties were able to transform themselves from underground cadre parties into mass parties with such rapidity. Even if the Communists themselves were disappointed with the electoral results in Hungary, Poland, and elsewhere in the region, the fact remains that a strikingly large number of voters freely went to the polls in 1945-1946 and elected Communists. The beginnings of Soviet rule in Eastern Europe did not automatically eliminate the ability of new social formations to influence their own destinies. Workers and peasants, artists and writers, returning prisoners-of-war and former underground fighters attempted to shape their nascent polities. Even the Stalinization of the region, which prevailed after the expulsion of the Yugoslavs from the Cominform in the summer of 1948, cannot be understood exclusively in terms of the manipulations of Soviet politicians. The ways in which the societies of Eastern Europe influenced and adjusted to Soviet demands affected the individual character of each of the countries in the period of de-Stalinization, and continues to affect them today.

Opportunities for Research

The opening of the archives in Russia and in the countries of Eastern Europe have allowed historians to get a much firmer grasp on both Soviet policies in the region and on East European responses and initiatives. Vexing questions about Soviet intentions in the region can be much more fully answered as a result of the accessibility of the former Party archives (RTsKhIDNI), which holds documents from the Comintern, Cominform, and a variety of special committees responsible for foreign Communist parties.[25] In the best of cases, historians can compare the holdings of Party archives in Moscow and in the East European capitals to check the sometimes differing versions of common meetings.[26] More than any other single source base, these archives reveal the extent of direct Soviet involvement in day-to-day decisions which effected the communization of Eastern Europe. They also demonstrate the continuity of the goals, personnel and institutions of the Moscow-led international Communist movement, from the days of the Comintern, through the war and the establishment of the Cominform.

Thus, the Western "Cold War" historiography of Soviet domination of the region was fundamentally on target. From the very beginning of their occupation of Eastern Europe, the Soviets manipulated East European leaders, bullied and deceived the populations, arrested and sometimes shot political opponents. They operated cynically and forcefully to accomplish their aims. For most Central Committee leaders, there is no question that the period of diversity from 1944-45 to the end of 1947 was nothing more than a tactical maneuver to prepare for the final communization of the region. Foreign ministry archives in both Russia (AVPRF) and in the countries of Eastern Europe support this conclusion.

Our understanding of the history of postwar Eastern Europe has grown by quantum leaps as a result of this new access. But the historian must also be aware of the limitations of archival work. Communist Party (and state) documents must be read with particular care. If Communist newspapers tended to describe contemporary life as it should have been rather than as it was, Party documents were often the product of internal squabbles and resolutions rather than the source of concrete policy initiatives. The language of the documents is laden with ideological Party-speak, which needs to be read with an eye towards political undercurrents and a good measure of skepticism. It is especially important to analyze documents critically in terms of "the rules of the game" played by Soviet Party and government institutions. For example, it would be easy to present a distorted view of East European realities after the war by relying exclusively on Soviet diplomatic documents sent by representatives of the Foreign Ministry back to Moscow.[27]

Despite improved archival access, critical documents remain off-limits. It is virtually impossible to get to important NKVD/MVD documents about Soviet security police actions in the countries of Eastern Europe. Although the historian can draw inferences from Polish and East German archives (and from limited NKVD collections in the Russian State Archives) the opening of the KGB holdings is indispensable to an accurate assessment of the role played by the security police in creating Communist Eastern Europe.[28] The same holds for military archives, especially in those countries – Poland, Eastern Germany, and Romania – where the Soviet armed forces played a crucial role in establishing Communist institutions.

Stalin is also a spectral figure in those Russian (and East European) archives to which we have access. The "Presidential" archives, which apparently hold critical executive documents from the wartime and postwar period, are closed to all but a few selected historians.[29] Even at that, there appears to be no opportunity to research systematically Stalin's role in the communization of Eastern Europe. There can be no question that the *vozhd'* made all important decisions regarding the fate of the region. We know that he was kept informed by his lieutenants of the major (and even minor) developments in the parties and societies of

Eastern Europe. We now have numerous sources – from Djilas and Tito to Rákosi and Pieck – that recount meetings of East European leaders with Stalin in the Kremlin and reproduce Stalin's thoughts or words. But we are still missing the kind of information about Stalin and his immediate circle of advisors and cronies that we have, for example, about Roosevelt and Truman, and that makes the historiography of American policy in Europe so much complete and credible than contemporary versions of Soviet policy.

Even with critical gaps in access to relevant archives, there is an enormous amount of work that is being done and that can be done in the future. Relatively open archives, like those in East Germany and Poland, can be used to investigate problems related to countries like Romania or Albania, where the archives are still hard to get at. Soviet involvement in the construction of critical national institutions – the military, the police, the banks, the parliaments, the parties – can be investigated using many of the national archives in Eastern Europe. Relations between East European nations can be traced, as can the deteriorating contacts with the West.

The striking diversity within the region, even within the constraints of Stalinism, can and should be the subject of research and analysis. There is a great deal of room for studies that examine regions or localities. The histories of Kraków or Sophia, barely touched by the war, are very different than those of Warsaw or Budapest, which were devastated in the fighting. Comparative work can be done not only within the region, but between Western and Eastern Europe, where the effects of the war and the dynamics of reconstruction involved many of the same processes. As Gross reminds us, there is much that can be done to further our understanding of the social history of the "Communist revolutions" in Eastern Europe. The goals and actions of workers, peasants and the postwar institutions that represented them can now be researched as never before.

New cultures were being constructed and shaped during and after the war in Eastern Europe. Fresh ideas about the role of the East European intelligentsias in their respective countries were heatedly debated on the pages of newspapers and journals. The East Europeans were actors in a drama that was conceived, if not completely scripted, by the Soviets. The way in which they chose to play their roles made a difference to the relative success or failure of the play, even if the end was never in doubt – at least in Moscow. Given the fact that the East Europeans are actors again, this time in a drama where they can largely determine their own futures, it is important to return to the immediate postwar period for both warnings and guidance.

As the organizers and editors of the project, we would like to thank those who gave the papers at the 1994 conference for making them available for publication. We are also beholden to those who helped organize the conference and prepare the volumes for publication:

olluck and Lynn Ellen Patyk of Stanford University;
ereshchenko, Nina Ivanova, and Margarite Len'shina of the
f Slavonic and Balkan Studies of the Russian Academy of
and Anna M. Cienciala of the University of Kansas. In many
ynn Patyk is the real editor of the book. Not only did she
mas. the intricacies of preparing the manuscript for publication, she
contributed greatly to making the chapters readable and consistent. The
sponsors of this project have made it possible to bring it to a successful
conclusion. We are glad to acknowledge the enthusiastic support the
Institute of Slavonic and Balkan Studies of the Russian Academy of
Sciences, Stanford University's Center for Russian and East European
Studies, Stanford University's Dean of Humanities and Sciences, the
Joint Committee on Eastern Europe of the American Council of Learned
Societies and Social Sciences Research Council, and IREX (the
International Research and Exchange Corporation).

Notes

1. See, for example, the monograph by Vladimir Dedijer, *Josip Broz Tito:
Prilozi za biografiju* (Belgrad: Kultura, 1953) which was also published in the
U.S.A. and Great Britain in a somewhat altered form: Vladimir Dedijer, *Tito*
(New York, 1953,) and *Tito Speaks* (London, 1953,). See also the pamphlet
published in English by the Yugoslavs, *The Correspondence between the Central
Comittee of the Communist Party of Yugoslavia and the Central Committee of the
All Union Communist Party (bolsheviks)*, (Belgrade, London, 1948); and *The
Soviet-Yugoslav Dispute*, The Royal Institute of International Affairs (London,
1948).

2. Research containing significant material from the Czechoslovakian
archives relevant to the establishment of the Communist regime, were published
in part or in whole in collections of documents, for example: Jiří Pelikán, ed.,
*Zakázaný dokument: zpráva komise ÚV KSČ o politických procesech a
rehabilitacích v Československu, 1949-1968* (Vienna: Europa-Verlag, 1970);
idem (ed.), *The Czechoslovak Political Trials, 1950-1954: the Suppressed Report
of the Dubček Government's Commission of Inquiry, 1968* (London: Macdonald,
and Stanford: Stanford University Press, 1971); Karel Kaplan, *Die Entwicklung
des Rates für gegenseitige Wirtschaftshilfe (RGW) in der Zeit von 1949 bis 1957*
(Ebenhausen: Stiftung Wissenschaft und Politik, 1977); idem, *Dans les archives du
Comité central: trente ans de secrets du Bloc soviétique* (Paris: Michel, 1978);
idem, *The Short March* (London: C. Hurst, 1987; idem, *Report on the Murder of
the General Secretary* (Columbus: Ohio State University Press, 1990).

3. Information supplied by L. Ia. Gibianskii.

4. See, for example, the editions of books by Mito Isusov published before 1990,

e.g., *Politicheskite partii v Bulgariia, 1944-1948* (Sofia: Nauka i Izkustvo, 1978); and *Komunisticheskata partiia i revolyutsionniiat protses v Bulgariia, 1944-1948* (Sofia: Partizdat, 1983), and those afterwards: *Poslednata godina na Traicho Kostov* (Sofia: Khristo Botev, 1990) and *Stalin i Bulgariia* (Sofia: Universitetsko Izdatelstvo "Sv. Kliment Okhridski," 1991). The author, in fact, had access to the same archival materials, but could write one thing before 1990, and another after.

5. Krystyna Kersten, *Narodziny systemu władzy, Polska 1943-1948* (Paris, 1986). [English] *The Establishment of Communist Rule in Poland, 1943-1948* (Berkeley: University of California Press, 1991).

6. Veselin Djuretić, *Saveznici i jugoslovenska ratna drama.* Knj. 1-2, (Beograd: Balkanološki institut SANU, 1985). A decade ago, the arbiters of Yugoslav historiography organized a cruel campaign against books by Rasim Hurem, especially *Kriza narodnooslobodilačkog pokreta u Bosni i Hercegovini krajem 1941 i početkom 1942 godine* (Sarajevo: Svjetlost, 1972), which deviated from the official portrayal of Communist Party politics in the early phase of the revolution in Yugoslavia. See, for example, the lecture of the former director of the Institute of Contemporary History in Belgrade, Pero Morača, "O jednoj interpretaciji razvitka NOP-a u Bosni i Hercegovini krajem 1941 i početkom 1942 godine" at the November 1973 conference in Sarajevo, and the discussion of this lecture at the same conference: *A VNOJ i narodnooslobodilačka borba u Bosni i Hercegovini (1942-1943). Materijali sa naučnog skupa održanog u Sarajevu 22 i 23 novembra 1973 godine* (Beograd, 1974).

7. Some 650 topics of research have been registered with the Deutsche Bundestag *Enquete-Kommission: "Aufarbeitung von Geschichte und Folgen der SED Diktatur in Deutschland." Forschungsprojekte zur DDR-Geschichte im Mannheimer Zentrum für Europaische Sozialforschung (MZES).* Bearbeitet von Thomas Heimann unter Mitarbeit von Ralf Eicher aund Stefan Wortmann (Der Universität Mannheim, 1994). An example of actual recent research is *Historische DDR-Forschung: Aufsätze und Studien.* Herausgegeben von Jürgen Kocka (Berlin: Akademie Verlag, 1993).

8. For example, the Institute of Political Research of the Polish Academy of Sciences has published the series *Dokumenty do dziejów PRL* (Documents on the History of the Polish People's Republic). The series has included such collections of materials from the Polish archives as A. Kochański, ed., *Protokółobrad KC PPR w maju 1945 g.* (Warszawa: Instytut Studiów Politycznych PAN); A. Kochański, ed., *Protokoły posiedzeń Biura Politycznego KC PPR 1944-1945* (Warszawa: Instytut Studiów Politycznych PAN, 1992); Z. Palski, ed., *Agentura informacji wojskowej w latach 1945-1956* (Warszawa: Instytut Studiów Politycznych PAN, 1992). Other examples are two series published by the Institute of Contemporary History of the Academy of Sciences of the Czech Republic. One of them, *Dokumenty o perzekuci a odporu.* For materials from this series pertaining to the establishment of the Communist regime, see: K. Kaplan, ed., *Zemřelí ve věznicích a tresty smrti 1948-1956. Seznamy* (Praha: Ústav pro soudobé dějiny, 1991); K. Kaplan, J. Váchová, eds. *Protistátní letáky 1948.*

Dokumenty (Praha: Ústav pro soudobé dějiny, 1995). Another series, *Sešity*, includes the following collections of documents relevant to that period: Sv. I. R. Jičín, K. Kaplan, K. Krátký, J. Šilar, eds., *Československo a Marshallův plán.* *Sborník dokumentků* (Praha: Ústav pro soudobé dějiny ve spolupráci se Státním ústředním archivem, 1992); Sv. 2, K. Kaplan, ed., *Kádrová nomenklatura KSČ 1948-1956. Sbornik dokumentů* (Praha: Ústav pro soudobé dějinu ČSAV, 1992); Sv. 4, K. Kaplan, ed., *Pražské dohody 1945-1947. Sborník dokumentů* (Praha: Ústav pro soudobé dějiny ČSAV, 1992); Sv. 7, K. Kaplan., ed. *Připrava Ústavy ČSR v letech 1946-1948. Diskuse v Národní frontě a názory expertů. Soubor dokumentů* (Praha: Ústav pro soudobé dějiny. AV ČR ve spolupráci se Státním ústředním archivem, 1993); Sv. 15, K. Kaplan, ed., *K politickým procesům v Československu 1948-1954. Dokumentace komise ÚV KSČ pro rehabilitaci 1968,* (Praha: Ústav pro soudobé dějiny. AV ČR, 1994).

9. In Bulgaria, this collection of documents about the establishment of the ideological control of the Communist Party over the research and instruction of the history of the second half of the 1940s: B. Mutafchieva, B. Chichovska, ed., *Sudit nad istoritsite. Bulgarskata istoricheska nauka. Dokumenti i diskusii. 1944-1950.* V. I. (Sofia: Akademichno izdatelstvo "Prof. Marin Drinov," 1995). In Yugoslavia, at the time of the collapse of the former government in 1991, a volume of protocols and other Communist Party documents from the end of 1943-1945 was published: B. Petranović, Lj. Marković, eds., *Zapisnici NKOJ-a i Privremene vlade DFJ, 1943-1945* (Beograd: Memorijalni centar "Josip Broz Tito," 1991).

10. See for example: B. Bonwetsch, B. Bordiugov, N. Naimark, eds., *SVAG: Upravlenie propagandoi (informatsiei) i S. I. Tiul'panov. Sbornik dokumentov, 1945-1949* (Mosow: "Molodaia Rossii," 1994). A. F. Noskova, ed., *NKVD i pol'skoe podpol'e, 1944-1945. Po "ocobym papkam" I. V. Stalina* (Moscow: 1994). The result of the cooperation of Russian and Polish historians and archivists is a volume of documents from the funds of RTsKhIDNI on the mechanisms of the subordination of Poland to the Soviet Union from 1944-1949, published in Moscow and Warsaw: G. Bordiugov, G. Matveev, A. Koseskii, A. Pachkovskii, eds., *SSSR –Pol'scha. Mekhanismy podchineniia. 1944-1949. Sbornik dokumentov* (Moscow: AIRO-XX, 1995); G. Bordiugow, A. Kochański, A. Koseski, G. Matwiejew, A. Paczkowski, eds., *Polska-ZSRR. Struktury podległości. Dokumenty WKP (B). 1944-1949* (Warszawa: Institut Studiów Politycznych PAN, 1995). In addition to this, the Institute of Political Studies of the Polish Academy of Sciences has published a five-volume series, "Z archiwów sowieckich," (From the Soviet Archives), which consists of Russian archival materials that Moscow transferred to the Polish government in 1992, and the three last volumes contain documents pertaining to the period of the Communist seizure of power in Poland: Vol. III, W. Roszkowski, ed. *Konflikty polsko-sowieckie 1942-1944* (Warszawa: Instytut Studiów Politycznych PAN, 1993); Vol. IV, T. Strzembosz, ed., *Stalin a Powstanie Warszawskie* (Warszawa: Instytut Studiów Politycznych PAN, 1994); Vol. V, A. Paczkowski, ed., *Powrót żołnierzy AK z sowieckich łagrów* (Warszawa: Instytut Studiów Politycznych

PAN, 1995).

11. G. Procacci, G. Adibekov, A. Di Biagio, L. Gibianskii, et al., *The Cominform: Minutes of the Three Conferences 1947/1948/1949,* (Milan: Feltrinelli Foundation, 1994).

12. Unfortunately, it is impossible to offer a complete list of the materials which have been published in the past few years. For this reason, we will limit ourselves to a few examples which are characteristic to particular countries of East Europe. Aside from new editions of works by certain Eastern European historians – for example, Krystyna Kersten and Karl Kaplan – who were previously published in the West prior to the collapse of the Communist regimes, the series "Sešita" deserves mention. Published by the Institute of Contemporary History in Prague, it includes not only individual documents, but also monographs and collections of articles about the establishment of Communist power. This series includes: Vol. 6, K. Kaplan, ed., *Majetkové zdroje KSČ v letech 1945-1952,* (Praha: Ústav pro soudobé dějiny ve spolupráci se Státním ústředním archivem, 1993); Vol. 8, Š. Šutaj, ed., *"Akcia Juh". Odsun Mad'arov zo Slovenska do Čiech v roku 1949* (Praha: Ústav pro soudobé dějiny, 1993); Vol. 10, K. Kaplan, ed., *Aparát ÚV KSČ v letech 1948-1968. Studie a dokumenty* (Praha: Ústav pro soudobé dějiny AV ČR, 1993). Volumes 14, 20, and 22 of this series also contain extensive documentation on various questions from this period.

On the establishment of the Communist regime in Poland, see, for example: S. Kondek, *Władza i wydawcy. Polityczne uwarunkowania produkcji książek w Polsce w latach 1944-1949* (Warszawa, 1993); W. Tkaczow,. *Powstanie i działność organów informacji Wojska Poskiego w latach 1943-1948. Kontrwywiad wojskowy* (Warszawa, 1994). For Romanian works see: Gh. Buzatu *Istoria interzisa* (Craiova: Curierul Cojean, 1990); and N. Baciu, *Agonia Romaniei, 1944-1948* (Cluj-Napoca: Editura Dacia, 1990). In addition to these last Romanian titles, Romanian historians devoted a special issue of the journal *Revista istorica,* No. 7-8 (1993) to the establishment of the Communist regime in Romania. See also the collection of articles by Romanian and some foreign authors about the communization of Romania: *6 Martie 1945. Inceputurile comunizarii Romaniei* (Bucuresti: Editura Enciclopedica, 1995). For works by Bulgarian historians, see the previous reference to the books by Mito Isusov. For works published by historians from the new countries of the former Yugoslavia, see: B. Petranović, *Balkanska federacija 1943-1948* (Beograd, 1991); J. Vodušek-Starič, *Prevzem oblasti 1944-1946* (Ljubljana: Cankarjeva založba, 1992).

13. T. V. Volokitina, G. P. Murashko, A. F. Noskova, *Narodnaia demokratiia; mif ili real'nost? Obshchestvenno-politicheskie protsessy v Vostochnoi Evrope, 1944-1948 gg.,* (Moscow: "Nauka," 1993); L. Ia. Gibianskii, ed., *U istokov "sotsialisticheskogo sodruzhestva": SSSR i vostochnoevropeiskie strany v 1944-1949 gg.,* (Moscow: "Nauka," 1995).

14. See, for example, Volokitina, Murashko, Noskova, *Narodnaia demokratiia.*

15. Hugh Seton Watson, *The East European Revolution,* (London: Methuen, 1950); Francois Fejto, *Histoire des demoraties populaires,* (Paris: Editions du

Seuil, 1952); Adam Ulam, *Titoism and the Cominform*, (Cambridge, Mass.: Harvard University Press, 1952)

16. See Hugh Seton-Watson, "Thirty Years After," in Martin McCauley, ed., *Communist Power in Europe, 1944-1949* (London: Macmillan, 1977), 220-221.

17. Zbigniew Brzezinski, *The Soviet Bloc: Unity and Conflict*, (Cambridge, Mass.: Harvard University Press, 1960).

18. Geir Lundestad, *The American Non-Policy towards Eastern Euorpe, 1943-1944*, (Oslo: Universitetsforlaget, 1978).

19. Charles Gati, *Hungary and the Soviet Bloc* (Durham, N.C.: Duke University Press, 1986).

20. Wilfried Loth, *Stalin's ungeliebtes Kind:Warum Moskau die DDR nicht wollte* (Berlin: Rohwolt, 1994).

21. Vojtech Mastny, *Russia's Road to Cold War* (New York: Columbia University Press, 1979).

22. Adam Ulam, *Titoism and the Cominform* .

23. R. V. Burks, *The Dynamics of Communism in Eastern Europe* (Princeton, N.J.: Princeton University Press, 1961); Jan T. Gross, "Social Consequences of War: Preliminaries to the Study of the Imposition of the Communist Regime in East Central Europe." *Eastern European Politics and Societies*, vol. 3 (Spring, 1989).

24. Martin Broszat, *Von Stalingrad zu Währungsreform* (Munich: R. Oldenbourg Verlag, 1988); and Martin McCauley ed., *Postwar Eastern Europe*.

25. See J. Arch Getty and V. P. Kozlov ed., *A Reseach Guide. The State Archival Service of the Russian Federation. Russian Center for the Preservation and Study of Documents of Contemporary History* (formerly the Central party Archive). (Moscow: Blagovest, Ltd. U.S.A.: Center for the Study of Russia and the Soviet Union, 1993).

26. The Cold War International History Project Bulletin has made important efforts to compare documents from archives in Moscow, Eastern Europe and the U.S.A. See, for example, issues 1-4, 1993-94.

27. T. V. Volokitina, G. P. Murashko, A. F. Noskova, *Narodnaia Demokratiia*.

28. Norman M. Naimark, "'To Know Everything and to Report Everything Worth Knowing': Building the East German Police State, 1945-49." Cold War International History Project. Woodrow Wilson International Center for Scholars. Working Paper No. 10.; and his "Revolution and Counterrevolution in Eastern Europe" in Christiane Lemke and Gary Marks ed., *The Crisis of Socialism in Europe* (Durham and London: Duke University Press, 1992), 61-83.

29. See Dmitri Volkogonov, *Triumpf i tragediia* (Moscow: Izd-vo Agenstva pechati Novosti, 1989).

1

War as Revolution[1]

Jan Gross

The general thrust of my thinking on the subject matter that concerns us here is to conceive of a society's experiences of war and occupation as if they were endogenous. This may not be a particularly original insight, but it departs from routinely adopted historiographical approaches in which states or societies *drawn* into war or put under occupation are studied primarily as objects exposed to external, imposed, circumstances. What this means in practical terms is that we are much more likely to find political histories of occupation regimes, than social histories of countries under occupation.

And yet all social systems, at all times, operate within sets of constraints that they do not control, or cannot anticipate.[2] This is a trivial point again, and one should be reminded that in some historical circumstances (such as war between states, for example) these externalities might be uniquely non-negotiable and intrusive. But then, conversely, we might think of internal circumstances that are uniquely, so to speak, non-negotiable and intrusive. And the impact of some such factors would be no less decisive and disruptive on the course of – [otherwise "normal"?] societal development. *Pace* assorted Marxist writings about the role of individual in history, no serious student of the 20th century would hesitate to list Hitler's willfulness as a major force shaping the destiny of Russia.

I would propose, accordingly, that the wartime history of Poland, for example, ought to be written within the same mind-set and methodological approach as the wartime history of, say, Germany. Even though the substance of respective narratives would be unique, we would still seek answers to similar sets of questions. What effect does prolonged stress has on collective life? Where do people look for authority under stress or terror? When new elites emerge in various walks of life, given new opportunities for social mobility, what are they like? What happens when adult men are absent from their households? How is the labor force, and family structure and life, affected by the unprecedented activation of young people and women?

Such a research agenda, expanded and refined well beyond a few sample questions, would enable us to view how a given society copes with the enormous jolt which a war delivers to its various institutions and patterns of interaction. In this sense a social history of society/state subject to war and/or occupation could make us think of war as a revolution. Before they were confined to a common lot in the Soviet bloc, the countries of East Central Europe were not particularly interested in one another. What little regional cooperation there was among them during the interwar period – the Little Entente – was directed against one of the countries of the region, namely Hungary. Attempts to develop federalist solutions during World War II were also scuttled, this time by Soviet diplomacy.[3] From the perspective of the year 1950, when all countries of East Central Europe had been securely fitted into the "camp" of People's Democracies with a remarkably similar framework of mono-party institutions ("geographically contiguous replica-regimes" they were called in a recent study)[4], it would have been impossible to guess how much these countries' internal developments had differed throughout the decades prior to the consolidation of Communist rule. Their wartime histories were as varied as could be. Some ended up in the Axis camp, some with the Allies; some occupied, some not; some dismembered, some with their territory actually expanded. When the Ribbentrop-Molotov pact was signed in August 1939, it met with gloom and confused disbelief all over Europe, except in Bulgaria. There, the pact was widely acclaimed and the position of the CPB significantly enhanced. Soon, several hundred Bulgarian leftists who fought in the Spanish Civil War had their citizenship restored, while Russian books, films, and newspapers were allowed into the country. A loyal Axis member, Bulgaria nevertheless managed to maintain diplomatic relations with the Soviet Union through the summer of 1944. It did not send troops to the Eastern front, or its Jewish citizens to extermination camps.[5]

Bulgaria's neighbor, Romania, and also Hungary, would not tolerate any overt pro-Russian activity. Politics in both countries were quite lively, with cabinets changing, coalitions being worked out, and opposition politicians speaking out. The leaderships oscillated between the conservative and the radical right, with the latter gaining the upper hand in the last months of the war in Hungary. This, as we know, led to horrible consequences for the Jewish minority there. Romanian Jews, though not surrendered to the Germans, suffered murderous pogroms by the Iron Guard and mass deportations to Transistria where many thousands died.

Yugoslavia vacillated at first between a pro-Western and a pro-Axis orientation. It was then occupied and dismembered, and a ferocious civil war ensued in which the Communist underground, in the context of a complex tribal and national mosaic, proved victorious in the end. Over 10% of Yugoslavia's population died of war-related causes. This was the second highest casualty rate in World War II, surpassed only by the tragedy in Poland.[6]

Divided in September 1939 between the USSR and Germany, Poland suffered proportionally the greatest material and population losses of all belligerents in the Second World War.[7] In a unique response to the long lasting terrorism of the German occupation, Polish society went underground and built a complex set of institutions encompassing a framework of political parties, welfare administration, cultural outlets, numerous daily and periodical publications, a school system, a parallel economy, and a clandestine volunteer army.

Czechoslovakia, dismembered even prior to the outbreak of the war, had a segment of its territory integrated into the Reich, another one set-up as a new state, and yet another given the transitory status of Protectorate and placed under a "Quisling" administration. But it was a "Quisling" administration which deferred for a long time to the exiled President of the Republic who headed a pro-Allied government in London, while the leader of the newly created puppet state defied German orders from the time he became convinced that they were incompatible with Slovak patriotism or Christian ethics. After the summer of 1942, Father Tiso halted further deportations of Jews to extermination camps, and only after Germany had occupied Slovakia in September 1944 to suppress the Slovak National Uprising did the killings resume. Still, one third of Slovak Jews survived the war.[8]

Already from these brief outlines we can see that there *were* indeed many different national roads to socialism.

So much for variety. But the same story can be told in a number of ways. What I have sketched so far conforms to the more or less standard account of wartime experiences in East Central Europe. Yet when we adopt another lens, we can focus on the social fabric of these societies rather than on political outcomes – on material life and processes rather than on the facades of institutions and policies. If we further consider the meaning of demographic trends rather than police actions, and that of public opinion rather than government's declarations, we are likely to get a different handle on the story. Let me direct attention first to the political economy of the war years, to the material life, where even a brief perusal of a few important themes reveals the complexity of the issues. We know, of course, that the region's economy suffered a widespread destruction of infrastructure under Nazi domination. But this result of the war, which we all grasp intuitively, should not prevent us from scrutinizing the economic processes that went on for the half a decade when Nazi influence was paramount. War is a powerful stimulus of economic growth. It turns out that a significant part of the area in question was not an exception to this general rule.

Perhaps the most dynamic growth was in the production of raw materials. Extraction of hard coal in Poland increased by 50% from 1939 to 1944, and the production of brown coal increased at a similar pace in Czechoslovakia. Polish oil fields increased production by 60%, while in Hungary the oil industry was virtually created during those years and by 1944, had attained a respectable one-fourth of the annual Romanian output. The production of natural gas doubled in Poland and in Romania. The production of chrome trippled in Yugoslavia, while production of bauxite (the basis of the aluminum industry and a substitute for copper) doubled in Hungary where, incidentally, the production of aluminum during those years increased nine-fold. Taking 1939 as the base, the combined index for electrical power produced in Bulgaria, Czechoslovakia, Hungary, and Poland reached 141 by the year 1944.[9]

The years 1938-1944 in Hungary, for instance, were a boom period of industrialization financed in large part by German capital. In only two years, from 1938 to 1940, the growth of manufacturing industry exceeded that achieved over the preceding two decades. In 1943, at the peak of production, industrial output was 38% higher than before the war. "Livestock increased by 11 percent during the war and at the time of the Russian invasion [i.e. at the end of the war] eighteen million metric quintals of cereals were housed in public stores."[10] On a smaller scale, Bohemia, and Moravia registered a robust growth at the time as well (particularly in the 1941-1944 period). Even in such backwards regions as Slovakia "the regime managed to solve economic problems to the surprise even of those who were favorably inclined to the regime... the situation in Slovakia is better from the point of view both of real wages and of the supply of goods,"[11] wrote a Slovak Communist functionary, Gustav Husak, in a secret report dispatched to Moscow in July 1944. Starting with a very low base in 1939, industrial production during the war increased in Slovakia more rapidly than in the Protectorate. The index of total industrial production for Bulgaria: industrial production shows less robust change after a significant spurt in 1939-1941 but, nevertheless, it stands at 112 for the year 1945 (with 1939 taken as a base). And among important the economic legacies of war in Albania should be counted considerable road networks and numerous bridges constructed by the Italians.[12]

Depending on the degree of integration, or planned future integration with the Reich,[13] the overall pattern of development in a given area (such development as there was) targeted intensification of agricultural production and favored raw-materials production to the neglect of consumer goods or industry. But even with respect to parts of Poland – that is, the most devastated country during the war – incorporation into the Reich was followed by a policy of comprehensive development. In what was called Warthegau (an area wedged between the Vistula and Oder rivers) industrial employment increased threefold – from 90,000 to 263,000 workers – between 1940 and 1943.[14] As a general indicator of trends, let me quote the cautious assessment of economic historians regarding Bulgaria, which was least affected during the war by occupation and military activity, and where "agricultural development was less favorable than that of some other countries which were more directly involved in the war."[15]

Clearly, one must recognize that there were processes under way at the time in East Central Europe which cannot be simply subsumed under some notion of "war ravages." Of course, we must take this "rosy" account with a grain of salt. I drew a deliberately one-sided picture to be polemical with standard accounts. But what moves me to do so is not simply contentiousness but also the conviction that conventional narratives lose sight of a process that lasted several years and left important imprints on the affected societies.

What kind of insights can we gain by considering the political economy of the war years? With respect to structural changes, for instance, I would point out that economies of the region experienced growing autarky and a decoupling from international trade comprising the whole continent. Most of the industrial potential of the area was harnessed to supply the needs of the German war economy. In the territories directly under German control, such as Poland or Bohemia and Moravia, this was a simple matter resolved through administrative measures. But massive German acquisitions of French-, British-, and Belgian-held capital took place in Yugoslavia, Romania, and Hungary as well. "In 1940, 44 percent of Romanian exports went to Germany, compared to 19 percent in 1937. In the same year 59 percent of Bulgarian, 49 percent of Hungarian, and 36 percent of Yugoslav exports went to Germany." German capital participation in Slovak industry increased from 4 percent in 1938 to 52 percent in 1942.[16]

Accordingly, we ought to note that the area partook during this period in a new international division of labor designed to support the imperial ambitions of the German Reich. It was an ideologically motivated division of labor as the economic role of various territories was to a significant degree determined by Nazi racial doctrines, or, should we rather say, Hitler's idiosyncrasies.[17] Furthermore, throughout the period, local economies were gradually taken over by the state. This was most conspicuous in the countries under direct German occupation, and in the expropriation of Jewish property. But measures to this effect were executed in every country in the region.

Hence, at least five years before the Soviet Union established its domination in the region, local economies were redirected away from the West and gradually taken over by the state. And as government intervention in an economy fosters coordination and planning – indeed German planning for coal and steel production, for example, was particularly effective in stimulating Czech and Polish output – we may surmise that the conclusions of a leading authority on Balkan economic history, that "the Bulgarian experience during the Second World War laid important economic groundwork for the postwar practice of central planning,"[18] could apply equally to other countries in the region. They apparently do, as another author attests, in the case of Romania where "the dictatorship of King Carol II, reinforced by the demands of Nazi Germany, had built the rudiments of a central planning system which the Communists were able to exploit and were encouraged to do so by Stalin."[19]

Were we to move from the consideration of the region's economies' institutional framework to that of individual behavior, we ought to take note, for example, of the effect that expropriations and take-overs must have had on the inhabitants of East Central Europe. Such actions conspicuously demonstrated that property rights were dependent on a state's good will and could be eliminated with the stroke of a pen. This, of course, effectively undermined confidence and dampened the entrepreneurial spirit of indigenous would-be capitalists. Labor discipline and the work ethic collapsed (a significant drop in labor productivity was universally reported from the region) as people realized that the German war effort for which their work was being harnessed did not coincide with their own long-term interests (that Germany would lose the war was commonly believed from about mid-1942 onward) or, even worse, reduced their own prospects of survival. Second economies, with all the demoralization that they entail, prospered as never before. In an admirable book a literary critic showed how the Poles had experienced, among other effects of the occupation, alienation from work in the purest Marxist sense of the term.[20] Work – one of the major means for socializing people by creating a basis for cooperation among them, providing links between the satisfaction of individual needs and the common effort, as well as a forum for status seeking and social mobility – suddenly lost its capacity to do so, and labor was used contrary to the interests of the group performing it. *In hindsight, then, we ought to note that a complex process of structural and social change was underway that facilitated the etatization of the economy to be implemented a few years later according to principles of scientific socialism.*

Likewise, the immense population losses and shifts which occurred during the war and immediate postwar years had a profound impact on the process of consolidation and on the character of postwar regimes. The sheer volume of death inflicted selectively upon the peoples of the area significantly altered the composition of the labor force. The destruction of the East European Jewry alone created opportunities for upward social mobility for skilled workers, artisans, entrepreneurs, and professionals that would not have been made available by any postwar reform or change in the economic regime. Additional vacancies opened up because nationalities not scheduled for total annihilation were killed off selectively, with the elites of each nation targeted in successive waves of repression. Jews and Germans, ubiquitous throughout East Central Europe before the war, were no longer there, or were radically reduced in numbers in the postwar era. They had been urban populations *par excellence*. An important nucleus of the bourgeoisie, of the middle class, was removed from the region as a consequence of their disappearance. In general, all countries of East Central Europe, except Yugoslavia, experienced a shift from being multi-ethnic to being nationally more homogeneous. Czechoslovakia, split three ways before the war (ethnic Germans constituted 23 percent of its citizenry), was bifurcated in 1947 between Slovaks and Czechs who together made up 90 percent of the population. National minorities added up to one-third of Poland's population before the war. In the postwar period, the country was an ethnic monolith – over 97 percent Polish. Romania emerged from the war with only one numerically significant national minority, the Hungarians. Together, the two ethnic groups made up 95 percent of the population, while before the war they added up to 80 percent. What did these changes mean? Simply that the legitimacy of Communist regimes was enhanced because they could take credit for providing opportunities for mobility and for satisfying nationalist aspirations?

Between the outbreak of the war and the beginning of 1943, "more than thirty million Europeans were transplanted, deported, or dispersed." Certainly, as this was a process that fed on itself, from 1943 through 1948 another twenty millions were "on the move."[21] To fill the space vacated by 2.5 million expelled Sudeten Germans, 1.8 million Czechs and Slovaks were transferred into the area. In Poland four million settlers were sent to the "Western" lands. In Germany a steady westward flow of refugees drained the Soviet zone of the most qualified manpower. In 1950, almost one-third of the population of the Bundesrepublik had not been born in the territorial area of the existing state. Edward Shils, who studied "Social and Psychological Aspects of Displacement and Repatriation," found that this continent-wide transcience generated "a widespread psychological regression, i.e. a collapse of adult norms and standards in speech, behavior and attitude, and a reversion to less mature patterns."[22] Certainly people who found themselves in these circumstances were much more dependent on the support of each state administration (and, therefore, were more pliable to its wishes) than they would have been had they lived in their native communities undisturbed by the high tides of history.[23] A grand theme still awaits its social and cultural historian: what was the meaning and impact of exile from East Central Europe?

Or think of the violence which people either suffered or witnessed at a close range. By analogy with the well established paradigm attributing the vulnerability of European societies to fascism in the 1920s and 1930s to the generalized violence experienced in Europe during World War I,[24] we can posit that the unwelcome familiarity with the violence unleashed under World War II regimes of occupation made the methods of Communist *Machtergreifung* in the subsequent period more acceptable than they would have been otherwise. One could not hope to understand the period without realization that the wartime experience of spiritual crisis, crisis of values, and normative disorganization, profoundly affected representations of the commonweal, collective good, and group interests in the societies of the region. The old operative definitions of legality, justice, legitimacy, common purpose, national interest, or *raison d'état* were put in doubt, shattered. As a consequence, there was more room for new normative ideas to form the basis for life in common. Or think of the youths who leap-frogged over decades in their life cycle to become soldiers, breadwinners, or conspirators. Thus, many were forced to assume positions of responsibility for families, organizations, or causes that their elders would never have relinquished in normal times. The social revolutions that were imposed in the postwar period allowed youth to continue occupying the center stage of society, and as such, they tapped into generational energies released by the war. And one should also mention the labor activation of women during these years. All these processes, though unwittingly, had a pronounced leveling effect on the social structure and initiated transformations that were continued – this time with explicit ideological justification – in the postwar years.

Even this superficial overview shows how, in the period of Nazi domination of East Central Europe, comprehensive processes of social change conducive to etatization of the affected societies were set in motion. Apparently, the Soviet victory over the Nazis did not entail such a radical break as is customarily portrayed. Indeed, one could point to the continuities in the dynamic of social change set off by Nazi policies, and then resumed, albeit with an altogether different ideological and organizational inspiration, by Communist parties.

Thus, a social history approach unveils an ongoing process, whereas political history suggests a more drastic rupture. The conclusion emerges that for adequate conceptualization of Communist takeovers in East Central Europe, we must change the periodization and begin the analysis with the outbreak of the Second World War. And one would be well advised to raise a another doubt about traditional periodization. When, exactly did the war end in East Central Europe? Should we not view two years beyond 1945 – give and take a few months in each of the countries – as a closing chapter of a process begun in 1939? It was only then that the destruction *cum* transformation of institutions, political forms, and social strata constitutive of pre-war polities looses its impetus and a consolidation phase of a new kind of regime begins. These two claims may seem contradictory. But so is revolution, with its contradictory claims to being, simultaneously, a closing coda for the *ancien regime* and an opening chord of a social order to come.

One must, finally, address the issue of support for policies implemented during the war by organizers of the public order, whoever they might be in a given territory. This is a very complicated matter that can be only crudely handled with concepts such as obedience, collaboration, or treason. It spills over after the war into the murky domain of "political justice." Even to deal with the responsibility of *the Germans* (on the face of it, the least problematic category of perpetrators) a new jurisprudence had to be developed for the benefit of Nuremberg Trials. On the other end of the spectrum, when Hannah Arendt brings out the role of Jewish councils in the Nazi engineered destruction of European Jewry, a heated debate flares up in journals two decades after the war has ended.[25] I wish to make a very modest contribution with respect to this issue, by signaling its complexity.

We should keep in mind that during World War II arrangements defining the source of political authority – or, more exactly, designating incumbents of positions customarily endowed with political authority – in the occupied territories were determined by the occupier. Whether there had been a Hacha, a Quisling, a Pavelić, a Petain, or a Tiso was indicative primarily of German will, not of the will of the French, Czechs, Croats, Slovaks, or Norwegians. Collaboration, in other words, was "occupier-driven." Which means also, that pointing to its absence – as, for example, in the phrase "certainly, Poland did not have its Quisling" – is of a limited heuristic value. It merely tells us that the Germans, locally, had not made the offer.

In effect, to speak of collaboration is informative in one respect – it reveals the presence, or absence, of a country (community?)-wide bureaucracy. This, of course, alludes to a complex enough social phenomenon with accompanying ethos, vested interests, considerable material resources to distribute, etc. But in the absence of collaboration, how do we conceptualize the role and function of urban administrations, for example? In Warsaw alone it numbered about one hundred thousand employees; it was not significantly smaller than the administration of the entire Protectorate of Bohemia and Moravia under Hacha. And what do we do with *Judenräte* set up in Nazi-ordered ghettos in preparation for the Final Solution? And, also, in response to the *divide et impera* strategy of totalitarian social control, how do we conceptualize the role and behavior of one segment of the local population vis-á-vis another, set apart and targeted by the new masters for more radical measures of oppression than any other group? "Collaboration" does not give us enough flexibility to grapple with such issues. I suggest that a more colloquial expression, such as collusion or complicity, would serve this purpose better.

To show the complexity of the issues at stake, and because I want to bring the Holocaust into our discussion, let me pause and shift away from the general tone of this inquiry. Let us immerse ourselves in the wartime life of provincial Poland with the help of journals kept by Dr. Zygmunt Klukowski, an amateur historian and an ardent local patriot of zamojszczyzna.[26] He was director of the county hospital in Szczebrzeszyn and a serious man. Moved by a sense of duty and civic responsibility, he enjoyed the respect of his fellow-citizens. Klukowski noted his daily actions and moods, wrote regularly about hospital business and the condition of his patients. But he also collected information from other people and reported the content of innumerable conversations as well as personal observations as he went about town. Since he was competent, courteous, reliable, and provided indispensable services, he knew pretty much everybody and people confided in him. He was a formidable informant about local affairs.

Szczebrzeszyn experienced more than the usual share of turmoil in these troubled times. Germans came there first, then relinquished the area to Soviet occupation for about two weeks, and only to return in early October. In a later phase of war, zamojszczyzna suffered German colonization experiments with the accompanying terror and breakdown of "public order," leading to the proliferation of banditry as well as guerrilla activity and everything in-between. Klukowski captured the rapid collapse of the norms of civility under the impact of war. "Shops were looted in town yesterday," he writes on September 18, 1939. "Both Jewish and Polish shops were looted. But since Jewish shops are much more numerous one heard that Jews were being robbed. It happens like this. A few soldiers come in first, take something for themselves, and then they proceed to throw the merchandise out into the street. There, crowds of Christian (!) [author's emphasis] population are already waiting, both city people and country folk. They grab whatever they can and quickly take it home. Then others rush into the store and jointly with soldiers rob and destroy everything. If a shop is closed soldiers break the doors open and it gets robbed even faster." Five days later he noted that the robberies continued, and since the shops had already been emptied, the looters broke into people's apartments.[27]

Already in this early period of the occupation, Jews were beaten up and harassed by the German authorities in numerous ways, and Klukowski duly took note of this. He also recorded episodes when the Polish population applauded or joined in these brutalities. He further drew attention to the symptoms of breakdown of social solidarity within the Polish community itself. "I never suspected that broad segments of the Polish population would be so weak in spirit and have so little personal and national dignity."[28] He went on to deplore voluntary sign-ups for work in Germany, large audiences filling a movie theater, female fraternization with German soldiers, and the plague of denunciations. "As a consequence of denunciations, gendarmes all the time take away from various people some hidden items. And they don't have to look for them. They come into a house and say up front that in such and such a place, such and such an item, is to be found."[29] This pattern of cooperation with the German authorities, even against the welfare of fellow citizens, is so routine by the summer of 1940, that we are barely surprised when reading about a manhunt for hiding Jews, of whom only fifty (rather than three hundred) showed up for the scheduled departure to a nearby labor camp. "So a manhunt began in town and in surrounding hamlets. Alongside with the police and two militiamen, quite a few volunteers from among town inhabitants took part in it, including the mayor, Borucki."[30]

Through early 1942, the Polish and Jewish populations of Szczebrzeszyn were subjected to commensurate levels of terror by the occupiers. More restrictions were placed on the Jews, they were more casually beaten up in the streets and humiliated, and they had been stripped of their possessions (although most managed to make arrangements with their Polish neighbors), but the dangers to which they were exposed were not of a different order of magnitude. "Everybody is anxious that Germans might come to fetch him at any moment. I am so well prepared that I always keep a packed suitcase ready," writes Klukowski.[31]

In Szczebrzeszyn periods of heightened terror alternate with days, sometimes weeks, of relative calm. Then, around March 1942, terror against the Jews intensified abruptly. Train-loads of Jews from abroad passed through the railroad station. Jewish residents of various little towns in the vicinity were being resettled. Belzec appeared to be their destination. Horrifying stories about resettlement from Lublin had reached Szczebrzeszyn. By early April people already knew that full trainloads arrived daily at Belzec and then returned empty. On April 11, most Jews from Zamość were taken away, and news of unspeakable horrors committed on this occasion paralyzed the little town. The arrival of the gendarmes was expected at any moment. "Most Jews keep out of sight, they either left town or hide. Some were frantically carrying things away and attending to some urgent business. All the hoodlums ["szumówiny"] are milling around, a lot of [peasants with] wagons came from the countryside and kept waiting the entire day for the moment when they could start looting. News keeps reaching us from all directions about scandalous behavior of segments of the Polish population who rob emptied Jewish apartments. I am sure our little town will be no different... Everybody in town is very tense. Many people would like this to end one way or the other because panic among the Jews spreads around and affects all inhabitants."[32] And then for a few days the tension let up. There were no more passing trains to Belzec. Until May 8, when at "about 3 o'clock in the afternoon all hell broke loose in town. A few armed Gestapo men arrived from Zamość. First they requested 100 Jews to show up for work within an hour, and then, assisted by local gendarmes, they took to their bloody work. Shots were ringing continuously. People were shot at as if they were ducks, they killed also in apartments, anybody – women, children, men without discrimination. It is impossible to estimate the numbers of dead and wounded. There must have been over a hundred."[33] The hospital and Klukowski were forbidden to tend to the wounded Jews. He is shaken by this injunction, but afraid to break it, especially after two Gestapo agents had come to look for Jews that they were told were there.

Klukowski noted at this time a general breakdown of "law and order" in the surrounding countryside. "Guerillas were all over. They took from peasants primarily food. It is impossible to tell who is who – there are Polish guerrillas among them, Soviet guerrillas, German deserters, regular bandits, what not."[34] Germans seemed unable to stop this progressive disorganization. They frequently resorted to measures of collective responsibility, killing scores of randomly picked peasants for allegedly abetting bandits. And yet the Jews had nowhere to go, they could not find shelter in the midst of this deepening disorder. "On the next morning – after the murderous eighth of May – behavior of a certain part of the Polish population left a lot to be desired. People were laughing, joking, many strolled to the Jewish quarter looking around for an opportunity to grab something from deserted houses."[35]

A new wave of mass killings of the Jews took place in the area – in Krasnobrod, again in Zamość, and in Tomaszów. In early July, some 1,500 Jews of Józefów were killed on the spot.[36] On August 8, all Jews of Szczebrzeszyn were ordered to assemble in the square, near the Judenrat, with a few belongings, in order to be taken to work in the Ukraine. Nobody showed up voluntarily. From mid-day on, local gendarmes, Gestapo, Sonderdienst soldiers, as well as Polish policemen, Judenrat members, and Jewish policemen went around taking Jews out from their apartments and hiding places. Terrorized Jews brought to the assembly point remained there in complete silence. "Quite a few Poles, especially boys, eagerly help in the search."[37]

When finally led out of town late in the evening, some Jews tried to run away. Shooting started in all directions. Poles in the streets panicked. The column of Jews was driven with blows and shots to the station. Some one thousand Jews from Bilgoraj and vicinity were taken out to the train station in Zwierzyniec on this day, as well. After this *Aktion* only "productive" Jews were allowed to remain in town. Everyday a few Jews were shot, but people no longer paid any attention. And so it goes on for a couple of weeks. The final round-up began on October 21. Nine hundred Jews were led out of town in the afternoon. Some four to five hundred had been killed right away. "Nobody ever dreamed that things like that are possible. I am completely overwhelmed, I cannot find a place for myself, I cannot do anything."[38]

The bloody spectacle continued for several days. Jews were hunted down, killed on the spot, or brought to the cemetery in groups for execution. On October 26, "I saw near the hospital, in the compound of well known rope makers named Dym, 50 Jews were found and taken out. We counted as they were led to the police station. A crowd of spectators stood around and watched. Some volunteered assistance: they ripped through walls and roofs searching for Jews, and then beat them with truncheons From opened up Jewish apartments people grab everything they can lay their hands on. Shamelessly they carry loads of poor Jewish belonging or merchandise from little shops... All of this together makes an unbelievable spectacle, hard to describe. Something equally terrifying, horrible, was never seen or heard about, by anybody, anywhere."[39]

And the same spectacle repeated itself all over the area. Under the November 4 entry, Klukowski noted a three-day long *Aktion* in Bilgoraj and Tarnogrod. Afterwards, the road from Bilgoraj to Zwierzyniec, where Jews were loaded on the trains, was covered with corpses. Those who had scattered throughout the countryside were hunted down by everybody. "Peasants afraid of reprisals catch Jews in hamlets and bring them to town or sometimes kill them on the spot. In general some terrible demoralization has taken hold of the people with respect to Jews. A psychosis took hold of them, and they emulate the Germans in that they don't see a human being in Jews, only some pernicious animal, which has to be destroyed by all means, like dogs sick with rabies, or rats."[40]

Klukowski leaves an unusually comprehensive account. He makes no apologies for anything that he had witnessed or done (as when he refused to treat wounded Jews, for example, or accepted for his hospital a "donation" of linen and household goods from the gendarmes after the *Aktion*.[41] What did he tell us then, which makes his memoirs so important? We learn from Klukowski a simple fact – that Poles have witnessed the Holocaust. This, to my mind, is the most remarkable significance of the document he left behind. For he does not tell us, in substance, anything we didn't know about the mechanism of destruction. His testimony only proves *that this entire process had taken place in full view of the surrounding population*. The most revealing information in Klukowski's memoir are two numbers he quotes from a conversation with Szczebrzeszyn's mayor: that 934 Jews were deported on the first day of the *Aktion* and that about 2,300 had been killed in town over the next two weeks.[42] These proportions may vary from town to town and from ghetto to ghetto. I would guess that from the largest agglomerations a greater proportion of the Jewish population was deported rather than murdered on the spot. But in countless small towns, where from a few hundreds to a few thousand Jews were confined to their quarters - by no means walled-in and out of sight of the Gentile population – a significant proportion, if not the majority, were killed right there. The Holocaust, in other words, was not confined to the pitch dark interiors of gas chambers and covered vans. It took place in full daylight, and was witnessed by millions of Poles who – and this will be a very minimalist interpretation – by and large did little to interfere with it. In Polish historiography, the significance of these circumstances has not been evaluated, and only barely recognized.

What happened in this little town cannot be captured by reference to the concept of collaboration. What happens to people who passively witness the brutal murder of their fellow citizens? But there was broader collusion in Szczebrzeszyn, complicity of various kinds, in the victimization that took place at the instigation of the occupiers. Again, the framework "war as a revolution" beckons our attention, for it turns out that, including the most radical measures, the war experience to a significant degree was endogenous, i.e. self-inflicted. How did this bear on the capabilities of the local population to organize their collective life after the war?

In conformity with the periodization suggested earlier, let us briefly analyze political developments in East Central Europe beyond 1945. To begin with, the mere fact of a Soviet presence in this territory after German capitulation needs to be seriously considered. In the earliest period it took the form of direct arbitration and decision making by SVAG and individual Soviet advisers placed throughout the newly established state administrations. But in addition to informal, *ad hoc*, or discreet penetration, Soviet influence in East Central Europe was well institutionalized. Thus, in the former Axis countries of Bulgaria, Romania, and Hungary, Allied Control Commissions (A.C.C.'s) were set up following armistice agreements. These commissions were *de jure* responsible for validating all decisions of the indigenous administrations. This gave the Soviet authorities an official instrument to steer policies, veto or authorize appointments, and in other ways gradually ensure Communist Party domination over local bureaucracies. A.C.C.'s were staffed jointly by the Allies, but the British and the American representatives played only perfunctory roles in East Central Europe.[43]

Spread all over each country, A.C.C.'s exercised supervisory functions on local levels without a clearly delimited sphere of responsibility. On occasion, Yugoslav and Czech representatives sat on the commissions to make sure that their countries' share of war indemnities was safeguarded. Needless to say, they had scores to settle with the former Axis satellites who had participated in the dismemberment of their countries. Now, empowered by the Soviets, they eagerly turned the tables on their neighbors. Ferenc Nagy, the Hungarian Prime Minister in 1946-1947, had many unkind words to say about the Commissions' comportment. A high foreign ministry official, Stephen Kertesz, offered an innocuous but telling example of the arbitrariness with which they exercised their duties on occasion. A commission spawned by the A.C.C. to supervise the purging of "fascist" literature in Hungary requested, among other things, that "Horthy" and all derivative catalog entries be removed from libraries. As a result, holdings on horticulture were removed since they were believed to contain Horthy propaganda materials.[44]

The point I want to make is that the A.C.C. apparatus, like the Red Army commands in the earliest period, provided local Communists in all of these countries with a wild card that they could always use against their opponents. The Allies' responsibility under the Declaration on Liberated Europe was to make sure that the reconstruction and return to normal life on the continent proceeded through a joint effort of democratic elements in society. It was also the Allies' responsibility to decide what was "democratic" in each of the countries involved. Thus, ironically, in East Central Europe the Soviet authorities were the arbitrators of this question.

A.C.C.'s were an institutional vehicle through which the acceptability or unacceptability of a decision, a program, a publication, or a person was decided. Their own rules of decision making could not be challenged and these were, as we have seen, rather arbitrary. But most frequently the commissions promoted what the Soviets or local CPs deemed to be in their interest. Thus, when involved in negotiations, joint projects, or competition with all the other political forces allowed in their countries, the CPs could invalidate outcomes that they disliked. In other words, they were bound by different rules than were all the other participants in the game. In the November 1945 Hungarian elections, the Smallholders Party received a 57.5 percent majority, and when negotiating the composition of the coalition government, it insisted on keeping the Interior Ministry portfolio. The Communists finally relented. But just before the new government was to be presented to the parliament Mátyás Rákosi, leader of the Hungarian CP, paid an urgent visit to Ferenc Nagy and informed him that the Communists must have the Interior Ministry after all. And they got it.[45]

But the decisive factor which led to the incapacitation of democratic forces in East Central Europe was neither the absence of tangible Western support nor the Red Army's firepower, but rather a new conceptualization of politics that the non-Communists were confronted with when CP organizers set out to establish a new public order. A Polish author, Paulina Preiss,[46] has provided the most concise measure of Stalin's version of totalitarianism. It was, she wrote, the sum of unwritten books. The phrase is a figure of speech, a *pars pro toto*, and she meant, of course, the sum of lives unlived to their natural end, of thoughts that remained unthought, of unfelt feelings, of material goods not produced. There is important heuristic advice in this simple diagnosis: a credible theory of totalitarianism must capture totalitarianism's historically unprecedented waste of human potential.

This is where CPs scored their decisive victories over traditional political actors. For once these actors had harnessed entire sectors of society into political organizations, they could no longer conceive of a government capable of dispensing with them entirely. Experience indicated that once constituted and framed into political parties, social forces could be called upon to govern, brought into a ruling coalition, finessed into a minority position, or they could be weakened or strengthened at the expense of some other actor. But it was inconceivable – or, in any case, contrary to experience – that they might be dispensed with entirely, obliterated, and scrapped. After all, they had functioned under local despotisms, and they had also functioned when their countries were client states entirely dependent on a foreign power. In both contexts they could always carve out some social space where they either hid or led a low-key existence. Not so under CP dominated regimes in the Stalinist period, when these various nuclei of collective life were deliberately disorganized. To put this insight on a firm footing we must reexamine the notion of monopoly of power held by Communist parties. We should note a striking aspect of the phenomenon, which is usually overlooked: the concept of a monopoly simply refers to a mode of distribution, logically and phenomenologically independent from the volume or the process of accumulation of whatever is being monopolized. This has important consequences, as it implies that a state organization which monopolizes all power in society is not necessarily that "all-powerful." In effect, the architects of the Soviet state discovered early that one accumulates power simply by denying it to others. It is only in this framework that the concept of absolute power becomes clear. What else is absolute power but that others do not have any? Thus, absolute power is produced by the incapacitation, i.e., by a process of reduction, not amplification, of the existing or potential *loci* of power in society.

The goal of accumulating absolute power in society does not get accomplished by a Communist state through careful grafting and transfer of existing capacities onto itself. Socialist parties all over East Central Europe were not unified with local Communist parties in order to win over their constituencies, to accommodate parts of their programs, or to transfer their members' allegiance to the new organization. On the contrary, in each case the move was intended as a liquidation, not a real merger. And since power derives from association ("freedom," wrote Edmund Burke, "when men act in bodies, is power"),[47] it cannot be created, moved around, transferred, or accumulated by decree. But it can be destroyed by decree, as organizations can be outlawed and people arrested, or killed. Hence the perplexing "weakness" of these all-powerful regimes. The history of the Soviet bloc offers generous evidence that shows how the Communist governments of East Central Europe consistently failed to meet their own criteria of satisfactory performance in the domains of culture, politics, or the economy. As to the Soviet Union itself consider, for example, the military disasters suffered by the Red Army at the beginning of the German offensive, now all but forgotten in the glory of the ultimate Allied victory.[48] And remember that in his own little war which he fought against Finland in 1940-1941, Stalin was forced to a draw.[49] Have not Communist regimes in East Central Europe proved exceedingly fragile? It took only a week for the Hungarian state to collapse in 1956. Eight months of popular pressure in Czechoslovakia prompted the measure of last resort, the Soviet military intervention of 1968. In 1980, two months after the conclusion of the August strikes, the majority of the Polish working class walked out on the system. We were given many hints about the coming of the 1989 *annus mirabilis*, but we somehow were unable to read them.

The quest for absolute power renders the institutions of a totalitarian state "freedom sensitive" as they are geared towards detecting and preventing spontaneous association. That the overall system's capacity to accomplish constructive tasks is thus substantially diminished is not recognized as a serious dysfunction, since the totalitarian state in its Soviet variation is not interested in power as the capacity to reach positive goals.[50] It sees power primarily as a relative attribute, which reaches perfection when the state is its exclusive repository. This novelty, I believe, took all the traditional actors on the East European political scene by surprise in the immediate postwar period. There was no space for politics left when one actor was determined to destroy all others, regardless of the social cost that this entailed. This was, if you wish, a war waged from within, and disguised as a revolution. Throughout the years 1944-1948 in East Central Europe, political parties, organizations, various kinds of voluntary associations and territorial communities were cleverly steered to incapacitate, dissolve, and spend themselves in one way or another by their own efforts. "Gradually," notes a student of Hungarian politics, "the Smallholders Party was maneuvered into a self-liquidating process which began in March 1946 with the expulsion from the Party of twenty-one deputies, attacked by the Communists as 'reactionaries'."[51] There were of course outright bans, arrests, murders, and deportations which put an end to organized life from the outside, as it were, i.e., by the secret police. But the main effort was *to get people to unhinge their own communities and associations*. They were induced to do so, writes a Czech civil servant, "for the sake of issues which seemed more vital than the ones immediately at stake – a chain of withdrawals which ended in the loss of the whole country."[52] One of the ruling *troika* in Poland, Jakub Berman, repeatedly used the word *zroznicowac* (differentiate) when describing the official policy vis-à-vis social milieus in those years. We wanted, he said in his long conversation with Teresa Toranska, *zroznicowac* – the Catholics, socialists, writers, public opinion, the peasants (and the list could have gone on until the name of every nucleus of group life had been provided), i.e., to induce each milieu to quarrel, to divide, to dissociate, to make people grow to dislike one another.[53] The "true purpose" of the KPD-led "Bloc of anti-Fascist, Democratic Parties" in the soon-to-be established German Democratic Republic, "was neither to give expression to non-Communist political interests nor to share power with them, but rather to share *responsibility* for the KPD transformation program.[54] Complicity *cum* social atomization.

In the foremost *Bildungsroman* of socialist realism, *Mother*, Maxim Gorki formulated a revealing and ominous prescription: "we are forced to hate people so that the time will come when we can love them all."[55] This preeminent "engineer of human souls" extolled Lenin posthumously for his very ability "to hate in order to sincerely love."[56] Generally speaking, the foundation of the Communists' conceived society – and one can see this during the period of state sponsored revolution quite clearly in the official propaganda which used a vile, indeed filthy language – was resentment.[57] Thus, appropriately, a prototypical activist of this regime (in addition to professional revolutionaries who stage managed the spectacle) was an *enrage* – an angry youngster – the "acme generation" they were called lovingly by a Polish litterateur.[58] Indeed, in addition to class resentments, Communist regimes freely tapped into ethnic prejudices for purposes of social engineering. Postwar population transfers provided convenient propaganda material in this context. Anti-Semitism was skillfully used to provoke pogroms intended to compromise anti-Communist opposition in the eyes of the Western opinion.[59] Appeals to xenophobia underlay rhetoric deployed against political opponents: pro-Western, ergo reactionary; reactionary, ergo fascist; fascist, ergo allied with Germany. Władysław Gomułka called the opposition Peasant Party during the June 1946 plebiscite in Poland (the plebiscite contained three questions and was run by the Communists under the slogan "Three Times 'Yes'") the camp of "Drei Mal Nein".

With this slogan we have come full circle. Apparently, the Nazi-instigated war and the Communist-driven revolution in East Central Europe constituted one integral period. We could note this by pointing out continuities in the transformation of social fabric, as well as affinities in deployed strategies of subjugation. And we also know that important protagonists viewed their post-1945 struggles as a resolution of conflicts which culminated in the catastrophe of the war. One could even argue that legitimacy of "People's Democracies" was instrumentalized via regime sponsored interpretation of the collective experience of war, rather than Marxist ideology. "Even for the postwar generation in Yugoslavia, the War was not a futile and senseless blood-letting, but on the contrary, a heroic and meaningful experience that was worth more than its one million victims. The idea was hard to challenge because our whole education – lessons, textbooks, speeches, newspapers – was impregnated with it as if our history prior to 1941 barely existed."[60] Any Pole born after the war can corroborate this assessment by Slavenka Drakulić. And a glorified mythologization of the Great Patriotic War must have been an equally prominent foundation of the Soviet regime after 1945. It was certainly a cornerstone justifying the Soviet imperial domination of East Central Europe in the perception of its own citizens. And thus we find the politically constructed experience of war in the space usually reserved for revolutions, i.e., that of a foundation myth of a new regime or imperial order. Half a century later the time has come to deconstruct it.

Notes

1. In the first and in the concluding parts of this paper, I draw heavily on my earlier study published in the *East European Politics and Societies,* entitled "Social Consequences of War, preliminaries to the Study of Imposition of Communist Regimes in East Central Europe."

2. For individual and collective actors who might think in a fit of *hubris* that they fully control their destiny, one may recommend ample sociological literature on "latent functions" and "unintended consequences" of social actions.

3. See for example Edward Taborsky, *President Edvard Beneš. Between East and West 1938-1948* (Stanford: Hoover Institution Press, 1981), chapter 4.

4. Ken Jowitt, "Moscow 'Centre'," *Eastern European Politics and Societies,* 1:3 (1987), 311.

5. It ran out of luck eventually and in the autumn of 1944 managed to gain "the dubious distinction of being simultaneously at war with Great Britain, Germany, Russia, and the United States" (Marshall Lee Miller, *Bulgaria During the Second World War* (Stanford: Stanford University Press, 1975), 1.

6. As Istvan Deak pointed out in *The New York Review of Books* (November 5, 1992) more recent scholarship concerning casualty figures incurred by various societies during World War II indicates that original statistics ought to be readjusted downward. This would be certainly justified with reference to Poland. But the order of magnitude, or relative rankings of casualties suffered, would not be affected.

7. One may add, parenthetically, that during the first two years of the war, prior to the mass murder of Jews by the Nazis, when German and Soviet occupations ran concurrently, the impact of the Soviet occupation – as measured by civilian deaths, deportations, and material losses – was far more injurious to the local population. For details, see my *Revolution from Abroad. The Soviet Conquest of Poland's Western Ukraine and Western Belorussia* (Princeton: Princeton University Press, 1988), especially the "Epilogue."

8. See Livia Rothkirchen, "Vatican Policy and the 'Jewish Problem' in 'Independent' Slovakia (1939-1945)," in *Yad Vashem Studies,* vol. 6 (Jerusalem, 1967), 27-53.

9. M. C. Kaser and E. A. Radice, eds., *The Economic History of Eastern Europe 1919-1975,* vol. 2 (Oxford: Oxford University Press, 1986), 398-417.

10. Stephen D. Kertesz, "The Methods of Communist Conquest: Hungary 1944-1947," *World Politics,* 3:1 (1950), 36.

11. Quoted by Eugen Steiner, *The Slovak Dilemma* (Cambridge: Cambridge University Press, 1973), 55.

12. Kaser and Radice, *The Economic History,* 445-448.

13. And in all fairness it must be said that such plans were not firmly set concerning territories that were not immediately incorporated. For instance, the *Generalgouvernement,* central Polish lands, were first designated as a *Nebenland,* an "over-there" territory, somewhere on the periphery, and treated accordingly. In time the *Generalgouvernement* was promoted to a *Zwischenland,* a more glamorous status of an area "in-between," presumably between the Reich and some other "over-there" yet further removed. And since in the *Zwischenland* German colonists were supposed eventually to reside, the occupation administration adopted a more conservative attitude vis-á-vis its material resources

14. Kaser and Radice, *The Economic History,* 431.

15. Kaser and Radice, *The Economic History,* 389.

16. Alan S. Milward, *War, Economy, and Society 1939-1945* (Berkeley and Los Angeles: University of California Press, 1979); Steiner, *The Slovak Dilemma,* 39.

17. Thus Kaser and Radice, students of economic history of Eastern Europe, are at a loss for any other explanation as to why Germany encouraged development of an armaments industry in Hungary while remaining cool to Rumanian entreaties to be allowed to do the same, even though Antonescu was Hitler's firmest ally and fielded the second largest military force in the war with Russia. The Fuhrer as a former subject of the old empire, Radice speculates, apparently regarded Hungarians as in some sense a master race, superior to Slavs and also to Romanians.

18. John Lampe, paper delivered at the conference on "Effects of Communism on Social and Economic Change: Eastern Europe in Comparative Perspective," at John Hopkins University Bologna Center, June 1986.

19. See the review of D. Turnock's *The Romanian Economy in the Twentieth Century* (Basingstoke, Kent: Croom Helm, 1986) in *Soviet Studies* 40:1 (1988), 160.

20. Kazimierz Wyka, *Życie na niby* (Warszawa: Książka i Wiedzą, 1959).

21. Eugene M. Kulischer, *Europe on the Move; War and Population Changes 1917- 1947* (New York: Columbia University Press, 1948), 264. For information on population transfers in subsequent years, see Joseph B. Schechtmann, *Postwar population Transfers in Europe 19451955* (Philadelphia: University of Pennsylvania Press, 1962). The redistribution of ethnic groups which followed the end of World War II in Europe affected over eighteen million people. Schechtman, p. 7.

22. Edward A. Shils, "Social and Psychological Aspects of Displacement and Repatriation," *Journal of Social Issues* 2 (1946).

23. Communist Parties immediately seized on this opportunity. In Czechoslovakia "the Communist Party, which before the war was the only party containing both Czechs and Germans, became in 1945 a most enthusiastic supporter of the transfer scheme [of Sudeten Germans], regardless or perhaps because of its Czech-German past. The Communists profited well by this period of patriotic fervor and postwar excitement, often expressed by a thirst for revenge and for easy acquisition of other people's property. The atmosphere of violence and lawlessness terrorized not only the Sudeten Germans but the majority of Czechs as well" (Ivo Duchacek, "The Strategy of Communist Infiltration: Czechoslovakia, 1944-1948," *World Politics*, 2:3, (1950), 363.) On the same principles underlying the politics of expulsion of Germans from Hungary see Stephen Kertesz, "The Expulsion of the Germans from Hungary: A Study in Postwar Diplomacy," *The Review of Politics*, (1953), 15:2, 179 - 208.

24. See for example, George L. Mosse, *Nazism. A Historical and Comparative Analysis of National Socialism* (New Brunswick: Transaction Books New Jersey, 1978), 55.

25. I have in mind, of course, her *Eichman in Jerusalem. A Report on the Banality of Evil.*

26. Zygmunt Klukowski, *Dziennik z lat okupacji zamojszczyzny,* (Lublin: Ludowa Spółdzielnia Wydawnicza, 1958.)

27. Klukowski, *Dziennik,* entry of 23.IX.1939.

28. Klukowski, *Dziennik,* entry of 19.II.1940.

29. Klukowski, *Dziennik,* entry of 25.IV.1940; see also pages 113, 149, 183.

30. Klukowski, *Dziennik,* entry of 12.VIII.1940.

31. Klukowski, *Dziennik,* entry of 10.III.1941.

32. Klukowski, *Dziennik,* entry of 13.IV.1942.

33. Klukowski, *Dziennik,* entry of 8.V.1942.

34. Klukowski, *Dziennik,* entry of 17.V.1942.

35. Klukowski, *Dziennik,* entry of 9.V.1942.

36. Klukowski, *Dziennik,* entry of 24.V.1942 and 17.VII.1942.

37. Klukowski, *Dziennik,* entry of 8.VIII.1942.

38. Klukowski, *Dziennik ,* entry of 21.X.1943.

39. Klukowski, *Dziennik,* entry of 26.X.1942.

40. Klukowski, *Dziennik ,* entry of 26.XI.1942.

41. Klukowski, *Dziennik,* entry of 29.X.1942.

42. Klukowski, *Dziennik,* entry of 4.XI.1942.

43. "In 1943 an Allied Control Commission had been established in Italy under joint American and British command and with no formal participation by the USSR. An Allied Advisory Commission for Italy was also established, with Soviet participation, but it had no executive authority. These arrangements in Italy, which reflected the view that occupation policy was the exclusive prerogative of the governments exercising military control, served as the precedent for the armistice terms in Eastern Europe, and later for the unilateral

U.S. control of Japan. In September 1944 the United States and the United Kingdom agreed to armistice terms with Romania in which the Soviet representative on the A.C.C. was to exercise exclusive executive authority. It was explicitly understood that, by analogy with the Soviet status in Italy, the role of the American and British representatives in Romania would be limited to maintaining liaison between the A.C.C. and their governments." (Cyril E. Black, "The Start of the Cold War in Bulgaria: a Personal View," *The Review of Politics* (1979), 41:2, 167). Similar arrangements were adopted in Bulgaria. Likewise, when a complaint was lodged in Hungary about this state of affairs, the Soviets replied that they were merely following precedent established earlier in Italy where the opposite situation prevailed and where their presence on the A.C.C. was purely ornamental. See also, Stephen Kertesz, *Between Russia and the West: Hungary and the Illusions of Peacemaking, 1945-1947* (Notre Dame: University of Notre Dame Press, 1984), 39

44. Interventions at the ministerial level from the Hungarian cabinet were to no avail, see Ferenc Nagy, *The Struggle Behind the Iron Curtain* (New York: The Macmillan Co., 1948), chapters 37 and 47. Stephen Kertesz, *Between Russia and the West,* 85.

45. Nagy, *The Struggle,* chapter 37. A high Czech official, Ivo Duchaek, who fled from his country after the February 1948 coup wrote this conclusion: "For a successful revolution the Communists must have among other things a clearly favorable balance of potential outside aid. The democratic majority must feel isolated *internationally*, while the Communist minority is sure of direct or indirect support from Soviet Russia or other Communist states." For the Czechs it had been clear since Munich that the West was not genuinely interested in what regime would be forced on them. Ivo Duchacek, *The Strategy of Communist Infiltration: the Case of Czechoslovakia,* (New Haven: Yale Institute of International Studies, 1949), 2.

46. Paulina Preiss, *Biurokracja totalna* (Paris: Instytut Literacki, 1969).

47. Edmund Burke, *Reflections on the Revolution in France* (Garden City, N.Y.: Doubleday - Dolphin Books, 1961), 20.

48. One can argue persuasively that in addition to the military valor of the Russian people, the victory on the Eastern front was due primarily to Hitler's obsessions (which made him veto the initiative to create the Russian Liberation Army out of willing Soviet POWs) and Western generosity.

49. The term "Finlandization" has been coined with disregard for historical record and Finland's reputation.. The Finns fought against the Soviets and were able to win for themselves limited sovereignty when the Soviets wanted to subjugate them. "Finlandization" ought to stand for steadfastness and cunning rather than faintheartedness and misconceived compromise.

50. "While violence can destroy power, it can never become a substitute for it. From this results the by no means infrequent political combination of force and powerlessness, an array of impotent forces that spend themselves, often spectacularly and vehemently but in utter futility, leaving behind neither

monuments nor stories, hardly enough memory to enter into history at all. In historical experience and traditional theory, this combination, even if it is not recognized as such, is known as tyranny, and the time-honored fear of this form of government is not exclusively inspired by its cruelty, which – as the long series of benevolent tyrants and enlightened despots attests -- is not among its inevitable features, but by the impotence and futility to which it condemns the rulers as well as the ruled." Hannah Arendt, *The Human Condition* (Chicago and London:: University of Chicago Press, 1958), 202.

51. Stephen D. Kertesz, "The Methods of Communist Conquest: Hungary 1944-1947," *World Politics*, 3: 1 (1950), 43.

52. Ivo Duchacek, "The Strategy of Communist Infiltration: Czechoslovakia, 1944-1948," *World Politics*, 2:3 (1950), 353.

53. Teresa Toranska, *Oni* (London: Aneks, 1985), 272, 284, 285, 287.

54. Gregory W. Sandford, *From Hitler to Ulbricht. The Communist Reconstruction of East Germany 1945-1946* (Princeton: Princeton University Press, 1983), 52-53.

55. Maxim Gorki, *Mother* (Moscow: Progress Publishers, 1949), 145.

56. Maxim Gorki and V. I.. Lenin, *Letters. Reminiscences. Articles* (Moscow: Progress Publishers, 1973), 273.

57. Many decades later Georgi Markov in his wonderful book of reminiscences recounted a conversation one of his friends had with an officer of Bulgarian militia: "And now tell me who your enemies are?' the militia chief demanded. K. thought a while and replied: 'I don't really know, I don't think I have any enemies.' 'No enemies!' The chief raised his voice. 'Do you mean to say that you hate nobody and nobody hates you? You are lying, what kind of a man are you not to have any enemies? You clearly do not belong to our youth, *you cannot be one of our citizens* [author's emphasis], if you have no enemies! And if you really do not know how to hate, we shall teach you! We shall teach you very quickly!'" Georgi Markov, *The Truth That Killed* (London: Weidenfeld and Nicolson, 1983), 16.

58. Alicja Lisiecka, *Pokolenie "pryszczatych"* (Warszawa: Państwowy Instytut Wydawniczy, 1964).

59. See, for example, Krystyna Kersten's analysis of the Kielce pogrom in her book *Narodziny systemu władzy. Polska 1943-1948* (Paris: Libella, 1986); on Communist instigated anti-Semitic pogroms in Hungary, see Nagy, *The Struggle*, chapter 56. A Columbia University historian Istvan Deak wrote in a letter to *The New York Review of Books* (vol. 35, no.18): "The Communist slogan, 'We shall not give anything back,' was directed not against the former landowners, who would not have dared to come back from the West in any case, but against the Jewish shopkeepers and homeowners who, having survived Auschwitz, were so bold as to lay claim to their stolen property. The result was a number of Communist-inspired minor pogroms in the Hungarian countryside in 1945 and 1946."

60. Slavenka Drakulić , *The Balkan Express. Fragments from the Other Side of the War* (New York, London: W.W. Norton and Co., 1993), 12.

2

The CPSU, the Comintern, and the Bulgarians

Yelena Valeva

Soviet historiography's first attempts to reevaluate the history of the Communist International began in the mid-1980's, when the Communist Party Central Committee archives were opened to a broader circle of scholars.[1] The materials from these archives dating from World War II persuasively demonstrate that the Stalinist Politburo of the CPSU(b) and the Soviet government manipulated the Comintern in order to further Soviet foreign policy interests, that is, to insure the territorial expansion of the USSR and the victory of Communism in Europe and throughout the world. Even after Germany's attack on the USSR, Stalin held fast to this course, although the new situation required essential changes in the tactics of the international Communist movement.

On June 22, 1941, Stalin summoned to the Kremlin Georgi Dimitrov, General Secretary of the Executive Committee of the Comintern (ECC). In his diary, Dimitrov recorded Stalin's instructions on how to proceed in the new situation: for the time being, the Comintern was not to maneuver openly, and the Communist parties should desist from pursuing socialist revolution.[2] Immediately after his conversation with Stalin, Dimitrov called a session of the ECC Secretariat, where he summed up the radical change in Communist tactics with the maxim: everything that hastens the defeat of fascism is correct and useful. For that reason, the Communist Party should not call for the overthrow of capitalism and the triumph of world revolution;

rather, it should issue a call to arms in the struggle for national liberation. That very day, corresponding instructions were sent to the sections of the Communist parties, including the Bulgarian Workers' Party.[3]

In the 1930's, the Communist Party of Bulgaria (CPB) was one of the more active and influential sections of the Comintern. This was, to a great extent, due to the large contingent (according to some estimates, around 2,500 people) of Bulgarian political refugees who fled to the Soviet Union in the wake of the failed Communist-led uprising in 1923. The majority of Bulgarian émigrés became Soviet citizens and dedicated themselves to the promotion of the interests of the Soviet state. From 1930 to 1944, the Foreign Bureau of the Central Committee of the Bulgarian Workers' Party, led by Georgi Dimitrov and Vasil Kolarov, was located in Moscow. After Dimitrov was elected to the post of General Secretary of the ECC, the leadership of the Comintern and that of the CPB, had, for all practical purposes, merged. Clearly, under these circumstances, the Comintern assumed a decisive role in the formulation of the CPB's political line.

On the day of Germany's attack on the Soviet Union, Dimitrov spoke on a CPB radio broadcast in which he called upon the Party to "take all measures in order to facilitate the battle of the Soviet people, to oppose the anti-Soviet plans of the Bulgarian reaction, strengthen a united national front in the battle against German fascism..." In the spirit of the Stalin's instructions, he declared: "Bear in mind that at the current stage it is a question of liberating nations from Nazi enslavement, and not of socialist revolution."[4] The Party line was spelled out in a resolution from the Foreign Bureau of the Bulgarian Central Committee entitled "The Attack of Fascist Germany on the Soviet Union and our Tasks" (At that point the Bureau included G. Dimitrov, V. Kolarov, St. Dimitrov and G. Damianov). The document, received from Sofia on July 1 via radio links between the Foreign and Domestic Bureau of the Bulgarian Central Committee, defined the tasks of the revolutionary movement, the forms and means of the struggle at that stage, the prospects for the development of the anti-fascist movement, and the character of the future government. Without question, the first priority of the Bulgarian Communists was cooperation with Allied forces in the total defeat of Nazi Germany. "To this end, it is necessary to involve *everyone and everything*, without diverting the efforts of the popular front to other, ultimately more important but less immediate, purely socialist tasks. *The tasks of the proletarian dictatorship, Soviet power and socialism are not critical at the current stage of world war*," the resolution stressed.[5] By describing "the struggle against the Nazis and their Bulgarian henchmen and accomplices" as the critical issue, the Foreign Bureau laid the groundwork for a transition to the strategy of a broad national anti-fascist front: "Now we must have only one front – an *anti-fascist front*, and no others." Thus the imperative that the Party renounce "all prejudices, all vestiges of sectarianism.", "put an end to any campaign against Britain and the United States of America", and "change the attitude to the *Anglophile Opposition* in Bulgaria." "Our tactical maxim should be this: he who assists the USSR in the war against Nazi Germany shall be our ally, regardless of Party affiliation, social background or social views," the document concluded.[6]

The resolution of the Foreign Bureau testified to the fact that the Party did not intend to renounce its main, strategic goal – the struggle for the victory of socialism – but was merely postponing it until more auspicious circumstances prevailed: "In the course of events, as conditions become more favorable at home and abroad, the mass movement of the people and army should be directed against the Bulgarian government, with Boris at its head." A national anti-fascist government should be established in which the working class and its Party shall be "ensured the appropriate position" commensurate with its efforts, as well as its resolute and selfless actions.[7]

The CPB leadership in Sofia had been coordinating its activities with Moscow from the outset of the Great Patriotic War. On June 22, 1941, the Politburo of the Party published an appeal which called upon the Bulgarian people to take up arms against Nazi Germany and support the just struggle of the Soviet people. In preparing this appeal, the Bulgarian Communists used the address broadcast by the Soviet government as its basis. Dimitrov's encoded radiogram, received in Sofia on the night of June 22, outlined the anti-fascist program which had been elaborated at the June 24 sitting of the Bulgarian Politburo. According to the program, the anti-fascist resistance would seek to win over the Bulgarian army to the side of the people, disrupt the supply of munitions to the German troops, launch a large-scale partisan movement and involve all democratic and patriotic forces in the resistance movement.

The CPB decided upon this course of action in a situation that was extremely unfavorable to its realization. At a time when almost all of Europe was involved in the brutal war or under occupation, Bulgaria seemed to be a relatively peaceful oasis, where the economic situation was still rather stable. Bulgaria's status as a German satellite differed from that of other countries occupied by Germany, because Bulgaria was able to preserve its state apparatus, and the German troops located on its territory did not perform occupation functions. Furthermore, many strata of the Bulgarian population had succumbed to the nationalist wave. For, apart from the fact that in September 1940, Bulgaria had received Southern Dobruja from Romania with Germany's support, Macedonia, Western Thrace and areas adjacent to the Western border with Yugoslavia had "joined" Bulgaria upon completion of the Wehrmacht's Balkan operations. Taking advantage of the peaceful resolution of the nationality question and of the fact that the country had managed to avoid the horrors of war and occupation, the government and Tsar Boris had managed to win the trust of considerable numbers of people. The initial victories of the Nazi troops on the Soviet-German front was another factor that impeded the development of the resistance movement in Bulgaria.

In adopting the policy of armed struggle in June 1941, the CPB acted in accordance with the general line of the world Communist movement, elaborated in Moscow, and not in light of the prevailing domestic situation.This influenced the nature of the Bulgarian resistance movement from the outset. Ultimately, the CPB-led movement was aimed at the transformation of the existing system and the creation of a new society, where the Communist Party was to play at first a prominent, and eventually, the leading role. The Bulgarian Communists regarded the struggle for a government of national anti-fascist unity solely as a necessary and inevitable stage which would be followed by far-reaching social reforms, and finally, socialism. In initiating the resistance movement, the CBP intentionally exaggerated the prevalence of fascist tendencies in the country, erroneously equating the Bulgarian regime to Italian fascism and German Nazism. Seeking to involve the broad masses, the Communists called upon the working people to struggle against the "reactionary monarcho-fascist dictatorship." Thus, without belittling the importance of anti-fascist elements in the Bulgarian partisans' struggle during WW II, it should be emphasized that from the outset, the resistance was characterized as a class struggle, and as such was directed against the existing system

Because the resistance movement in Bulgaria was directed against the Bulgarian regime rather than the foreign occupation, it was hampered in its attempt to become a nation-wide movement. The resistance fighters consisted largely of Communists and "young Communists." Non-Communist anti-government forces constantly vacillated in their positions, so it was no easy task to involve them in effective action. Aware that the complicated situation in the country would inhibit the commencement of armed operations, many Communist Party leaders realized that the Party would be forced to fight single-handedly in the initial stages.

In the first months following the declaration of its commitment to armed struggle, the CPB was divided by differing approaches to technical questions regarding the timing and methods of the proposed uprising. Some Communists asserted that preparations should start immediately. In this connection, they requested instructions from the Foreign Bureau in Moscow. Dimitrov, however, was not prepared to assume responsibility without consulting "the highest instance." Therefore, on August 2, 1941, he wrote Stalin:

> According to information supplied by the CC of our Bulgarian
> Party, the situation in the country is extremely tense. The Germans

are relentlessly pressuring the Bulgarians to take an active part in the war against the Soviet Union. Although Tsar Boris and the government are still vacillating, they are making preparations to join the war. Meanwhile, the overwhelming majority of people and the masses of soldiers are against it.

Dimitrov went on to write about the situation in the Bulgarian army, particularly about the Velchev Group (Velchev was a leader of the former Military League and the political movement "Trend") which opposed Tsar Boris. "This Group," Dimitrov wrote,

wields considerable authority in the army, especially among reserve officers. It has offered to cooperate with our Party. We are holding talks on the subject. The issue of an uprising against Boris and his German patrons has been raised directly in Bulgaria. In this connection, the Party's Central Committee would like to know – *how, and to what extent, the USSR will be able to render assistance in the event of an uprising in Bulgaria.* I am in urgent need of your instructions on that score.[8]

The answer came promptly, for on August 5 Dimitrov sent the following instruction to A. Ivanov, a member of the CPB Central Committee: "After a thorough discussion of the issue in the upper echelons, we have come to the unanimous conclusion that it would be premature to organize an uprising now, for it would be doomed to failure. We shall start preparations for an uprising when it proves possible to coordinate actions inside and outside the country, which, at this juncture, is impossible. We must build up our strength, prepare thoroughly, consolidate our positions in the army and at strategic points."[9] Dimitrov also advised that Ivanov stick to that line in the talks with the Velchev Group.

A week later, Ivanov informed the CPB Foreign Bureau on behalf of the Central Committee of the Party that the Party was working precisely in that direction:

We are making comprehensive preparations for an uprising of the army and people at the appropriate moment *and in cooperation with external forces,* as well as for the respective organizational restructuring and military-technical training of the Party and the masses. We are combining those preparations with the launching of a large-scale struggle and the disruption of the Nazi rear. With this aim and in the course of the struggle, militant groups and partisan detachments are being formed.[10]

Thus, from the outset the Bulgarian Communists prepared to overthrow the existing regime, but only when they had been assured of the Soviet troops' support for the uprising. Both Stalin and Dimitrov were equally aware of the fact that in the absence of such support, the Bulgarian Communists' action would be doomed to failure. The Communists had to clarify their tactical line for those who supported the armed struggle: the left activists of the former Military League and the political movement Link, among whom were radical intellectuals and officers opposed to the idea of the masses' participation in preparations for the uprising, which they viewed as a single military act. On August 20, Ivanov informed Dimitrov of the mood prevailing among the members of the Velchev Group (which, in light of the conspiracy, he referred to as the "special" group) and solicited his opinion on that score:

> The 'Special' group insists that since we are oriented towards major action on a national scale...we should refrain from small-scale active operations aimed at the disorganization of the Nazi rear in order to avoid arousing the enemy's suspicions and interfering with the actual action, when the time for that action arrives. We believe... that well-considered and prepared discreet actions... will not interfere with, but will contribute to the success of the common action.[11]

The Foreign Bureau expressed its support for the CPB Central Committee's line. For the radio transmission of September 1, 1941, Dimitrov wrote:

> Your stand is correct. If it were a matter of a palace coup, then discreet military actions would be counter-productive. But in the current situation this is not the case, since we have in mind an uprising of the army and the people, not a palace coup. Actions to disorganize the enemy bases and rear, which rouse the masses to action, are not only not counterproductive, but are necessary preconditions of success. That there is a significant difference between a palace coup and a popular uprising is apparently not clear to the 'Special' group, and they do not take it into account.[12]

In May-June 1942, when the defeat of Nazi forces at the outskirts of Moscow indicated a turning-point in the course of the war, the CPB Foreign Bureau raised the question of inaugurating a transition from resistance to an offensive against the pro-Hitlerite Bulgarian government, with the aim of its total liquidation. Under Dimitrov, the CPB leadership elaborated a Fatherland Front program, which was oriented towards the creation of a broad anti-fascist front established on a democratic basis. The program was transmitted via the clandestine radio station, "Khristo Botev," from Moscow to Bulgaria. The program's demands were formulated so that they suited all democratic and patriotic forces. When the committees of the Fatherland Front were initially created, they included representatives of the left wing of the Bulgarian Agricultural Popular Union, left Social Democrats, members of the political circle Link and several independent public figures. For the time being, at least, the CPB deferred pursuit of its hegemonic ambitions in the interests of consolidating an anti-fascist coalition.

The seizure of power was first characterized as an urgent task for the Bulgarian Communists in Circular no. 2 of the CPB Central Committee. "On the Tasks of the Party in the Mobilization and Preparation of Anti-fascist Forces for the Nation-wide Armed Uprising."[13] The circular announced that "the Party takes a firm stand on the organization of specific actions, towards the expansion and intensification of the battle in all of its forms and in all areas of public life, with the aim of the immediate overthrow of the present government and the establishment of a popular-democratic government of the Fatherland Front" The Party, the document stressed, "shall bear great historical responsibility for the future of the country, for the future of the Bulgarian people."[14]

At this critical juncture for the Bulgarian Communists, when preparations for the seizure of power were accelerated, it was extremely difficult for the Central Committee to maintain contacts with the Foreign Bureau and Dimitrov. After the CPB radio center in Sofia had been raided (September 1941), the direct radio link was severed. Information was relayed between the Bulgarian Communists in the country and the General Secretary of the Comintern primarily by the Soviet secret service. In December 1943, P. Fitin, head of the first Department of the NKGB of the USSR, gave Dimitrov a letter from the Party leadership which had been sent via a NKGB resident in Sofia. The letter, dated November 10, 1943, began:

> Dear Comrades,
> All our attempts to restore contacts with you have thus far been fruitless. Last year you managed to find us and convey Comrade Dimitrov's message, but after the arrest of our comrade with whose assistance we maintained contacts with you, we have lost that possibility. And at present we are in great need of such direct contacts.... If you do not object, we might make use of high places [they probably meant the Soviet Embassy.– Ye.V.] which are quite safe. We think that such contacts will be of use to you, as well... We ask that you send us the cipher, bands and the time of transmission by which we will be able to communicate as soon as possible. Moreover, inform us whether you would be able to send us some ammunition and arms, both of which we need badly. The terrain for the parachute jumpers is ready.[15]

In February 1944 Dimitrov received the following information from Fitin: "Zakhari Bakov, a tailor from Sofia who is well-known to you [as the Party liaison man, – Ye. V.], has told our man in Sofia that a certain Karo Stoianova Gits wishes to establish contacts with you as soon as possible, and with this aim in mind, wants to meet with an employee of the Soviet Mission in Bulgaria."[16] On February 23, G. Karastoianova sent a message through the same channel, saying that "the members of the organization" (the Communist Party leadership) would like to learn Dimitrov's opinion on "whether the organization has taken the correct line on the armed uprising with the aim of seizing power. What kind of assistance are you able to render us in people and arms?" Further she noted that "at present the organization is 7,000 strong, the young members of the organization come to about 10,000, and all together they can't amount to more than 20,000 people. We do not have weapons, we are unable to supply arms even to the 3,000 people who are fighting in partisan detachments. The organization has established contacts with the British via Marshal Tito, and the former have sent Tito arms and uniforms for Bulgarian detachments." Dimitrov was consulted as to whether it was appropriate to accept arms from the British.[17]

On March 7, Karastoianova sent two messages from D. Terpeshev (a member of the Bulgarian Central Committee who was responsible for the operations of the Peoples' Liberation Insurgent Army – [P.L.I.A.]) addressed to Dimitrov. The first message reemphasized the seriousness of the situation due to lack of arms in the P.L.I.A., and asked Dimitrov to inform them how assistance would be rendered through Yugoslavia, and who should be informed of secret addresses and passwords for that purpose. The Bulgarian Communists also requested that the P.L.I.A. General Staff be sent military experts to guide preparations for the uprisings in large cities. The following question, addressed to Dimitrov, is very telling: "Please inform us whether it would be correct to refer to you as the leader of the Bulgarian people. Until now we have been talking about you as the leader of the Party."[18]

Terpeshev's second message provided data about the numerical, Party and age composition of partisan detachments as well as their organizational structure and activities.[19] That message was a reply to Dimitrov's questions, addressed to the Bulgarian Central Committee, about the Party, the scope of the partisan movement and composition of its leadership. Dimitrov conveyed all the information obtained from Bulgaria regarding the scope of the partisan movement to Molotov on March 13.[20]

Dimitrov received the next message from Sofia on March 19. "We are firmly resolved to prepare for a nationwide uprising not only by carrying out propaganda, but also through action (meetings, etc.). This will help the people and the army overcome their indecision and take part in the uprising," wrote Terpeshev on behalf of the Party leadership. "Our political line has convinced our allies among the political parties and public leaders that we are fighting for the popular democratic power of the Fatherland Front." The last sentence demonstrates that the Communists regarded the Fatherland Front as a "front" behind which they could conceal the real strategic goals of the CPB; namely, the establishment of the socialist system. "Partisan detachments have red banners with 'Fatherland Front' written on them and partisan badges," Terpeshev continued. "Some detachments had five-pointed stars made for them, but we gave orders for them to be removed. The banners were replaced by three-colored ones. That should satisfy the military. We shall stick faithfully to the program broadcast by the 'Khristo Botev' radio station," Terpeshev assured. "We are looking forward to receiving news from those whom you sent to Tito. We badly need their assistance."[21]

In April 1944 Fitin informed Dimitrov that at his request "a radio station shall be handed over to C-de Petrov [Terpeshev's alias]."[22] In early July, a NKGB resident in Sofia informed Terpeshev of the cipher for direct contacts with Dimitrov.[23] The Soviet secret service, in their turn, were in need of direct assistance from the Comintern General Secretary. On April 4, 1944, I. Bolshakov, head of the Department of Strategic Intelligence of the Main Intelligence Administration of the General Staff of the Red Army, applied to him with the following request: "We are in need of several Bulgarians to carry out intelligence assignments in Bulgaria. If possible, please issue your instructions regarding the selection and transfer of three to four people for training."[24]

In response to Party Circular no. 2 regarding preparations for an armed uprising in the spring of 1944, the Communists launched a campaign to recruit people to partisan detachments. The Red Army's spring offensive and the acute domestic political crisis in Bulgaria contributed to its success. To a considerable degree, the crisis was triggered by the sharp deterioration of Soviet-Bulgarian diplomatic relations. In a series of notes (in January, March, April, and May 1944) the USSR demanded that Bulgaria stop building warships for Germany, and prohibit the use of Bulgarian territory, ports and airports as springboards for waging war against the Soviets. The diplomatic steps taken by the Soviet Union had a strong impact on the political situation in Bulgaria, and actually triggered a government crisis in April-May 1944. Even the Bulgarian ruling circles were inclined to show less support for pro-German policy. Political forces advocating a reorientation of Bulgaria's foreign policy in order to save the country from disaster were now in the ascendant.

On June 1, 1944, a new Cabinet of Ministers, led by I. Bagrianov, came to power. Because of the changes in the international situation, the new government was intent on radically altering its foreign policy line: to put an end to Bulgaria's involvement in the war with the assistance of the U.S.A. and Britain, and, at the same time, maintain its relations with Germany. In that way, the Bagrianov government hoped to prevent the Soviet Union from becoming the arbiter of Balkan problems, and defuse the threat of imminent revolution in Bulgaria. The advance of the Red Army towards the Balkan peninsula added to the tensions in Bulgaria. The Bagrianov government was losing control of the situation while the Fatherland Front, led by the Communists, was increasingly active.

On August 20, Dimitrov sent a letter with new instructions to the Bulgarian Central Committee.[25] In it, he spoke of the need to expose Bagrianov's policy and reject his offers to form new government coalitions aimed at splitting the Fatherland Front. "At the current stage, the line of strengthening the Fatherland Front, increasing its action and energy, setting up a Fatherland Front government that would be a truly national, popular-democratic government, should be the main tactical line of the Workers' Party." The Workers' Party could take part in only such a government, he stressed. Dimitrov asked the Party to acknowledge the receipt of those instructions and inform the Foreign Bureau of all actions taken by the Central Committee. The Bulgarian Communists embraced Dimitrov's letter as a guide to action. On the basis of his instructions, the Central Committee refused to participate in the future government of the bourgeois-liberal opposition, describing it as unacceptable and calling for its overthrow.

On August 24, a delegation of the Fatherland Front, which had in the interim renounced its clandestine status, paid a visit to Bagrianov and demanded that he transfer power to the Fatherland Front immediately. The premier refused, but did not dare arrest the delegation. As a result, the Front decided to dispense with peaceful means and take power by force. The Bulgarian Communists began preparations for the overthrow of the regime at a time when the advance of the Red Army towards the Bulgarian border made it almost impossible for the Nazi troops to attack the insurgents, while the forces loyal to the government were likewise paralyzed. Under these circumstances, on August 26, 1944, the Bulgarian Central Committee issued its Circular no. 4, which was both a plan and signal for the beginning of a nationwide uprising.[26] Guided by that document, the General Staff of the P.L.I.A. gave orders that all partisan detachments commence offensive operations.[27]

Dimitrov was informed in detail about the political line of the Central Committee. In early September, Fitin sent information (dated August 29) that he had obtained a communication from Terpeshev via a NKGB man to Dimitrov. "We have received your instructions of August 20," the letter said.

> We are exposing the Bagrianov Cabinet and reject the attempts by
> Bagrianov, the regents and the bourgeois opposition to make us join

the Bagrianov-Gichev-Mushanov Cabinet. We are fighting for the independent power of the Fatherland Front both in the center and in the localities. We've stepped up our work in the army, involving career officers and allies in our staffs... Our allies [in the Fatherland Front] wish to become ministers, but so far they cooperate with us and obey us. They are marching with us, but they look back, for they are afraid of the masses and the possible struggle in the future.... The government is wracked by crisis. Since August 24, the regents and Bagrianov have been holding talks with representatives of political parties on the formation of a new government. [28]

In their desire to avoid a domestic conflagration fueled by external forces (the Red Army), the authorities struck a political deal with the so-called bourgeois opposition. On August 30, 1944 a new cabinet was formed with K. Muraviev at its head, and the Bulgarian Agrarian Popular Union assumed leadership. The formation of the Muraviev government was an attempt to resolve the domestic political crisis according to the plans of the bourgeois-liberal opposition. For this reason, all attempts by the government to involve the Fatherland Front in it were doomed to failure. The CPB and the Fatherland Front were engaged in preparations to establish their own rule.

On September 5, the day of the Soviet Union's declaration of war on Bulgaria, Dimitrov sent an urgent radiogram to Bulgarian Communists concerning preparations for and the execution of an armed uprising. "The Bulgarian people," wrote Dimitrov in the directive, "and its armed forces must resolutely take the side of the Red Army, which is liberating Bulgaria from Germany's oppression, and together with it, will chase the German brigands and their nefarious accomplices from Bulgarian soil."[29] On September 6 Dimitrov informed Stalin about the radiogram and relayed its full text.[30]

On the same day, the Bulgarian Communist Politburo and the P.L.I.A. General Staff met and adopted a specific plan of action. In response to an appeal by the National Committee of the Fatherland Front, nationwide strikes began, and demonstrations were held under the slogan: "All power to the Fatherland Front!" Partisan detachments stepped up their actions. They received instructions and arms from the Soviet Union. In early September, I. Vinarov, Sht. Atanasov and D. Dichev, acting on Dimitrov's instructions to unite partisan forces, formed the largest military unit (about a thousand strong) of the Bulgarian Peoples' Liberation Army on the liberated territory of Yugoslavia – the First Sofia Partisan Division. A few days before its formation, the three Bulgarian Communists sent a radiogram to Dimitrov with the request to be supplied with Soviet arms and ammunition. Dimitrov wrote in reply: "Be prepared to meet the planes... starting tomorrow evening, arms and ammunition will be air-dropped the next three nights... "[31] Scores of Soviet transport planes dropped the large quantity of armaments required by the partisan divisions in the area of Dobro Polie and Tsrna Trava (near the Yugoslav-Bulgarian border).

Between September 6 and 8, Fatherland Front power was established in more than 160 Bulgarian population centers.[32] The balance of political forces in the country had tipped sharply in favor of the Fatherland Front and the CPB. The fact that the Red Army had advanced to Bulgaria's borders by September 6-7 created favorable conditions for the seizure of power by the Bulgarian Communists. On September 8, Soviet troops entered Bulgaria without firing a single shot. The local CPB committees acted in compliance with the Central Committee's instructions to prevent military operations against the Soviet troops and offer them every support. On the eve of the Red Army's ingress, the Soviet Command established contacts with the Liberation Army's General Staff. Subsequently, in accordance with the previously elaborated plan of action, military units of the Bulgarian army which had gone over to the side of the Fatherland Front captured the Ministry of War, the radio station, the telegraph office, and other strategic facilities. At 6:00 a.m., radio broadcasts announced that the popular uprising had been successful, and that the Fatherland Front had taken power.

The documents currently available to historians clearly demonstrate the critical role played by external factors in the establishment of the Communist regime in Bulgaria. From the beginning, the anti-Hitler resistance in Bulgaria, comprised largely of Communists, was intent upon the abolition of the existing system. Guided by Dimitrov's directives and Kremlin strategy, the CPB created the Fatherland Front, and bided its time until it was assured of Soviet military support. When Red Army troops finally entered Bulgaria as liberators, German troops had, in fact, already withdrawn. Nevertheless, a Soviet military presence remained to bolster the fledgling Communist regime, which later imposed the Soviet model upon a country that had never engaged in hostilities.

Notes

1. See for example: R. N. Sokolov, "Istoriia kominterna:novyie pod-khody,"*Voprosy Istorii KPSS*, no. 7 (1989), 142 - 150; "Muzhestvo protiv bezzakoniia. Dokumenty arkhiva kominterna o bor'bie za spaseniie komunistov-internatsionalistov ot stalinskikh repressii," *Problemy Mira i Sotsializma*, no. 7 (1989), 89-92. "Komintern i sovetsko-germanskii dogovor o nenapadenii analiticheskii material," *Izvestiia TsK KPSS*, no. 12 (1989), 202-215; F. I. Firsov, "Arkhivy kominterna i vneshnaia politika SSSR, v 1939-1941 gg.," *Novaia i Noveishaia Istoriia*, no. 6 (1992), 12-35.

2. F. I. Firsov, "Arkhivy kominterna," 34.

3. Rossiskii Tsentr Khraneniia i Izucheniia Dokumentov Noveishei Istorii (Russian Center for the Preservation and Study of Recent Historical Documents) [RTsKhIDNI], Fond (Fund) 495, Opis' (Collection) 18, Delo (File) 1335, List (Page) 1-10.

4. RTsKhIDNI, f. 495, sent documents, 1941, N. 420.

5. Tsentralen Partiien Arkhiv pri TsK na Bulgarskata Sotsialisticheska Partiia [Central Party Archives of Central Committee of the Bulgarian Socialist Party] (Hereafter, TsPA pri TsK na BSP) f. 3, op. 4, d. 586, 1.1; *Antifashistkata borba v Bulgariia. Dokumenti i materiali,* vol. 1 (Sofia, 1984), 176.

6. TsPA pri TsK na BSP, f.3, op.4, d.586, l. 2-3.

7. Ibid., l. 5.

8. RTsKhIDNI, f. 495, op. 74, d.84, l. 5.

9. RTsKhIDNI, f. 495, sent documents, 1941, no. 567.

10. Ibid., op. 184, received documents, 1941, no. 689.

11. Ibid., no. 731.

12. Ibid, sent documents, 1941, no. 653.

13. See *Antifashistkata borba v Bulgariia,* vol. 2. (Sofia, 1984), 297-303.

14. Ibid., 299.

15. RTsKhIDNI, f. 495, op. 74, d. 93, l. 17.

16. Ibid. 1.18. The document provides valuable information about the well-known figure of Georgitsa Karastoianova, who established contact between the Central Committee of the BCP and the Foreign Bureau of BCP.

17. Ibid., l. 19.

18. Ibid., l. 20.

19. Ibid., l. 21-22.

20. Ibid., d. 95, l. 1-3.

21. Ibid., d. 93, l. 26-27.

22. Ibid., l. 29.

23. Ibid., l. 43.

24. Ibid., d. 94. l. 28.

25. *Antifashistkata borba v Bulgariia,* vol. 2, 5., l. 501-503. Since the latter was of special importance, Dimitrov asked that it be duplicated. It was then relayed by a special, secret communication channel with Sofia (i.e., via Soviet secret services) and by the the Vinarov group's radio station in Yugoslavia. A group of Bulgarian political emigres, led by the career intelligence man I. Vinarov, was airdropped in June 1944 in a partisan-held area in Yugoslavia and immediately established radio communications with Dimitrov. The radiogram, sent by Dimitrov to the Vinarov group, was dated August 23. However, the Bulgarian scholar D. Daskalov established that the radiogram and Dimitrov's letter of August 20 contained the same instruction to the BWP Central Committee. See: D. Daskalov, "Georgi Dimitrov, the National Crisis and the Victory of the Uprising of September 9,"*Istoricheski pregled.,* no. 9 (Sofia, 1989), 24.

26. *Antifashistkata borba v Bulgariia,* vol. 2, 505-507.

27. *Antifashistkata borba v Bulgariia,* vol. 2, 526-527.

28. RTsKhIDNI, f. 495, op. 74, d. 93, l. 49.

29. *Antifashistkata borba v Bulgariia*, vol. 2, 537.

30. D. Daskalov, *Georgi Dimitrov, the National Crisis*, 31.

31. Ts. Dragoycheva, *Pobedata. Povelia na dulga*, vol. 3. (Sofia, 1979), 586; and I. Vinarov, *Boitsi na tikhiia front*. (Sofia, 1969), 506.

32. See Sl. Petrova, *Borbata na BRP za ustanoviavane na narodnodemo-kratichnata vlast: mai - septemvri 1944*. (Sofia, 1964), 212-213.

3

The Soviet Leadership and Southeastern Europe

Vladimir Volkov

In recent years, researchers have gained access to new archival materials which reveal heretofore unknown aspects of the establishment of Communist regimes in Eastern Europe. In light of these, our old picture of events requires some revision to allow for a more complex, nuanced analysis of the Soviet leadership's views and actions. By scrutinizing the available materials for the details of relationships between the Soviet leaders and the Communist parties of Yugoslavia and Bulgaria, as well as between the leaders of the latter, we can discern much about the establishment of Communist regimes in Southeastern Europe, and about the perceived prospects for cooperation among them.

The evolution of the Soviets' relationship with their Yugoslav comrades accelerated as the war drew to a close, when the Yugoslav Communist Party functionaries began their transformation from partisan fighters into statesmen. As the Yugoslav leadership embarked upon the formation of a new Soviet-style federative state in the spring and summer of 1944, the divisive Macedonian issue reared its ugly head.[1] The Communist Party of Yugoslavia (CPY) and the Bulgarian Communist Party (CPB) were at odds over the election of D. Vlakhov, a Macedonian émigré, as vice-chairman of the Anti-Fascist Council of National Liberation of Yugoslavia. Since Georgi Dimitrov, leader of the Bulgarian Communist Party, remained resolute in his opposition to Vlakhov, Josip Broz-Tito turned to the Soviet leadership for mediation.

Tito's inquiry via Lieutenant General N. Korneyev, head of the Soviet Mission at the Supreme Headquarters of the People's Liberation Army of Yugoslavia, prompted the first of a series of telegrams from Stalin and Molotov to Tito on April 15, 1944. Leaving the question of Vlakhov to the Yugoslavs' discretion, these communications assured Tito that the Soviet Government would not adopt any decision on the Macedonian issue without consulting Yugoslavia. At the same time, Tito was informed that henceforth Dimitrov would not be in charge of Yugoslav affairs, and that Tito could address Molotov directly. This decision contravened the former hierarchy of relationships within the Communist movement, and effectively raised the status of the Yugoslav leadership. In practice, that meant that future relations between the Soviet and Yugoslav leaders would be regarded as interstate relations.

In addition, the telegram contained a rather programmatic statement, indicative of Soviet policy goals in the Balkans.

> We regard Yugoslavia as an ally of the Soviet Union, and Bulgaria as an ally of the Soviet Union's enemies. In the future, we would like Bulgaria to dissociate itself from the Germans and become the Soviet Union's ally. In any event, we would like Yugoslavia to become our chief mainstay in Southeastern Europe. And we deem it necessary to explain that we do not plan the sovietization of Yugoslavia and Bulgaria, but instead, prefer to maintain contacts with democratic Yugoslavia and Bulgaria, which will be allies of the USSR.[2]

Although the telegram mentioned only two countries – Yugoslavia and Bulgaria – by implication it encompassed all of Southeastern Europe. Until 1948, when Soviet-Yugoslav relations were disrupted, Yugoslavia was indeed the Soviet's main ally in the region, and in those years it served as a model for the other People's Democracies. The Soviets realized that they would only succeed in transforming Bulgaria into an ally if the Fatherland Front, led by the Communists, came to power. Yet they consistently denied any intention to sovietize Yugoslavia and Bulgaria, in accordance with the strategy devised by the Comintern and employed by the Department of International Information (DII) of the CPSU(b)'s Central Committee, which had inherited many of the Comintern's functions.[3] That strategy consisted of concealing the role that indigenous Communist parties were to play in Moscow's grand design, while advocating the establishment of "People's Democracies," the defeat of fascist blocs, and national liberation.

Subsequent exchanges between the Soviet and Yugoslav leadership reveal that both sides sought to cultivate the relationship, and even engaged in mutual compliments. On May 25, 1944, Stalin and Molotov sent birthday greetings to Marshal Tito via General Korneyev, wishing him "continued success in the fight against Nazi invaders and traitors to the Yugoslav people."[4] However, the day was marred by German air raids on the town Drvar, where Tito was quartered with the Yugoslav Army's Supreme Headquarters. In the wake of the air raid, Molotov wrote to General Korneyev in a telegram of May 28, 1944:

> We believe that the air raids were highly suspicious. It is strange that Maclean and Churchill[5] left the area before the strike. We recommend that you and Tito be extremely cautious and distrust those who made themselves scarce in the nick of time, without informing you about the imminent danger, although they must have known about it.[6]

In April 1944, the Yugoslav military mission, led by General V. Terzic and including M. Djilas, arrived in Moscow to further facilitate Soviet-Yugoslav cooperation. The relationship was strengthened by Djilas's meetings with top Soviet leaders: on April 24 he met with Molotov and on May 19 and June 4, with Stalin.[7] Upon Tito's request, General Korneyev, head of the Soviet Military Mission, also travelled to Moscow in mid-July 1944 to hash out problems which concerned the Yugoslav leadership. Tito sent a letter via the General to Stalin, in which he raised the issue of Soviet military assistance to the People's Liberation Army of Yugoslavia, and requested that the question be settled as soon as possible, for "on it depends the ultimate success of the establishment of a democratic federative Yugoslavia."[8] Tito also referred to the Western Allies' attempts to meddle in Yugoslav internal affairs, and stressed the need to proceed with a degree of circumspection, in order to preserve Yugoslavia's political and military independence without jeopardizing its relations with the West. "In this context, any, even very insignificant assistance from the USSR would be very valuable to us. And I ask you to render us this assistance," wrote Tito. He believed that a Red Army advance through the Carpathians and Romania to the south would be most effective, since it would fundamentally change the situation in the Balkans.

Tito also wrote about a possible meeting with Field Marshal Henry Maitland Wilson in Italy, and expressed his fears that the Western Allies' troops might land on Yugoslav territory. For the first time, Tito also suggested that he himself visit Moscow to discuss the postwar peace settlement (or, as Tito wrote, it was necessary, "to discuss certain problems and adopt a stand on them prior to peace talks"). Tito believed that the discussions would be "in the interest of the Balkan countries and the Soviet Union," and his wording indicates that he proposed to discuss a wide range of problems in the Balkans.

Before Tito's visit to Moscow, however, a number of important events took place. First, Tito met with Churchill in Italy on August 12, 1944. Before his departure for Italy, Tito asked the Soviet government for advice. In his telegram of August 5, Molotov thanked Tito for the letter sent with Korneyev, remarking that the information he had provided about the situation in Yugoslavia and its prospects for development was of great value. "We will do our best in order to assist you in the future, as well," Molotov assured him. However, he added, "As far as your meeting with Churchill is concerned, I will refrain from giving you specific advice, for I have insufficient information at my disposal. I am sure you will cope with the task well."[9]

Molotov's reserve is easily explained. For one thing, the Soviet leadership's stance on the two basic issues to be discussed at the talks – the fate of the king and the formation of a coalition government – was well known. According to the Soviets, the problem of the king should be dealt with after the war, and the functions of the provisional government should be performed by the National Committee for the Liberation of Yugoslavia. In the past, moreover, advice had been conveyed via official Party channels by Dimitrov. Tito interpreted the fact that Molotov offered no further advice as an unambiguous expression of trust. However, Molotov's vagueness may have reflected nothing more than the Soviets' desire to have *carte blanche* in their relations with Great Britain and the U.S.

The meeting between Tito and Churchill, held on August 12-13, 1944, cannot be considered a success for British diplomacy. The talks, which took place on the island of Vis (with the premier of the Royal Government-in-Exile, Ivan Šubašić, in attendance, confirmed the main provisions of the agreement which had been concluded by Tito and Šubašić on June 16, 1944. The communiqué, which was later published, emphasized the preservation of the National Committee's administration on Yugoslav territory and the formation of a united government, while the issue of monarchy was conveniently deferred to the postwar period.

The communiqué had a significant impact on the situation in the Balkans, given that the Soviets had launched a major offensive to drive the Germans out of Southeastern Europe. The offensive, known as the Jassy-Kishinev operation, commenced on August 20, 1944, and culminated in Romania's withdrawal from the war and its subsequent occupation by Soviet troops. On September 5, the Soviet Union declared war on Bulgaria, which caused the government of the Fatherland Front, with the Communists at its head, to come to power on September 9. The fates of Yugoslavia, Hungary, and Greece were next on the agenda. Tito and the Yugoslav leadership nurtured hopes that they would control the new government of the Communist regions, and these were adumbrated in a telegram from the Soviet military mission, sent to Moscow on September 8, 1944, in connection with the planned liberation of the country's eastern regions.[10] On September 11, Stalin and Molotov wrote in reply:

Inform Tito of the following. We have no obligations to Yugoslavia with respect to the Allies. We are not bound by any promises and might have commenced operations, but regrettably, we lack the necessary forces at present. We can supply arms to you and shall do so. The town of Krajova will serve as a center for your supplies, and Korneyev has been sent there, so you may contact him directly. If you wish to fly to Krajova, you may do so with our assistance.[11]

Upon receipt of that telegram, Tito began making preparations for the flight to Krajova and from there to Moscow. Tito's visit to the Soviet capital clearly had a major impact on subsequent events, but due to the absence of transcripts from meetings between Tito, Stalin, Molotov, and Dimitrov, we must reconstruct the discussions based on available sources. Tito visited Moscow at a time when Soviet troops had occupied Romania and established control over Bulgaria, and their advance into Hungarian territory remained only a matter of time. The Soviet government was informed by the British Ambassador, Archibald Kerr, of Great Britain's intention to occupy Greece, to which the Soviet government replied that it had no such plans.[12] However, the Allies had not reached any agreement on Yugoslavia, which was the only country in the Balkans whose fate hung in abeyance.

Strategic issues were the focus of attention at the Moscow talks. Finally, the Soviets decided to launch a large-scale offensive operation to liberate Belgrade and Eastern Yugoslavia, which determined the country's destiny. In a published communiqué, the Soviets applied to the AVNOJ and the Command of the People's Liberation Army for permission to conduct operations on Yugoslav territory. The communiqué stipulated that the Soviet troops would enter only the territory bordering on Hungary and would be withdrawn immediately upon the fulfillment of their tasks, while the AVNOJ civil administration would continue to operate in areas where Soviet troops were deployed. Not only did the communiqué set a new precedent in diplomatic relations by unilaterally raising the status of the Yugoslav Communists, but it was also clearly aimed at obstructing a British landing in Istria. Characteristically, the issue of the Yugoslav government in exile was passed over in silence, indicating that the "Yugoslav side" was to be represented by the AVNOJ and the Yugoslav Army Command.

In light of the Soviets' previously articulated desire to regard Yugoslavia as its mainstay in Southeastern Europe, the development of Yugoslav-Bulgarian relations naturally occupied a prominent place in the discussion of regional problems. From a brief entry in Dimitrov's diary, it is evident that they were a subject of discussion between Tito and Dimitrov:

September 29, 1944. Second conversation with Tito.[13] We discussed
all problems in detail, and agreement was reached on issues of
interest to the Bulgarian and Yugoslav Communist parties, as well
as on the main issues between the new Yugoslavia and the new
Bulgaria. Of course, there is complete mutual understanding
between us, but difficulties will arise in putting our plan into effect:
the establishment of an alliance between Bulgaria and Yugoslavia,
and possibly a federation of South Slavs (including Bulgarians,
Macedonians, Serbians, Croatians, Montenegrins and Slovenians)
from the Adriatic to the Black Sea. Difficulties are to be expected,
especially from the British side, and their pan-Greek (Hellenistic)
and pan-Bulgarian agents.[14]

Until the Soviet-Yugoslav rift in 1948, a trilateral military-political
alliance between the U.S.S.R, Yugoslavia and Bulgaria dominated the
strategic situation in the Balkans. As a direct consequence of the Moscow
talks, Tito met with a delegation from the Bulgarian government's
Fatherland Front on October 5, 1944, in Krajova, and on the same day,
concluded an agreement on the participation of the new Bulgarian army
in battles fought on Yugoslav territory. The three armies took part in
the Belgrade Operation, which was launched in late September 1944,
and Yugoslav-Bulgarian relations flourished with the patronage of the
Soviet Union. Southeastern Europe's fate was effectively secured.

In view of this three-way alliance, the Moscow talks between Stalin
and Churchill, held on October 9-18, 1944, appear in quite a different
light. This meeting has been extensively treated in the historiography,
although Soviet historians have denied that an agreement on the
allocation of spheres of influence was reached.[15] Available documents,
however, indicate that there can be no question that such an agreement
was concluded. The implications of the agreement have also been the
subject of considerable dispute. After the Yugoslav-Soviet split,
Yugoslav historians (primarily V. Dedijer) interpreted the agreement as
a betrayal of Yugoslavia's national interests by the Soviet leadership.
That evaluation was a product of its time, and was unabashedly
propagandistic. Later, Yugoslav historians revised this analysis;
Professor N. Popović, one of the foremost experts in Soviet-Yugoslav
relations, concluded that the 50:50 allocation of spheres of influence in
Yugoslavia was tantamount to Stalin's and Molotov's tacit agreement to
protect Yugoslavia from outside interference. In fact, the national
liberation movement of Yugoslavia "had no obligations [to the Allies],
nor did it confront an unfavorable military or political situation, which
was in fact real assistance."[16]

It is likely that Churchill's infamous formula, which divided the
Balkans into spheres of influence, came as a pleasant surprise to Stalin
and Molotov at their first meeting with Churchill on October 9, 1944, for
not only did it acknowledge Soviet influence in the Balkans, but it

completely coincided with their minimum program. The Soviet transcript is strangely reticent on the subject of the formula, and does not include a description of its contents, nor any mention of "the blue pencil mark" which Stalin silently inscribed on its corner. Only one, somewhat ambiguous remark by Stalin was recorded.

> Comrade Stalin says that the 25 percent to be controlled by Britain in Bulgaria does not harmonize with the other figures in the table. He, Comrade Stalin, deems it necessary to introduce some changes, that is, 90 percent of Bulgaria should go to the Soviet Union and 10 percent to Britain.[17]

Stalin's use of the word "harmonize" is slightly puzzling. Possibly, he was referring to an analogous allocation of spheres of influence in Greece. This seems likely in light of his expression of support for Britain's right to suzerainty in Greece earlier in the conversation. This transcript, like the others at our disposal, shows that Stalin was a consummate game player, one whose skill also manifested itself in his deft maneuvering with regards to Italy. Churchill had expressed the wish that the Soviet government would rein in Italian Communists, whose rhetoric might inflame passions and incite clashes with the Allied troops. The transcript provides a terse account of the following exchange between Stalin and Churchill.

> Comrade Stalin says that it would be difficult for him to exert influence on the Italian Communists, because he has not been informed about the internal political situation in Italy. Moreover, there are no Soviet troops stationed in Italy – in contrast to Bulgaria, where we are in a position to tell the Communists what to do. But if he, Comrade Stalin, attempted to advise Ercoli, Ercoli might tell him to go to the devil, for he, Comrade Stalin, knew nothing about the situation in Italy. He, Comrade Stalin, can only say that Ercoli is a clever man who would not act recklessly.
>
> Churchill says that he would prefer that the Italian Communists refrain from inflaming passions in Italy.
>
> Comrade Stalin notes that the figures referring to Bulgaria should be amended.
>
> Churchill replies that, generally speaking, he could not give a damn about Bulgaria, and that the issue would probably be discussed by Eden and Molotov.
>
> Comrade Stalin agreed.[18]

The Balkans were the subject of much debate at the Moscow talks, but aside from wresting formal recognition of Britain's influence in Greece, Eden walked away empty handed. Spheres of influence in Bulgaria were allocated in accordance with Soviet wishes, while a joint policy (50:50) in Yugoslavia was observed *de jure*, rather than *de facto*. The problem of a united Polish government remained unresolved, and there was no mention of the problem in Moscow. British diplomacy proved ineffectual in stemming the tide of Communism which eventually washed over the areas liberated by Soviet troops, and Churchill was much chagrined. He expressed his concern in a conversation with Stalin on October 14, 1944. The Soviet transcript records the conversation as follows:

> He, Churchill, believes that the world's future depends on friendly relations between the British and American sides and the Soviet Union. Churchill told Marshall Stalin with great sincerity that the small European countries had been scared to death by the Bolshevik revolution. [Later] this fear was exacerbated by the fact that before the dissolution of the Comintern, the Soviet government professed its intention to convert all European countries to their faith. Churchill remembers how the world trembled in fear of world revolution, although Churchill was sure that revolution would not take place in Britain.

> Comrade Stalin replies that now the world will not quake in fear. The Soviet Union does not intend to stage a Bolshevik revolution in Europe. He, Churchill, may look to Romania, Bulgaria and Yugoslavia as examples.

> Churchill replies that he believes Marshall Stalin.[19]

Clearly, Stalin had no intention of honoring these promises. But Churchill was not Stalin's dupe; rather, he participated in the diplomatic ritual of mutual reassurances and professions of good faith. Yet some aspects of the conversation remain opaque. If Churchill's anxiety about "Bolshevik revolutions" was genuine – and no doubt it was – what was his motivation for suggesting that the Balkans be conveniently carved up into spheres of influence? He was sufficiently experienced to know that Stalin was not to be trifled with. By this time, the Allies had already determined the occupation zones in Germany, and it was a matter of time before all of Poland was occupied by Soviet troops, which were also poised to liberate Hungary and a sizable part of Czechoslovakia. In effect, Eastern and Southeastern Europe had been ceded to the Soviets. This was Stalin's minimum program.

As the war drew to a close, all the East European countries faced similar problems, although each developed their own solutions. After the liberation of its eastern regions, Yugoslavia had to confront entirely new problems of administration and defense which required the complete restructuring of the army and the formation of a modern air force. On November 17, 1944, Tito sent a telegram to Stalin which detailed these new administrative problems, and noted the difficulty of restructuring the armed forces in these circumstances. Tito expressed his intention to begin restructuring the armed forces "by imposing a clear-cut administrative system in the General Staff, the central military apparatus, and the mandatory educational institutions." Tito proceeded to outline the structure of the military apparatus, and supplied a detailed description of the requisite military personnel, their ranks and number (222 people), which Tito admitted was insufficient. "I fully realize," wrote Tito, "that it will not suffice to restructure the army alone, for the army will be strong only if it has a reliable and well-organized rear. We shall tackle the difficult task of building such a rear, and improving organization in the country. In the meantime, I also ask that you assist us in forming a Navy."[20]

Stalin replied on December 13, 1944, explaining that the delay was due to his heavy workload and Molotov's illness. Stating that he was in principle prepared to comply with the Yugoslavs' requests, Stalin stressed the need for supplies to be delivered to the Yugoslavs on a regular basis, as a well as the need to come to an agreement on the organization of the Yugoslav ground forces. As for the requested Soviet military instructors, Stalin concurred that they should conclude an agreement on their rights and duties. "We should no longer tolerate the absence of coordinated decisions on those issues, for it inhibits the process." Stalin offered to assemble military and political representatives from both sides as soon as possible in order to settle these practical matters.[21]

In this case, Stalin was as good as his word. The meeting was held in Moscow in January 1945, with Andrija Hebrang, the chief delegate from the Yugoslav Party, and Arso Jovanović, Head of the Supreme Command of the People's Liberation Army of Yugoslavia, representing the Yugoslavs, and Molotov, A. Kiselev, V. Sakharov[22] and Stalin participating on the Soviet side. They discussed organizational problems plaguing the Yugoslav army, and Stalin called for a more realistic evaluation of Yugoslav potential. The meeting devoted considerable attention to Soviet economic assistance to Yugoslavia, which was badly in need of food and medical supplies, raw materials, and clothing for both the army and the populace.

Yugoslav demands with regard to foreign policy are of even greater interest to the historian, however. Hebrang presented a program that encompassed all of Yugoslavia's neighbors, and exhibited pronounced hegemonic tendencies, which were not lost on the Soviets. First, the Yugoslavs broached the issue of reparations from Hungary, asserting that Hungary had caused some $900 million in material damage. In reply to Stalin's rejoinder that total reparations would amount to $300 million (only the sum of Romania's and Finland's payments), Hebrang said that he considered this insufficient, although he understood America's and Britain's opposition to reparation payments.

Undaunted, Hebrang advocated the inclusion of a Yugoslav representative on the Allied Control Commission for Hungary, which precipitated an exchange of opinions by Stalin and Molotov on the possible inclusion of both a Czechoslovak and a Yugoslav representative. However, Yugoslavia's primary aim was the incorporation into Yugoslavia of the area surrounding the Hungarian city of Pecs, which was largely inhabited by ethnic Slovenians. The Yugoslavs had set their sights on the region's coal deposits, which were crucial for the rejuvenation of the economy, and they also coveted the "Baja Triangle," with the town of Baja at its center. "Have the Hungarians given their consent?" Stalin disingenuously inquired.

Hebrang was not to be deterred, and turning his attention to Austria and Italy, requested the incorporation of part of the Korucs region, which was populated by ethnic Slovenians. After World War I, the Austrian province of Karinthia had belonged to Yugoslavia, but by referendum it was ceded to Austria. Furthermore, Istria, with its ports of Trieste, Pola and Rijeka (Fiume), which currently belonged to Italy, should likewise be incorporated into Yugoslavia. The inhabitants of Istria were mostly Croatians and Slovenians; only a small number in the port cities were Italians. When Hebrang displayed an ethnographic map of those regions, indicating the desired borders, Stalin observed that it was necessary for these regions to express their wish to be incorporated into Yugoslavia. At this point, Stalin and Molotov referred to an unofficial conversation with Churchill, in which he had suggested that Istria be designated as an autonomous region, which would allow Austria an outlet to the Adriatic Sea. When Hebrang argued that only a few small groups in Trieste and Rijeka advocated the formation of a British Protectorate, Stalin "jokingly offered to drown them."

On the subject of Romania, the indefatigable Hebrang cited the necessity of incorporating certain areas of the Timisoara region inhabited exclusively by Serbs, as well as the town of Timisoara, whose population was largely German.

> Comrade Stalin inquired whether anything had appeared in the press on that score, and upon receiving a negative reply, noted that it was necessary for the Serbs of that region to raise the issue of incorporation into Yugoslavia themselves. However, that issue would be placed on the agenda of the future Peace Conference. But if you are to raise the issue, you must have certain arguments, [said Stalin, addressing Hebrang].

Hebrang had not yet exhausted his demands, and suggested amending the Yugoslav-Romanian border in the area of Resita in order to acquire the iron and steel works there. "If it is impossible to incorporate Resita into Yugoslavia, it would be crucial for Yugoslavia to obtain iron from those works by some other means."

Yugoslav-Bulgarian relations were a particularly contentious issue at the meeting. Hebrang asserted that relations were developing very slowly due to the fact that the Bulgarians had rejected the Yugoslav draft treaty for a federation. Stalin objected to Hebrang's rendition of events, countering that the Yugoslavs' draft treaty was unacceptable because it put the Bulgarians on par with the Serbs, Croats, Slovenes, and Macedonians, producing the impression that Yugoslavia intended to "swallow" Bulgaria. Hebrang, however, was not cowed by Stalin's criticism and insisted that the Yugoslav leadership had rejected the Bulgarian offer to conclude a treaty of friendship and mutual assistance because they regarded it as a presumptuous attempt to settle the Macedonian issue in their own favor, as well as to end the isolation resulting from its alliance with Germany. Thus, the Yugoslav leadership had rejected Bulgaria's treaty, and offered its own version of a federation treaty which ignored the bilateral principle. Hebrang blamed Dimitrov for the delay in establishing a federation, because Dimitrov had advised the Bulgarians not to sign the agreement, instead offering to conclude a treaty of friendship and mutual assistance.

Stalin was well acquainted with Bulgarian-Yugoslav differences, and presumably knew about Dimitrov's telegram. He took a definite stand on the issue, advocating gradual progress towards a Bulgarian-Yugoslav treaty of federation. Stalin viewed Bulgaria's readiness to accept an alliance as a positive development and expressed the hope that a treaty of mutual assistance might be concluded for a term of 10-20 years. In Stalin's view, a federation along the lines of the Austro-Hungarian model should be established – without its numerous drawbacks, of course. Molotov. interjected that even something as innocuous as a treaty of friendship and mutual assistance would alarm Turkey and Greece, as well as Romania, and Europe would certainly be thrust into a turmoil. Only the Soviet Union would remain unperturbed. The Soviet transcript continued:

> Comrade Stalin and Comrade Molotov exchanged opinions on the possible Czechoslovak reaction. The Czechs would not feel threatened, for they uphold the principle of Slav solidarity, but they would be alarmed by the prospect of a left-wing Slav federation. Moreover, it would affect internal relationships in Czechoslovakia – Slovakia might demand similar measures in Czechoslovakia.

Stalin inquired about the Yugoslav position with respect to Greece, and Hebrang replied, "Yugoslavia expects to obtain Greek Macedonia and Thessaloniki. Those demands have not yet been expressed in order to not to complicate matters for the Greek ELAS. Now we will put forward these demands." Stalin was a bit taken aback by Yugoslav demands, and he reminded Hebrang "that you will find yourself at loggerheads with Romania, Hungary and Greece, and [you] are going to do battle with the whole world; such a situation would be absurd."

In order to resolve the issue once and for all, Stalin inquired about Yugoslavia's relationship with Albania. Hebrang replied that "the Albanians are Yugoslavia's best friends," and noted that on their latest visit, the Albanian government delegation to Belgrade signed a Yugoslav-Albanian Treaty of Friendship and Mutual Assistance, as well as a separate trade agreement. Stalin responded that "since Yugoslavia has assumed obligations under the treaty, it will have to fulfill them. If any complications arise, it will have to fight, and whether it will be able to offer resistance to Britain remains to be seen. The Albanian issue should be considered more carefully. The British only respect strength." Stalin considered it fortunate that the treaty of mutual assistance had been neither ratified nor published, and he advised that the Yugoslavs cool their heels and give further thought to such close ties with Albania. In any event, the treaty should not be made public until February 1945.[23]

Stalin also wished to clarify the international legal ramifications of Yugoslavia's relationship with Albania and Bulgaria. Hebrang had informed him that the Provisional Government which had been set up in Albania a few months earlier had not yet received international recognition. Ironically, even Yugoslavia, which had stationed a military mission in Tirana, had not yet extended its recognition to the Albanian government. Stalin insisted that according to international codes of conduct, a country must establish diplomatic relations before concluding treaties with another country, whereupon Hebrang asserted that the British were intentionally delaying the formation of a united government in Yugoslavia. If a united government had not been formed by January 15, the Yugoslav leadership would declare the National Council for the Liberation of Yugoslavia the provisional government of Yugoslavia.

Stalin caught on immediately: the Yugoslavs looked to the Polish case for a precedent, and sought to emulate it![24] Of course, Stalin commented, the Soviet government might extend recognition to the Yugoslav Provisional Government, but for the time being it was still implicated in events in Poland. Churchill had swallowed the bitter pill, but Roosevelt was still sulking. Therefore, a Provisional Government in Yugoslavia was unlikely to receive recognition from Britain and America. Once again, Stalin advised the Yugoslavs to wait until February, and speculated that Churchill, inspired by the recent successes in Greece, sought a pretext to interfere in Yugoslav affairs, and the Yugoslavs should not provide him with one.

In general, Stalin must have been bemused by the scope of Yugoslav demands, their clumsy presentation, and their misguided plans for attaining their goals. According to the Soviet transcript, Stalin "expressed doubts about the advisability of starting a quarrel with Romania and Hungary." He felt that Yugoslavia's stance on a number of issues would entail complications for the Soviet foreign policy. As a prophylactic measure, Stalin suggested that in the future, the Yugoslavs consult with the Soviet leadership before making important decisions, "otherwise, we might find ourselves in an awkward position."

The roots of the Soviet-Yugoslav rift can be clearly discerned in this January 9, 1945 meeting. From his conversation with Hebrang, Stalin divined that the Yugoslavs' hegemonic ambitions would conflict with the Soviet Union's conception of the postwar world order, in which the Soviets were to play the leading role in shaping foreign policy for the entire socialist bloc. Subsequently, the Yugoslavs were forced to "fall in line" and rescind their demands, which engendered growing resentment among the Yugoslav leadership towards their overbearing "elder brother."

Considering that the federation treaty with Bulgaria was of central importance to Yugoslavia's foreign policy, Moscow's obstruction of it in late 1944-early 1945 did not bode well for Soviet-Yugoslav relations. According to Hebrang, the Yugoslav leadership was planning to sign a federation treaty on December 31, 1944, and announce it on January 1, 1945.

> Everything had been thought out in minute detail: we had decided which halls the ceremonies would be held in, who would deliver addresses, etc. However, the Yugoslav project was rejected, and our Bulgarian comrades reported that Dimitrov had opposed the plan from Moscow, and instead had suggested concluding a treaty of friendship and mutual assistance. [Upon consideration] the Yugoslav leadership found it unacceptable, and in early January presented another federation treaty."[25]

The Yugoslavs were not naive enough to suppose that Dimitrov alone had spoiled the deal. Since they had few doubts about who made decisions behind the scenes, they were obliged to give their consent to a treaty of friendship and mutual assistance. On January 24, 1945, a trilateral meeting was held in Moscow to discuss the treaty. The meeting was attended by Stalin, Molotov, and Vyshinsky on the Soviet side; M. Pijade, vice-chairman of the Anti-Fascist Council for the National Liberation of Yugoslavia, and Hebrang on the Yugoslav side; and Premier K. Georgiev,[26] Bulgarian Minister of Internal Affairs, A. Yugov, and D. Mikhalchev, a representative of the Bulgarian government in Moscow, on the Bulgarian side.

In his opening statement, Stalin responded to Bulgaria's inquiry regarding the Soviet government's stance on the inclusion of territorial concessions in a Soviet mediated Yugoslav-Bulgarian treaty, and the possible conclusion of a secret agreement on federation.[27] Stalin observed that whatever was done in Yugoslavia and Bulgaria was ascribed to the USSR, the Soviet Union had to know for what it would bear responsibility. This should not be regarded as meddling in the affairs of Bulgaria and Yugoslavia, he added. On the subject of federation, he advised that the treaty of alliance and mutual assistance avoid any mention of preparations for the establishment of a federation, since this might alarm Britain and America.

During the ensuing discussion, Bulgarian representatives expressed their support for a bilateral federation, while the Yugoslav representatives asserted that Bulgaria should join Yugoslavia on par with Bosnia and Croatia. Otherwise, claimed Pijade, in an effort to bolster the Yugoslav position, other areas of the country would demand the same status as Bulgaria. Stalin, however, supported the Bulgarians.

> The Yugoslav side is oversimplifying the issue, losing sight of the fact that Bulgaria is a state with embassies, with its own army and navy. If such a state were included in a federation on a par with Bosnia and Croatia, its intellectuals and the bourgeoisie, which has not yet been eliminated in Bulgaria, would sabotage such a measure. And another thing should be borne in mind. People holding hostile views will say that the Bulgarian government has lost the war and now they're losing their state.

Stalin advocated flexibility, since the establishment of a federation would necessitate appropriate preparations, including the resolution of territorial problems. While on the subject of Macedonia, Stalin advised that it would be more politic to refer to the reunification of its regions rather than the creation of Macedonia as an independent state. The British and Americans would be hard pressed to object to this slogan.

Following this exchange of opinions, Stalin offered to draw up a draft treaty of alliance and mutual assistance between Yugoslavia and Bulgaria which would be couched in conciliatory, inoffensive terms. A federation was absolutely necessary, but at this stage, it was better to exclude mention of it, and continue negotiations by correspondence between the two premiers. In conclusion, Stalin entrusted Vyshinsky with the task of "assisting the Bulgarian and Yugoslav delegations in drawing up a draft treaty of alliance."

The conversation related above is telling in many respects. Stalin seems to have delivered a monologue, which consisted of prepared questions and answers, to the Bulgarians, while the Yugoslav delegation (judging from the transcript) remained somewhat taciturn. The transcript relates only one short comment by Pijade, who presented

Yugoslavia's views of the federation. But the Yugoslavs' silence was in itself eloquent. By that time, the Yugoslav leadership could not be swayed: since Bulgaria was smaller than Yugoslavia, it could only be considered a constituent part of a federation. Later, in 1948, this view seemed vindicated by growing suspicions that the Soviet insistence on a bilateral federation was merely a ruse designed to bring Yugoslavia under Soviet control. It is impossible to say whether the Soviet leadership was aware of the resentment and suspicions harbored by Tito and his entourage at this point.

On January 28, 1945, further trilateral discussions were held in Stalin's country house in the Moscow suburb of Kuntsevo. This meeting was more inclusive than the previous ones: Stalin, Molotov, Malenkov, and Beria represented the Soviet side; Pijade, Hebrang, and the Yugoslav ambassador in Moscow, S. Simić, represented the Yugoslav side; and Dimitrov, T. Kostov, K. Georgiev, A. Yugov, and D. Mikhalchev represented the Bulgarians. Nevertheless, the draft treaty failed to meet with the approval of all sides, and the issue of federation was left to be decided in an exchange of letters. The final texts of these letters would be agreed upon in early February.

The Yugoslav-Bulgarian treaty was not signed in February 1945, however, due to U.S. and British protests that as a defeated power, Bulgaria was not in a position to sign international agreements before the conclusion of a peace treaty. As a result, ratification of the treaty was delayed for over a year, and was signed in the completely different political context of late 1947.

This episode illustrates the degree of control that the Soviets exercised in the Balkans, which in fact precluded any influence by the Western powers. Because the Soviets did not want to complicate their relationship with their Western allies, however, they proceeded with great circumspection, taking the Western position into account while shaping their own policy. But this in no way deterred the Soviets from pursuing their own aims in the region, which consisted, first and foremost, of consolidating Communist regimes where they already existed (Yugoslavia, Bulgaria, and Albania) and aiding Communists in wresting power where they did not (Hungary and Romania).

At the same time, conflicts arose between the Soviets and their allies that the Soviets not only failed to diffuse, but exacerbated. A telegram sent by Stalin and Molotov to Tito while preparations for the Yalta conference were underway illustrates this nascent conflict of interests. The telegram informed Tito of the February 10, 1945 conference's decision to implement the Tito-Šubašić, agreement. On the basis of the agreement, a new government would be formed which would be charged with opening the AVNOJ to members of the former government who had not compromised themselves by collaborating with the enemy.

Indicating that Tito would receive similar directives from the governments of the U.S. and Britain, and that these would also be included in a communiqué released by the Big Three, the Soviet leaders stressed that the clause would in no way jeopardize the future government. "Those two clauses have been adopted... as a concession to the British, [so that] they stop procrastinating and agree to the immediate formation of a united government on the basis of the Tito-Subašić agreement. We do not doubt that you will use the two clauses to your advantage, and to the detriment of your enemies." [28]

The concluding words of this telegram are indicative of the Soviet leader's confrontational mentality, which the Yugoslavs also shared. Despite the defeat of their mutual enemy, the mentality remained, and played a critical role in deteriorating Soviet-Yugoslav relations. Eventually, the Soviets would count the Yugoslavs among their "enemies," as they drew an increasingly tightly-knit circle of obedient satellites around them to form the "Socialist camp" in the 40-year stand-off known as the Cold War.

Notes

1. There is considerable material on the Yugoslav-Bulgarian dispute. See for instance: Kostadin Paleshutski, *Iugoslavskata komunisticheska partiia i makedonskiaat vupros 1919-1945,* (Sofiia: Izd-vo na Bulgarskata akademiia na naukite, 1985); Georgi Daskalov, *Bulgaro-Iugoslavski Politicheski Otnoshenia, 1944-1945,* 1. izd., (Sofia, Universitetsko izd-vo "Kliment Okhridski," 1989). For Yugoslav studies, see: V. Chashule, *The BCP and the Macedonian Issue, 1944-1968,* (Skoplje, 1968); Slobodan Nesovic, *Jugoslavija-Bugarska, Ratno Vreme 1941-1945,* 1. izd., (Beograd: Narodna knjiga, 1978).

2. Archive of the President of the Russian Federation (hereafter, APRF), Fund 56 (Molotov's Fund), op. I, d. 1369, l. 129.

3. On the founding of the DII, see: N. S. Lebedeva, "The Shadow of the Comintern. 1943-1945," in *Komintern i vtoraia mirovaia voina.* Sostaviteli, avtory vstupitelnoi stati i kommentariev, N. S. Lebedeva, M. M. Narinskii; otvetstvennye redaktory, K. M. Anderson, A. O. Chubarian, (Moskva: "Pamiatniki istoricheskoi mysli," 1994).

4. APRF, f. 56, op. 1, d. 1370, l. 65.

5. The persons referred to here are F. Maclean, head of the British Military Mission at the Supreme Headquarters of the People's Liberation Army of Yugoslavia, and Randolf Churchill, Winston Churchill's son, who was serving at the Mission.

6. APRF, f. 56, op. 1, d. 1370, l. 66.

7. The transcript of Stalin's conversation with Djilas is absent from Molotov's archives. The contents of Stalin's conversation with Djilas, held on June 4, 1944, were summed up in Molotov's telegram to General Korneyev (APRF, f. 56, op. 1, d. 1370, 1. 79-80.). Djilas's reports on the meeting can be found

in Yugoslav sources. See: *Documents of Foreign Policy of the Socialist Federative Republic of Yugoslavia. 1941-1945,* Document No. 85, pp. 116-117; Document No. 94, pp. 142-143 (in Serbian).

8. The letter in question was published on several occasions, including in Tito's *Collected Works.* Tito also sent letters to Molotov and Dimitrov via General Korneyev.

9. APRF, f. 56, op. 1, d. 1371, l. 117.

10. APRF, f. 56, op. 1, d. 1372, l. 1-3.

11. APRF, f. 56, op. 1, d. 1372, l. 10.

12. This fact was reported by Andrei Vyshinsky in his memo to Archibald Kerr of September 23, 1944 (APRF, f. 3, op. 64, d. 994, l. 40).

13. Dimitrov recorded only a couple words about his first meeting with Tito, which took place on September 25, 1944: "Talked with Tito."

14. Dimitrov's Diary. Entry of September 27, 1944.

15. I. Zemskov, "On the So-Called 'Division' of Yugoslavia into Spheres of Influence," *Mezhdunarodnaya Zhizn,* no. 8, 1958; Yu. Girenko, "Against Falsification of the Soviet-British Talks. October 1944," *Mezhdunarodnaya Zhizn,* no. 6, 1983.

16. Nikola Popović, *Jugoslavensko-Sovjetski odnosi u drugom svetskom ratu (1941-1945),* 1. izd., (Beograd: ISI, 1988), 165. This subject had been previously treated in Soviet literature. See: Leonid Gibianskii, *Sovetskii Soiuz i novaia iugoslaviia ,* (Moscow, 1987), 124-126.

17. APRF, f. 45, op. 1, d. 238, l. 3-16.

18. APRF, f. 45, op 1, d. 238, l. 3-16.

19. APRF, f. 45, op. 1, d. 238, l. 18-21.

20. APRF, f. 45, op. 1, d. 390, l. 52-58.

21. APRF, f. 45, op. 1, d. 390, l. 60.

22. General Korneyev was replaced by General A. Kiselev as head of the Soviet Military Mission in Yugoslavia; V. Sakharov was a staff member of the Mission. The conversation recorded in the transcript is also described in Stalin's personal archives. (APRF, f. 45, op. 1, d. 397, l. 1-16).

23. In much of his advice and recommendations, Stalin obviously has in mind the impending meeting of the Big Three, which was scheduled to be held in February 1945. He was averse to further complicating negotiations.

24. The Polish National Liberation Committee, as is known, was transformed into the Provisional Government of Poland on December 31, 1944. On January 4, 1945, the Soviet Union extended recognition to it, and exchanged official representatives at the ambassadorial level. At the same time, the USSR requested that the governments of Czechoslovakia and Yugoslavia recognize the Provisional Government of Poland.

25. APRF, f. 45, op. 1, d. 397, l. 1-16.

26. The Yugoslav delegation's stay in Moscow was prolonged until February 14, 1945, and judging by subsequent events, it was quite fruitful for the development of Soviet-Yugoslav cooperation, primarily in the military sphere. (see: N. Popović, *Jugoslavensko-Sovjetski otnosi,* 205-206).

27. According to the Soviet transcript by Vyshinsky (APRF, f. 45, op. 1, d. 397).

28. APRF, f. 45, op. 1, d. 397, l. 27-29.

4

Postwar Hungary, 1944-1946

Bela Zhelitski

With the Red Army's rapid advance westward in 1944-1945, the situation in the eastern part of Central Europe was undergoing dramatic change. The possibilities open to the political forces of the small Central European countries – which were ultimately circumscribed by their dependence on the belligerents – were increasingly limited in the course of military operations. After the war, the fates of these countries would be determined by a whole complex of external factors and by the victorious powers – among them, the Soviet Union. Nevertheless, as the war drew to a close, the leaders of Romania and Czechoslovakia attempted to exert influence on the Great Powers in order to ensure their national interests and determine their relations with postwar Hungary.

In August 1944, Romanian troops joined German forces to prevent the Hungarian government, headed by Géza Lakatos, from withdrawing from hostilities. Subsequently, the Romanian government severed ties with its former ally and turn its forces (which were already fighting on the side of the Red Army) against the German occupiers in the Northern Transylvania region. Thanks to this wily maneuver on the part of the Romanians, the Soviets supported Romania's claim to "Transylvania or its major part" when the USSR and Romania concluded an armistice agreement.[1] This issue became a serious bone of contention between Romania and Hungary, since there were 2.5 million Hungarians inhabiting the designated area. Moreover, in establishing

Romanian administration in North Transylvania, the "Maniu guards" maltreated the indigenous Hungarian population, especially in the regions of Kolozsvar (now Cluj-Napoka) and Bihora. The Allied Control Commission and the Soviet Military Headquarters were forced to intervene to put a stop to these atrocities.

Hungary also suffered the consequences of the Czechoslovak government-in-exile's territorial ambitions, which were fostered by Edvard Beneš. As early as December 1943, Czechoslovakia had concluded an agreement with the Soviet Union, according to which its 1937 borders would be restored. This effected some 700,000 ethnic Hungarians, who lived in Southern Slovakia and the Lower Carpathians.

On February 13, 1945, the advance units of the Red Army occupied Budapest, and after approximately two months, all of Hungary was free of the Nazi occupation. Hungary had suffered great damage during the war, and was a scene of devastation and destruction. The country lost about one million lives, in addition to approximately 40% of its national wealth, amounting to 4.4 billion dollars.[2] Every family suffered the hardships of the war and its aftermath. Hungary's postwar democratic government was forced to take these factors into consideration in drawing up both its domestic and its foreign policy agenda. Until the signing of the armistice (April 1946) and the conclusion of the Hungarian peace treaty (1947), territorial questions loomed large on the political scene, and there remained uncertainty whether the vast number of Hungarians in the territory of Transylvania belonged to Hungary or Romania. This uncertainty manifested itself in messages from the representatives of the Soviet military command in Hungary to Moscow in the Spring of 1945.

In a report forwarded to the Central Committee in Moscow (May 23, 1945), a leading political officer of the Second Ukrainian Front wrote:

> The most important factor influencing the political sentiments of the population is the expected and endorsed armistice treaty between the Soviet Union and Hungary. The very fact of its conclusion, and that Hungary has ceased to be the enemy of the United Nations, has met with nation-wide approval. The population considers the terms of the treaty to be severe, but just and workable – the sole exceptions being the clauses concerning reparations and North Transylvania. Many Hungarians think that under present economic conditions, Hungary is unable to pay 300 million U.S. dollars, or that it will be able to do so only if rendered external assistance. People are also of the opinion that the question of North Transylvania should be reconsidered after a time and decided in favor of Hungary.[3]

The Soviet account accurately characterized the prevailing mood in Hungary. The formation of a new, democratic government in Romania (led by Petru Groza) evoked little enthusiasm in Hungary, but it brought some relief, since it promised to ensure peace in the disputed territory and broad rights for the nationalities inhabiting Transylvania. Yet national political circles were anxious about Hungary's interstate relations, especially with its neighbors and the Soviet occupiers. This is illustrated by secret dispatches from the Hungarian Communist Party leader, Mátyás Rákosi, to Georgi Dimitrov in Moscow on May 5, 1945, in which he reported on the complicated political and economic problems, transport difficulties, and thorny relations with Czechoslovakia. "Martial law in Hungary has led to ever new difficulties," Rákosi wrote to Dimitrov.

> The Red Army needs some means of transportation for use in Austria and Czechoslovakia. What remained of Hungarian transport has been commandeered and driven West, so the country finds itself in a catastrophic situation. There is no transportation in Budapest and the industrial towns... The situation has worsened because the factories are being dismantled and taken to the Soviet Union. Every day delegations of workers visit, and, reminding us that they have worked well for the Red Army for months, ask us to reserve at least some factory equipment so that they may continue with their work.[4]

Economic problems in postwar Hungary were compounded by political ones, many of which resulted from the actions of Hungary's neighbors. The position of the Czechoslovak government with respect to the Hungarian population in Czechoslovakia caused particular problems for the new Hungarian government. "Recently, in political circles here, the news that the Hungarians were being deported from Czechoslovakia (with the exception of those who have performed services in defense of the Czechoslovak Republic) made a very unpleasant political impression," Rákosi reported to Moscow. "The public is not opposed to the deportation of Hungarians who settled in the regions torn away from Czechoslovakia in 1938. But if Hungarian peasants and workers (approximately half a million persons) who have lived there since time immemorial, are deported, this would be a severe trial for Hungarian democracy. At the same time, this circumstance would play into the hands of the reaction."[5]

On January 20, 1945, representatives of the Hungarian national government signed an armistice agreement in Moscow. In accordance with the terms of the agreement, Hungary declared war on Nazi Germany and was obliged to prosecute those Hungarians suspected of war crimes, as well as to pay for the maintenance of the A.C.C. located on its territory. It also promised to pay certain reparations to the USSR,

Czechoslovakia, and Yugoslavia; and to place all industrial, transport, energy systems, equipment, radio, and telecommunications, etc. at the disposal of the Allies. According to Clause 12 of the armistice agreement, Hungary's reparation payments amounted to 300 million U.S. dollars, 200 million of which were earmarked for the USSR, thirty million for Czechoslovakia and seventy million to Yugoslavia. Reparations payments were to be paid in full within six years.[6] This time frame was unrealistic in light of the war-ravaged Hungarian economy, and would have required that Hungary pay fifty million dollars, or 20 percent of its national income, in 1945.

Needless to say, at the Potsdam Conference the victorious powers did not honor Hungarian claims against Germany. Moreover, German property on the territory of Hungary was decreed to belong to the Soviet Union. In the summer of 1946, the Soviet Union agreed to extend the period of reparations payment from six to eight years, stipulating only a slight increase in the total amount paid. However, after the Communist regime was established in Hungary in 1948, the Soviet Union, having received the first third of the reparation payment (134.3 million dollars), canceled the remaining debt of 65.7 million dollars by a decision of the USSR Council of Ministers on August 18, 1953.[7]

By concluding an armistice agreement with Hungary, the Allied Powers recognized it as a sovereign state, but since Hungary's political actions were under A.C.C. control until a peace treaty was signed in 1947, its sovereignty was actually quite limited. In 1945, a network of local administrative bodies was created; however, the formation of a new government "had no positive effect on the political mood of the people," according to a report issued by the Political Administration of the Red Army.[8] In the spring of 1945, public opinion was rather indifferent to that government. "The interests of the government and the difficulties which inhibit its effective action have led the population to consider it as a symbolic phenomenon demonstrating the intention of the Red Army to preserve the independence of Hungary," stressed the report. "The most important step taken by the government – the declaration of war on Germany – was assessed positively."[9]

Nevertheless, political activity in Hungary gradually gathered momentum, and various democratic parties came into being or resumed their activities. The Communist and Social Democratic parties, the Smallholders Party and the National Peasant Party were the most active parties in postwar Hungary. They immediately began to vie with one another for the support of the people. Among the parties and other political forces, the Communist Party, which was organized and mobilized by Communist emigrés who had returned from the USSR, assumed a special role. Its members immediately occupied important posts which allowed them to wield considerable influence within the coalition government. Although the Hungarian Communist Party (CPH) was not large, it was one of the most active and confident political forces in the country. "The Party's numerical strength is well on the increase," wrote Rákosi to Dimitrov on April 14, 1945. "There are, evidently, over 20,000 of us in Greater Budapest, and on a national scale, probably over 100,000 Party members."[10] The General Secretary of the CPH proudly reported to Moscow that all power had been concentrated in the hands of his Party, but he was forced to admit the existence of certain problems facing the country and the CPH. Thus, among other things, he wrote to Dimitrov: "The problem of the police is becoming more cause for concern. We hold the vast majority of the organs of the political police in our hands. Of course, it is still very inexperienced... For the most part it performs its duties well, but at the same time, it makes many mistakes, sometimes even tremendous blunders."[11]

According to Soviet military analysts operating in Hungary, the following factors of public life exerted a negative influence on the political sentiments of the Hungarians at that time: "1) economic hardships; 2) mistakes committed in the deportation of Hungarians, when those bearing German names were arrested and deported; and 3) arbitrariness, pillage and violence on the part of certain Soviet soldiers." The authors of the analysis came to the conclusion that as a result of the above-mentioned factors, "the political sentiments of the population towards us could be appraised as negative." The report further noted that if "the population appears quite loyal, that is only because they are powerless."[12]

The analysis of the Red Army administration in Hungary coincides with the memoirs of a leading member of the CPH, Zoltán Vas. Characterizing the situation in 1945, Vas asserted: "In Hungary, political as well as economic power is completely in the hands of Moscow."[13] Vas, widely respected for his competence in political, economic and Party matters, recalled in an interview how he had managed to prevent Soviet representatives from completely dismantling and hauling off factory equipment. The Soviets then complained about Vas's interference to Voroshilov, who was then chairman of the A.C.C.. Voroshilov, who according to Vas, liked him and often invited him to lunch, then took Vas to task: "You see, Comrade Vas, don't be so stubborn! We trust you, you must agree with what we ask you to do." But Vas was afraid to jeopardize the popularity of the Party by giving in to all of Voroshilov's demands.[14]

With time, the situation changed, although Moscow's priorities continued to hold sway in both the domestic sphere and foreign policy. This was facilitated by the presence of Soviet troops and the A.C.C., as well as by the activities of the CPH, which was rendered every possible form of assistance by the CPSU(b). The only party capable of serving as a counterweight to the CPH, and to some extent challenging its hegemony among the Hungarian democratic parties, was the Smallholders Party (PSH).

The potential influence of the PSH was demonstrated by the results of the elections to the Municipal Assembly of Greater Budapest in October 1945. The Hungarian Communists who had returned from Soviet emigration believed that the Communist Party enjoyed great sympathy and support; therefore, its leader Rákosi predicted its overwhelming victory on the eve of the elections. However, the election results deeply disappointed Rákosi. Commenting on their reaction, Z. Vas later recalled:

> It was a catastrophe. We were sure that the joint Communist and Social Democratic ticket would win. Rákosi personally guaranteed Voroshilov our victory. The reports coming in that evening raised our hopes, and at eleven o'clock in the evening, Rákosi, Gerö, Farkas, Révai, and I toasted to our victory at Party Headquarters. Dawn brought sobering disillusionment and embarrassment. Rákosi, as pale as a corpse, sunk onto the chair without saying a word.[15]

The results of the elections confounded the expectations of Rákosi and the other Communists. The PSH won an absolute majority (50.54%). For the Communists, the situation was further complicated by the upcoming parliamentary elections. Marshall Voroshilov, as chairman of the A.C.C., attempted to help the Communist Party. With his assistance, on October 16, 1945, representatives of the coalition parties began talks with the aim of securing the appearance of all democratic parties on a common ticket. The proposal, however, was opposed not only by a number of political parties, but also by the Western powers.

During the parliamentary elections in November 1945, all the parties vied for voters independently. The results of the voting were as follows: the PSH had 245 seats in the parliament, the CPH - 70, the SDPH - 69, National Peasants' Party - 23, and the Bourgeois-Democratic Party - 2. The fact that 57 percent of the vote went to the Smallholders clearly demonstrated Hungarian society's support of pluralistic parliamentary democracy.

On November 15, 1945, a new coalition government was formed in Hungary, headed by the Protestant pastor Zoltán Tildy, a member of the Smallholders Party. Ferenc Nagy, the leader of the PSH, was not included in the coalition cabinet, and only after Hungary was proclaimed a republic and the post of president created (Z. Tildy was elected president), did Nagy become Prime Minister. After numerous discussions, the Communists managed to seize the chief posts in the Ministry of Internal Affairs and in two other ministries, while the Social Democrats got three ministerial posts. Considering that Z. Vas, the Communist leader, headed the Higher Economic Council, which *de facto* functioned as a key ministry, we can say that the left-wing forces (i.e. Communists and Social Democrats) had strengthened their position relative to the former provisional cabinet. And this occurred after the PSH had won a resounding victory in the parliamentary elections.

The leaders of the CPH, enjoying the support of important patrons such as the Chairman of the A.C.C., the CPSU(b), and Red Army units stationed on Hungarian territory, became confident of their ability to consolidate their positions and to oust methodically all competing political parties from the power structure. As long as the membership of the CPH was relatively small, the Communists pursued these goals with a degree of circumspection, but as time went on, the CPH increased its pressure on other political parties and public organizations in order to establish the dictatorship of a single party.

Occupying the key positions in the Ministry of Internal Affairs (which was headed by the Communist László Rajk), the Communist Party was able to embark upon the realization of its plans. By 1946, it had already liquidated many autonomous public organizations and movements, thereby taking another step in creating a totalitarian state. Characterizing the situation at one of the inter-party conferences, Minister of Justice Istvan Ries (a member of the SDPH) noted: "From the point of view of the Law, the situation is such that the Russian [Soviet] Administration has the right to give us instructions" that the government was obligated to carry out.[16] It should be noted that the representatives of Western Powers in the A.C.C. did not exercise any influence in matters of domestic policy, and in fact relied upon the appraisals of Soviet representatives. The persecution of various religious and public organizations by the Ministry of Internal Affairs in 1946 was only the beginning, and these were followed by political purges of prominent figures from various democratic parties as the leaders of the CPH attempted to defeat their rivals and establish a totalitarian regime. The tactics of the CPH consisted in fomenting disagreement within the ranks of the rival leadership. To this end, the Communists employed the most diverse methods.

In the sphere of foreign policy, the most pressing issues facing Hungary were the preparations for a peace treaty and the normalization of relations with its neighbors. Hungary's leadership was particularly concerned with the fate of the Hungarian minority living in Czechoslovakia. Among the coalition partners, various solutions to this problem were proposed in connection with the preparation of the peace treaty. The Communists focused on the observance of national and territorial principles, the elimination of confrontation among the neighbors, and close economic cooperation with them. The PSH did not conceal the fact that it intended to raise the question of possible alterations in the Hungarian-Czechoslovak and Romano-Hungarian borders, taking into account the ethnic composition of the population of the regions situated near the state borders. The CPH's approach to this problem would depend largely upon the results of forthcoming talks with Moscow.

On July 29, 1946, the conference of victorious powers commenced in Paris. The conference proclaimed its official aim: to create and secure a situation in Europe in which the revival of fascism would never occur; to lay the foundations for the economic and political cooperation of states with different social systems, and, in so doing, to secure peace for many years to come. The fates of the vanquished states, the former allies of Germany (i.e. Italy, Romania, Bulgaria, Hungary and Finland) would be decided with an eye to achieving these objectives.

At the plenary meeting of the Paris conference, as well as in its committees, the representatives of the victorious powers did not consider it necessary to consult with representatives of the vanquished states when drawing up the peace treaty. They were only given the right to present their point of view at the conference. At that time, it was out of the question to hold a referendum among the populations involved in the controversial issue of territorial redistribution. This approach provoked serious misgivings among the democratic parties of Hungary on the eve of the Conference.

The Hungarian government expended great effort in its attempt to be included in the preparation of the peace treaty so as to somehow influence the resolution of territorial questions. However, the democratic government was not aware of the fact that the West was leaving all decisions concerning Hungary to the discretion of Soviet leaders. For this reason, Hungarian diplomats sought to determine the positions of both Western and Soviet politicians on the question of Hungarian minorities living beyond Hungary's borders. Of course, they had no idea that Soviet leaders had already reached an agreement with E. Beneš on the Czechoslovak-Hungarian border and methods of "solving the national question." Nor were they aware of the continuous Czechoslovak lobbying and the secret directives of the Soviet delegations at the Paris meetings in March 1946, when it had been agreed to uphold "the transfer to Romania of Transylvania"; "the deportation of Hungarians from Czechoslovakia"; as well as the "re-establishment of Hungary's 1937 borders."[17]

Before the Paris conference the government sent its delegation to Moscow to discuss the problems connected to the signing of the peace treaty. The Hungarian delegation stayed in the Soviet capital from April 9 to April 18, 1946. According to existing documents (namely, E. Gerö's notes), during the delegation's meeting with Stalin, the Hungarian Prime Minister and other members of the delegation raised a series of questions regarding Hungarian-Soviet relations, and the status of the Hungarian minorities in neighboring countries. In the course of the talks, Nagy informed the Soviet representatives about the situation in the country (land reform, the purges of the state apparatus, plans for the recovery of the national economy), as well as about foreign policy, including relations with neighboring countries. Stalin, taking into consideration the economic situation in Hungary, promised to defer the country's reparations payments, and declared his intention gradually to withdraw Soviet troops from Hungary. "We cannot withdraw all of them at once. But gradually, yes. Some troops will remain there. Thus, this will ease your difficulties, as well," he replied to the Hungarian Prime Minister's remark concerning the expense involved in maintaining Soviet troops on Hungarian territory. According to F. Nagy, this expense "meant a tremendous burden for us under the current economic conditions."[18]

The problems which bedevilled drawing up the peace treaty occupied a special place in the talks with Stalin. "We have not raised the question anywhere," said the Hungarian Prime Minister. "We considered it our duty to raise the question here. We do not lay any claims to Yugoslavia. We lay claims only to our two neighbors – Czechoslovakia and Romania. There are 650,000 Hungarians in Czechoslovakia... Czechoslovakia has decided to liquidate its Hungarian minority."[19] Stalin, in his turn, requested more complete information: "And what does liquidation mean?" Nagy answered: "It means deportation, separation, the eradication of national characteristics." Stalin suggested that Hungary and Czechoslovakia agree on the exchange of populations, following the example of that taking place between the USSR and Poland, as a result of which, according to Stalin, "more than a million Poles have been sent to Poland, while they sent us only 400,000 Ukrainians and Byelorussians." Stalin further expressed his concern about the situation and advised his interlocuters: "That would be the correct national policy. That would be a bold decision. You must understand that the Hungarians who remain in Czechoslovakia will lose their national identity."

János Gyöngyösy, Hungarian Minister of Foreign Affairs, was present during this exchange and noted that in the difficult economic situation "there is no possibility of moving Czechoslovak Hungarians to Hungary," and further, "the Hungarians do not want to leave their native realm, where they have lived for centuries."[20] The Prime Minister of Hungary added that Hungary wished to live in peace and friendship with Czechoslovakia, yet it was not indifferent to the fate of the national minority living there. For this reason, he drew attention to two possible solutions of the problem, and said to Stalin that "either it is necessary for the peace treaty to establish that all Hungarians living in Czechoslovakia are guaranteed full equality with all citizens of Czechoslovakia, or the Czechs, wishing to get rid of the Hungarians (as they have repeatedly declared) must give us enough territory to accommodate the Hungarians deported from Czechoslovakia."

Stalin immediately remarked that the Czechs would never agree to give their territory to Hungary. "They are afraid of the Slovaks, and therefore want to meet all their demands," he said. "Naturally, it is not right that they deprive the Hungarians of civil rights, do not allow them freedom of speech, etc. Your claims concerning their civil equality are well-founded," he concluded. "We'll raise this question with them and try to come to a peaceful settlement."[21]

In postwar Czechoslovakia, denazification was used to "settle" the nationalities problem by force; in other words, the political leadership of the country decided to eliminate not only the fascist and German element, but also the significant Magyar population. In the early 1970s, the Czechoslovak historian Jan Šindelka commented that "there was no great desire to guarantee broad civil rights to national minorities,"[22] the more so becauseBenešand his supporters cherished the idea of creating a single "Czechoslovak nation." In its Košice program (April 1945) the Czechoslovak democrats of that time practically declared all the Hungarians (except the groups of active anti-fascists) who lived on the territory of that country to be members of a "criminal nation"[23], who should be deprived of citizenship or deported from the country. Beneš's overt efforts to get rid of the Hungarian population living compactly in Southern Slovakia along the Hungarian border resulted in a population exchange and forced deportation of twelve to fifteen percent of the Hungarian national minority in the country at the end of 1948.[24]

As the peace treaty was being prepared, Hungary also had to deal with the problem of Transylvania, and of the Hungarian people inhabiting these regions. In the documents of the 7th Department of GlavPURKKA dated May 23, 1945, there are letters, notes, and appraisals concerning that problem, the history of Hungarian-Romanian relations, and the status of the Hungarian population of Transylvania. One Soviet military report to the Central Committee noted: "The situation in North Transylvania, is, on the whole, analogous to the situation in Hungary, but it is aggravated by growing Romanian-Hungarian antagonism, which has become even stronger after the signing of the armistice agreement between the USSR and Hungary." The note continued:

> The Romanians have cited the agreement as evidence... that all Transylvania should belong to Romania; hence, the expression of Romanian chauvinism has become sharper and more open. The Hungarians reacted to the agreement with great alarm – they are especially afraid of the return of the Romanian administration, which would lead to robbery, violations of human rights, and the humiliation of Hungarians.[25]

Such was the situation in the spring of 1945. However, the problem of Transylvania remained one of the most important and controversial issues in inter-party debates on foreign policy. Therefore, when the Hungarian government delegation visited Moscow, this problem was of necessity touched on in the discussions with Stalin. Presenting the Transylvanian issue to the Soviet leader, Nagy pointed out: "The second, even more serious problem, concerns Romania, since in connection with this we must consider the return of the indicated part of Transylvania to us. We don't mean to inflict any harm upon the Groza government or Romanian democracy. We know that the voluntary transfer of territory to us would be an impossibility. It would likewise be impossible for Hungarian democracy to relinquish its territorial claims. 1.5 million Hungarians are currently living in Romania."[26] Stalin responded to this statement, noting that Romania would not voluntarily relinquish Transylvania, and then he asked V. M. Molotov to remind him what had been decided upon in the Soviet-Romanian Agreement on this matter. The notes of Ernö Gerö included the text of the following dialogue between Stalin and Molotov:

> V.M.: The territory of Transylvania or its greater part
> should belong to Romania.
>
> J.S.: Then there is reason to raise the territorial question. The
> problem is now the focus of the Conference of Deputy Foreign
> Ministers.
>
> V.M.: It seems the question has not yet been discussed,
> but it is next on the agenda.
>
> J.S.: Then on April 25, Molotov will visit Paris and will
> raise this question at the Conference of Foreign
> Ministers. We will consider it again.[27]

In the end, the Hungarian government's delegation to Moscow facilitated the establishment of relations between the USSR and Hungary, and the resolution of a number of economic questions. Its effect on problems of foreign policy was less significant. The Soviet Union assured Hungary of its support in retrieving national treasures and state property that had been taken to the West. As for amending the most galling points of the peace treaty, the visit had no appreciable results.

Upon his return to Budapest, Nagy gave the following assessment regarding the results of the Soviet-Hungarian talks: "We considered a great number of problems of interest to Hungary... We received concrete and satisfactory answers to all the questions, which may be decided between two countries, and reached a mutual understanding on other subjects, as well."[28] The diplomatic statement of the Hungarian prime minister aroused hope in political circles. The concluding sentence of the statement, as became apparent at the session of the State Assembly on May 2, 1946, was an oblique reference to the problem of Hungarians residing beyond the state border. Nagy made it clear that in Moscow, they had also touched upon questions of the "unavoidable territorial claims," and he noted Moscow's profound understanding of the Hungarians' peaceful aspirations.[29]

At the above-mentioned session of the State Assembly the Prime Minister characterized the main objectives of Hungarian foreign policy in the following way: "The peaceful aspirations of Hungary refer, first and foremost, to the defense of the legitimate civil interests of Hungarians living outside the country," including the urgent settlement of territorial claims in order to ensure the future development of the nation. The deputies emphasized the need to "take into account the ethnic principle, and on this basis, demarcate the borders" in the hope that millions of Hungarians would receive the opportunity to return to the Fatherland.[30]

The first Hungarian ambassador to the USSR in the postwar period, the historian Gyula Szekfü, was more realistic in his appraisal of the results of the Hungarian delegation's visit to the USSR, which he summarized in his annual report to Budapest. He stressed that the most important problem discussed at the Hungarian-Soviet talks in Moscow was that of the peace treaty, although the delegation did not achieve any appreciable results in the settlement of this problem. In his summary report for 1946, he pointed out that "these talks paved the way for the development of normal Soviet-Hungarian relations, and it can be expected that the Soviet side will be friendly and cautious in its approach to the problems of occupation, reparations, prisoners of war... and in the matter of the forthcoming peace treaty."[31] Indeed, reparation payments were actually deferred, and the Soviets promised partial troop withdrawal from Hungary. Moreover, from October 1945 to October 1946, of 550,000-570,000 Hungarian soldiers taken prisoner on the territories of the USSR, Hungary, Austria, Czechoslovakia, and Germany, 300,000 were allowed to return to their native land, and by the end of 1947, 120,000 more were released.[32] At the same time, the Hungarian Ambassador in Moscow pointed out:

> 1) The Soviet government has not accepted either of our proposals concerning the division of Transylvania. We were given the opportunity to ask the peace conference to settle the problem of territorial concessions on the basis of the text of the armistice agreement with Romania;
>
> 2) It [the Soviet government] has not expressed readiness to be, in some form or another, an intermediary between us and the Romanians, or between us and the Czechs, in settling these problems, and although [the Soviet government] considered that the matter will be settled with the participation of both sides, Hungary is expected to take the initiative;
>
> 3) The Soviet government considered the exchange of populations a correct and expedient action. However, it has in mind the territory of Hungary after the Trianon Peace Treaty, whereas

the Hungarian government would like to realize the following plan: if 22,000 sq. km. of Transylvanian territory were returned to Hungary, the Hungarian population could be transferred from the territories remaining in Romanian hands;

    4) It definitively declared that it would be quite lawful to demand equal rights for the Czechoslovak Hungarians.[33]

Ambassador Szekfü came to the following conclusion: "The peaceful initiatives of the Hungarian government, the division of Transylvania, the protection of Czechoslovak Hungarians, and possible modifications of the border with Czechoslovakia did not meet with the support of the Soviet government. Positive results consist in the following: 1) they approved the equality of the Hungarian minority; and 2) in accordance with the recalled text of the armistice agreement with Romania, they considered it possible to raise the question concerning Hungarian claims. However, they did not state that they intend to support these claims, and did not indicate that they were ready to take any concrete steps in the interests of the Hungarian minorities."[34] The Hungarian diplomats and Szekfü himself also repeatedly directed the attention of the workers of the Foreign Commissariat offices in Moscow to the situation of Hungarians in Czechoslovakia. Concerning one such discussion in the Foreign Commisariat's Department of Balkan States, A. P. Vlasov wrote: "The Czechoslovakian government is employing not entirely humane methods in the transfer of Hungarians; for example, villages inhabited by Hungarians are surrounded by troops at night, and the entire population, regardless of sex and age, are herded into cattle cars and transported to the regions Sudet, while their remaining property is divided amongst the local Slovak population."[35] The methods used by the Czechoslovaks were reminiscent of the Stalinist deportations of some Caucasian nationalities at the end of the war.

After the Moscow talks, the Hungarian coalition partners began to formulate more moderate territorial claims. On May 7, 1946, the Paris Conference of the Council of Foreign Ministers considered the Hungarian draft of the peace treaty, but it had no effect on the deliberations. The draft of the peace treaty was drawn up by special commissions. Neither the plenary session, nor the committees formed by it expressed any wish to discuss territorial questions with the representatives of the defeated states.

Reports from the Paris conference disappointed Hungarian politicians, and forced them to amend their already more moderate claims. In conformity with the decision of the parliamentary commission for foreign affairs, Hungarian representatives at the peace conference reduced their claims to only 20,000 square kilometers of Transylvanian territory, referring to one of the articles of the Romanian armistice agreement which stated that the greater portion of this territory would remain in Romanian hands. On May 7, however, the conference adopted the final decision on the restoration of state borders in accordance with those of December 31, 1937. This meant that Hungarian claims to Transylvania were completely rejected.

Subsequently, the political parties which comprised the Hungarian coalition government took different approaches to the question of national minorities in neighboring countries. The Communist Party confined itself to the problem of legal guarantees for the Hungarian populations in other countries. The Smallholders considered the territorial problem and the revision of borders to be of paramount importance. Meanwhile, the Social Democrats' position was close to that of the Communist Party, and the National Peasants' Party considered both legal guarantees and a revision of borders to be equally necessary. In the summer of 1946, the Nagy government decided to send a delegation to Washington and London in order to consult with Western politicians, and if possible, obtain their support for Hungary's peaceful initiatives. On June 12 the Hungarian governmental delegation, headed by the Prime Minister, departed for the USA, where it met with political figures and acquainted them with Hungary's position on the peace treaty. Nevertheless, the question most critical for Hungarian foreign policy – the revision of the May 7 decision of the Council of Foreign Ministers concerning borders – did not meet with any support there, either. The delegation did not receive any concrete promises with regard to this problem, or to the status of Hungarians in Czechoslovakia. The American politicians advised the Hungarians to take into account the different spheres of influence, and indicated that the settlement of these problems depended, in many respects, on the Soviet leadership.

Reporting to Moscow on the visit of the Hungarian delegation to the USA, the leader of the Hungarian Communists, M. Rákosi, wrote to Stalin on June 30, 1946 (during his visit to Moscow):

> Outside of acquainting the Americans with our goals in relation to the peace treaty and Hungarian domestic problems, the delegation's efforts yielded no results. When asked their position on the signing of a peace treaty with Hungary, the Americans gave an evasive answer and hinted rather cautiously that in this case the Russians had the decisive word. The Americans were very restrained vis-á-vis the Soviet Union. Officials made no attempts to set Hungary against the USSR.[36]

The results of talks between the Hungarian delegation and British politicians proved even less promising, since the position of Labor Party leaders actually obstructed the Hungarians' attempts to address the issue of the Hungarian minority in Czechoslovakia. It is interesting to note how the behavior of the British was appraised by Rákosi in the above-mentioned letter to Stalin: "In England the picture was quite different. The leaders of the Labor Party stressed their Czechophile sentiments. For example, they did not want to listen to anything concerning the inclusion of guarantees for the protection of the Hungarian minority in Slovakia in the peace treaty, believing that the common declaration of the United Nations would be quite enough. They attempted to express anti-Soviet sentiments."[37] In fact, this indicated that Beneš's position concerning the solution of ethnic problems had the full support of British Laborite circles, and therefore the visit to London was doomed to failure.

As a whole, the results of the Hungarian delegation's visits to the USA and Britain demonstrated the futility of efforts to win the support of those countries on problems of the legal status of the Hungarian national minority in Czechoslovakia. At the meeting of the Communist Party leadership on August 2, 1946, Rákosi expressed himself even more openly on this subject. "Especially the British part of our visit was a complete fiasco, as it became clear that the English government and the present Laborites had an agreement with the Czechs not to countenance any requests made by the Hungarians. The aim of this agreement was to prevent the inclusion [in the peace treaty] of any clauses concerning the rights and freedoms of the Hungarian minority in Czechoslovakia. This was somehow unexpected, even for us Communists."[38] Even the chairman of the Labor Party, Neal Becker, was "somehow embarrassed" by these circumstances, and "told us honestly" that he supported the Czechs, since they had already pledged their support, although they understood that more than 650 thousand Hungarians lived in Czechoslovakia. Another leader of the same party, Ernest Bevin, addressing the representatives of the Hungarian delegation, remarked maliciously that the given question "had already been solved with Beneš during the war."[39]

The position held by the English leaders naturally distressed the Hungarians. They realized that the former rulers of Hungary were responsible for the country's participation in the war, but they could in no way agree to the position of the new Czechoslovak government as expressed in its Košice program, which underscored "the criminal character of the whole Hungarian nation."

On the other hand the Hungarian delegation's visit to the USA was not completely useless; in fact, the visit concluded with an agreement to return to Hungary those valuables (gold bars, coins and jewelry) which were taken from the country by the Nazis, and ended up in the American zone. Further, the United States promised assistance in reviving the Hungarian national economy and stabilizing its curency. In this connection Rákosi wrote to Stalin:

> Our visit to America has had some success as far as the economy of
> the country is concerned, in the sense that the Americans have

promised the return of Hungarian property taken after January 20, 1945, including the Hungarian river steamers, without disputing property rights. And finally, the Americans expressed a readiness to discuss the return of Hungarian property taken after October 15, 1944. If the promises to return the gold and steamers are fulfilled, it would be significant help. I said 'if', because the property removed after January 20, 1945, should have been returned by the Americans three months ago, as promised, but as yet nothing has been returned.[40]

The government delegation returned to Budapest on June 25, 1946, stopping in Paris in order to consolidate their moderate gains by conducting talks with the Foreign Ministers of the Great Powers. These talks did not yield any concrete results, either. Nagy decided to inform V. M. Molotov about the results of his visits to Western countries in order to dispel his doubts and suspicions. He assured Molotov that the discussions in England and the U.S.A. had not in any way altered relations between Hungary and the USSR.

Thus, the delegation's visits to Washington, London, and Paris ended in political failure, and put the Soviet, as well as the Czechoslovak, Romanian, and Yugoslav politicians on their guard. Hungary remained in political isolation and its efforts seemed rather futile on the eve of the Paris Peace Conference. If the Hungarian delegation's visit to Moscow had aroused hopes that at least some of Hungary's objectives regarding the just establishment of borders with its neighbors would be attained, then the journey to the West confounded hopes that Hungary's foreign policy objectives would be supported by the Western Allies. It had become clear to Hungarian politicians that the resolution of peace problems in their neck of the woods depended to a considerable extent on the USSR. In this regard, Szekfü drew Budapest's attention to the fact that in the opinion of G. M. Pushkin, the Soviet Ambassador to Hungary, the visits to Washington and London made the Soviet top leadership suspect that Hungary continued to pursue a "see-saw policy."[41] Szekfü believed that were it not for this circumstance and speeches given by alleged reactionary forces in Hungary, it would have been possible to avoid the "growing distrust" on the Soviet side and to toughen its stance in favor of the Hungarians at the peace conference. In fact, the American dele-gation protested the deportation of Hungarians from Czechoslovakia, while the Soviets remained silent.[42]

On August 3, 1946, the Hungarian National Assembly familiarized itself with the draft peace treaty, and two days later, it had already elaborated its final position on the territorial problem. In conformity with the proposal submitted by the Minister of Foreign Affairs, J. Gyöngyösy, it was decided that at the forthcoming peace conference, Hungary would not demand the return of the Transylvanian territory

(22,000 square kilometers), but instead would refer to "certain modifications of the border." Czechoslovakia's claims to five additional Hungarian settlements on the right bank of the Danube provoked less argument among the parliamentarians, since they considered these new territorial claims to be utterly groundless.[43]

On August 6, prior to the visit of the Hungarian delegation to the Paris conference, the draft peace treaty and Hungary's position were discussed by the Council of Foreign Ministers on the initiative of the Parliamentary Committee for Foreign Affairs. At the plenum of the Paris Peace Conference on August 14, 1946, the Hungarian Minister of Foreign Affairs set out the position of the Hungarian government in connection with the draft peace treaty. The Hungarian project was discussed in the commission on the settlement of territorial and political problems, where the Hungarian representative declared that Hungary claimed only 3,000 square kilometers of Transylvanian territory, and requested the inclusion of clauses guaranteeing the civil rights of the Hungarian population living in Romania. On August 28, the problem of the Romano-Hungarian border was settled by the commission within a few minutes, since Hungary's minimal demands generated little support. It should be noted, however, that the previous day, during the discussion of Hungarian territorial claims against Romania, U.S. Secretary of State James Byrnes was prepared to introduce some corrections with respect to the borders, which, according to him, "could help return half a million Hungarians," to their homeland, but his proposal was not supported by Molotov. The Soviet delegation had deemed it necessary to restore the borders of 1937, and, as a result, 102,000 square kilometers in Transylvania was once again given to Romania. On September 5, 1946, the Romanian-Hungarian border, which had been arbitrarily established by the Habsburgs, was restored.

The settlement of the Czechoslovak-Hungarian conflict was more problematic. In September-October 1946 the Commission of the Peace Conference was faced with the deportation of 200,000 Hungarians from Czechoslovakia. Czechoslovakia's territorial claims vis á vis Hungarian settlements on the right bank of the Danube resulted in its acquisition of an additional 43 square kilometers, while Trans-Carpathia became part of the USSR. The deportation of Hungarians met with resistance from U.S. representative Bedell Smith, who stated that the problem was "more than unpleasant to his country." He suggested that the Hungarians and Czechoslovaks conduct bilateral talks, in which the issues of border amendments and population exchanges could be discussed. These questions, however, remained unresolved for a long time (up to the time when the Czechoslovak leader Edvard Beneš was forced out of office), and were a destabilizing factor in the relations between the two countries.

As a whole, the terms of the Paris peace agreement proved even less favorable for Hungary than the terms of the Trianon Peace Treaty after World War I. The territorial claims of its neighbors and the attitude of the victorious powers were harsh and inflexible. Just as it had in 1920, Hungary suffered relatively more in 1947 than the culprits who had unleashed the world war. The Paris Peace Conference ignored the rights of those national minorities living beyond the state borders of their motherland, and left this problem to the discretion of certain states as a matter of internal affairs. This decision complicated the situation of these minorities, and its consequences continue to be felt to the present, making the protection of national minorities one of the most urgent political problems in Europe today.

In conclusion, the Paris Peace Conference determined the fates of Central and Southeastern European nations without sufficient forethought; as a result, interethnic conflicts in the region will certainly continue in the future. The Paris Peace conferences (in 1920 and 1947) proclaimed the noble principle of national self-determination, but in fact they violated it themselves. Those peoples whose fates were decided by representatives of the Great Powers were deprived of the opportunity to express their will – the decisions were made without the benefit of plebiscites or popular referendums. The shortcomings in the peace treaty's provisions regarding the small states of East Central Europe have become even more apparent, as the collapse of the ideological rationale employed to create a single "Czechoslovak" or "Yugoslav" nation have been exposed as artificial constructions bol-stered by totalitarian regimes.

A final analysis of the domestic and international situation in which Hungary found itself after the Second World War seems to reveal that a sound basis existed for the formation of a democratic, multi-party political system in a neutral, democratic state. From 1944-46, coalition forces of the young Hungarian democracy successfully held onto power, began the process of reviving the national economy and assisted in concluding a peace treaty in Europe. In the midst of this democratic system, however, Communist political forces attempted to strengthen their commanding positions in the government and institute a dictatorial regime. With the assistance of a mighty foreign patron, they were able to establish a dictatorship in 1948. The fledgling Hungarian democracy of the mid-40's was still very weak, and it received little understanding or support from the Western democracies. The internal and external situation did not allow Hungary to become strong enough to withstand ultra-left, totalitarian tendencies, or the prevailing Soviet influence. These circumstances and factors decided the fate of Hungarian democracy in the 1940s.

Notes

1 . Zoltán Szász. *Iz Obshechego Istoricheskogo Proshlogo Vengrii i Rumunii,* (Budapest: Külpolitika, 1989), 16.

2. Mihály Korom , *A magyar fegyverszünet, 1945* (Br. 1987). 174. old.

3. Rossiiskii Tsentr Khraneniia i Izucheniia Dokumentov Noveishei Istorii (Russian Center for Preservation and Study of Recent Historical Documents – RTsKhIDNI), f. 17, op. 128, ed. khr. 38, l. 16.

4. RTsKhIDNI, f. 17, op. 128, ed. khr. 37, l. 14-15.

5. RTsKhIDNI, f. 17, op. 128, ed. khr. 37, l. 20

6. The Foreign Policy Archive of the Russian Federation, hereafter – AVP RF. f. 021, op. 6, p. 77, d. 69, l. 1-7.

7. Center for the Preservation of Contemporary Documents, hereafter – TsKhSD), f.5, op. 30, ed. kh. 148, 1. 41.

8. RTSKhIDNI, f. 17, op. 128, ed. khr. 38, l. 16.

9. RTSKhIDNI, f. 17, op. 128, ed. khr.. 38, l. 16.

10. RTSKhIDNI, f. 17, op. 128, ed. khr. 38, l. 4.

11. RTSKhIDNI, f. 17, op. 128, ed. khr.. 38, l. 13.

12. RTSKhIDNI, f. 17, op. 128, ed. khr. 38, l. 17.

13. László,Varga "New Yorki Bészelgetés Vas Zoltánnal," *Magyar Nemzet,* October 31, 1992.

14. Varga. "New Yorki Bészelgetés ."

15. Varga, "New Yorki Bészelgetés. "

16. Magyar Országos Levéltár, f. 285, ö.e. 6, p.32.

17. AVP RF, f. 012, op. 6, p. 106, d. 171, l. 2, 5.

18. Ernö Gerö *Ismeretlen feljegyései. Közli:* Éva Szabó, *László Szücs . Erdély és a Felvidék Sorsa.* 1946-ban 1 rész. (Uj Fórum, 1989), 2.sz., 44. old.

19. *Ibid.,* 2.sz., 44. old.

20. *Ibid.,* 2.sz., 44. old.

21. *Ibid.,* 2.sz., 44. old.

22. Jan Šindelka *A nemzeti kérdés problematikájának megoldása Csehszlovákiában 1945 és 1968 között.* (Társadalomtudományi Közlemények, 1972), 1. sz. 63. old.

23. *Ibid.,* 1.sz. 63. old.

24. *Ibid.,* 1.sz. 63. old.

25. RTsKhIDNI, f. 17, op. 128, ed. khr. 38, l. 17.

26. Gerö, *Ismeretlen,* 44. old.

27. Gerö,, *Ismeretlen,* 44. old

28. Sándor Balogh. *A párizsi béke, 1947. A felszabadulás utáni történetünkről,* I. köt., (Budapest, 1987), 107.old.

29. Balogh, *A párizsi béke,* 107. old.

30. Lajos, Izsák.*A koalició évei Magyarországon 1944-1948.* Bp. 1986, 100. old.

31. Ernö Gerö *Ismeretlen feljegyései. Közli:* Éva Szabó, *László Szücs . Erdély és a Felvidék Sorsa.* 1946-ban 1 rész. (Uj Fórum, 1989), 2.sz., 44. old.

32 Mihály Korom, *A Magyar fegyverszünet, 1945* (Budapest: 1987), 175-176 old.

33. *Szekfü Gyula moszkvai,* 44.old.
34. *Szekfü Gyula moszkvai,* 44.old.
35. AVP RF, f. 012, op. 7, p. 105, d. 165, l. 84-85.
36. RTsKhIDNI, f. 17, op. 128, d. 915, l. 82.
37. RTsKhIDNI, f. 17, op. 128, d. 915, l. 82.
38. RTsKhIDNI, f. 17, op. 128, d. 915, l. 211.
39. RTsKhIDNI, f. 17, op. 128, d. 915, l. 212.
40. RTsKhIDNI, f. 17, op. 128, d. 915, l. 82.
41. *Szekfü Gyula moszkvai,* 44. old.
42. *Szekfü Gyula moszkvai,* 45. old.
43. Balogh, *A párizsi béke,* 110. old.

5

"Bandits and Reactionaries": The Suppression of the Opposition in Poland, 1944-1946

John Micgiel

During World War II, the belligerent and occupied nations suffered enormous casualties, particularly Poland, which had been a battlegound since the Nazi offensive on September 1, 1939. The organized Polish resistance to the occupation is well known and well documented. During the great Soviet offensive in 1944, Polish Home Army units attacked the German rear and cooperated with the Soviets in the capture of many towns and cities. Resistance was not limited to any particular political party or group, but while the majority of political parties eventually subordinated their paramilitary units to the Home Army the radical left and the Communists organized separate "people's armies" which only occasionally cooperated with the Home Army.[1] By late summer 1944, Soviet troops occupied eastern Poland as far as the Vistula river, and as they advanced, they actively supported the Polish Communists by disarming, arresting, and deporting members of the Home Army who had emerged from the underground and offered to cooperate in the struggle against the Germans. Home Army leaders were relentlessly hunted down, arrested and/or deported. Many of them simply disappeared into the hands of the Soviet-led security police.

In an effort to save as many Home Army members as possible from charges of operating behind Soviet lines, Home Army Commander General Leopold Okulicki officially disbanded the organization in January 1945. But the dissolution of the Home Army and the end of the struggle against Hitler some four months later did not mean the end of bloodshed and terror in war-torn Poland. During the next three years, the Communist takeover and the resistance it engendered resulted in continued carnage. Indeed, some scholars consider this period to be one of civil war, claiming that as many as 30,000 people perished in the struggle. Poland was not a unique case, however. After the surrender of Germany, guerrillas continued to battle Tito in the mountains of Yugoslavia. Likewise, in the Transylvanian mountains, guerrilla bands doggedly opposed the Romanians and Soviets.

The Polish regime's determination to subdue its political opponents initiated a broader reign of terror aimed at intimidating a society whose values and traditions were at odds with Communist ideology. This essay briefly examines how the Communists cowed an already embattled society into compliance (or at least into silence) during their struggle against the legal political opposition and the covert armed underground – the so-called "reactionaries" and "bandits" to which the title of study refers.

The primary instrument for waging this covert war against the opponents of the new order in Poland was an institution with which the Poles were generally unfamiliar. Nevertheless, it was one which would quickly become the foundation and guarantor of the new system. The official name of this abhorred institution changed several times over the years, but for a long time it was commonly known as the Security Office or UB (Urząd Bezpieczeństwa). Tellingly, the UB was modelled on the Soviet secret police, the NKVD, whose specialists had helped forge the new "shield of the state."

The chief of the Soviet NKVD in Poland was General Ivan Serov.[2] Known to the Poles by the pseudonym Ivanov, Serov was one of the more adept students of "Bloody Felix" Dzerzhinsky, the Polish founder of the Cheka, the Soviet secret police.[3] Long before the Soviets actually liberated Poland and Serov launched NKVD operations there, the Soviets had already begun training Polish recruits in NKVD methods. In September 1940, near Smolensk, not far from the forest at Katyn where over 4,000 Polish officers had been shot just a few months earlier, the NKVD organized a training center. The 200 recruits had been recommended by the NKVD authorities in Minsk, and consisted of Poles, Byelorussians, and Ukrainians, all former residents of the eastern areas of the Polish republic. Following six months of military, intelligence and political training, graduates were either sent back to work in their home areas,[4] or selected for further schooling in a special NKVD center in Gorkii.[5] The German attack on the Soviet Union in June 1941 interrupted these courses for a time. The NKVD sought collaborators from among the Polish officers captured in September 1939 and held in prisoner-of-war camps. However, volunteers did not flock to enlist. Despite the harsh living conditions in the camps and the constant pressure from the NKVD, only a handful of officers were willing to cooperate. In mid-1942, this small group helped organize the Soviet-sponsored Polish First Army, which was trained, supplied, led, and indoctrinated directly by the Soviets. Polish recruits volunteered for the new army for the same reasons that they had flocked to General Anders's army the year before; it seemed to offer the only opportunity to get out of the Soviet Union and eventually return to Poland. In the summer of 1943, a special commission of Soviet officers arrived at the newly formed First Division's camp on the Oka river at Sielce to interrogate individual officers and enlisted men. The nearly 50 men who were selected as a result of these discussions were summoned to Kuibyshev in the spring of 1944, when the division found itself near Smolensk.

An NKVD training center had already been established there. During the spring of 1944, the first three-month training course was run by Soviet Colonel Dragunov.[6] The Central Bureau of Polish Communists sent 217 trainees to attend the three-month course at NKVD Officers' School Nr. 366.[7] Graduates were sent to the Polish city of Lublin at the beginning of August 1944, where they immediately joined the ranks of the new security apparatus. Still more recruits were sent to Kuibyshev for training. The second, considerably shorter, three-week course took place during the summer.[8]

The main task of the Security Office was to pursue those individuals who committed political or anti-state offenses. It strove to extend its control over the public sphere as well as the private sphere. Thus, in 1945 the Minister of Security placed representatives on the Commission to Combat Abuses and Bribery, the Commission to Combat Economic Abuse and Sabotage, the Supply Commission, the Office for Combating Usury and Speculation, the Commission for Housing Affairs, and the Main Office for Control of Press, Publications, and Public Performances.[9] This is not a complete list. Essentially the Security Office had agents and/or informants almost everywhere.[10]

In turn, the Security Office itself was under the constant and direct supervision of the West European Section (no. 4) of the NKVD. Officers and agents of the NKVD were employed in all offices and at all levels of the UB as advisors, instructors, or functionaries. Of course, NKVD "advisors" and agents were to be found not only in the Ministry of Public Security, but in all the Polish ministries and government offices. General Serov, and the six Soviet officers who succeeded him as Advisors to the Department (later Ministry) of Public Security until 1956, were subordinated directly to the Second Main Board of the NKVD/MVD. In the second half of 1944, in the various levels of the Ministry of Public Security alone, from headquarters down to the County Security Office level there were some 350 Soviet advisors. In addition, Serov had the 64th Infantry Division of the NKVD/MVD Internal Army at his disposal, and probably the 90th and 218th regiments of the NKVD/MVD, as well, which were assigned to patrol the Polish rear areas of the Soviet Northern Army Group.[11]

In 1944, life in the liberated area known as "Lublin" Poland developed dichotomously. On the one hand, there were the supporters of the Polish Committee of National Liberation, whose power was based in the Red Army, the Department of Public Security, and the other coercive organs of the Polish government. On the other hand, there was the majority of Polish society, in a state of at least passive resistance. General Zygmunt Berling described those turbulent times twelve years later in a letter to Władysław Gomułka.[12] He wrote "as a Marxist," but this did not prevent him from referring to those earlier years as "terrible."

Meanwhile, despite the official propaganda published by the Soviet-sponsored Polish Committee of National Liberation (and, after January 1, 1944, by the Provisional Government), which proclaimed that the Poles had embraced the new system, after the initial euphoria of liberation had passed, the vast majority of Poles remained, in fact, resolutely opposed to the system. Many of the dissatisfied supported open, legalized action, which, it was hoped, would result in fewer casualties. Others – chiefly young men and former officers of the Home Army and the National Armed Forces (NSZ), who were unable to take advantage of the amnesty of August 1945, fled to join the resistance units in the forests. With the help of information supplied by local underground Communist groups, Soviet partisans – and later, by their own friends, confidantes, and traitors in their midst – they were relentlessly hunted down. Data supplied by willing and unwilling informants was assiduously collected and processed in various branches of the increasingly ubiquitous bureaucracy.

The Poles had been physically and psychologically battered during the war, and following liberation, the population eagerly absorbed the Communist slogans. But after just a few weeks, one observer reported that "drunken Bolsheviks were yelling that despite the blessings that they had brought, the Poles were relating to them quite indifferently."[13] The Soviets and their protégés, the Polish Communists, faced the enormous challenge of convincing the public to accept Communist precepts. Those who remained indifferent or hostile to the new order became candidates for repression. During the German occupation, the Polish Communists had worked underground alongside the Home Army and had the opportunity to learn many of the Home Army's secrets. They were able to discover the true identities of those bearing wartime pseudonyms, as well as to pin-point high-ranking officers in the Home Army. Even at the time, it was clear that the Polish Communists would share this information with the Soviets and, of course, with the NKVD.

Some of the most interesting information on the activities of the UB and NKVD in Poland was provided by a direct participant and eyewitness, Józef Światło.

> For five months before the entry of the [Red] Army into Nowo-Radomsk county, 900 parachutists were dropped in and worked in various groups, each of which had its own task . . . "Captain Fiedor's" group had 80 people and its task was military intelligence . . . "Captain Wiktor's" group's job was to determine local relations. After the Red Army came, this group pointed out those members of Polish society which it deemed dangerous, arrested, and shot them.[14]

At this time, Polish soldiers and officers who had spent years (or months, in the case of Home Army members taken prisoner following the collapse of the Warsaw Uprising) in German *oflags* or *stalags*, returned to Poland. The Polish government-in-exile received reports from the remnants of its agencies in Poland describing the situation: "Many Polish soldiers returning from German imprisonment were arrested by the NKVD on the charge of collaboration with the Germans. Youths freed from German camps in East Prussia are being deported to the East."[15]

The Soviets, of course, had the necessary resources in Poland to deal with the real and supposed enemies of the fledgling Communist regime. In fact, the Polish Communists had given the Red Army legal jurisdiction over a fairly wide zone immediately behind the front line with the Germans.[16] As the front line moved westward, the NKVD's operational groups actively sought out members of the underground civilian administration, as well as the Home Army, Peasant Battalions, and other resistance groups. Perhaps the most infamous episode of this covert war was when the Soviets invited the leadership of the Polish Underground State (the "Sixteen") for discussions under a guarantee of personal safety. The Polish leaders were then arrested and kidnapped to Moscow, where they were tried as counterrevolutionaries.

The NKVD and UB interned suspected underground members in a number of camps, the best known of which where at Skrobów,[17] Lubartów, and Rembertów, near Warsaw, where approximately 1,500 Poles were incarcerated. Other camps included those at Rawicz, in Poznań province, where 800 Home Army prisoners were held; at Jaroslaw, with 300 AK prisoners; and Bakuńczyce near Przemyśl, with 1,500 Home Army prisoners. Former German concentration camps were used as well, the most famous being Majdanek and Auschwitz, as well as German jails, like the former Polish royal castle in Lublin. One should not forget about the cellars in the buildings occupied by Security Offices, where prisoners were isolated.[18] From the establishment of these camps, their prisoners were deported east, into the depths of

Russia. London was informed that:

> In the spring of 1945 thousands of prisoners were transported to
> Russia. At the Wilno train station in Warsaw, five freight trains
> with forty cars each, loaded with people from the AK, were noted...
> According to reports received, 170 freight cars were sent from the
> Białystok jails during this same period, packed tight with young
> people of both sexes from the AK.[19]

There were many other camps in Russia in which Poles were
imprisoned

> among others southeast of Moscow. About 25,000 Polish political
> prisoners are imprisoned there. This group includes a number of
> camps, separated from each other by 70-80 kilometers, each
> containing between 600 and 800 persons. The deportees live in
> barracks . . . There is insufficient food: 120 grams of bread daily,
> coffee in the morning, soup at noon, coffee or soup in the evening. [20]

Recent revised estimates concerning the extent of the deportations
have sparked controversy among historians.[21] No reliable estimate
seems possible until historians gain access to the relevant Russian
archives, which have only begun to yield precious information on this
and related topics. For example, thanks to the assistance of Russian
archivists, in 1993 the Polish Central Military Archive received the
records of approximately 500 Home Army soldiers who were interned
or jailed in the Soviet Union.

It will be illustrative to point out just a few of the more important
legal innovations of the Soviet-sponsored regime. On September 12,
1944, the PKWN established special courts to try Nazi war criminals,[22]
which became notorious for meting out swift "justice." Indictments had
to be presented within 14 days of the arrest; the case had to come to
court within forty-eight hours of receipt of the indictment by the court;
judgment was final and had the force of law; and there was no
provision for appealing the verdict. If a death sentence was handed
down by the court, the defendant had the right to appeal to the
chairman of the KRN for clemency.

The majority of capital cases tried by military courts were judged in
light of two important decrees. The first was the draconian Penal Code
of the Polish Army,[23] issued by the PKWN on September 23, 1944, but
formulated by the Polish Communists during their exile in the Soviet
Union. It provided for the trial of civilians in military courts in cases of
treason, and indeed the overwhelming majority of cases tried by these
courts involved civil-ians.[24] The Penal Code of the Polish Army became
the formal basis for sentencing those who actively criticized the PKWN,
Polish-Soviet relations or Soviet domination.[25] Its articles mandated the

death penalty far more frequently than had the pre-war army penal code.[26]

The second measure was the Decree Concerning the Defense of the State, passed on October 30, 1944, which was retroactive to August 15, 1944.[27] The first eleven articles of this decree encompassed political crimes, administrative and economic offenses, and disruptions of public order, and allowed the courts to sentence offenders to imprisonment or death. These crimes were removed from the jurisdiction of regular courts and placed within the purview of the military tribunals.

This decree threatened the vast majority of Poland's population with a death sentence, since it could be wielded against: members of underground organizations during the period of the German occupation who had not revealed themselves as such (and most did not, for fear of being arrested and deported to Russia); farmers who were opposed to land reform, or did not deliver requisitioned items; workers, engineers, and railroad workers who were charged with delivering faulty industrial goods or with shoddy work; as well as bureaucrats and officials. Moreover, this decree was the first to violate the principle that laws cannot be retroactively applied (more decrees of this kind followed later), and it virtually negated the civil rights guarantees provided in the March 1921 Constitution, which putatively was still in force.[28]

The introduction of a law establishing a new system of Military Courts and Military Prosecutors[29] officially relegated political matters to the province of military courts until early 1955, when the jurisdiction of these courts was limited following the dissolution of the Ministry of Public Security in December 1954. Thus, during the People's Republic of Poland's first decade, political crimes were treated as if the state was still embattled. The Polish military justice system served the objectives of the security forces, which were not subject to control by the bureaucracy, or, evidently, by the PPR. During the initial period of their existence, the military courts targeted former members of the Home Army and its successor organizations,[30] as well as right-wing paramilitary organizations,[31] and a host of regional and local outfits,[32] many of whom were tried and given severe sentences. Later, the courts focused their attention on the activities of Polish Peasant Party members and socialists who remained aloof from the PPR.[33]

Despite the fact that the President of the Republic had issued a formal revocation of the state of war in November, 1945,[34] new decrees were introduced which were premised on the continued existence of a state of emergency. The first, "on particularly dangerous crimes during the reconstruction of the Polish state,"[35] encompassed a number of articles in an earlier decree on espionage, some articles contained in the decree on the defense of the state, and portions of several other decrees.[36] It provided for the selective nullification of legislation from the interwar period and, more importantly, sanctioned military justice and the death penalty for a wide variety of offenses. Thousands of people received stiff sentences on the basis of this decree, among other things, for so-called gossip – that is, for conveying information on the situation in Poland. The decree commonly became known as the "little penal code" in Poland, and inspired fear among the population. The decree was later amended and supplanted by others which further intensified the coercive nature of the judicial system by stipulating the harshest punishment for a wide variety of offenses.[37]

A second important decree, on emergency or summary action, was published on November 16, 1945.[38] It dealt with various categories of offenses which did not lie within the jurisdiction of the military courts. The decree stated that those against whom summary proceedings had been initiated were subject to immediate arrest. The summary proceedings themselves were to "take place without an inquiry. The prosecutor could investigate directly, or indirectly through the Citizens' Militia... If the investigation has not or is not undertaken by the prosecutor, it can be undertaken by the public security organs. . ." The amount of time allowed for such investigations during the summary proceedings was very short and "the indictment should be presented within thirty days of the suspect's arrest... Following consultation, the court will immediately render its verdict..." and "the verdicts and decisions of the court are not subject to appeal."

This brief outline of landmark legislation would be incomplete without mention of the Special Commission to Combat Economic Abuses and Sabotage, established by decree on November 16, 1945.[39] The measure sanctioned the so-called penal forced labor camps that had been established and operating in Poland during the previous few months. According to one author, over 100 labor and other camps were established in Poland during this period, and the average number of prisoners interned there never fell below 150,000 annually.[40]

The Commission was established to uncover and prosecute crimes which jeopardized Poland's economic interests, and explicitly sanctioned denunciation, a form of information gathering that would complement the efforts of a large bureaucracy. Anyone seeking employment, housing or admission to a school or university was forced to fill out these lengthy questionnaires – in effect, informing on themselves. Regardless of the actions of the courts, the Commission could prosecute anyone suspected of alleged economic crimes, which were subject to definition by the Commission itself. The Commission's verdicts were not subject to appeal or judicial review of any kind. Further, the Commission was empowered to review and intervene in cases already being heard in court. In fact, at the Commission's request, the courts were required to turn over cases in progress.[41] There was no provision for appeal of the Commission's findings: "All decisions of the Special Commission are final; no legal recourse is possible."

The introduction of special courts, summary proceedings, and

Special Commissions were all important elements in the totalitarian system that was being constructed in Poland, and indeed, throughout the rest of postwar, Soviet-occupied East Central Europe. The Provisional Government created the Internal Security Corps [Korpus Bezpieczeństwa Wewnętrznego] on March 26, 1945.[42] Since it was well-known that the local population was feeding and providing intelligence to the underground groups, government organs countered with massive repression, which often made the resistance more determined.

Beginning with Operation Tempest, the underground had been dealt a series of serious blows, including the abortive Warsaw Uprising, the dissolution of the Home Army, the signing of the Yalta accords, the kidnapping and trial of the "Sixteen," and the withdrawal of Allied recognition from the Government-in-Exile. Stanisław Mikołajczyk shattered the underground coalition's unity when his Peasant Party left the government-in-exile and entered the Provisional Government of National Unity. Last but not least, the underground endured the unremitting waves of arrests that had regularily swept over Poland since 1939.

However, with the prospect of upcoming elections and the government's need to guarantee suitable conditions, the military was called upon to evaluate its performance to date and formulate a plan to clear Poland of "terrorists" and "bandits" through concerted, organized action. In a memorandum dated February 25, 1946, Brigadier General Stefan Mossor, then deputy chief of staff of the Polish Army, criticized the methods being used to liquidate the underground and concluded that the main reasons for such a poor showing were:

1. The continuing poor coordination between the Army, the Security Office, the Citizens' Militia, and civilian authorities, and above all the lack of a unified, efficient overall leadership. A government commission cannot serve as an efficient executive organ;
2. Gaps in the Army's stationing, above all in the Białystok and Lublin regions, where as a result of the removal of military garrisons from vast tracts of difficult terrain, diversionary action is not decreasing, but increasing ;
3. The lack of unified leadership, or command in the most important areas which would have in its hands the requisite powers and means to introduce law and order.

In addition, a new emphasis was placed on propaganda and intelligence work. A massive propaganda campaign was mounted just before the referendum, involving about 30 percent of the Polish Army's troops, which were used between May 15 and June 30 in an effort to convince people to vote in favor of the regime's proposals. Almost 110,000 troops were deployed to protect the polling stations from underground attack, and the exercise was repeated for the January 1947 elections.[43] But they accomplished much more than this: in Rzeszów province alone, they prompted the dissolution of seventy-five Polish Peasant Party clubs, organized over 1,913 village meetings in which over 285,000 people participated, and removed twenty-seven communal administrators and sixty-one village administrators. The Defense and Propaganda Groups were equally effective elsewhere.[44]

After the referendum, stream-lined intelligence units intensified their efforts to smoke-out the individual underground units targeted by Provincial Security Committees. The State Committee on Security analyzed the performance of the operational groups and issued new directives.[45]

It is clear from the daily, fortnightly, monthly, and quarterly reports documenting "the results of the struggle against the bandits" that in the latter half of 1946, the State Committee on Security was gaining the upper hand on the organized political underground. The fight was brutal, with no quarter given. According to one author, who cites materials in the Central Military Archives (but gives no collection, box, or folder numbers), the armed underground lost 2,830 in 1945; 2,770 in 1946; 1,486 in 1947; and 306 in 1948. In addition, 71,336 persons were arrested.[46]

These statistics, like so many of those presented earlier in this study, are subject to verification. There are, for example, various estimates of the number of civilians tried and sentenced by military courts in the immediate postwar era: 45,000 persons from 1944-49,[47] 54,000 from 1945-49,[48] even a figure as specific as 45,706 from October 1, 1944 to December 31, 1954.[49] When one adds soldiers who were tried and convicted, the total increases by some 10-15%. The most recent and presumably most accurate estimate of civilians and military personnel tried, convicted, and sentenced by military courts from 1946 to 1953 is 65,000, with 22,500 in the period from 1950 to 1953.[50]

Many more people were actually detained – a substantial number without arrest warrants[51] – in county and provincial security headquarters as well as in jails, and are therefore not included in the figures above. Some were undergoing investigation, some awaiting trial, others were simply incarcerated as an administrative measure to take them out of circulation for a few months. As for the total number of Polish prisoners held at any given time by the NKVD/MVD in their numerous facilities throughout Poland, the historical literature remains silent.

How many persons received the death sentence? The first articles on this topic began to appear in the late 1970s when Maria Turlejska, a Polish historian using the pseudonym Łukasz Socha, published studies based on materials hitherto unknown to historians. Turlejska's work cited unique documents concerning the Polish judicial system during the years 1944-1946, the majority of which contained verdicts handed down by military courts.[52] Two kinds of courts functioned during the first half of 1946, both with the right to hand down death sentences. Summary departments of civilian District Courts, *Sądy Okręgowe*, were organized in January 1946 following the decree of November 16, 1945 to try civilians suspected of cooperating with the underground. They functioned until July, when summary departments were introduced into the military courts. Civilian summary departments were also attached directly to military units in the field. These were infamous for meting out swift and usually pitiless justice. In spring 1946, Military District Courts were established – the so-called Military Regional Courts and the Military Court of the Internal Security Corps. Polish army courts handed down 900 death sentences in 1944-1945,[53] of which 306 were for political crimes: 170 of the 306 (55.5 percent) death sentences were carried out.[54] In 1945-46, over 1,700 persons were sentenced to death, while between 1944 and 1948, the total was 2,500.[55] Jerzy Poksiński estimates that slightly over 3,000 death sentences were handed down between September 1944 and December 1946.[56] A document compiled in 1989 by the Polish Central Board of Penal Institutions lists by name 2,800 persons actually executed in Polish jails between 1944 and 1956.[57]

Most military trials were held in secret. Others took the form of show trials – usually in theaters or factories – in which case they were given a great deal of publicity. Trials were held in provincial capitals, in smaller towns, and even villages, where they were used to terrify the inhabitants. In a few villages, gallows were erected to hang those found guilty (contrary to the Penal Code of the Polish Army, which stipulated death by firing squad).[58]

Generally, requests for clemency in the early postwar period were denied. Colonel K. Lasota, the chief of the Internal Security Corps' Military Courts, had instructed his subordinates that in cases where the condemned person request clemency from the President of the Republic, his plea should be duly noted, appended to his case records – and filed.[59] Of those appeals which were actually forwarded to Bolesław Bierut, the records show that between 1947 and 1952 less than one out of three requests were granted.[60]

Although the armed underground continued its activities until the mid-1950s, it did so on a much reduced scale, and its activities took on the character of marauding. It is safe to say that by the end of 1947, both the overt political opposition and the armed political conspiracy had been defeated through a lethal combination of terror, military action, fraud, and two amnesties which lured approximately 100,000 out of hiding.[61] Many of those people were later incarcerated. About 1,000 people, including high-ranking officers who had loyally served in the Polish People's Army, were executed after 1950.[62]

With Mikołajczyk's electoral failure, and with the evident, ever-increasing weakness of the underground, more and more people turned their attention to everyday life, and to physical survival. In the late 1940s, fear was constant and palpable among those opposed to the regime. They were dogged by the fear of being labelled "bandits" and "reactionaries," and sharing the fate of those whose mortal remains were scattered throughout the cities, towns, villages, and countryside.[63] In the early 1950s, that same fear spread even to active, loyal supporters of the regime, as the terror was turned against the Communists themselves by the coercive system that they had constructed.

Notes

1. In the spring of 1944, the Home Army numbered over 350,000, while the Communist People's Army counted between 10,000 and 20,000 members.

2. Ivan Aleksandrovich Serov had a long list of accomplishments during his service, including commanding the firing squad which executed Marshall Mikhail Tukhachevskii in June 1937; in summer 1941 he organized the deportations of the Volga Germans; and between October 1943 and June 1944, Serov arranged the expulsion to Siberia or Soviet Central Asia of six entire nations (1 million people) residing in the areas near the Caspian Sea, the Crimea, and the Caucasus. In March 1954 he became the first chief of the newly organized Committee of State Security (KGB), where he served until February or July 1958, when he was transferred to military intelligence (the GRU) removed following the unmasking of Lieutenant Colonel Yurii Popov as a western spy. Serov was removed as head of GRU in February or March 1964 after a similar scandal involving GRU Colonel Oleg Penkovskii. Marek Ciesielczyk, *KGB* (Berlin: Poglad, 1989), pp. 37, 48, 59-61. Serov was in charge of the Soviet rear areas in Poland after their liberation, and was appointed NKVD Advisor to the Polish Ministry of Public Security on March 1, 1945. Andrzej Paczkowski, "Aparat Bezpieczeństwa," in *Instytucje państwa totalitarnego: Polska 1944-1956* (Warsaw: Instytut Studiów Politycznych PAN, 1994), p. 62.

3. Bąkiewicz Collection, 138/263, PISM, counterintelligence report from Poland, no. 5 /45, 22/VI/1945, 1.

4. Some of its graduates who later appeared in People's Poland as party activists and security officers included: General Aleksander Kokoszyn, head of the Military Internal Service (WSW); Colonel Stanisław Koncewicz, head of the minister of interior's office; and Major Władysław Sobczynski, head of the Provincial Security Office in Rzeszów and Kielce (where he was to become infamous for his role in the pogrom of July 1944). Tadeusz Żenczykowski, *Polska Lubelska 1944* (Paris: Editions Spotkania, 1987), 71.

5. They included: Mieczysław Moczar, partisan, head of the Provincial Security Office in Łódż, later vice-minister of public security, and minister of various portfolios; General Konrad Świetlik, vice-minister of public security;

and Colonel Józef Czaplicki, head of a department in the ministry of public security. Żenczykowski, *Polska Lubelska 1944*, 71.

6. They included: Eliasz Koton, head of the provincial security office in Białystok; Major Józef Krakowski, head of a security office operational group in Otwock; and Faustyn Grzybowski, head of the provincial office of public security in Lublin. Żenczykowski, *Polska Lubelska 1944*, 74.

7. Andrzej Paczkowski, "Aparat Bezpieczeństwa," *Instytucje państwa totalitarnego*, 62.

8. Tadeusz Żenczykowski, "Przyczynki do historii Bezpieki (I)," *Na antenie*, no. 140, (January, 1975) : 17-19; and "Przyczynki do historii Bezpieki (II)," *Na antenie*, no. 141, London (February, 1975) : 18-20.

9. B 2111, PISM, A.K. Opolski, *Sowietyzacja Polski* (London: November 1946), 7.

10. The impact of the security force's surveillance of and interference in everyday life was soon felt. Local authorities passed ordinances which, for example, extended the reach of the secret police to each apartment building. In mid-1945, the chairman of the National Council of the City of Warsaw issued "Instructions for Building Committees" in which he suggested that "the Building Committee should take care to see to it that the building not become a meeting place for criminals, that it not become a place to hatch criminal schemes. . . Toward these ends the Building Committee should keep a vigilant eye out for strangers, and immediately alert the local Citizens' Militia station of such visitors." Bąkiewicz Collection, 138/263, PISM, report from Poland by "Szkrab," 27/X/45, 4-5.

11. The latter were recalled in autumn 1946, the former in spring 1947. Andrzej Paczkowski, "Aparat Bezpieczeństwa," in *Instytucje państwa totalitarnego*, 62.

12. Jan Nowak, "Sprawa generała Berlinga," in *Zeszyty Historyczne* 37 (1976), 39.

13. Bąkiewicz Collection, 138/264, PISM, report by Tadeusz Chrzanowski, 19/ XI/1945, 6-7.

14. Bąkiewicz Collection, 138/266, PISM, interview with Alfons Kasza, 4/VIII/ 1945, 6.

15. Polish Government-in-Exile in London, 1939-1945, Box 71, HIWRP, *Poufny Biuletyn Informacyjny*, nr. 114a, telegram-szyfr z dnia 21/III/1945; *Poufny Biuletyn Informacyjny* , nr. 115b, telegram-szyfr z dnia 13/IV/1945; *Poufny Biuletyn Informacyjny*, nr. 117a, telegram-szyfr z dnia 26/IV1945; *Poufny Biuletyn Informacyjny*, nr. 118a, telegram-szyfr z dnia 10/V/1945.

16. See "Porozumienie między Polskim Komitetem Wyzwolenia Narodowego i Rządem Związku Socjalistycznych Republik Radzieckich o stosunkach między radzieckim wodzem naczelnym a polską administracją po

wkroczeniu wojsk radzieckich na terytorium Polski," July 26, 1944. *Dokumenty i materiały do historii stosunków polsko-radzieckich,* vol. 8 (Warsaw: Książka i Wiedza, 1974), Document Nr. 75, 155-157. The agreement was neither confirmed by the KRN nor published in the official law monitor, *Dziennik Ustaw.* Although the agreement did appear in the Polish-language journal, *Wolna Polska* 28 (August 3, 1944), published in the Soviet Union, it was not published in Poland until 1954. Maria Turlejska, *Te pokolenia żałobami czarne...: Skazani na smierć i ich sędziowie 1944-1954* (London: Aneks, 1989), 33-35.

17. See Jerzy Ślaski, *Skrobów. Dzieje obozu NKWD dla żołnierzy AK 1944-1945* (Warsaw: PAX, 1990).

18. Bąkiewicz Collection, 138/264, PISM, report by Tadeusz Chrzanowski, November 19, 1945, 22-23; 138/267, report by Jan Osowski, August 12, 1945, 2; 138/267, report by Wacław Mańkowski, August 30, 1945, 2-4; 138/267, report by Jan Łopuski, November 13, 1945, 2-3.

19. Bąkiewicz Collection, 138/264, PISM, intelligence report from Poland, no. 1/45, October 22, 1945, 22-23; 138/267, report by Jan Osowski, August 12, 1945, 2; 138/267, report by Wacław Mańkowski, August 30, 1945, 2-4; 138/267, report by Jan Łopuski, November 13, 1945, 2-3.

20. Bąkiewicz Collection, 138/263, PISM, intelligence report from Poland, no. 7/45, June 25, 1945, 9; 138/ 266, report by Jan Konopka, November 9, 1945, 1; 138/ 266, report by Zofia Kaczorowska, November 5, 1945, about Poles who returned from Soviet camps by rail on September 20, 1945, 2.

21. See, for example, the polemic between Krystyna Kersten, Albin Głowacki and Andrzej Korzon, respectively, concerning deportations in *Polityka* no. 2 (January 8, 1994), no. 6 (February 5, 1994), no. 24 and no. 21 (May 21, 1994), 25.

22. DzURP 1944, Nr. 4, item 21, 25-26.

23. DzURP 1944, Nr. 6, item 27, 35-54.

24. My own research shows, for example, that in the first eleven months of 1945, the Military Court of the Garrison at Przemyśl tried 456 people, of whom 416 (91 percent) were civilians. Centralny Archiwum Wojskowy, III/437/4, Wojskowy Sąd Garnizonowy w Przemyślu.

25. Turlejska, *Te pokolenia żałobami czarne*, 38.

26. In pre-war Poland, the death sentence was applicable in criminal cases involving murder by means of a weapon. Less than twenty death sentences per year were handed down during the 1930s, out of approximately 1,500 cases per year involving homicide. Turlejska,*Te pokolenia żałobami czarne*, 37.

27. DzURP 1944, Nr. 10, item 50, 97-98.

28. Turlejska,*Te pokolenia żałobami czarne*, 42-44.

29. DzURP 1944, no. 6, item 29, 55-64.

30. Including NIE [*Niepodległość* (Independence)], DSZ [*Delegatura Sił Zbrojnych* (the Armed Forces Delegacy)], and WiN [*Wolność i Niezawisłość*

(Freedom and Independence)].

31. Chiefly the NSZ [*Narodowe Siły Zbrojne* (National Armed Forces)] and the NZW [*Narodowe Zjednoczenie Wojskowe* (National Military Union)].

32. For a very good, concise discussion of the various underground organizations and their goals, see Andrzej Friszke, *Opozycja polityczna w PRL, 1945-1980* (London: Aneks, 1994), 45-66.

33. Turlejska, *Te pokolenia żałobami czarne*, 41.

34. Published on and effective as of December 17, 1945, *DzURP* 1945, Nr. 57, Item 320.

35. *DzURP* 1945, Nr. 53, item 300, 469-473.

36. It also rescinded several legislative acts including some dating from the prewar period:

1. the Polish Committee of National Liberation's decree on the defense of the state of October 30, 1944;

2. the decree of the President of the Republic of November 22, 1938 concerning the protection of state interests; and

3. the executive order of the President of the Republic of October 24, 1934, concerning crimes against the security of the state.

37. Dated, respectively, June 13, 1946, *DzURP* 1946, no. 53, item 300, 469-473; July 12, 1946, a decree *DzURP* 1946, no. 30, item 192, 347-352; and October 17, 1946 "abolishing special military courts." *DzURP* 1946, no. 59, item 324, 692-693.

38. *DzURP* 1945, no. 53, item 301, 474-476.

39. *DzURP* 1945, no. 53, item 302, 476-477.

40. Tadeusz Żenczykowski, *Dramatyczny rok 1945* (London: Polonia Book Fund, 1982), 198. Not all inmates of these camps were sent there by the Special Commission however. A recent article based on research in the Special Commissions' records asserts that in the early period only thirty such camps operated and that until 1949 the Commission sent 16,500 people to the labor camps. The later figure was confirmed by this author in the same archive. See Grzegorz Sołtysiak, "Komisja Specjalna do Walki," in *Karta* (January 1991), 83-86.

41. 2111, PISM, A.K. Opolski, *Sowietyzacja Polski* (London, November 1946); Poland, Ministry of the Interior Collection, Box 12, HIWRP, *Służba Bezpieczeństwa w Polsce 1945/46*, 31-32.

42. Its responsibilities soon comprised:

1) a protective service whose job it was to guard state dignitaries, particularly "dangerous" political prisoners, hightly valuable items in transport, etc:

2) liquidation units, whose task was "to liquidate socio-political elements hostile to the State";

3) Border Defense units, which, in addition to controlling border traffic, were to "prepare residents of the frontier area for complete cooperation with the authorities";

4) guard units, to watch over particularly important state property and to supervise camps and jails in which political prisoners and "individuals particularly dangerous to society" were incarcerated;

5) an information section, whose task it was to gather intelligence as well as domestic counter-intelligence.

43. From December 5-21, 1946, and January 3-21, 1947, 109,964 troops organized into Defense Propaganda Groups covered the country to agitate on behalf of the regime and later to defend the polling stations against attack.

44. Ryszard Terlecki, *Dyktatura zdrady. Polska w 1947 roku* (Cracow: Arka, 1991), 15. The reports of the Defense-Propaganda Groups located in the Centralny Archiwum Wojskowy provide ample evidence of their efficacy. Their activities were noted by the Polish Peasant Party and included in numerous protests lodged by that Party including, among others, the well-known memoranda submitted to the Soviet, British, and American ambassadors.

45. See "Wytyczne dla pracy Wojewodzkich Komitetów Bezpieczeństwa na okres przedwyborczy," dated July 17, 1946, Centralny Archiwum Wojskowe, Oddział Operacyjny Sztabu Generalnego, teczka 505, Akta PKB 26 VIII-22 X 46, 374-384.

46. This coincides closely with a figure given in proceedings against Lt. Colonel Czesław Szpądrowski, serving with the Chief Military Prosecutor's Office, and accused and convicted on May 25, 1949, by the Supreme Military Tribunal in Warsaw of providing state secrets to an enemy agent. In November or December 1947, Szpądrowski, who was in a position to know, revealed that in 1947:

there were 72,000 people arrested and jailed by military justice organs, of whom 15 percent were military, that 3,000 people had been sentenced to death, including 10 percent military, that among the 72,000 arrested and jailed, 12 percent were convicted of possession of a firearm without permission, that these figures could be off by at most 2 percent, that in addition there was a substantial number of people being detained by Security and about whom the military prosecutors know nothing and are included in the figures given.

47. Andrzej Werblan, *Stalinizm w Polsce* (Warsaw, 1991), as cited by Jerzy Poksiński, "Sądownictwo wojskowe," in *Instytucje państwa totalitarnego*, 7. Werblan admits, however, that the number may be higher by as many as an additional 10,000 people.

48. Jerzy Paśnik, "Prawne aspekty represji stalinowskich w Polsce," in *Dziś* 7, (1991), 101, and "Obig zamknięty. Sądy wojskowe w Polsce w latach 1944-1949," in *Prawo i Życie* 21 (1989), as cited by Jerzy Poksiński, "Sądownictwo

wojskowe," in *Instytucje państwa totalitarnego* , 7.

49. Jerzy Muszyński, *20 lat ludowego Wojska Polskiego, II Sesja naukowa poświęcona wojnie wyzwoleńczej narodu polskiego 1939-1945* (Warsaw, 1966), 1064, as cited by Jerzy Poksiński, "Sądownictwo wojskowe," in *Instytucje państwa totalitarnego*, 7.

50. Andrzej Paczkowski, *Półwieku dziejów Polski, 1939-1989* (Warsaw: PWN, 1995), 253. These political prisoners comprised 44 percent, or 26,400, of the 60,000 people who had been tried, convicted, and were serving their sentences in Polish prisons on January 1, 1948; a year later there were 32,200 of them (40 percent of 80,500 people) and in mid-1950, their numbers rose to 35,200, or 35.9 percent of 98,000. See Andrzej Paczkowski, *Półwieku dziejów Polski*, 259.

51. My own research into the military court system unearthed many reports of inspections which complained of this very problem.

52. By 1945, courts existed at the division, army, and branch levels, as did field courts and garrison courts. In Spring 1946, District Military Courts [Wojskowe Sądy Okręgowe] were established, followed by Regional Military Courts [Wojskowe Sądy Rejonowe] to judge civilians, and the Internal Security Corps' Military Courts. The President of the Supreme Military Court initially was Brigadier General Aleksander Tarnowski, and in 1946, Colonel Aleksander Michniewicz, both Soviet citizens and Red Army officers with 25 years service before "joining" the Polish Army.

53. 380 death sentences were handed down in 1944, of which 122 (32.1 percent) were carried out. Centralny Archiwum Wojskowy, teczka III/439/25, Naczelna Prokuratura Wojskowa, Imienny skorowidz wykonanych wyroków śmierci skazanych przez Sądy Wojskowe WP w 1944.

54. Stefan Zwoliński, "Skazani na smierć przez Sądy WP w latach 1944-1945. Wyroki, których być nie powinno," *Wojskowy Przegląd Historyczny* 1 (1992), 219-251.

55. Turlejska, *Te pokolenia żałobami czarne*, 98. Professor Turlejska's archival source has not been made public in the 17 years since she first began to publish articles on death sentences handed down by military courts.

56. Based on records in the Central Military Archive. See Jerzy Poksiński, "Sądownictwo wojskowe," in *Instytucje państwa totalitarnego* , 8.

57. *Straceni w polskich wiezieniach 1944-1956* (Lublin: Retro, 1994).

58. Turlejska, *Te pokolenia żałobami czarne*, 106.

59. Turlejska, *Te pokolenia żałobami czarne*, 370.

60. In 1947, however, the chances of receiving clemency were less than one in four, as 77.4% of the requests were turned down, and the chances for clemency in the earlier period were still slimmer. Grzegorz Wojciechowski, unpublished manuscript entitled "Wnioski o ułaskawienie w zespole Kancelarii Cywilnej Prezydenta RP wobec skazanych przez sądy wojskowe 1947-1952," 7-10.

61. That is, following the dissolution of the Provincial Committees of Security in most of the areas west of the Vistula River in October, the arrest of the Fourth Main Board of WiN (Freedom and Independence, the largest underground network) and finally, the escape of Stanisław Mikołajczyk to Great Britain in November.

62. Andrzej Garlicki estimates that between 1950 and 1955, 40,000 people were arrested, and nearly 28,000 convicted, *Stalinizm* (Warsaw: Wydawnictwo Szkolne i Pedagogiczne, 1993), 54.

63. Several hundred cities, towns, villages, and other locations where victims were found are listed in Zbigniew Taranienko, *Nasze Termopile* (Warsaw: Wydawnictwo Archidiecezji Warszawskiej, 1993), 40-46.

6

The Soviet Administrators and Their German "Friends"

Alexei Filitov

The Soviet occupation authorities' attitude to the German Communists in their zone is customarily depicted as extremely supportive, with the Soviets prodding their protégés to engage in the kind of intense activism that would culminate in their seizure of power. However, Soviet reports on the situation in Germany immediately following the end of hostilities present a dramatically different picture; rather than inciting their indigenous "party comrades" to radical actions, Soviet representatives deplored their zeal as inimical to the purposes of the occupation.

A report on events in Meissen during the second half of May 1945 portrays the situation as reminiscent of that prevailing in Soviet Russia during the Civil War: red stars were affixed to public buildings; "commissars" were installed to run enterprises abandoned by their owners; and intellectuals were arrested on serious, though trumped-up, charges. The Soviet reporter, however, cited these "Red" activities as lamentable examples of sectarianism on the part of German local "activists," which were facilitated by the negligence of the Soviet Military commandant.

In order to combat the problems in Meissen, the following measures were taken: the removal of stars and "other Communist symbols"; the abolition of the "commissars"; the prohibition of all civil organizations except for a City Magistrate entirely composed of "non-Nazis" (but not necessarily "anti-Nazis"); and the convocation, on May 30, 1945, of the "most respected citizens" representing all strata of the population.[1]

The misguided zealotry and bungling of German comrades in the northern part of the Soviet zone (Rostock-Stralsund-Greifswald) had fewer ideological implications, but was no less politically damaging. From the beginning, the local police force in Rostock exhibited numerous deficiencies. The police chief, a Communist, "does not understand his task," and had confiscated flats, removing the furniture and other movable property. Moreover, the Chief of Criminal Police, who was likewise a Communist, sought supporters "among the pimps, rather than among the workers." In Greifswald, the Communist ranks were also rumored to be recruited from "the pimps and criminals."[2] Even in Berlin, the "Ulbricht Group" (consisting of especially trusted German Communists) got bad marks for its lack of coordination with the Soviet commandants and with counter-intelligence units. [3]

Both the Meissen and Rostock-Stralsund-Greifswald reports were written by Germans who later became prominent in the KPD/SED, Anton Ackermann in the first case, and Gustav Sobottka/Willi Bredel, in the second. Nevertheless, the reports are undeniably "anti-Communist," and express more support for the Social Democrats, who were previously – during the Weimar Republic, and subsequently – during the Stalinist period – labeled "social fascists." For instance, the dismissal of the Communist chief and his replacement by a Social Democrat was recommended to remedy the situation in Rostock.

In the Ackermann report, the Chief of 7th Department of the Red Army's Main Political Administration, Major General M. I. Burtsev, categorically stated: "The situation in Meissen underscores the necessity of retaining a ban on all political organizations and parties until the political situation stabilizes, until the people are disabused of their deep-rooted and dangerous sectarianism, and are convinced of the correctness of our policies." Several days later, however, on June 10, 1945, the Soviet Military Administration (SVAG) issued Order no. 2, allowing for the creation of political parties in the zone.

The glaring discrepancy between the formal recommendation of SVAG's supervisory agency and SVAG's actions is perplexing. Clearly, the new policy that superseded the practice of "political quarantine" emanated from the highest echelons of the Soviet power structures, presumably from Stalin himself. Perhaps this decision was taken with an eye to the impending Potsdam Conference: Stalin wanted to pose as an advocate of democracy in Germany and was eager to set the tone for the whole country. Basically, he succeeded on both fronts. Political development was more advanced in the Soviet zone than in the Western zones, and the parties which emerged in the East (Communist, Social Democrat, Christian Democrat, Liberal Democrat) became the focal points of political activity in the West.

The early formalization of party divisions created, however, substantial handicaps for the Soviet administrators. They sacrificed flexibility in the hiring and firing of German officials. "Party solidarity" took precedence over the suitability of the prospective official. After the formation of the KPD, and its most formidable competitor (the SPD), the replacement of a bad Communist police chief by a good Social Democratic one became unthinkable. From this point on, the dismissal of a Communist official, even on non-political grounds, would be construed as evidence of an anti-Communist crusade, and even as indicative of re-Nazification.[4]

Accordingly, a high percentage of KPD members in any branch of government was viewed as an achievement in and of itself – quite irrespective of their performance – while the mere presence of "others" was considered an unavoidable evil, at best. For example, in a report by Major Kvassov, Chief of the 7th Section in the Political Branch of the 8th Army Guard, depicting the state of affairs in Thuringia, the tell-tale word "cleanest" was used to describe the composition of the Landespolizei staff (eighteen Communists and three Social Democrats, none of whom were ex-Nazis) as opposed to the Finance Department staff, which still counted fifty-two former NSDAP members out of a total of eighty-seven employees, and the Education Department (with eight Communists, seven Social Democrats and twently-seven former Nazis).

The activities of ex-Nazis were less a cause for concern than those of the Social Democrats. As the dubious theory that "the SPD received its support from the bulk of the politically unaffiliated and from the vast majority of former Nazis" gained currency[5], the Soviets fell prey to a polarized view of the political scene. This erroneous assessment, along with the German Communists' fetish for "party solidarity," inhibited the Communists' ability to maneuver deftly in delicate situations. When confronted with the unruly behavior of the Soviet occupation forces, for example, the Communist response was constrained by the dictates of Party propaganda and solidarity.

The Communists were, in fact, among the first to condemn and expose the outrages committed by the Soviet troops, both in conversations with local and central occupation authorities, in their correspondence with Soviet military commanders, and in the Soviet newspapers for Germans, such as *Tägliche Rundschau* (*Daily View*) and others. The letters were, as a rule, signed, which testified to the civic courage of the correspondents.[6] The Soviet authorities and their superiors in Moscow, for their part, did not hesitate to relay these reports to the zenith of the Party hierarchy.[7]

After the Communist Party was legalized, the situation became more delicate. Party members were compelled to avoid any reference to the abominable behavior of the occupation forces, and instead to extol the virtues of the Red Army in contrast to the vices of the Western soldiers. This was, perhaps, the first step in creating an unbridgeable gap between word and reality, which became characteristic of the SED/GDR modus operandi, and eventually contributed to the demise of the "Workers' and Peasants' State."

The extent to which this "double talk" was deleterious to the newly-founded KPD is poignantly illustrated in a report compiled by a SVAG operative on an SPD rally – one of the first after the formation of parties in the Soviet zone. Although the SPD meeting featured such attractions as reserved seating and a choir (KPD equivalents lacked both of these), the reporter singled out three political "weak points" in the address of a Communist who took the floor at the SPD meeting to elaborate upon his Party's platform.

First, there was the thorny issue of the Germans' responsibility for the war and its consequences. According to the reporter, "as the Communist speaker said: 'Many of you are not dressed in German clothes, but in someone else's,' to which his listeners replied: 'I have never seen a German in a *tulup* (sheepskin coat) and *valenki* (felt boots),'" thereby countering the Communist's implicit reference to Germany's exploitation of its occupied eastern territories during the war.

Secondly, there was some disagreement as to who played the decisive role in ending the war. "As the speaker talked about the liberating mission of the Red Army, voices were audible: 'And what about the Americans? Without America, Russia would never have won this war. He is defending the Red Army as if he's been paid to do it'."

The third bone of contention was the speaker's assertion that the building of socialism was not on the agenda, and that the Germans should concentrate instead on the establishment of a democratic order. This point caused considerable consternation in the audience. "No, we are for socialism. Democracy helped Hitler to come power. The working class does not require reeducation."[8]

Although there was some truth in each of the German Communist's assertions, he failed to reach his audience for completely obvious reasons. The listeners had compelling evidence to support opposite points of view: the undisciplined conduct of Red Army soldiers, the material and technical superiority of American forces, and the lack of democracy in the Soviet Union. Constrained by the dictates of Soviet propaganda, the speaker could neither admit the legitimacy of these views, nor successfully counter them. However, he did enjoy one advantage over his Social Democratic rival: his appearance. Whereas the departing SPD speaker was dogged by derisive comments: "He is already well-fed and has his own car. So he is able to build socialism," the Communist's appearance inspired greater sympathy and trust: "He came on foot and looks shabby. It is apparent that the Communists are humble people."[9]

This advantage did not last long, however. From the middle of July 1945 onwards, a clear shift can be discerned in the letters and reports sent to *Tägliche Rundschau,* as criticism focused less and less on the behavior of the Soviet military, and more on that of the German Communists. In his letter dated July 26, 1945, a certain Karl Ludz briefly referred to the Red Army's Bacchanalia, "I expected more disciplined behavior from the Red Army," but directed his most vituperative attacks at the German Communists, "this huge crowd of sycophants who, in shunning any productive activities and in seeking the 'warm places', are indistinguishable from the Nazis just expelled." These observations led him to decry "the complete bankruptcy of the German Communists," and the KPD's inability to steer an independent course.[10]

The criticism gained momentum after the creation of the SED, which – at least formally – liquidated the KPD-SPD duality and thereby raised the new party to the status of a quasi-governmental body. As a report on the SED compiled by Deputy Political Advisor of SVAG , I. F. Filippov, and dispatched to Moscow on October 9, 1946, stated: "Top [Party] officials are enjoying a luxurious lifestyle, while the majority of rank-and-file Party members are suffering from malnutrition and shortages... Corruption is on the rise in the Party apparatus. There are cases in which prominent leaders of the SED, taking advantage of their position, employed Nazis and speculators in order to secure comfortable living quarters... Most of the leading figures in the Berlin SED organization have quarters in Pankow, in the area reserved for the Soviet Kommandatura officers."[11]

Over the course of time, the Communist functionaries' image further deteriorated, until they were perceived as something like "Godfathers" (without the redeeming features of Puso's hero): the abettors and supporters of the mafia-like activities which proliferated throughout the zone. A September 4, 1947 report by the newly-appointed "Pravda" correspondent in Germany, Yuri Korol'kov, upon his visit to Mecklenburg, relayed interesting – albeit sensationalist – information to Editor-in-Chief Pospelov. Korol'kov dwelt at some length on the story of a "big businessman," Rudolf Bentisch, who "with the support of SED authorities, obtained the monopoly rights to the tobacco trade." He himself became an SED member, and both the First Secretary of the SED organization and the Prime Minister presented him their portraits – complete with warm dedications – which were then hung in his study to impress visitors with the visages of his "friends."[12]

In turn, this representative of the new "monopolist capitalism" assiduously greased his sponsors' palms, German and Soviet alike. The Deputy Chief of the SVAG and Economic Department, Colonel Mikhailov, was said to have received 118 pairs of stockings, forty-six meters of fabric, unspecified quantities of women's underwear, etc. According to his entries, specific quotas of "staples" were set for the Generals: from 750 thousand cigarettes to the Commander-in-Chief of the 5th Army, General-Colonel Gorbatov, to five thousand for General

Shchelakovskii. "All this looks like corruption," reported Korol'kov, stating the obvious.

The practice of exacting reparations from current production had largely replaced the dismantling which prevailed in the initial phase of the occupation, and facilitated the criminal practices of the SED-SVAG "connection." A September 26, 1946 memorandum entitled "A Critical Assessment and Constructive Proposals Concerning Economic Performance in the Soviet Occupation Zone of Germany," written by Ulbricht himself, alluded to this state of affairs.[13] The memorandum provided examples of how German enterprises, under the pretext of complying with Soviet reparation orders, evaded the planned distribution system and peddled their merchandise on the black market. Their *modus operandi* was very simple: a fictitious contract was concluded by a representative of one of the numerous Soviet economic agencies active in Germany and a manager of a German firm; the required work force, money, and raw materials were mobilized to fulfill the order; and both sides signed a document – likewise fraudulent – confirming that the supplier had delivered and the customer received the contracted quantity. In fact, the "customer" received a portion of the profits from reselling the commodities on the black market. The value of these goods was added to the sum of reparations received by the USSR, even though not a single item ever crossed the Soviet border.[14]

The mafia-like activities of SVAG-SED representatives provoked the natural resentment of the German population, in light of which Korol'kov issued the gloomy prediction that should German elections be held in the autumn of 1947, "the SED would obtain little more than ten percent of the vote."[15] These sort of reports from the field may help to explain the Soviet leadership's hesitant, zig-zag approach to the general, all-German elections which turned out to be a water-shed in Soviet diplomacy.

Of course, the reporters did not confine themselves to the mere depiction of ills; they advanced possible solutions, as well. However, the recommended measures usually entailed administrative pressure and reprisals, which only perpetuated the vicious circle. In fact, Korol'kov began his report with the complaint that too few arrests were actually made, and that the number of detainees relayed to the center was inflated to please superiors. Korol'kov's conclusion is clear: more reprisals, and all would be well.[16]

Ulbricht's conclusions are likewise clear-cut. Economic performance would improve, he argued, if and when the competing Soviet agencies ceased to violate the plans with their extra-plan orders. The motto of his memo "Germans themselves must run their economy" actually meant that all power should be concentrated in the SED apparatus.[17] A single-party dictatorship combined with the most rigid anti-market regulations is even more strongly advocated by F. Grosse, a prominent figure in the "second echelon" of the SED hierarchy, in his August 7, 1946 memorandum. He presented a long list of grievances (the disorderly conduct of the Soviet military, the dismantling of factories, the inefficient handling of the return of prisoners of war, etc.) but singled out the existence of the "so-called free market" as the primary nuisance. "Since May 1945, there has been no other manifestation which caused such hostility on the part of the Germans... The rich can afford to buy something while the worker has neither the money nor the time."

To remedy the situation he recommended that a "special unit" be set up (affiliated with the Organization Department of the SED, but with "no ties to the NKVD") with a three-fold purpose: to monitor the activities of the CDU and the LDPD, to expose "underground activities" on the part of former Social Democrats, and to investigate corruption cases.[18] These proposals amount to a program for the creation of a police state, and were ultimately incarnated in the omnipresent Stasi.

Initially SVAG supervisors deplored the sectarianism within the newly established SED, and castigated it for both minor faux pas (such as the under- representation of former Social Democrats at Hermann Matern's birthday celebration) and more serious political blunders (such as Franz Dahlem's recruitment of staff for the Central Department of Internal Affairs exclusively from the ranks of former Communists, and without consulting his counterpart in the Party secretariat, former SPD member Erich Gniffke).[19]

For some time, the SPD's readmission to the political scene was contemplated. While SED representatives never concealed their opposition to such a ploy, the Soviet position, articulated by Stalin himself, seemed to be more ambivalent. This author has previously speculated that the Soviets may have been crafting a "big deal" in which the SED would relinquish its political monopoly in exchange for the West's assent to Soviet reparations. The deal did not come off, however. In any case, the Soviets' arguments in support of this deal (the alleged "softening" of the SPD line vis á vis the Soviet Union, and the advantages for West German "progressive forces" resulting from the legalization of the SED in West Germany) were not very convincing.[20]

The drawbacks of the "Social Democratic card" became clear after the abortive Munich conference of German Minister-Presidents in June 1947. The report on the conference, compiled by the staff of the Information Department of SVAG and signed by Colonel Tiul'panov himself, is a valuable and largely untapped source on the history of politics in the Soviet zone. It confirms that SVAG and the Ulbricht group in the SED leadership harbored a basically hostile attitude to the conference. Moreover, it demonstrates that all the Minister- Presidents of the Soviet zone (not only the non-SED Minister-President Hübener) engaged in strong and effective opposition to the SVAG /Ulbricht line, due to which the resistance of the hard-liners was overcome and Eastern participation in the conference was secured.

The report further illustrates how this opposition was used by Tiul'panov's staff to concoct a "conspiracy" on the part of former Social Democrats within the SED leadership. The situation was depicted as all the more ominous in light of the "incorrect position" adopted by the West German Communists, who pleaded for the unconditional participation of the Eastern representatives in the Munich conference and were displeased by their rigid tactics. The alleged existence of an SPD "conspiracy" in the SED ruling body, and of "Social Democratic" leanings in the Western KPD were, perhaps, the main points of the report's summary.[21]

A flood of information from Germany elaborated upon the "Social Democratic threat," in particular, the Korol'kov report, which is distinguished not only by the large number of "Schumacher agents" it identifies, but by its exposé of the intricate "plot" allegedly directed from SPD Central Headquarters in the West and designed to infiltrate the Soviet zone's economic structures. According to Korol'kov, in the expectation of the imminent restoration of the SPD, its leaders set their sights on an early take-over in the Soviet zone in order to forestall the repetition of the "Berlin Case," in which the Social Democrats had won the majority in the Magistrate, yet failed to remove the Communist officials entrenched in the administrative machinery.[22]

Korol'kov's report, especially with regards to the SPD, prompts the following questions: was the SPD's readmission to the Soviet zone a real enough possibility to inspire suspicions of its "conspiratorial" use by the SPD leadership? Did the perception that the SPD planned to infiltrate East German administrate structures have a basis in reality, or was it sheer fantasy? Was the "Berlin precedent" (the electoral victory for the SPD accompanied by SED entrenchment in administrative positions) a preferrable outcome from the Soviet point of view? Was it a viable alternative under the conditions of late 1947? Until new archival materials are explored, these questions will remained unanswered.

In the last months of 1947, and the first months of 1948, the SED's popularity suffered a further decline, precluding any compromise solution, which was, in any case, made all the more impracticable in light of international developments. The Marshall Plan, the Tito-Cominform rift, and the Berlin blockade all contributed to destructive trends in the SED – not to mention a sharp decrease in Party membership. The Berlin Crisis, which began in late June 1948, triggered mass defections from the Party, as is evidenced by statistics from Thuringia.[23]

Naturally, the situation was nothing short of catastrophic for the SED in Berlin, and the Party practically ceased all activity in the Western sectors. SED officials accounted for their passivity with the following rationalizations: "the population is in any case opposed to the SED" and "the situation will change only after the Western Allies abandon Berlin." The latter supposition initiated a dynamic which persisted for years to come, and consisted of the SED/GDR leaders urging the Soviets to "smoke out" the Western forces from West Berlin. Ironically, that assumption ("no prospects for the SED in West Berlin until the Western presence there has been liquidated") was not shared by Soviet analysts as late as 1948.

Nevertheless, no positive solutions were put forth – apart from the September 2, 1948 conference in Berlin, held under the auspices of a new SVAG political boss, General Russkikh. "The results of the discussion will be reported," is the tantalizing margin note on the "Berlin Report"; however, no such report (if indeed there was one) is actually available in the file. Obviously, no means were found to rectify the situation. The Berlin crisis ultimately sealed the fate of the German Communists. They succeeded in one respect – in changing their role from the supporters of the occupiers to that of recipients of the latter's support, on which they vitally depended. Of course, it was a dubious achievement.

Despite the banality of the question, one is tempted to ask: was this outcome unavoidable and the only possible? The Soviet occupation practices were not unique in their negative traits, and they also possessed some positive features lacking in the Western zones. There was significant troop misconduct, corruption, and party intrigue in the Western zones, and the general economic performance there – at least until mid-1948 – was much worse than in the Soviet zone, despite all of the above-mentioned irregularities and problems. Nonetheless, Western policies turned out to be more promising and appealing to the populace. Why?

Of course, material wealth was an important factor (CARE packages!). Aside from this, the most effective means to combat corruption in the Western zones was the "fish bowl," that is, the frank and open coverage of scandalous cases involving the occupation forces in the (relatively) free press. And, certainly, the Western powers showed much more flexibility in their treatment of the indigenous political forces. As a rule, they avoided the practice of "putting all their eggs into one basket," which would result in the politically undesirable association of the German partners with the unpopular actions of the occupation authorities.

Could SVAG have pursued a similar course? The material incentives at the Soviets' disposal were quite limited, "glasnost" was unthinkable in the Stalin era, and narrow ideological confines inhibited political maneuvering. It should be borne in mind that these confines were not indicative of ill-will on the part of the Soviets; rather, the Tiul'panov-Ulbricht group could not envisage anything but a single-party dictatorship and a Germany oriented "towards the East." There were people amenable to other solutions both in SVAG and the SED, but their scope of action was severely constrained by international developments, as well as by German actions and mentality.

In reflecting on the road not taken, the historian must ask why SVAG eschewed any alliance with the "bourgeois" parties, an alliance which may have preserved Germany's integrity and preempted the Cold War. Johannes Becher, a SED dignatary put a similar question to the Soviet Political Advisor, Semyonov. Why did SVAG repulse the loyal elements of the bourgeois parties and ally itself exclusively with the SED? Semyonov accepted the critique implicit in his interlocutor's question, and answered by reminding Becher: "The policies of the CDU and the LDPD exhibit a lot of disloyalty to SVAG." (e.g., the organization of an illegal printing press in Rostock, support for the revision of the Eastern borders, insincerity regarding the German specialists who left for the USSR). Becher did not refute Semyonov's assertions, but merely recommended that SVAG openly chastise the leader of the CDU, Kaiser, for his tolerance of those "who openly called for the creation of the German Army and armed revision of the Eastern frontier."

Just as SVAG was intractable in its view of the bourgeois parties, Germans were firmly wedded to their unflattering image of the Soviets as men in "sheepskin coats and felt boots." Until this image was revised with the passage of time, there could be no rapprochement between the Germans and their "liberators."

Notes

1. Burtsev to Central Committee (CC), June 1, 1945. Russian Center for the Preservation and Study of Documents of Contemporary History (RTsKhIDNI), f. 17, op. 128, d. 39, l. 15.

2. Account of the Visit by Political Emigrés. G. Sobotka and W. Bredel. RTSKhIDNI, f. 17, op. 128, d. 39, l. 37-38.

3. Some Facts on the Work of Comrade Ulbricht's Group in Berlin. RTsKhIDNI, f. 17, op. 128, d. 39, l. 32-33

4. Report on the Events and Political Situation in Berlin, November 17, 1945. RTsKhIDNI, f. 17, op. 128, d. 39, l. 141-157. The original text of the report, compiled by K. Maron, A. Pieck and H. Jendretzki, was entitled: "Crusade Against the Communists in the Berlin Magistrate." The authors were the leading figures in the Berlin mayorial office, and had been appointed by the Soviet military commandant prior to the Western Allies' entering of the city.

5. Major Kvassov to A. Panyushkin, November 24, 1949. RTsKhIDNI, f. 17, op. 128, d. 39, l. 165-169.

6. For a ground-breaking study of Red Army misconduct in the Soviet zone of occupation, see Norman M. Naimark's *The Russians in Germany. A History of the Soviet Zone of Occupation, 1945-1949* (Cambridge: The Belknap Press of

Harvard University, 1995). An approximate quantitative estimate may be deduced from the Report on Activites of SVAG Military Commandatura (it performed the functions of Military police). According to this source, a total of 120,268 officers and enlisted men were apprehended and detained for disorderly conduct. This data seems to refer only to 1946. Major-General Andreyev (Chief, SVAG Political Administration) to A. A. Kuznetsov and I. V. Shikin, January 11, 1947. RTsKhIDNI, f. 17, op. 123, d. 357, l. 12.

7. See, for example, Burtsev to CC, August 20, 1945. RTsKhIDNI, f. 17, op. 128, d. 39, l. 51-52.

8. On the SPD Mass Rally Conducted on July 13 in the Lichtenberg District. RTsKhIDNI, f. 17, op. 128, d. 39, l. 68-69.

9. On the SPD Mass Rally Held on July 13.

10. On the SPD Mass Rally Held on July 13.

11. Memorandum on the SED, October 9, 1946. RTsKhIDNI, f. 17, op. 126, d. 147, l. 125.

12. Letter by "Pravda" correspondent Yu. Korol'kov to comrades Korotkevich and Kraminov, September 4, 1947 (incorporating his September 3, 1947 memo to Pospelov). RTsKhIDNI, f. 17, op. 128, d. 358, l. 4-5.

13. Suslov to Zhdanov, October 5, 1946. RTsKhIDNI, f. 17, op. 128, d. 147, l. 70-87. Ulbricht's memo was sent to eight persons: Stalin, Molotov, Beria, Mikoyan, Zhdanov, Voznesenski, Bulganin, and Malenkov. Zhdanov does not seem to have read it until November 1.

14. It is in fact difficult to estimate how wide-spread such deals were. Ulbricht himself believed that they comprised a considerable proportion of total output, and the statistical data provided in his memo suggests a figure of two-thirds to nine-tenths of total production. Discrepancies in the available official Soviet figures for the costs of deliveries from German current production support a "corruption quotient" within this range.

15. Korol'kov. Korol'kov saw the eviction of Germans from living quarters reserved for the Soviet officers as a primary cause in the SVAG-SED's decline in popularity. The SED Chairman in Saxony, Wilhelm Könen, and Deputy Minister-President Fischer, attributed it to reneging on the pledge to give the people every third bushel of potatoes picked. In the opinion of Thuringia's Minister-President, Hübener, which was shared by the local SVAG chief, Major-General Kolesnichenko, "the actions of the NKVD" were the culprit: "the disappearance of people, whose fates are unknown to their relatives and any German organ for years, is the primary cause of the anti-Soviet propaganda, and of the decline in SVAG's prestige." See M. Gribanov (Deputy Political Advisor) to A. Panyushkin, from V. Kuznetzov's diary, July 14, 1947; A. Kolesnichenko to Ponomaryov, November 29, 1948. RTsKhIDNI, f. 17, op. 128, d. 357, l. 121, d. 572, l. 90. The

relative weight of these factors is difficult to assess; certainly, they all contributed to SVAG-SED's image problems.

16. Korol'kov, l. 2.

17. Suslov to Zhdanov, l. 87. Characteristically, Ulbricht invites his Soviet counterparts to discuss all relevant matters with "The Deputy Chairman of the SED and the Chief of the SED Economic Department" – rather than with any of the Zone's provisional administrative organs.

18. Memo by F. Grosse, August 7, 1946. RTsKhIDNI, f. 17, op. 128, d. 147, l. 28-62, (esp. 11, 37, 53).

19. Memo on the SED, l. 115-116.

20. Suslov to Stalin, Molotov, Zhdanov. On the Social Democratic Party of Germany, January 29, 1947; Transcript of a Conversation with Comrade I. V. Stalin, January 31, 1947. RTsKhDNI, f. 17, op. 128, d. 1091, l. 25, 51-52.

21. Tiul'panov to Suslov, June 11, 1947. Memo on the SED and the Munich Conference of Minister-Presidents of Germany. RTsKhIDNI, f. 17, op. 128, d. 357, l. 76-83 (esp. ll. 82-83).

22. Korol'kov, l. 12-13.

23. Kolesnichenko to Ponomaryov, November 29, 1948. The average rate of defection from the SED in Thuringia in the first months of 1948 was 500, in contrast to 680 in July, 1,193 in August, and 900 in September.

7

The Gomułka Alternative: The Untravelled Road

Inessa Iazhborovskaia
translated by Anna M. Cienciala

For almost half a century, Soviet scholarly treatment of the regimes of People's Democracies was dictated by apologetic interpretations, ideological caveats, and the inaccessability of important sources. After the liberation from ideological pressures, and the opening of formerly inaccessible archival materials, historians finally were able to undertake a more objective analysis of the establishment and development of the regimes of People's Democracies in Central and Southeastern Europe. In the case of Poland, the key task is to elucidate the following issues: what was the model of political relations; how did the Stalinist regimes of the People's Democracies take root; and in what manner did totalitarian mechanisms and methods of rule become consolidated in them?

The development of political relations in Poland, and the formation of the Polish People's Democracy, are of particular interest because the conditions in which they came in to being could be likened to "laboratory" conditions. That is, the political arena in Poland had been swept virtually clean with the "liquidation" of the Polish state. Moreover, the authority of the Polish government in London had been undermined, and only a narrow spectrum of forces remained in the resistance movement. As a result, the task of shaping the new regime was left largely to the Polish Workers' Party (PPR), which did not possess any significant political base.

In the post-Yalta world, these factors determined that Comintern principles would exert the decisive influence on the structure and functioning of the political system. The condition of the Polish economy at the end of the German occupation also facilitated the impostion on the Party of the administrative-command model, and the institution of private property was easily replaced by the incursion of state power into all aspects of life.

The PPR (Polska Partia Robotnicza, Polish Workers' Party) was not formally part of the Comintern, but in fact, its dependence on that organization was no less than that of other Communist parties. The PPR was fully subject to the Comintern's organizational principles. This meant that the formation of Party elites, and the imposition of the administrative-command model on the Party, as well as its cadres policy, was to be based on the strict hierarchy of an autocratic-totalitarian character. A favorite Stalinist cliche: "The Cadres decide everything," gave expression to this model.

The consolidation of this model in the Comintern portended the victory of a strict system of hierarchical discipline, and the proliferation of those mechanisms which perpetuated it. In practice, the fate of the cadres – and of the parties themselves – was decided by the Stalinist leadership. Appointments and transfers were determined by personal loyalty to Stalin. Resignation from any kind of office or post was not allowed. The parties were deprived of the right to propose cadre changes. Their leaders were instructed to be constantly present in Moscow and to transmit the Center's policy downward. They were to carry out the command decisions prepared by EKI, while observing absolute obedience and "unanimity" (edinomy'slie).

In this system of rule, Stalinist methods of elite group formation played the decisive role. The "clique" model was therefore dominant in the Comintern. It was characterized by informal relationships and camouflaged group interests, and was built on the principles of personal loyalty, dependence, obedience, and servility – in accordance with the totalitarian model of political culture. The adoption of the "clique" model meant the suppression of any potentially democratic models of "coalition," in which the elite group is constructed according to a "delegation" of power. When power is delegated, cadres are promoted from below, and lines of authority are clearly visible, offering the possibility of control. Moreover, democratic procedures may prevail, which could be premised upon cadre competence and strong, reciprocal ties with the population.[1]

After Stalin had dissolved the Polish Communist Party (Komunistyczna Partia Polski, KPP), which had begun to show "excessive" independence after the 7th Congress of the Comintern, he began to build the Polish Workers' Party, PPR, forcing its kernel into the procrustean bed of the clique model. Having initiated, at the beginning of 1942, the transfer of the first leadership group of the PPR to Warsaw, Moscow simultaneously "hacked off" the Communists who were trying to re-establish the KPP in occupied Poland. Discovering that the resurrgent Communists were headed by the proletarian leader Leon Lipski ("Łukasz") who in 1938 had tried to save the Party by convening a conference to elect a new leadership, Georgi Dimitrov denounced this organization as "anti-Soviet" and "provocateur." Recently accessible materials in the Russian Center for the Preservation and Study of Documents of Contemporary History describe this episode. In July 1943, Lipski, who intended to work within the PPR, was "liquidated," which Dimitrov duly reported to Stalin and other members of the Soviet Party's Central Committee.[2]

In 1942-1943, the PPR leadership suffered catastrophic losses. Marceli Nowotko, who had pursued an independent political line, was assassinated in November. The Gestapo put to death his successor, Pawel Finder, along with Małgorzata Fornalska, who were both captured in November 1943 and executed in July 1944. Still, the Center's line on the selection of cadres remained the same: the Party was forbidden to elect its leadership locally. Instead, their replacements were groomed in Moscow, and in the process, were advised to avoid contact with the lower Party *aktiv* in Poland.[3] Moscow obviously preferred this method of cadre replacement to the"delegation" of cadres from below, because it was key to the imposition of an authoritarian regime beholden to the Soviets. The International Information Section (OMI) of the Soviet Central Committee inherited from the Comintern the functions, forms, and methods of work previously existing in the international Communist movement. Thus, in the process of gestation, the future regime of postwar Poland was shaped by the Comintern practices of elite group formation. The developmental logic of this model determined the internal structure of the political system, which envisioned the fusion of inter-state and inter-party relations based on the party-state.

At the end of 1943, Stalin took steps to build on his own ground, in Moscow, the Polish National Committee (Polski Komitet Narodowy, PKN) and, along with it, the Central Bureau of the Communists of Poland (Centralne Biuro Komunistów Polski, CBKP). Meanwhile, the Central Committee of the PPR sought to promote a new leader from its own midst. On November 23, 1943, after elections which had not been sanctioned by Moscow, the post went to Władysław Gomułka, a working-class leader who had come up through the Trade Union ranks. Gomułka's electoral success was the natural outgrowth of his role in the Party; of his initiative in organizing the representation of the left wing of the resistance movement, the Home National Council (Krajowa Rada Narodowa, KRN); and of his programmatic statements in the underground press. Gomułka's candidacy, however, had not been approved by the "Center." This was a violation of the basic tradition of inter-party relations.

Moscow reacted accordingly. The coded message of December 29,

1943 signed "Vesl," which reported the arrest of Finder and Fornalska, aroused great anxiety among the Soviet leadership. The Soviets mobilized all channels to elucidate the identity of this Vesl (that is, "Wiesław" – Gomułka's underground pseudonym). Moscow soon learned that the KRN had been established in Warsaw, although the Soviets had not assented to Finder's request for its creation. The Soviets first learned that Gomuka was the head of the PPR in February, 1944.

Although Gomułka had entered the Central Committee on the recommendation of M. Nowotko, Stalin exhibited a distrustful and even negative attitude toward the new leader's undertakings. Stalin's attitude was undoubtedly a result of the PPR's insubordination in electing a leader without first consulting Moscow, as well as of doubts that Gomułka would toe Moscow's line in organizing the post-Yalta system. Confronted with Gomułka's potential unreliability, the Soviet leadership decided to provide "doubles." This was the Leon Kasman group, sent not only to establish communications between Poland and Moscow, but also to secure a reserve "of Polish Communists, who have completed the Party School." Kasman was even forbidden to contact the Central Commitee of the PPR before clarifying "who leads there, and what is the situation."[4]

As the head the PPR, Gomułka was quite unlike the typical leader promoted from among the workers, who had gone through the Comintern school in the period of "bolshevization", and had been molded by a system designed to perpetuate itself. His stay in the Lenin School [1934-36] was a brief one and occurred at a time when the Polish Communist emigration was working out new solutions to social problems, regrouping its political forces, and forging a new political course based on the growing worker, peasant, and national liberation movements. During the war years, as Gomułka reaped the benefits of new experience, M. Nowotko saw in him a leader with strength commensurate to the needs of the time, and drew him into the Central Committee. Having assumed the leadership of the Party, Gomułka immediately showed himself to be an independent and more broad-minded politician, who was able to take the initiative, pursue his goals, and seek creative means to accomplish collectively determined Party objectives.

In a letter of July 10, 1944, Bolesław Bierut pointed out these characteristics to Dimitrov, because they did not accord with the Comintern model of a Party leader. Gomułka had his own opinion of events; he did not hasten to send reports to Moscow; and he made decisions based on the majority view, thus violating the principle of "unanimity." Guided by the schema of hierarchical subordination reigning in the Comintern, Bierut believed it was absolutely necessary to find a way of controlling Gomułka, for example, with help of a plenipotentiary sent officially to Poland from Moscow, as had been done in previous years.[5]

In accordance with this same tradition, Stalin personally confirmed the membership of the Central Bureau of the Polish Communists in Moscow (CBKP) and the document concerning its status as a exclusive, top secret, intermediary agency, charged with carrying out directives on organizational-political matters. This was done without consulting either the leadership of the PPR or the leaders of the Polish Communist emigration in the USSR. After a careful verification of the candidates (as Dimitrov wrote to Stalin, "there were no others more fit than these"), the following persons, who had been schooled in Comintern structures, were selected: Aleksander Zawadzki, Karol Świerczewski, Stanisław Radkiewicz, Jakub Berman, who had worked in the Comintern: and the post-Comintern Institute (NII) no. 205. Wanda Wasilewska headed the Bureau.[6] In this way, the kernel of the future leadership was united not only by its shared experience in the KPP – and the painful lesson of its dissolution at Moscow's behest – but also by the "clique" principle. They were further united by their education in the Comintern principles of Party building; by their mastery of the basics of organizational work acquired in the period of the Party's "bolshevization;" and by their familiarity with the Stalinist model of internal and inter-party relations.

Of course, it would be an over-simplification to claim that the members of the CBKP consciously betrayed their country and its interests by accepting orders, "unanimity," behind-the-scenes activity, subordination, and increased servility. Any kind of organization trains, subordinates, and, to some extent, deforms the views and goals of the individual, dictating his or her model of behavior. In the Comintern, this tendency was particularly pernicious because the individual activist's faith was placed at the disposal of the international Communist movement, with the goal of advancing it at any price. All this was combined with strict, autocratic customs and a discipline which bordered on direct coercion, demanding absolute obedience. Elite groups in the Comintern were educated in such a way as to believe that they acted for the good of their country. Thus, they identified the latter with the policy of the Stalinist, totalitarian leadership of the "fatherland of the world proletariat," and sought to further their country's interests on the basis of the totalitarian principles of rule inculcated into them.

The relations between the PPR and Moscow, and Gomułka's personal relations in particular, developed in a complicated manner. He insisted on the primacy of the Polish leadership. Unaware of the existence of the Central Bureau, he viewed the ZPP as representing Poland and believed it was imperative to have a KRN plenipotentiary there with full, legal, powers. In the meantime, the Soviet Central Committee's International Information Section was giving its "advice" and "recommendations" in an ever more authoritarian form, imposing its own interpretation of programmatic directives on the PPR leadership. The PPR's independent line was criticized as sectarian. The innovations of the PPR, which were tailored to prevailing conditions in Poland, were countered by Dimitrov's progressive but dogmatic ideas on the national front.

The imperious tone in which the directives were relayed did not allow consideration as to whether these ideas would work in practice, thus condemning the policy to voluntaristic deformations. At the same time, Moscow took care to preserve the appearance of democratic decision-making. Thus, when preparing the Plenum of the ZPP Executive Committee for April 5, 1944, Dimitrov asked for Molotov's agreement to change the text of the demands regarding transformations in the countryside and the nationalization of industry. He promised that: "We will, through the Central Buro of the Communists of Poland, make the appropriate changes in the projected resolution."[7]

After the arrival of the KRN delegation in Moscow on May 16, the Stalinist leadership allowed it to have contacts only with the ZPP. Manuilskii suggested to Molotov that the KRN be treated as "a center concentrating political forces," oriented only to participation in the partisan war, to supplying the Armia Ludowa (People's Army) with armaments and specialists, and to transferring PPR activists unable to bear arms to the USSR. Nevertheless, the goal of removing the leading kernel of the PPR proved unrealistic. Stalin then chose another course. On July 17, 1944, the Soviet leadership sent a directive to Gomułka and the KRN demanding that the KRN proceed to Moscow. The leaders of all the parties, the candidates for ministers and deputy ministers were to come to the Soviet Union to establish a Polish National Commitee.[8] This ruse was designed to give the impression of a democratic "delegation" of power – which was impossible in practice – as well as to secure prominent positions for those groomed by Moscow: Edward Osóbka-Morawski in the Department of Foreign Affairs, and Michał Rola-Żymierski in the Department of National Defense. Indeed, their signatures are found at the bottom of the telegram, together with those of Wanda Wasilewska and Aleksander Zawadzki for the ZPP (and CBKP).

On July 21, the Polish Committee of National Liberation (Polski Komitet Wyzwolenia Narodowego, PKWN) met in a founding conference. It accepted the Manifesto published the following day in liberated Chełm, together with the proclamation on the establishment of the PKWN and the transfer of power into its hands. In its formulations, the Manifesto stood closer to the declarations of the Polish National Commitee (PKN) than to the documents of the KRN.

Events now proceeded rapidly. Stalin was master of the situation, and both the selection of PKWN cadres, and the formation of the PKWN itself, was securely in his hands. But he manuevered very deftly, demonstrating his ability to anticipate the opposition, while creating the appearance that the whole process was a voluntary one. Nevertheless, Gomułka was completely excluded.

On July 26, *Pravda* published the declaration of the Soviet People's Commissariat of Foreign Affairs, which stated that the Soviet government considered military activities on Polish territory as taking place on the territory of a sovereign, allied, state, and that it did not intend to establish its own administration there. On the same day, Osóbka-Morawski and Molotov signed an agreement between the Soviet government and the PKWN on the relations that would obtain between the Soviet Commander-in-Chief and the Polish administration after the advance of Soviet armies into Polish territory. The first article gave supreme power and responsibility in all matters relating to the conduct of war to the Soviet Commander-in-Chief, that is, Stalin. In reality, Stalin's powers on Polish territory extended far beyond the conduct of war.

The building of the party-state in liberated Poland began almost from ground zero, without stable power structures enjoying popular legitimacy. Pre-war structures no longer existed and the "underground state" was effectively shattered by the Red Army. The task of building the new regime was entrusted to a small group from the left-wing of the resistance movement, which was driven by the PPR and supported by the Army. In view of the PPR's key position in the political and administrative system then being formed, the further development of the national-democratic regime depended on its leading cadres. Inevitably, the new regime in Poland, its party-state structures, and the regulation of their functions, bore the stamp of the organizational models familiar to PPR leading cadres. The cadres' experience and views on these questions were not, however, homogeneous. For some of them, the interwar heritage was decisive, while for others, it was the multi-party tradition. Yet another group was influenced by the Comintern imperative, which had been strengthened by the repression and the dissolution of the KPP. A not insignificant part of this group was able to overcome this legacy to a greater or lesser extent, in the death-struggle with the Nazi occupiers. A third group had emerged during the struggle for liberation and was well-equipped to meet the challenges of a new historical epoch.

The character of the newly consolidating regime, as well as its evolutionary prospects, was affected to a large extent by the conflict between these different tendencies. In the first stage, it was the PPR itself, or rather, its elite group, which was responsible for the reactivization of these political traditions. The PPR was likewise responsible for the embryonic form of the party-state, and for its subsequent transformation with the help of experienced Party cadres and their allies.

In the PPR leadership, two basic tendencies came into conflict with one another. Gomułka and his collaborators strove to steer a course toward building a democratic Poland; to establish as many varied forms of a National Front as possible under the circumstances of 1944-1945;

and to delegate the exercise of power to its four constituent parties. At the February (1945) Plenum of the PPR Central Committee, Gomułka emphasized the fact that such a National Front constituted a voluntary agreement between parties, which had concluded a healthy compromise and acted independently on the basis of their own programs. The Front's task was to include other national political forces as well.

At the same time, however, a second tendency was being successfully advocated in the PPR by an elite group formed during the liberation of the Lublin region of Poland. The members and leaders of the Central Bureau (CBKP) were brought into the PPR Politburo and Central Committee, where they formed the majority, while other CBKP representatives occupied key positions in the PKWN and in the army. These forces determined the composition of the PPR as it rapidly grew into a mass Party; they laid the political foundations and steered the course of the regime. The Politburo busied itself with the immediate formation of administrative structures for ruling the country, seeking to strengthen the Party's central and regional organizations by establishing Party committees and distributing Party cadres. In essence, the Politburo dictated the political culture that would prevail in postwar Poland.

In several areas, the PPR, to which Soviet military commanders often transferred local power, could rely on its cells and committees, as well as on the People's Army garrisons, and the *aktiv* of national councils and factory committees. Elsewhere, especially in western Poland, such structures were lacking. All levels of Party and administrative organs were established from the top down, by way of nomination, not delegation. The KRN, as the supreme organ not only of representative, but also administrative power, established executive organs which were fully subordinated to it. The governing concept was not of dividing power, but of strengthening executive power. The idea of general elections to national councils was rejected; instead, the national councils were augmented on the principle of proportional representation of the bloc parties. They exercised only limited power, and primarily served the purpose of transmitting directions from the top downward.

From the beginning, the system was endowed with a series of autocratic characteristics and inflexible structures, beginning with the KRN and ending with the Constituent Assembly. Furthermore, the executive organs – the PKWN, the Provisional Government, and then the Government of National Unity – were armed with even greater prerogatives. Parliamentary traditions were extremely fragile. A significant part of the PPR *aktiv* occupied key positions in the state and economic bureacracy, constituting, together with the Party bureaucracy, up to one-third of the cadres. Naturally, it implemented the same principles of cadre policy and rule on all levels of government.

Having assumed key positions in the state-party structures, the cadres raised on Comintern models concentrated real power in their hands. This exclusive group was able to expand and strengthen its influence by bureaucratic methods. The ruling group was based on strict subordination, personal loyalty and obedience, as well as on the confidentiality and "unanimity" of the clique model. Needless to say, these characteristics were a harbinger of Stalinist totalitarianism. The absence of democratic political structures; the conspiratorial character of relations which persisted even after the end of the occupation; the lack of public and open discussion, all facilitated the proliferation of totalitarian political culture in the Party, government, and economic bureaucracy, thus laying the foundations for building the party-state.

Gomułka was guided by other tendencies. His cadre policy was clearly distinguished by a strongly expressed rejection of "clique" principles, and by an emphasis on efficiency rather than on personal loyalty. He showed tolerance for different points of view, and was not inclined to dispose of those who held different opinions – or displayed initiative – on the pretext of insubordination.[9] His convictions accorded with the democratization of internal Party relations, that is, with the "delegation" model. Gomułka clearly proclaimed these principles early in the process of building Party structures on liberated territories. At the first meeting of the PPR *aktiv* in Lublin on August 5, 1944, Gomułka advocated the election of Party organs. Essentially, this was an attempt to adopt the "delegation" model, and thereby introduce a new procedure for elite group formation, as well as for governance.

But how did things work out in practice? Election procedures were introduced only gradually. By the end of 1945, the Politburo, the Secretariat, and the Central Control Committee had split off from the Central Committee. Furthermore, only the *aktiv* and Party functionaries participated in local elections, and they elected as Secretary the plenipotentiary who had been sent to them by the voevodship Party committee. The election was not conducted by secret ballot. Delegates to the first PPR Congress held at the end of 1945 were elected in the same way. The result was that 60% of the delegates were members of the PPR, while at the same time they made up 53% of the PPR bureaucracy and only 14. 6% of the lower*aktiv*. [10]

Throughout the immediate postwar period, there was an on-going struggle in the government, the KRN, the Central Committee bureaucracy, the central Party press, the trade union *aktiv*, and in various social organizations. It crystallized into a conflict between advocates of the "clique" model and the supporters of the "delegation" model. The subsequent introduction of centralism, hierarchical principles, and administrative-command methods thwarted the development of fragile democratic tendencies. As a result, the rapid increase in Party membership was not accompanied by "delegation" in the higher and middle Party echelons. New cadres lacked the necessary experience, and therefore subordinated themselves to those occupying a higher place in the hierarchy, as was expected of them. In view of the complexity and on-going modification of political structures, it was absolutely necessary to reinforce the Party *aktiv*, to increase its efficacy as well as the political consciousness and organizational maturity of the cadres. However, practices persisted which inhibited democratic norms from taking root in Party organizations and discouraged "experiments" designed to introduce innovations and advance Polish national interests.

The Gomułka group tried from time to time to analyze the processes taking place in the Party and to counteract what they saw as deformations, such as the proliferation of previous models of internal relations within the Party, and the establishment of totalitarian methods of rule. Gomułka's effort to democratize Party life reflected popular demands and addressed the specificities of postwar Polish society. However, his attempts at democratization were marred by inconsistency and internal contradiction. They were further undermined by the weakness of the PPR; the preponderance of old Party-political traditions; and delays in building democratically functioning structures. Indeed, the narrow spectrum of forces in the political arena, and the substitution of armed force for a popular base constituted the real obstacles to the establishment of a truly democratic regime.

After the conclusion of the Soviet-Polish Treaty of Friendship, Mutual Aid and Postwar Cooperation on April 21, 1945, and after clearing up old business left over from the first months of building the PPR and the state, Gomułka began to focus on the negative phenomena which had manifested themselves in the Party, such as the premium placed on ideological "unanimity" within the Party. Gomułka was also concerned with the Party's drive to consolidate political power in its hands, and to reject cooperation with other bloc parties and enforce unpopular social-economic reforms. At the May 1945 Plenum of the PPR Central Committee, Gomułka's report condemned certain cadres for the existence of sectarian deviations from the general Party line, qualified in the Plenum resolution as "especially harmful and dangerous today."[11]

Gomułka stressed the need to break with administrative and command methods in the Party. He proposed not only to neutralize this pernicious influence, but also to quell the leftist tendencies of part of the *aktiv* – even as far down as cadre rotation – and effectively to deprive their proponents of influence on Party life. He threatened that the Politburo would wage a decisive battle in this direction, "by drawing conclusions regarding individual Party members, down to and including kicking them out of the Party, bringing people to trial, and conducting public trials."[12] In this way, the General Secretary showed that he fully realized the danger presented by the proliferation of these tendencies – but he did not understand the basic mechanisms for their consolidation. Moreover, he expected the Politburo to lower the curtain on them. Realizing the pervasiveness of these tendencies, Gomułka nevertheless intended to employ extreme measures in a harsh, Stalinist-Comintern style, for he was convinced that no other methods would yield the desired results. This path, however, could not guarantee a fundamental, democratic renewal of the PPR and of the whole political regime if it were taken without introducing cardinal changes in the formation and functioning of the Party elite.

At the lst PPR Congress in December 1945, it became clear that along with the manifold increase in Party membership, there was practically no development of a central activist group on the voevodship level; instead, the existing leaders had transformed themselves into a *nomenklatura*. This demonstrated the extent to which the Party had adopted the "clique" principle, that is, the establishment of a narrow circle of "verified," "loyal," and "trustworthy" members. They exhibited their opposition to the promotion of new members by arguing against "messing up the aktiv and the bureaucracy with unverified people" with little training and experience. The goal was to bar access to young people, to limit "delegating," and to thereby impede renewal of cadres from below.

At the Party Congress, Gomułka directly linked Party strategy and tactics with their successful implementation in practice – which, as he said, "depended on people, on those who carried out and fulfilled the Party line."[13] With the goal of increasing Party membership to one million, Gomułka advocated the consolidation of new models of political culture; a new quality of party-political life; and the successful integration of democratic elements into the political system. Despite the complex political situation, Gomułka oriented the Party and the state toward peaceful, evolutionary reforms tailored to the conditions of postwar Poland.

The discussion before and at the Congress itself – two fifths of whose delegates had been absent from Poland during the war and did not belong to the PPR – revealed the Old Communists' opposition to Gomułka's course. They preferred to solve problems by undemocratic means; to force the transformation of the emergent multi-party system into a mono-party system; and to use repressive methods to consolidate the dictatorship of the proletariat. Gomułka succeeded in opposing these attitudes. He countered the demand for doing away with "the cretinism of legality" by condemning the "office-holder fetishism," the totalitarian "fetishism of those sitting at the top," and the persistence of old stereotypes.[14] He unequivocally linked the difficulties in securing the political power base, both in Poland and in the Party, with the miscalculations of the old cadres, who could certainly learn something from the younger ones, including the organization of political work. At the same time, Gomułka emphasized the importance of the strict observance of legality, and the necessity of creating a democratic political system.

Gomułka openly conceded that the previous habits of the Party *aktiv* were very much alive at the top and at the lower levels of the administration bureaucracy, where "our comrades... are committing all kinds of stupidities." Alongside creative and effectively working persons, "there are, among former KPP members, those unable to get a feel for the new situation, to understand it, and those who have not stopped being narrow sectarians. It is necesssary that they too begin to think in terms of the nation, of the state in whose administration we are participating at this time." Both in his report, and in his persuasive rhetoric, Gomułka stressed the absolute necessity of abandoning dogmatic thinking and the attitudes of many pre-war Communists. He pointed out that the formidable task of building a common Polish national home had to be accomplished according to the needs of the Polish people, after analyzing both the positive and negative experiences of other nations.[15] Finally, Gomułka called for cadres to think independently, and advocated educating new cadres to resist blind subordination. Instead, they should be encouraged to feel real responsibility for Party work.

In its resolution, the Congress prescribed the bold promotion of new cadres to responsible positions in the government, administrative, and Party bureaucracy, and passed a statute broadening and defending the rights of Party members. This policy line received the support of the majority of delegates – even though 15% of them had written the names of active opponents of the Central Committee on the election ballots. Because the tradition of obedience and "unanimity" proved stronger for many, however, this was not enough to guarantee a subsequent revision of opinions, habits, and attitudes.

The personnel of the leading organs was not qualitatively renewed. No opponent of the Gomułka line was "removed" or "hacked off." Bolesław Bierut as well as other leading military and government leaders (above all, generals and functionaries of the Ministry of Public Security), entered the higher Party organs, although they had not been elected to them at the Congress. The foundations of the Party-government structure crystallized around these cadres, and this elite inner circle dictated the style, forms, and methods of rule.

In closing the Congress, Gomułka sketched the contours of the democratization of the Party and the political regime. He emphasized the obligation to observe the principle of collective decision-making on all important questions and on all levels, and geared the Party toward strengthening ties with the masses. He also proposed that Party decisions should be scrutinized with an eye to prevailing conditions, and that any indications that the Party line was at odds with reality should be reported immediately to the leadership. Finally, he advanced the ideas of a national Party with close, organic ties to the people, which would not only encourage mass political activity based on cadre experience, but effectively convey the conditions in and needs of the country.

Despite Gomułka's intentions, there was no major break-through, since among the leading cadres other orientations predominated which were at odds with Gomułka's vision. In fact, the ideological and organizational foundations of the party-state were already in the process of being laid down, including a compulsory social-economic transformation which was supervised by increasingly powerful organs of coercion. In postwar Poland, a significant part of the PPR leadership unquestioningly accepted both the Soviet experience in Party and state building, and the ideological stereotypes of its Great Neighbor, along with the traditional hierarchy in the international Communist movement.

Gomułka's relations with Stalin were also problematic. He was obliged to visit Moscow on an almost monthly basis in order to settle a multitude of concrete questions: reparations; the presence of Soviet troops on Polish territories; the removal of raw materials; the dismantling of enterprizes; the activity of Soviet security organs, etc. According to Jan Ptasiński's testimony, Gomułka summed up this rather difficult period as follows: "In fact, through all of 1945, I had difficult disputes with Stalin over Poland." He rejected the role of petitioner. His uncompromising attitude and obstinacy angered Andrei Vyshinsky to such an extent that he could not refrain from making the retort: "You are no better than Sikorski."[16]

After the conclusion of the Treaty of Friendship, Mutual Aid and Postwar Cooperation, Gomułka, intending to initiate a more egalitarian relationship with the Soviet leadership, suggested that the leaderships of the two countries coordinate their political lines and abandon administrative methods. Stalin responded with measures designed to preserve the hierarchical nature of Polish-Soviet relations. On May 10, 1945, Gomułka was obliged to report on the situation in Poland and on PPR policy in the International Information Section of the Soviet Central Committee, while Dimitrov "made corrections" in his position.

At this meeting, Gomułka insisted on enhancing the role of the Polish leadership and reiterated his opposition to forced industrialization and collectivization. Conversely, Dimitrov insisted on consolidating one-party rule, on repression, and on the acceleration of social-economic transformations. As was characteristic of Gomułka, in the course of the discussions he cited the need to take the Polish people's will into account. Gomułka emphasized the legality of his Party's decisions, and the importance of building relations on the basis of equality and partnership. In pointing out the harmful nature of the proposed line, he stated that its supporters were to be found both in the commanding ranks of the Red Army and in the PPR, but emphasized that he intended to root out this sectarianism.[17] In this way, Gomułka openly demonstrated that he would not accept the old ideas which dictated Party work and inter-party relations.

After returning to Warsaw, Gomułka implemented a series of measures designed to realize the goals he had enumerated in Moscow. He added members to the Politburo, the Central Committee Plenum, and the Party *aktiv*. After this, he unambiguously confirmed the Party platform on the key questions under discussion in a letter to Stalin. Here, he wrote of the need to adjust mutual relations in such a way as to stop the interference of Soviet representatives and the imposition of Soviet models, which encouraged sectarianism in the PPR. Gomułka also underscored his intention to eliminate administrative pressure and direct coercion from the functioning of the administrative bureaucracy.[18]

However, the basic features of the political system were already firmly in place. The leadership had adopted the "clique" model, while the Stalinist style of party-state work had also become well-entrenched. Thus, the possibilities for democratizing the political regime and Polish society were greatly reduced.

The adjustments in bilateral relations also proved to be half-measures, and short-lived ones at that. From time to time, Stalin showed patience, conducting relations with Gomułka in a calm, peaceable tone. Thus, "he tried to create the impression that he was seeking advice and consultation."[19] Gomułka preserved his dignity and independent judgment. He dealt openly and honestly with the Soviets, in keeping with his committment to democratic, equal relations. When he noted the re-emergence of Comintern traditions in the establishment of the Cominform, Gomułka openly questioned the traditional Comintern style and the advisability of establishing such an organization.

This confrontation over the structure and functions of the Cominform in September 1947 inevitably developed into an open conflict in the PPR Politburo and Central Committee. Formed on the basis of Comintern ideology, and embodying the Stalinist model of rule and the hierarchical relations, the PPR Old Guard unhesitatingly accepted the Stalinist *volte face*. Using Bolshevik terminology, Gomułka "fell off the cart." Behind Gomułka's back, Stalin made arrangements with the (PPR) Politburo for Gomułka to be "hacked off" from the Party leadership. The deformed political process, functioning according to the "clique" principle, manifested its hidden supremacy and insured Gomułka's downfall. Gomułka's line of democratization was denounced as a "rightist-nationalistic deviation."

One of the most serious accusations levelled at Gomułka was "distrust of the USSR," of the ideological principles and policy of the CPSU(b). This was, of course, connected with the Yugoslav conflict. He was also accused of underestimating the role of the USSR in the struggle with "international imperialism." These charges served to mask Gomułka's real transgressions in the eyes of the Stalinist leadership: his open opposition to elite formation based upon "clique" principles, to Stalinist-style administrative rule within the bureaucracy, as well as to hierarchical interstate relations based on the Comintern tradition. By 1948, these features were firmly embedded in the postwar Polish political order.

The struggle between the "clique" model, with its Stalinist-style of rule on the one hand, and democratization of the Party and society on the other, ended with the defeat of Gomułka and his supporters. As a result, the Stalinist regime, in which "the cadres decide everything," tightened its grip on Polish society. Later, Gomułka tried to resume his course, but the political system proved stronger. It pulled him into its orbit, and imposed its own rules on him.

Notes

1. For details see: Inessa S. Iazhborovskaia, "Nekotorie aspekty otbora, funktsionirovaniia i rotatsii kadrov v Kominterne," *Mezhdunarodnaia Organizatsiia Komunistov*, Moscow, 1990.

2. Rossiiskii Tsentr Khraneniia i Izucheniia Dokumentov Noveishei Istorii. The Russian Center for Preservation and Study of Documents of Contemporary History, Moscow, henceforth: RTsKhIDNI.

3. Ibid., d. 425, l. 9, 11, 30.

4. Ibid., d. 434, l. 37; d. 437, l. 9; f. 17, op. 128, d. 1161, l. 84, 87.

5. Ibid., f. 17, op. 128, d. 1161, l. 24.

6. Ibid., f. 495, op. 74, d. 431, l. 39; d. 441, l. 12-15.

7. Ibid., d. 439, l. 24; d. 440, l. 14.

8. Ibid., d. 435, l. 48-50, 58, 60, 64-65; d. 441, l. 89.

9. Jan Ptasiński, *Pierwszy z trzech zwrotów, czyli rzecz o Gomułce* (Warsaw, 1983), 120, 123.

10. Norbert Kołomejczyk, *PPR. 1944-1945, (Studia nad rozwojem organizacyjnym Partii)*, (Warsaw, 1983), 175, 176, 294.

11. PPR. Rezolucje, odezwy, instrukcje i okolniki Komitetu Centralnego. VIII. 1944 - XIII. 1945, (Warsaw, 1959), 140.

12. Protokółobrad KC PPR w maju 1945 roku, (Warsaw, 1992), 16.

13. Władysław Gomułka, *Artykuły i przemówienia*, vol. I, (Warsaw, 1962), 516.

14. Ibid., 510-512, 523-527; Archiwum Ruchu Robotniczego, vol. X, (Warsaw, 1986), 210.

15. Gomułka, *Artykuły*, 530, 535, 540.

16. Ptasiński, *Pierwszy z trzech zwrotów*, 115-116.

17. RTsKhIDNI, f. 17, op. 128, d. 750, l. 146-156 ob.

18. "Nieznany list Władysława Gomułki do Stalina," Dziś, 1992, no. 7, 96-103.

19. Ptasiński, *Pierwszy z trzech zwrotów*, 116.

8

Polish Workers and the Stalinist Transformation

Padraic Kenney

The search for the origins of Stalinism is a dangerous minefield for a social historian. Any discussion of the first years of Communism in Eastern Europe will find it difficult to avoid a simple truth: without the occupation of the Soviet Army, there would have been no Communism in the region – most certainly not in Poland. Stalinism is of course by its very name a Soviet phenomenon, its origins bound up in the history of the CPSU. The existence of the Soviet Bloc naturally inspires a search for similarities in rule and resistance, lessening the importance of differences among societies, though those societies are understood to be quite dissimilar from their Soviet counterpart.[1]

It would be simple to state merely that we must learn something of the "other side" of Stalinist systems; that study of society will give us a more complete understanding of the history of Communist rule. This approach, however, exposes a basic misunderstanding of Stalinism as it was practiced in Eastern Europe.[2] Stalinism was an ideology of social transformation; therefore if we do not understand society, we can hardly understand Stalinism. Political histories have told us a great deal about *how* Communists ruled: they cannot explain *why* they ruled as they did; why Stalinist practices varied so much among states; and why Stalinist or post-Stalinist states fell apart as they did in 1989. For answers to these questions, society – and in particular the working class – must become our primary focus. The working class and its transformative (revolutionary) power was central to Communist thought, and above all to that of the Stalinists. Communists took worker support for granted over the long run, to be sure; in power, they sought to win the workers' support, regarding such support as necessary to their success. Thus, in the Polish case (where Stalinism lasted roughly from 1948 to 1956) which will be considered here, we must re-think the political narrative[3] by considering how workers (willingly or not) shaped the system which dominated their lives. We cannot be content to think of the workers as passive victims of Stalinization – because the Stalinists could not let them remain passive, as they required workers' active participation. But requiring that participation, the state could not control what forms it would take; this left open a path for the Polish labor community to influence and shape the development of the Communist system. As a result, relations between the Communist state and Polish society in the Stalinist years were a mutual creation.

The focus for this paper is Wrocław, a city born on the ruins of the nearly empty German city of Breslau in 1945. A city with a reinvented national identity, it was the capital of Poland's "Wild West," [dziki zachód][4] a free-spirited city of brigandry and rugged pioneers. The case of Wrocław reminds us that there were two quite different Polands in 1945. The Poland which Wrocław represented could not be more different from central Poland. The heart of the interwar Republic was largely destroyed by the war, and an enormous number of its inhabitants killed or displaced. Still, it was a settled Poland, with continuity. The changes in postwar Poland were symbolized by the addition of vast new territory to the west and north as a result of the agreements ending World War II, as a compensation of sorts for the loss of Poland's eastern lands to the Soviet Union. The new territory amounted to nearly one-third of the territory of the Third Republic. The Recovered Territories, as they were called, were populated mostly by migrants from eastern and central Poland. The region was economically more advanced than most of pre-war Poland; the taking of this area was thus a geographic parallel to the Stalinist project of industrialization. In many ways, this region was central to Poland's postwar transformation.

Wrocław/Breslau was the largest city in the Recovered Territories. In Polish memory, the city barely existed before 1945; its meager Polish ties, stretching back to the medieval Piast dynasty, were unfamiliar to most. Nowhere was there a feature one could recognize and call Polish without hesitation; the city was German in form and content. A factory was a factory, especially to those who had spent the war as forced labor in similar factories in Berlin and the Ruhr, but the churches, schools, shops, and neighborhoods were all products of a different culture. Just as city blueprints were lost in the flames of the siege or taken by the retreating Nazi Army, so too were the cultural blueprints of this city lost to those who came on the heels of the victors. Breslau's transfer to Polish hands was simple, in comparison to the task of creating – physically and culturally – a Polish city and a Polish community on alien terrain. For state planners, the idea of Wrocław as a template for Poland's rebirth was imbued with ideas of utopia. Sociologists, urban planners, and government leaders debated such topics as whether to populate first the countryside or the cities, whether to encourage mobility, and whether to screen settlers in order to control the make-up of model communities.[5]

Wrocław, a city unlike any other in Poland (indeed in Europe), was also crucial to the Stalinist transformation of Polish society. Support from the people of Wrocław was extremely important to the regime, as a confirmation of the Polishness of the region; the 1946 referendum results, for example, were nowhere more falsified than in Lower Silesia. The real results were not greatly different from those elsewhere: a narrow defeat of question one (abolishing the senate), a narrow victory for question two (upholding the regime's major economic reforms), and a decisive victory for the third question (on the new borders). Reported results, however, showed roughly 95% support for each question.[6] Wrocław voters, concluded Party observers, were "hostile to People's Poland," "distrustful, and restrained." Subsequent years did not much change the popular perception that "democracy is weak because it cannot overcome the difficulties in normalizing life."[7]

The patterns of migration and settlement, and the ways migrants interacted with each other, with their environment, and with the Communists presented unexpected problems for the new state. In the end, however, these same "difficulties" provided the underpinnings for the formation of a Stalinist social system. The experiences of Wrocław also reveal much about the way the Communist Party (PPR = Polish Workers' Party; after unification with the socialist party [PPS] in December 1948, it was renamed the Polish United Workers' Party, or PZPR) grew: it was neither a collection of outsiders and careerists, nor the embodiment of rural militancy. Rather, it was the reflection, and the beneficiary, of a new kind of society.

The Creation of Identities:
Polish Wrocław

Home of almost one million in January 1945, at the start of the Soviet Army's four-month siege of "Fortress Breslau," Wrocław contained only 150,000 Germans, mostly elderly, women, and children, among its ruins upon liberation on May 8. The city center was severely damaged, and two huge swaths of residential neighborhoods to the west and south, where fighting had been fiercest, were leveled. Even in ruins, Wrocław was impressive. Huge mountains of rubble blocked the streets, and the empty shells of great buildings loomed above. A printer from Lwów recorded his first impressions of Wrocław: "Endless ruins, the stink of burning, countless huge flies, the clouded faces of the occasionally encountered Germans, and, most important: the emptiness of the desolate streets."[8]

By 1949, Wrocław was again a city of some 300,000, filled with migrants who brought to the new city the most varied experiences. Most had never been in such a large city, nor such a western one. Some were returnees from forced labor in Germany who stopped in Wrocław or returned there after a quick reconnaissance of their old hometowns. Many newcomers had survived the war in the Eastern borderlands – the *kresy* – which had now been ceded to the Soviet Union. Expelled from their homes and assigned to new lives in the West, they arrived in Wrocław at the end of cattle-car journeys which often lasted several weeks. Most migrants, however, came on their own from the villages and small towns of central Poland, escaping overcrowded farms and ruined lives to find work or get rich in a land of freedom and opportunity.

The belongings left behind by the evacuating Germans proved a powerful attraction. The President of Wrocław estimated that 60% of those who came in 1945 came to loot – for *szaber*, as it became known.[9] While press reports of the time often presented *szaber* as the work of a corrupt minority, the urge to get back something from the Germans and make up for the difficult war years seems to have been universal. "The attraction to *szaber* is epidemic," complained the director of Pafawag in a letter to the Minister of Industry. "The mad desire to grab someone else's abandoned property is beyond all means of control."[10] Wrocław was also a mecca for traders and shopkeepers, lured by the promise of an opportunity to make a lot of money with little effort, or to make a new start far from home. Finally, Lower Silesia also became legendary as a hiding place for former Home Army partisans and others who counted on the relative lack of police and civil administration to survive undetected. The authorities claimed to find evidence of "enemy propaganda" spread by these same people, and tied it to the *szaber* problem. Lower Silesia, and particularly Wrocław, was full of "those destructive elements of Polish society which do not want to join in rebuilding the ruined nation."[11]

Perhaps surprisingly for a city so central to Stalinist industrialization, Wrocław could not easily be identified by newcomers as a city of labor. Most factories were on the periphery; the larger ones in heavy industry were islands – some would say cities – unto themselves. Small workshops, and a network of clothing factories, were the only signs of industry in the center. But the Stalinist world of labor was everywhere built on new territory, in Magnitogorsk, for example, rather than Leningrad. Wrocław, where most early migrants were unfamiliar with both urban culture and the factory, was an ideal site; thus, the experience of migration to Wrocław was framed not in the traditional terms of labor but in terms of the frontier. Wrocław, was not so much rebuilt, a term that might imply knowledge of its past, and reclamation of that past, as it was discovered and claimed. As a Wrocław daily editorialized in September 1945: "We are rebuilding Wrocław, or rather, we are building a new Wrocław – ours, and genuinely Polish."[12]

Workers in early Wrocław were in many ways denied the opportunity to form a labor identity. For example, the resonance of the pioneer image reveals much about the place of labor in early postwar Poland. Legends of the adventurous "pioneers" – those who came before the spring of 1946, when wages were scarce, no factories were open, and Germans in the city overwhelmed Poles by a ratio of 2:1 – say little about labor. These heroes, who worked all day clearing rubble or rebuilding factories for a bowl of thin soup, were portrayed as performing a national service rather than a physical one. While the theme of building was recurrent in propaganda of the time, the builder himself was not a hero – in contrast to subsequent moments in Polish history, where the image of the laborer in the act of building was clearly drawn and glorified.[13] The nationalist image of rebuilding made sense in those first years and undoubtedly made it easier for migrants to adapt to their new surroundings. Eventually, however, the lack of a labor identity would have profound implications for the Stalinization of Polish society.

For those who came to look for work, life in Wrocław was brutal and frustrating. The mad competition for apartments and shops left little for the average work-seeker. Returning Germans reclaimed their old apartments, often evicting the Poles who had been assigned there. This was a dangerous place: as late as December 1946, there were reports of attackers in police uniform robbing passersby of their money and clothing.[14] Whether these were policemen or impostors, the message was that there was no one in charge in Wrocław, no representative of the state upon whom one could rely. Nor could state and city authorities provide a sufficient standard of living. There were no ration cards issued until November 1945, leaving workers to rely on the meager offerings of the factory cafeteria – if there was one. State industry wages in the city ranged in November 1945 from 23 to 160 zł. per day (German laborers made as little as 10 zł.; private industry wages reached 200 zł.), while a kilo of bread cost 23 zł., and a kilo of kielbasa, 320-360 zł.[15] Even if conditions were acceptable, there might still be no work. Most factories did not begin operation until early 1946, while there were many other opportunities throughout Poland.[16] The "pioneers" of Wrocław were especially discouraged. Neglected by local administration, "their zeal has cooled," reported the Wrocław UB.

> They return to central Poland or give in to the most varied pursuits – anything which will bring them enough to live. Of course they are embittered, and listen willingly to all kinds of reactionary rumors. In this way, a society convinced of the impermanence of the government and of the temporary nature of Polish authority in this region is slowly but surely being formed.[17]

Those who left Wrocław often said they were returning "to Poland."[18]

The confusion and disorder of Wrocław's birth was a mixed blessing for Communist leaders. While it meant that a new, Stalinist identity could be imposed upon the migrants (as would later be the case in the great Stalinist industrialization projects), it also meant that Wrocław workers became fierce individualists, more comfortable relying upon themselves than trusting the state or the Party. The task of resettling millions of Germans and Poles was more than administrators could handle. Unlike the boom cities of the Stalinist Soviet Union, Wrocław grew without an organizing force. The state clearly had much less control over its growth than might be expected in Communist Eastern Europe. Neither industry nor the state nor the parties had real control over the organization of urban life during the early phase of Wrocław's Polish rebirth. While there were countless bureaucracies to distribute apartments, ration cards, and jobs, their reach was severely limited by the war's damage to Wrocław's infrastructure, by the chaotic influx of people, and by the city's distance from Warsaw. Labor organizations such as factory councils and trade unions were particularly helpless, lacking the community ties which gave them some voice elsewhere in Poland at the time.

The lack of reliable pay, food supply, or housing, the absence of sympathetic authority in the city and the factory, and the success of looters and shopkeepers constituted a message about individual resources and self-reliance in Wrocław. Patterns of individualism acquired in the war, the underground, and the postwar migrations were hard to unlearn, the more so in a strange environment, where the geography did not evoke pre-war social organization, but only ruins to be picked over and looted. These patterns inhibited the development of working-class culture in that city. The collective identities workers preferred were in fact anti-labor. The common experiences of migration made Wrocław a city representative of Poland as was no other, yet also one whose residents had little in common with one another. Wrocław was a conglomerate of different communities, resistant to the formation of broader allegiances of class or even of nation. In a sense, this resultant mix of regional and social origins accomplished something of what the social planners may have envisioned. Wrocław was the new Poland, and very malleable. Pre-war allegiances were left behind, leaving an empty space for the new engineers of society.

Factory workers were most divided along regional lines. Each group – the 'Poznaniaks' of ex-Prussian Poland, those from Warsaw, the peasants of the central provinces, the Galicians, and those from Lwów and the *kresy* – possessed a distinct culture which they felt separated them from others. This perception of difference is hard to define, in particular because the intervening years have successfully promoted a myth of social integration from the very start. An exchange with interview subject Stefania K., a peasant from Kielce who worked in the kitchen at Pafawag, reveals both the persistence of that myth and the reality underneath.[19]

[question]: Did you feel any difference between yourself and the other women?
SK: No. Everyone was equal. [...] Almost everyone was from a village. [...] And there were some from Warsaw ...
[Q]: The ones from Warsaw – did they put on airs?
SK: Oh yes, they put on airs – terribly – that they were from Warsaw.
[Q]: What did they say?
SK: Well, that we are 'Kongresówka,'[20] and they're from <u>Warsaw</u>. [...]
[Q]: Were there people from the *kresy*, and from Lwów?
SK: A lot. [...] They were second-class. We paid no attention to them – so to this day.
[Q]: Why?
SK: I don't know ... That's the way it was.
[later in the interview, the topic recurred, in an exchange about conversations at the workplace] [Q]: [Did] people talk about – 'I'm from those parts', and 'I'm from there' – that 'here it's better, there it's worse' ...?
SK: Yes! If someone was from Poznań province, then they were from Poznań province! Because if [one was] from Kielce or Lublin province, it was all the same.

The immediate result of these perceived differences was that workers kept to small circles of fellow migrants, suspicious of those from other backgrounds. Thus a young Silesian worker (from an interview conducted in 1947 or 1948): "In general, I hang around with mates who came from my part of the world, and whom I knew before. Sometimes I even like people from elsewhere, but I sense regional differences."[21] Irena Turnau points out that this caution is remarkably common among younger migrants, whom one might expect to have fewer qualms about meeting strangers. Among older migrants, the reason for keeping a distance was often linked to morality. Thus a bricklayer from Lwów: "I keep in touch with old acquaintances from Lwów who live nearby. I have nothing to do with my neighbors, because they are from central Poland, and don't even go to church."[22] Real differences in age, experience, education and culture between regional groups were magnified in a city foreign to nearly everyone. They forced migrants to rely on those ties which were easiest to recreate. These connections could be crucial to finding an apartment or a job.

In the absence of a common background, migrants formed communities in other ways. The most basic of these was the neighborhood. Workers of peasant background tended to choose apartments in the city center, in the neighborhoods built for the German workers of the first industrialization several generations earlier. Many from the same region were drawn together by a church – by the presence of a familiar priest, for example.[23] In outlying areas, neighborhood ties were especially likely to be constructed along regional lines. Here migrants could in effect recreate their home villages within the city. The family of Stanisława J., a young migrant from near Lwów whose father was a railway man, chose such a neighborhood in order to tend the cow and chickens they had brought from home.[24]

The most important institution in the lives of the workers ought to have been the factory. Factories were intended to enable the social organization and integration of the individual migrant into Polish society. In a transient society, work tied migrants to the city; however, the factory was only effective so long as it could keep its workers. As will be seen below, this was a nearly impossible task. Factories helped to structure the city, building tram lines and clearing rubble. They housed, fed, and clothed their workers; factory cooperatives could be the only place where necessities could be had at affordable prices. Even the available culture was provided by the factory: the largest ones organized and supported the city's first cinemas, theaters, and sports teams. As a result, a kind of "factory patriotism" did emerge in the largest factories.[25]

As noted earlier, national identity was central to Wrocław's rebirth. What is striking, however, is that this national consciousness did not produce more conflict. On the Western frontier, Wrocław was the site of national contacts unlike those anywhere else in Poland at the time. Germans, Russians, and Jews were prominent in the city through at least 1947. A regionally heterogeneous community, though rent with traditional suspicions, might eventually develop a strong idea of national identity, around the fear of common opponents.

The German border which lies less than 150 kilometers from Wrocław was in 1945 far from certain. Fears that Poland's tenure in the West was but temporary – that the Allies would give the region back to the Germans – were strong throughout the 1940s. The Soviet Army, meanwhile, encouraged this perception: local commanders attempted to strip Western Poland of much of its industrial capability, shipping machinery and raw materials to the Soviet Union.[26] Most who returned were women and old men. Yet they gave the city a distinctly German character for at least the first year. In Polish eyes, Germans acted like victors, biding their time until Poland was forced to surrender Wrocław. Poles guarded their apartments from returning German owners, and found many essential supplies could only be bought from Germans on the black market. Many Germans also believed that the region would soon be returned to them. A poster advertising the "Recovered Territories Festival of Polish Culture" offered a wry metaphor for the thin veneer of Polish culture in Wrocław in the summer of 1946. It was printed over a German announcement from the war, with the signature of the SS commander plainly visible, as if endorsing the Polish facade.[27]

The primary point of contact between Pole and German was at the workplace. A large number of Germans capable of working did remain or return to Wrocław. These fell into two groups: a small cadre of skilled workers or experts whose knowledge was needed to restart the factories and keep them running until Polish replacements could be persuaded to come west; and a much larger group of unskilled laborers, used primarily for jobs Poles were less willing to perform, on rubble-clearing crews and as janitors. In Pafawag, for example, German workers, employed mostly to clear rubble and rebuild machines, were the majority in the work force until November 1945.[28] The Polish worker's early experience was that employers preferred German labor. "German workers rest on beds covered with down quilts," complained a factory council representative at the Klecina sugar refinery in early 1946, while "Poles bunk on the floor, with nothing to cover them."[29] Many Poles were unable to find work and left the city, while factories preferred less-expensive Germans. City officials began to refuse firms permission to employ Germans, as factories were using highly-skilled German worker for "dirty work" – clearing of rubble, for example – in order to protect them "in anticipation of the beginning of production – since it is obvious that at the moment of beginning production the firm will not get a Polish expert on demand."[30] Poles, claimed industry officials, refused to accept work which was too hard or which they considered beneath them; Polish workers would quit soon anyway, so it was safer to retain Germans.[31] The employers set aside national considerations, in other words, as they recognized that the frontier afforded them an opportunity to benefit from the cheap labor of a defeated nation.

This apparent contradiction between the professed national goals of city and industry leaders, and actual economic policy was precisely the oppositional experience of nation which might provoke national identification among Polish workers. Even more provocative was the uncomfortably close contact with the semi-demobilized soldiers of the Soviet Army. Throughout the region, the Soviets played an ambiguous role, one which neither they nor their Polish hosts ever resolved. They acted officially as caretakers of German territory and industry until Polish authorities could assume control. Soviet soldiers were a ubiquitous feature of the landscape. Even today, jokes about their simple fascination with watches and bicycles are common in every repertoire; at the time, the humor was darker. These soldiers were feared; the archives of the City Administration are filled with reports of muggings, burglaries, and murder attributed to Soviet soldiers. They were particularly threatening to Polish workers, on the street after dark on the way to or from the factory.[32] The Polish police were powerless, or seemed so. "Every case of robbery or theft," noted the Provincial Information and Propaganda Bureau in 1946, "has been ascribed to the soldiers of the Red Army, towards whom hatred and distrust has grown."[33] The political consequences of anti-Soviet nationalism would later be evident; in Wrocław's first years, resentment of the Russians and the Germans were linked in everyday experience.

Yet these resentments and fears were more the product of the frontier than of a national community. Rather than being inspired to new national unity, Poles felt that they had found themselves in a land with two occupiers. Wrocław was understood by most who came there as a transitional city, where divisions meant more than community. Great chasms of distrust existed between the skilled and the unskilled, the worker and the looter or shopkeeper, the pioneer and the newcomer. Equally important was the tension between the migrants to Wrocław and the state. The new citizens of the city had been misled about the riches which awaited them, were neglected and underfed, and used as token Poles among Germans and Russians, cut off from the rest of Poland. The only common identity which linked Wrocław's workers, however tenuously, was one which held them apart too: the identity of the physical and temporal frontier. That frontier profoundly affected the way workers saw themselves, each other, and the authorities; it was at the heart of all their differences, and shaped patterns of resistance and accommodation.

The PPR and Labor in the "Wild West"

The importance of the frontier identity can be seen in the way it inhibited the development of other identities, especially that of class. A strong communal sense among Polish workers in Wrocław would surely have been manifested in conflict with employers who hired Germans, who were advised by Russians, who did not supply the food, shelter, and security which the migrants sought. Yet such conflict was virtually invisible at the Wrocław factory, in marked contrast to other cities in Poland.[34] While there were over a dozen strikes in 1946-47, this was but a weak echo of the strike waves which swept other Polish cities at the time. The strikes which did occur were generally short, lasting no more than a few hours. The experiences of frontier cities elsewhere – the American West, for example – lead one to expect rapid formation of conflict-based worker identities. This was not the case in Wrocław, though workers faced perhaps the worst conditions in Poland. The workers' putative opponents, moreover, were as new to the city as were the workers. Desperate to rebuild and to get production going as quickly as possible, they found it difficult to dictate labor terms. Nor was the Wrocław worker of the kind one might expect to find accepting conditions in his or her new home. Most were peasants, but in the past peasants in Poland had often resisted noble landowners, imperial governments, interwar capitalism, or the Nazis.

The lack of protest can partly be ascribed to the strength of the Wrocław PPR organization, but in a way which points up the Communists' shortcomings as much as their strengths. The only thing certain in this occupied land was the Party, and its power was unchallenged given the lack of an established community. One might then expect to find evidence of swift Party action to contain disputes or suppress dissent. But there is no evidence that the PPR organization was more powerful than elsewhere; rather, it is clear that the Communists in Wrocław did not in fact possess this kind of power within the factories.

The explanation of working-class quiescence on the Polish frontier lies not in a higher level of repression or discipline there, but in the nature of the work force. Although the Communists ultimately benefited from this circumstance, it was not one they created, and it led to a different kind of Party than they desired. Party membership did not bring about organizational discipline because it was not the result of ideological allegiance. Party members did not strike or express dissent in Wrocław not because they were forbidden to or were successfully indoctrinated. Rather, extremely high levels of membership were indicative of the extremely low level of political and organizational culture in the Wrocław working class. Still, even such a weak membership was beneficial to the Party, for it meant that a large proportion of the work force came into frequent contact with the Party and its culture. The result, as will be shown, was the laying of the social foundations of Stalinist Poland.

The numbers of Party members in Wrocław were indeed impressive. From 1,181 members in January 1946, the PPR grew to almost 19,000 by January 1948; nearly two-thirds of these were workers. The PPS, meanwhile, claimed 4,570 members in Wrocław in September 1946, and 14,377 a year later. Assuming that a similar proportion of PPS members were workers, and accounting for the differences in membership between 1947 and 1948 (including a verification campaign which reduced PPS numbers by 35%), this means that between 18 and 21 thousand workers in Wrocław were Party members, while there were only 30 to 35 thousand employed in industry as a whole.[35] These were among the highest rates of membership in the country. Nationwide, 18% of those employed in factories belonged to the PPR in January 1948. Membership in some Wrocław factories was often much higher: 70% of the work force at the State Hydrometer Factory, for example, and 59% at the Garment Factories.[36] By comparison, in mid-1946 less than 6% of the workers in twenty largest factories in Łódź belonged to the PPR; even by 1948, the average in four large factories for which data is available had only reached fourteen percent.[37]

Most workers joined a party when they began work. It was common practice among personnel directors, most of whom were members of the PPR, to make membership an unofficial prerequisite for employment. A Wrocław metalworker retells in his memoirs the story of a semi-literate

peasant named Koń. When Koń came to the factory, "the PPS and PPR
Secretaries were on duty in the personnel bureau; [Koń] happened to be
received by the PPR Secretary, [who said] 'If you want work, join the
PPR.' He joined."[38] A potential worker could join even sooner, in order to
find work. The personnel departments of the PPR, PPS, and later the
PZPR acted as employment bureaus, despite government efforts to
discourage this practice.[39] Stefania K. found work in Wrocław in this
way:

> When I was living in that [workers'] hostel, two men came – they
> also lived there. But they were some sort of, how can I put it – they
> were armed, you know? [...] and they asked what we're [SK and a
> friend] doing. We say that we don't have work yet, that we had
> worked on the trams, but there you had to come home from work
> very late at night, and that we're afraid, and we can't work like
> that. And they say that they'll arrange work for us in Pafawag.
> And they arranged it. We went there, and they hired us.
> [question: did they tell you to join the Party to get that job?]
> SK: I was already in the Party, I had already signed up. Because
> when we hadn't anything to eat, you know, there wasn't any
> money, and we went to the [PPR City] Committee, they signed us
> up right away, and that's why they gave us two weeks' worth of
> food, for free. [...] Because there was no other way.[40]

As factories rapidly expanded their work force, they could hardly
require membership of every new worker. These workers were targeted
later. Within the factory, as Stanisława J., a clothing factory worker,
recalls, recruiting went on during work; she herself hid in the bathroom
whenever Party recruiters appeared in her shop. Most workers, young
and inexperienced, joined partly to get some peace from the recruiters, as
well as out of fear. But membership in an organization also promised
introduction to a social world which was slightly intimidating to these
newcomers to city and factory.

Who were the workers in the so-called working-class parties? To
some extent, the profile in Wrocław proves the hypothesis that
Communism is strongest in underdeveloped areas.[41] Wrocław was
hardly underdeveloped, but its proletariat certainly was. A profile of
sorts can be sketched from personnel data from two Wrocław factories.
Party members differed from their non-party colleagues in ways which
reveal much about motivation for joining. The economic and social
background of the party-member worker, as compared to that of the
worker who did not join a party, thus provides an explanation for the
lack of protest by the Wrocław working class. Official histories of the
PPR emphasize the Party's working-class content. Data from Wrocław
suggest otherwise. Workers who joined a party were indeed less
experienced than non-party workers. Nearly half the workers in two

sample factories had been living in villages in 1939; less than a third of these workers had lived in a medium- or large-sized city, where most political activity would be concentrated. And between two-thirds and three-quarters of all workers, regardless of origin, had been in school, on a farm, or not working at all in 1939. Finally, most workers were very young, and single. About three-fifths of the workers were unmarried when they began work; workers from villages were most likely to be single or widowed. In both sample factories, more than three-fifths of the workers were under thirty when hired.

It is precisely these workers who would have been least likely to have been affected by Party organization and propaganda before their arrival in Wrocław; they were also the most likely to join a party. More than half the Party members in two sample factories come from villages or small towns. The paths to party membership in the PPR and the PPS, meanwhile, were very different. PPR workers were more likely to come from villages and small towns than were non-party workers.[42] PPS-member workers, meanwhile, were more likely to be of urban origin than other workers, and thus probably familiar with the pre-war PPS, if they had not been members themselves. The most likely to join the PPR were workers with no pre-war work experience at all. The combination of work and home experiences in 1939 seems a particularly strong indicator of party membership.

That ideology was not a reason for party membership is shown by examination of workers who spent part of the war in Germany or other European countries, nearly all on forced labor in militarized factories or mines, on farms, or in concentration camps. They were likely to have a very different perception of the wartime experience, and of the meaning of Soviet liberation, than would those in eastern or central Poland. In the two sample factories, however, they were not more likely to join a political party. Membership rates among this group are virtually identical to those of workers without German experience. As with labor experience, what might be termed a 'positive' reason (that is, one consonant with an 'ideological' model of party membership) to join a left political party (familiarity with German terror, gratitude for the Soviet liberation) is not a significant factor.

Wrocław workers, then, did not join the PPR for ideological reasons; the smaller PPS membership followed pre-war lines. The high PPR membership rate in Wrocław is not, therefore, an indicator of a strong labor or class identity in that city, but in fact a manifestation of the lack of a labor culture. It was precisely those workers without a prior labor identity who joined the PPR. While the Party organization itself was not particularly powerful in Wrocław, its membership was far easier to recruit, organize, and control than elsewhere. The workers in Wrocław were something of a blank slate: rural, young, poorly educated, and lacking in experience. Contact with the PPR was for many the first contact with this kind of comprehensive organization. The same phenomenon which led Wrocław workers to join the Party, then, also made it unlikely that they would strike.

The contrast between Wrocław and the cities of central Poland was not so much a contrast between two labor cultures as between a labor culture and its absence. The presence of the PPR in the factory was so great primarily because there was no alternative which might draw workers away from the Party. Such an alternative would have been a traditional working-class culture of skill and experience, of relations within the factory and neighborhood, and of shared and remembered custom. This culture, in a new city, might be passed on or spread by a cohort of workers who shared these or similar traditions and cultures.

However, while nearly one-third of the workers in the sample metal factory, and almost one-quarter in the textile factory, had some factory experience before the war, the pre-war working-class culture which these experienced workers remembered was actually the cultures of a dozen different cities. Their traditions, weakened by the move to Wrocław, did not necessarily translate into influence in the Wrocław factory. In a large factory, this cohort was isolated and divided. This group of workers – if it may be termed a group – could not play an important role. For example, the practice of leaving work together at the end of the day for a drink in a nearby tavern, so common elsewhere, was virtually unknown (or at least not memorable) in Wrocław. A group of metalworkers in Łódź enthusiastically recalled the camaraderie of those days:

> [worker 1]: [Workers] went to restaurants more often than today, because there were very many restaurants, and they were cheap, you could go there; one usually went to stand [at the counter] for five minutes, or one went to stand for two hours, or to sit. For some herring, for example, there was a restaurant on the corner of Obywatelska [Street]. The foundry workers went to that one on Końska, or on Obywatelska – and the supervisor, and one or two foremen [went too].
> [second worker]: Listen mister, when one of the guys had his nameday, then he bought rounds [*się stawiało*] on Obywatelska like you wouldn't believe.
> [third worker]: People worked together when a group was [leaving work, some one would say] 'Let's go to the restaurant *[knajpa].*'

Metalworkers in Wrocław, in contrast, were equally emphatic that they had never done the same:

> [Question]: Would you go to a *knajpa* [after work]?
> [worker 1]: No, because you didn't have the cash – we made pennies. It was like this: You go to your garden plot, you don't meet your acquaintances, and you won't say anything.
> [second worker]: There was nowhere to go. [...]

[third worker]: If there was a nameday, or a child's birthday, [...] then you had a family gathering, and a few neighbors, because that was cheapest.[43]

A better illustration of the atomization of society under Stalinism would be difficult to find – except that the first interview excerpt describes the same era as the second. The reason was not the efforts of Party leaders, but the nature of the frontier. Protest did not take place as in other cities, despite conditions which were, it would seem, ripe for large-scale protest, for the same reasons that workers did not gather after work for a drink: not because of the PPR's numerical superiority, but in spite of it. That is, this passivity was reflective of a lack of community identity which persisted despite the Party's efforts to impose an identity on the workers. Moreover, the Party and the employers had to contend with forms of resistance which were equally as damaging to the formation of a Stalinist society as were strikes. There were alternatives to open conflict available in postwar Poland; they require us to reconsider the nature of protest and consent between the working class and the state/employers at the birth of Polish Stalinism.

Alternative Forms of Resistance

The Wrocław worker was in fact no more willing to accept conditions in his or her new home than workers elsewhere. A closer look at the Wrocław work force finds, in fact, that workers were as troublesome to the authorities here as in more established cities. The nature of their resistance was, however, very different from more common modes of factory protest.

Above all, their means of expressing grievances tended to be individual rather than collective. Recalling their peasant backgrounds, one might expect significant levels of individual indiscipline, often manifested as disinclination to work according to a schedule. Because of poor living and working conditions; because of most workers' unfamiliarity with factory work; because of general expectations that life ought to be better after the war; and because of the weak ties among workers and between workers and supervisors, the inclination to work hard, and to form an attachment to a factory, was weak. Party observers and employers commented on the indifference of the Wrocław laborer to work, and the lack of attachment to the workplace. Labor discipline was the greatest problem – "the most burning issue in Lower Silesia," in the words of one PPR inspector in late 1946, who was shocked to find at an aircraft parts factory "workers resting and sleeping at 13:30 – that is, during the workday."[44] A Ministry of Industry report on another metal factory attributed workers'

lack of subordination to the orders of the factory council to the fact
that the factory work force is made up of a migrant element (from
various districts of the country), demoralized by easy money early
on, and by the general lack of discipline.[45]

Factory and Party authority was simply insufficient, these observers
discovered, to force workers to produce in the way the regime required.

The meaning of discipline, of course, is highly subjective. Worker
solidarity and collective responsibility (which was soon to be recast as
labor competition) could seem like insubordination to a production-
oriented state. Pafawag provides an interesting case of the tension
between still unenforceable planning goals and propaganda on the one
hand, and workers' indifference, misbehavior, and stubbornness on the
other. Amid national fanfare in January 1946, the still under-re-
construction factory produced its 100th wagon. This moment was
portrayed as a symbol of Poland's rebirth, an implicit sign of the
adaptation of the migrants to their new home. "Since that ceremony," the
factory's director wrote just a few weeks later,

> we have observed apathy, lack of enthusiasm, and lack of a sense of
> responsibility to one's work. Employees complain about low wages,
> claiming that the Western bonus [paid to workers in the Recovered
> Territories] does not even cover the difference in prices of basic
> necessities; moreover, the approaching spring brings the promise of
> the start of construction work, in which there are no set pay tables,
> and wages tend to be several times higher than in [manufacturing].
> Unexcused absenteeism has risen in several departments to 20.3%.
> The threat of being fired generally makes no impression, given the
> ease of finding employment in other industries.[46]

Older skilled workers or supervisors who spoke at a Pafawag
technical conference later in the year also saw a divide between them and
new workers. They recalled the pioneer days, when most Polish workers
at Pafawag were the skilled cadres sent from Warsaw or Silesia. The new
workers, they claimed, showed contempt for work rules and regulations:
"a worker says he's done his job because he's met the norm, that is,
100%." Many workers were finished, washed, and dressed an hour before the end of the shift, though the porter would not unlock the gates.
Some broke open their lockers in their haste to leave. Many workers
refused alternative tasks assigned during work delays caused by power
failures or material shortages. "A large part of our work force has never
worked in large groups before," explained one speaker, "and does not
understand the necessity to work together and to assume joint
responsibility for their work."[47] Labor competition, introduced in
Pafawag and in many factories across Poland in late 1947, would only
begin to address these problems, while creating new difficulties as well.

But lack of discipline in all its forms – including theft, looting, and even the black market – should not be understood, as Party officials wished it to be, as merely the product of untrained hands. More important, it functioned as an alternative which obviated the need to protest in a more formal way. A chemical industry representative inadvertently made this connection in 1947: while "the Lower Silesian chemical industry can boast that nowhere until now have there been any serious conflicts," thefts were often on a mass scale:

> workers steal both products and small tools. Party members and even guards steal, too. At the same time, Lower Silesian chemical factories have experienced high labor turnover. Young single workers secure a job, work for a short period, then quit; some factories have experienced a 100% turnover in the course of one year.[48]

As this official realized, the labor market, which in the Recovered Territories was quite advantageous for the worker, was Wrocław workers' most potent ally. While most forms of informal resistance are difficult to measure, labor turnover is much clearer. The entire Recovered Territories had an insatiable need for workers; this was a land of opportunity, filled with jobs for the taking. Leaving an unsatisfactory job in search of another remained a wide-spread, almost universal method of adaptation by Wrocław workers throughout the 1940s. Turnover across Lower Silesia throughout the 1940s was over one-and-a-half times the national average.[49] By March 1946 Pafawag, which employed at the time about 3,000 workers, had employed 15,000 workers in ten months.[50] The yearly turnover at Wrocław metal factories was estimated in early 1948 to range from 26% (at Pafawag) to 84.5%.[51] In the sample metal factory, nearly three-fifths of those employed at some time between 1945 and 1949 worked for less than one year – a five-fold turnover in just over four years, given a total of about 2,500 workers. Skilled workers were especially likely to switch jobs.

These workers (again, most were young and single, to a greater degree than their counterparts in other cities) had few commitments; with the German Army expected back any day, they preferred to spend what they earned, or send it back to families. In the region's textile industry, an observer noted, the workers were people, lamented a Party official in another Lower Silesian city, "whom nothing tied to their factory. They generally have families settled in central Poland on farms; thus the moment farm work begins, they quit their jobs in the factory and leave."[52] The wide-open labor market gave workers a clear advantage which neither authority nor incentive could easily diminish. There was always another factory, another city where management might be willing to pay a little more to lure desperately-needed workers.

Still, the PPR found it had some slight influence on this aspect of labor discipline. Members of the two major parties at the two sample factories were rather more likely to remain at work for a longer period than were non-party workers, although more than half of each group still left within one year. Members felt the parties' influence in various ways. They may have considered, or been told, that it was their Party duty to stay; many surely recognized that it would be difficult to leave work without facing an inquiry from the Party, as happened to Stefania K. Those who joined the Party expecting to advance certainly would stay longer than other workers. For whatever reason, Party workers found that membership had certain obligations; it turned them, whether they liked it or not, from anonymous newcomers into members of an organization. Thus, by simple virtue of the fact that the Communists had first attracted the younger, inexperienced workers to their ranks and then been able to keep them in the factory longer, the culture that would take root in the factory was that of the PPR, or rather, of the less urban and less educated workers who were Party members. The Wrocław factory, and the culture of Wrocław industry, was their creation.

However, while the PPR was able to assimilate a large proportion of the Wrocław work force into its organization, this was not the same as developing a disciplined Party cadre. In fact, the Party was able to grow precisely because of the indiscipline of the inexperienced workers who came to the city. To accept this point is to revise thoroughly our understanding of the role of the Communist parties in Eastern Europe. The PPR in Wrocław did not, through repression or agitation, create the factory relations found there; instead, its experience was a product of those relations. The effort to explain the lack of strikes has led beyond the PPR to the demographic and cultural shifts associated with the Recovered Territories and the great migration west. The lack of community in Wrocław proved to be its defining characteristic. But at least through the first years, the workers of Wrocław did have the resources to resist the state, though as individuals and not as a collective. Ultimately, this resistance would be easier to break.

What Kind of Stalinism?

At first, though, numbers were for the PPR an acceptable substitute for activist commitment. But beginning in 1948, for many reasons which are perhaps too familiar to go into here, a more active model of membership and of workplace commitment was necessary. To that end, the Party began to try to extend its reach deep into the factory, attempting to take control of the process of social transformation. PPR activists in Wrocław now discovered that imposing their culture on such a disaggregated, apolitical society was not so simple. These workers had been willing to join the Party in large numbers, and attend meetings. But now that the Party required more organized, "positive" participation – a tendency which increased as Stalinism deepened – the workers of Wrocław proved unable to meet Party standards. They lacked the collectivity essential for small Party campaigns like collections, volunteer work, and organized enthusiasm.

The overwhelming attitude of the workers toward the activist PPR was indifference, as much as it had been before. Locking gates to keep party members at a meeting was a recurrent motif in PPR reports of 1948. Distress over worker indifference represented both genuine apathy as well as the Party's raising of the stakes. And as strong as the concern might have been elsewhere, Wrocław was a PPR city, where membership was highest and the growth of a new, disciplined Party culture should have been the most easily accomplished. Yet everywhere the Party turned, its members were in disarray, uninterested in showing a higher degree of discipline – whether at work or at meetings – than their non-member colleagues. The leadership's call for discipline or agitational militancy clashed with the desires of the rank and file. In one factory, the popular leader of the PPR factory committee was planning to quit work and open a store; in another, only four of 100 PPR members had completed a Party course, leaving the rest unable to "take appropriate positions" on labor issues and "militant feelings."[53] A report presented to a meeting at a ceramics factory, at which just half of membership was present, raised the locked-gates refrain: "If we are Party men [*partyjniaki*], then we should come to meetings voluntarily, and it should not be necessary to stand by the gate and tell each one to stay because it is a Party meeting." Added another: "Comrade Party members are not disciplined at work; they leave their job to go into the city during work." This brought a heated response from the floor: "there's a lot of gab at this meeting about discipline, [yet though] my husband works, we don't have an apartment – how can we work; it'll come to the point that we'll have to quit work and leave Wrocław." In response, members were then admonished to speak with a Party sense [*poczucie partyjne*], and speak only when given the floor; though there was no sign of general protest, it was clear that members were not taking the call for greater discipline easily.[54]

At the same time, it was clear that these workers were attempting to find ways to reconcile the tensions between Party norms and their conception of the Party. A similar conflict emerged at a self-criticism session of the PPR circle at the Klecina sugar refinery in October 1948. Speakers talked about the conflict between Party discipline and social obligations, in particular their drinking habits:

> I've been working in the sugar refinery two years. There were cases where someone came with vodka, and it was 4PM, so I drank. There were four such cases where someone came and offered me a drink. But drinking all the time, no. My father [was] a shoemaker, I myself was a shopkeeper before the war. I am 61 years old.

I admit that I drank vodka, but I don't admit that I lead workers to
drink. As far as fulfilling my work duties – I do what I can, putting
parts together, repairing engines and automobiles.[55]

These speakers were in effect trying to defend their relationship to other
workers (in part by depicting themselves in a passive role in social
relations) and reconcile this with the duty of belonging to the Party. This
does not mean that they recognized the right of the Party to censure their
social habits; however, they attempted to state their cases in Party
language:

I joined [the Party, in 1946] out of conviction [explained a member
of the Industrial Guard]. Only now am I learning to write and read.
I will never forget that my father wielded a scythe all day for 90
groschen; I will always be a proletarian.[56]

The wooden language of allegiance to the proletariat indicates a desire to
remain accepted by the PPR, and a willingness to conform, at least
outwardly, to its rules.

The difficulties the Party would encounter in enforcing those rules
were dramatically illustrated in a violent protest in a garment factory
(the one used for statistical samples earlier) in December of 1948. As a
portrayal of worker-party relations, it deserves closer scrutiny. Perhaps it
was only possible in Wrocław, where the PPR was determined,
dominant, and distant from the workers, while the workers were equally
distant from a factory culture, and ready to defend values important to
their church- and village-based communities.

Garment Factory #1 employed about 3,700 workers in November
1948, 75 percent of them women. The PPR had 1,360 members there –
"completely unformed politically," as a Central Committee investigation
put it. In Division E, where the incident took place, half of the 400
workers belonged to the PPR, with another 20 percent in the PPS. It was
a situation typical for Wrocław: a high degree of Party membership,
with, as it turned out, a low degree of appropriate political
consciousness. In 1947, the workers of Division E had collected money to
buy several religious pictures to hang in each workshop of the division.[57]

The September 1948 PPR plenum was apparently the catalyst for the
extremely lax PPR factory organization to decide to crack down on these
displays.[58] On November 30, after the workers had gone home, PPR
secretary Błażejewski ("known as a 'crazed' anti-cleric"), with the
personnel director and a PPR activist-seamstress named Rdzanek,
removed the pictures. A report filed by two Central Committee
inspectors best describes the scene:

On December 1 at 6:30, at the moment of beginning work, the
[women] workers noticed the pictures were missing. A roar arose,

and shouts of "someone took the pictures," "they're taking God away from us," and "we want God." At the shout "Rdzanek did it," most of the workers ran to the shop where Rdzanek works and threw themselves on her, shouting "give up the pictures." Rdzanek, terrified, escaped to the sorting room, with a frenzied crowd of *dewotki* [pious biddies] after her. In the sorting room, [they] began to beat Comrade Rdzanek; members of the PPR and PPS led the attackers, pushing aside non-Party [workers], [saying that they] "must settle accounts themselves, and would not be punished for it [as Party members]."

At this moment, comrade Błażejewski entered the factory, then the whole crowd threw itself at him; [they] began to beat him and tear at him, shouting "give up the pictures," and "you burned them." Błażejewski, terrified, led them to his office and gave back the pictures.

During the whole incident, substitute pictures and medallions appeared and were hung in the place of those which had been removed. After receiving the pictures, [the workers] hung them back in their place, and they returned to work. The entire fracas lasted about two hours.[59]

Relations in this factory were, to say the least, confused. The PPR appeared completely out of contact with the workers, most of whom were members. Perhaps such a conflict could take place in a city in central Poland. The outcome there, however, would be quite different from that in Wrocław – as could not be otherwise, given the mass Party membership in most Wrocław factories. For however uncontrollable the membership may have been, the Party did have the resources of Party discipline at its disposal. At a joint PPR-PPS meeting that afternoon in the factory, a number of workers from both parties were expelled, with the promise of further vetting of the ranks. Later, a representative of the City PPR Committee threatened to close the factory and lay off all the workers; foremen and brigade leaders in Division E were degraded to ordinary workers; several workers and administrators were fired. The PPR, in other words, used this moment to make clear to workers what their obligations as Party members were: that contrary to rumor, they could certainly be punished for beating a Party activist, and Party membership meant not immunity, but certain sacrifices, if one were to remain a member. Workers in Wrocław had not joined the Party for ideology, and were unlikely to leave it for ideology, either. Rather, they would remain in the Party and follow its rules.

The result, even in Wrocław, was a rather complex interaction between the rules of the Party, which only now was beginning to enforce its culture explicitly upon its membership, and social relations in the factory. The Party was more easily able to dominate in Wrocław than in a city like Łódź; thus what took place on the western frontier, where social and communal ties were yet so fragile, was at the very least a possible future for Party-worker relations everywhere. Yet even in Wrocław, the transition from a community-circumscribed society to one where social norms were outlined by the Party was not easy. As the idea of Party membership evolved from one of sheer numbers to an activist regime, Wrocław workers, so adaptable to the first model, proved much more reluctant toward the second. After all, they could simply leave the city, or open a store, if work was unsuitable or the Party too harsh. The hold of the Party over society was not yet strong enough to impose models of behavior. This would change with the unification of the two mass parties into the PZPR, in December 1948; the Polish United Workers' Party would demand and get much greater activism from its membership. Meanwhile, the state found ways to appeal to these workers, rewarding activism with pay, promotion, and prestige. The growth of that system, of activism and production, must be understood in the context of the pressures placed on the system, and the opportunities afforded it, by the mixed migrant work force of cities like Wrocław. Thus we cannot begin to understand Stalinism until we have accounted for the experiences of those around whom the system was built.

The workers of Wrocław were not entirely different from the workers of the rest of Poland. They lived in the same political system; the newspapers they read, the films they saw, and the lectures they attended conveyed the same messages. But the relationship between workers and Party or state was fundamentally different. A labor or factory culture usually develops within a community well before the evolution of a party or political culture. In Wrocław, the two arrived at the same time. The creation or establishment of working-class traditions in the new city, therefore, was hindered and altered by the simultaneous evolution of labor institutions, and at the level of the state, no less. Two modes of culture – a transmitted culture of labor and tradition, and an organizationally-generated culture of membership – competed in a way unique to Wrocław and to the Recovered Territories. The established labor culture, as much as it was conveyed to Wrocław by experienced workers from other cities, was completely alien to the mass of inexperienced workers of rural origin who dominated the factories. So, generally, was organizational culture, for that matter, but it was organizational culture, in the form of the PPR, which met them at the train station, or at the door of the personnel office, or at the sewing machine. It was that culture which offered a job, a home, and a community.

Community, in its absence, was the essence of Wrocław culture. The workers of Wrocław came from all over Poland, searching to reform community in ways which would lend stability or logic to their lives after six long years of war. The most powerful force, regional allegiance, was also the most divisive. The shopkeeper or priest from the same district in Lwów province was more important than the workmate from Poznań who spoke and acted differently. The result was a city-wide work force which could not easily form a community around shared labor experience or class, and which did not seem interested in the wider city or national community, either. Another kind of community was provided by the PPR, something tangible to which one belonged, and which gave structure to one's life.

Shared experience is most powerfully produced by conflict. Class struggle, or conflict easily perceived as such, helps to shape class consciousness. The resistance in which workers engaged, though passive and individual, was potentially the beginning of such conflict. But this resistance, as it deflected conflict, provided a foundation on which a Stalinist society could be built. These single, newly-arrived workers could as easily leave, and many did. If the work in a metal factory was too harsh, or too poorly paid, there was work in a clothing factory, or on a construction gang. To strike when there were so many jobs available elsewhere was senseless. It might also be ineffective, because there were always new workers arriving. One could instead get one's due by stealing, looting, coming to work late, leaving early, or just leaving. Yet when these avenues were eventually cut off by growing repression and the growing economy, only the Party was left.

Was Wrocław typical of Poland in the years 1945-1948? Perhaps not. Most industry was still performed in the old industrial centers, relatively stable labor communities framed by the same relations as before the war, where workers were ready to strike. But Poland was only beginning to change. As new workers flooded into Wrocław, so they were arriving in another destroyed city, Warsaw. Soon, migrants like these would be arriving in the new centers of industry, in the expanding coastal industries of Szczecin, Gdynia, and Gdansk, in the mines of Silesia, in the new factories of Poland's future. Much of this expansion and migration took place on the other side of the Stalinist divide, in the early 1950s and after. Wrocław was the first example of the new migrant city in postwar Poland, and its experience says much about the worker culture of the future.

In laying the foundations of Stalinist society, the state needed to harness the potential of the new workers like those in Wrocław. The solution would be social advance, especially through various forms of labor competition, a movement which celebrated individual achievement and self-improvement over community ties and apprenticeship. This would provide a way for new workers in Poland's factories to succeed, in defiance of the older, experienced workers. It promised a great deal of money, and adulation like that for sports figures. Labor competition would, in effect, make Poland into Wrocław, while giving the workers of Wrocław something to keep them in the factory, and in the Party. The lasting pioneer myth, meanwhile, tells us something about the models the state would eventually rely upon: images of progress, technology, and education would eventually push the worker to the background. Wrocław, indeed, was the future of Stalinism in Poland, as that political system was constructed both from above and below.

Notes

1. The classic comparative text is Zbigniew K. Brzezinski, *The Soviet Bloc: Unity and Conflict* (Cambridge, MA, 1967). Other comparative accounts of the revolutions of 1945-49 are Hugh Seton-Watson, The East European Revolution (New York, 1951); and Jerzy Tomaszewski, The Socialist Regimes of East Central Europe: Their Establishment and Consolidation, 1944-1967 (London, 1989).

2. I follow Brzezinkski's distinction between the Communism introduced in Eastern Europe in 1944-45 and Stalinism , which arrives in 1948. See Brzezinski, *The Soviet Bloc: Unity and conflict.* Essential formulations of the Stalinist model are presented in the volume of essays edited by Robert Tucker (*Stalinism: Essays in Historical Interpretation* [New York, 1977]). For a review of the totalitarian theory, see Adam Westoby, "Conceptions of Communist States, in *States and Societies*, ed. David Held, et al. (New York, 1983), 227-30.

3. Krystyna Kersten, in *Narodziny systemu władzy. Polska 1943-1948* (Paris, 1985), in English as *The Establishment of Communist Rule in Poland, 1943-1948,* trans. John Micgiel and Michael H. Bernhard (Berkeley, 1991).

4. Jędrzej Chumiński, "Czynniki destabilizujące proces osadnictwa we Wrocławiu (1945-1949), " Acta Universitatis Wratislaviensis 1512: Socjologia X (1993), 64.

5. Tomasz Szarota, "Rada Naukowa dla Zagadnień Ziem Odzyskanych wobec osadnictwa miejskiego," *Polska Ludowa* IV (1965), 83-89; Szarota, Osadnictwo miejskie na Dolnym Śląsku w latach 1945-1948 (Wrocław, 1969), 75-82. The planning was not dominated by ideological engineers; Wrocław was not to be a socialist planned city, but a symbol of a new Poland. Not until the early 1950s, with such projects as Nowa Huta in Kraków and MDM in Warsaw, would socialist planning come to the fore. A good deal of sociological literature in Polish has studied the region as an example of the integration of society in Communist Poland. A guide to this literature is *Ziemie Zachodnie w polskiej literaturze socjologicznej. Wybór tekstów,* ed. Andrzej Kwilecki (Poznań, 1970)

6. AAN "Referendum" II/29, kk. l. 49. Results for the city itself have not been found, except for extremely negative results from two repatriate trains stopped in Wrocław for the vote. KW PPR Wroclaw, report September-October 1946, AAN KC PPR 295/IX/362, kk. 47-8; Chumiński, "Motywy migracji," 139.

7. Instructors report, July 9, 1946, AAN KC PPR 295/IX/49, k. 95; WK PPS Wrocław, election campaign report, November 14, 1946 - January 20, 1947, WAP

WK PPS 36/VI/21, k. 10; KCZZ inspector, report from Wrocław November 16, 1945, AAN KC PPR 295/XIII/28A, kk. 197-98.

8. W. Kania "Pamiętnik z lat 1945-1948," *Sobótka*, VII (1952), 229, quoted in Marek Ordyłowski, *Życie codzienne we Wrocławiu 1945-1948* (Wrocław, 1991), 13.

9. Stanisław Jankowski, *Przejmowanie i odbudowa przemysłu dolno śląskiego 1945-1949* (Warsaw 1982), 223.

10. Report to Minister Hilary Minc, October 10, 1945, in MPiH 31, kk. 14-15.

11. WUIiP, report January 1946, AAN MIiP 550, k. 23.

12. *Pionier*, September 7, 1945. Quoted in "Wrocław 1945: Wydanie specjalne" (Wrocław, 1985), 3.

13. Most of the memoirs in *Trudne dni*, the three-volume set of memoirs issued in the 1960s by the Society of Friends of Wrocław, are those of white-collar pioneers: organizers of the first newspapers, the first government administrators, and the surveyors of the city's industry.

14. Report on the political situation in Lower Silesia, December 11-20, 1946, AAN MIiP 552, k. 130.

15. Report from Wrocław, November 16, 1945, AAN KC PPR 295/XIII/28A, kk. 196-7.

16. Workers were well aware that conditions were easier elsewhere in Poland. See protests by construction workers making this point: Construction Machine Industry Central Administration, Lower Silesia Delegation, letter to Ministry of Industry, November 8, 1945, AAN MPiH 1171, kk. 133-4.

17. Situation report, November 1-15, 1945, WUSW Wrocław, KWMO 146/10, kk. 71-2.

18. Chumiński, "Czynniki destabilizujące," 75.

19.The interview was recorded on June 4, 1990. Stefania K. was 28 at the time of her arrival in Wrocław in the fall of 1946. She worked at Pafawag until 1949.

20. "Congress Kingdom" : pre-1918 Russian Poland. The term was used derogatorialy to mean outside of Wrocław

21. Irena Turnau, "Tworzenie się wielkiego miasta z różnorodnej ludności naplywowej (Wrocław – miasto przemian społecznych)" (PhD, Wrocław University, 1950), 149; other examples, 138-152.

22. Similar attitudes could be found among migrants from other areas. Turnau, *Studia nad strukturą ludno ściową polskiego Wrocławia* (Poznań, 1960), 227-80.

23. Bp. Wincenty Urban, Duszpasterski wkład księży repatriantów w Archidiecezji Wrocławskiej w latach 1945-1970 (Wrocław, 1970), 27-30; Turnau, "Tworzenie się," 131-3.

24. Interview conducted August 18, 1990.

25.Jędrzej Chumiński, "Kształtowanie się śrdowiska robotników przemysłowych Wrocławia w latach 1945-1949" (PhD, Akademia Ekonomiczna we Wrocławiu, 1992), 205. On state intentions, see Dulczewski and Kwilecki, Społeczeństwo wielkopolskie w osadnictwie Ziem Zachodnich, 166 passim.

26. See Chumiński, "Kształtowanie się," 47-54; and idem, "Przejmowanie przemysłu wrocławskiego przez władze polskie (maj-wrzesień 1945) in *Studia nad społeczenstwem Wrocławia, Prace Naukowe Akademii Ekonomicznej*, 543 (Wrocław, 1990), 23-50.

27. Report from Lower Silesia, July 30-August 6, 1945, AAN MIiP 90, kk. 21-2; Inspection report, June 13, 1946, AAN MIiP 75, k. 88. On Polish-German relations in Wrocław and the expulsion of the German population, see especially Elżbieta Kaszubska and Jędrzej Chumiński, "Nastroje, postawy i położenie materialne ludości niemieckiej we Wrocławiu w latach 1945 i 1946," in *Kształtowanie się społeczeństwa i gospodarki na Ziemiach Zachodnich ze szczególnym uwzględnieniem Śląska , Prace Naukove Akademii Ekonomicznej*, 608 (Wrocław, 1992), 93-100; and Sebastian Siebel-Achenbach, *Lower Silesia from Nazi Germany to Communist Poland, 1943-1949* (New York, 1994).

28. Pafawag director, reports to Minister Minc, August 31, 1945-April 10, 1946, AAN MPiH 31.

29. Meeting, Lower Silesian factory council and union representatives, February 5, 1946, WAP WRZZ, 49, kk. 398-9.

30. Socio-Political Department, report December 1945, WAP ZM 131, k. 53. Provincial Bureau of Public Security, Report, October 31-November 10, 1945, in WUSW, WUBP, 2/1, k. 54.

31. Clothing Industry Association, Wrocław, memo February-March 1946, AAN MPiH 200, kk. 24-5. On German labor, see Chumiński, "Kształtowanie się," 188-92.

32. Pafawag Director, letter to Minister of Industry, October 31, 1945, AAN MPiH 31, k. 25; meeting in Kowale district, November 18, 1945, WAP KM PPR, 30/V/3, k. 25.

33. AAN MIiP 549.

34. See Padraic Kenney, "Working-class community and resistance in pre-Stalinist Poland: The Poznański textile strike, Łódź, September 1947," *Social History* 18:1 (January 1993), 31-52..

35. Anastazja Kowalik, *Zdziejów Polskiej Partii Robotniczej na Dolnym Śląsku w latach 1945-1948* (Wrocław, 1979), 41; Karol Boromeusz Janowski, *Polska Partia Socjalistyczna na Dolnym Śląsku w latach 1945-1948* (Wrocław, 1978), 36; 52% of PPS members in Lower Silesia were workers, and the number was probably higher in large cities. Workers in Wrocław: Estimated from Chumiński, "Kształtowanie się," tables 30, 34.

36. *Partia w cyfrach 1944-1948* (Warsaw, 1948), 34. 8.5% of Wrocław's total population, one of the highest totals in the country, belonged to the PPR in August 1948: ibid., figure 19. Factory numbers from WAP WK PPS 36/XIV/20, k. 130 (May 1948); and WAP KW PPR 1/XII/28 (June 1948), respectively.

37. These statistics most likely include office workers. Membership tended to be lower at smaller factories, since large factories were of greatest concern to PPR leaders. Numbers of the PPS are scarcer; PPS membership averaged roughly two-thirds to three-quarters of PPR membership. 1946 figures: *W dymach czarnych budzi się Łódź. Z dziejów łódźkiego ruchu robotniczego, 1882-1948* (Łódź, 1985), 460: KŁ PPR report August 1946, AAN KC PPR 295/IX/227, kk. 52-3. Figures for 1948 are from ŁAP KŁ PPR 1/VI/142, k. 184 (Vima); ŁAP KŁ PPR 1/VI/143, kk. 99. (Biederman) and 133 (Gampe); and Wiesław Puś and Stefan Pytlas, *Dzieje Łódźkich Zakładow Przemysłu Bawełnianego im. Obrońcow Pokoju "Uniontex" (d. Zjednoczonych Zakładow K. Scheiblera i L. Grohmana) w latach 1827-1977* (Warsaw, 1979), 446.

38. Later, Koń himself became the factory's PPR secretary, having "learned the multiplication tables and some simple economic rules." Marian Kamiński, State Hydrometer Factory, CRZZ memoir 640, kk. 3-4.

39. Chumiński, "Kształtowanie się," 184-5.

40. The PPR had also given Stefania K. her apartment and her first job; later, she moved to the apartment of a friend from back home, before finding an apartment in the district controlled by Pafawag.

41. R. V. Burks, *The Dynamics of Communism in Eastern Europe* (Princeton, 1961), 65-6.

42. In the metal factory, 34.6% of the metal workers from a village background belonged to the PPR, while 25.4% of those from a large city belonged. In the textile factory, the numbers were more even – 40.8% and 37.2% because of the uniform lack of work experience of these workers. The data here is a summary of material explored in greater length in my forthcoming book, *Transforming Poland: Workers in Revolution, 1945-1950*.

43. Łódź: workers at John metal factory, interview January 18, 1990; Wrocław: workers at Pafawag, February 8, 1990.

44. Report from a trip to Lower Silesian province September 27-October 11, 1946, AAN KC PPR 295/IX/49, k. 124.

45. Tin and Enamel Factory, AAN MPiH 4260, k. 28.

46. Report to Ministry of Industry, February 10, 1946, AAN MPiH 31, k. 61.

47. Technical conference, July 20, 1946, in WAP Pafawag 173, k. 3.

48. Management conference, Lower Silesian chemical industry, August 24, 1947, WAP KW PPR 1/X/4, k. 37.

49. Chumiński, "Kształtowanie się," 177-8, and see Table 21.

50. KM PPR, meeting with union, factory council, and PPR representatives from four metal factories, March 7, 1946, WAP KW PPR 1/XII/31 k. 63. Archimedes, a factory of 200-700 workers, had employed 4,000 by 1948: report on investigation of OKZZ, March 3, 1948, WAP KW PPR 1/XII/24, k. 80.

51. Report, Metal Industry Section, February 6, 1948, WAP KW PPR 1/X/7, k. 24.

52. PPR Industrial Department, Jelenia Góra, protocol February 16, 1948, WAP KW PPR 1/X/7, k. 190.

53. Garment factory and artificial silk factory, in report from trip to Wrocław province, August 27-September 7, 1948, AAN KC PPR 295/IX/51, kk. 39-40; Centra battery factory, inspection November 23, 1948, WAP KW PPR 1/X/5, kk. 152-4.

54. PPR Circle Faience Factory, Wrocław, meeting September 1, 1948, WAP KD II PPR 32/VI/7, kk. 292-4.

55. 4th Party Circle, meeting, October 15, 1948, WAP III KD PPR 33/VI/6, kk. 56-7.

56. Ibid, k. 57.

57. This account is based on the following sources: Ptasiński and Miechno (Central Committee inspectors), report on the incidents in the Garment Factory, AAN KC PPR 295/IX/51, kk. 365-70; report filed for KW PPR Wrocław, AAN KC PPR 295/IX/370, kk. 43-5; Labor Department, KW PPR Wrocław, WAP KW PPR 1/XII/2, kk. 85-6.

58. This plenum saw the ascendance of the Moscow faction of the PPR. Gomułka was forced to engage in self-criticism, the first step toward his removal from power, Kersten, *Narodziny systemu władzy*, 346-9.

59. Ptasiński and Miechno report, kk. 367-8.

9

Peasants and Partisans: A Dubious Alliance[1]

Melissa Bokovoy

In the historiography of the creation and consolidation of Communist Yugoslavia, scholars have focused primarily on the subject of the party-state, its elites, its structures and institutions, its ideologies, its state-building processes and strategies, and the place of the Communist Yugoslav state in international politics.[2] In the immediate postwar period, the Yugoslav Communist Party (CPY) adopted and then adapted a state and party model bequeathed to them by the Soviet Union: a highly centralized, unitary party-state, adhering to democratic centralism, that ensured no significant devolution of power from its center; a five-year economic plan which allocated resources to heavy industry; and educational and cultural policies which celebrated the victory of the Yugoslav Partisan army over reactionary, fascist forces, and then extolled the virtues of the Soviet Union, Stalin, the Communist partisans, and Tito.

These state structures and the elites which constructed them are portrayed in the literature as monolithic, immutable, impermeable, and impervious to societal forces. It appears as if the Communist elites had little connection to or were influenced very little by the society over which they ruled. External forces such as Stalin, the Red Army, the United Nations Relief and Rehabilitation Agency, the Communist Information Bureau, and the events of the Cold War, influenced and affected policy debates and decisions of the CPY.

Yet inside their state, the Yugoslav Communists appeared untouched by any social forces. Workers, peasants, women, young people, and national elites were considered in terms of the state-building activities of the CPY. Policies, programs, plans, laws, ideological disputes between domestic and international Communist elites, and institutions become the benchmarks of Yugoslav history. What is lost in this history are the people and groups that were affected by the state-building activities of the CPY, their responses and resistance to the implementation of policy, and how their responses and resistance influenced the party-state's elites and the politics of state building. What needs to be illuminated is the reciprocal nature of the relationship between the Yugoslav Communists, their party-state, and society in all its diversity. Given the CPY's own interpretation of its rise to and consolidation of power, it is only logical to examine the CPY's relationship with what it considered its most ardent supporter within the National Liberation Struggle (NOB), the peasantry.[3]

This chapter explores the CPY's discussions and actions surrounding land reform, colonization, mandatory collections of agricultural goods, state agricultural agencies, state farms, collective farms, and cooperatives. After four years of war, the CPY wanted to explore ways that would bind the private, individual landholder to the state without resorting to coercion and violence. The CPY leadership did not make these decisions easily or in a vacuum. The country had been devastated by war, and pockets of opposition existed. They had to contend with these realities. In addition, agrarian experts, economic advisors, and local cadres all expressed opinions concerning the proper or improper path the CPY was taking. Sometimes their voices were uncomplimentary and critical or disagreed with the leadership's position.

During the first years of the new Yugoslav state, the peasantry also made its opinions known, often indicating through their actions that it wished to remain outside the CPY's reach. How the peasantry acted, reacted, and resisted the CPY's colonization plans, agrarian reforms, and mandatory collections also played a substantial role in the implementation and modification of agrarian policy, especially in the CPY's deliberations on how to socialize the countryside. The Yugoslav peasantry remained a powerful political force; they would not submit docilely to the maneuverings of the Communists if their interests were threatened.[4]

The Creation Myth: Peasants and Partisans

Any regime seeks sources of legitimacy and the Yugoslav Communists were no exception. By the end of the war, the CPY had perhaps the most important source of legitimacy: "a total and all-pervasive political monopoly."[5] In addition, they had the international recognition and legal continuity with the former Yugoslav state. However, these factors would hardly win the hearts and minds of the

Yugoslav people. Power, in the eyes of the Yugoslav Communists, should not rest on coercion, or brute force. They sought legitimacy in an explanatory creation myth: the new Yugoslav state had been created as a result of "two kinds of solidarity, that of the Yugoslav nations who had united to fight the enemy, and that of the Partisan veterans, the *stari borci,* who had done the actual fighting."[6] This creation myth was unique among the other East Europe states, and Tito, Djilas, and the other leaders promoted this uniqueness. They had come to power on the strength of the Partisan Army, the majority of whom were peasants, and the CPY was not about to disavow a revolution and victory which had been "achieved alone and against all odds."[7] There was one problem, the Partisans were primarily peasants and not workers. Room had to be found in the revolutionary ideology for this one unmistakable fact.

Early in 1945, Tito claimed the peasants as an indivisible part of the NOB and the new state:

> In this state, the worker with the peasant must be one monolithic rock which will guard the course of the revolution and we must give all of ourselves in order to repair that which is destroyed. The indestructible union of peasants and workers is the condition for guarding [the gains] of the NOB.[8]

Milovan Djilas, in a Moscow meeting with D. Z. Manuilsky in spring 1945, defended the role of the Yugoslav peasant in the NOB. Djilas stated:

> I made a special point of stressing the new revolutionary role of the peasantry; I practically reduced the uprising in Yugoslavia to a tie between a peasant rebellion and the Communist avant-garde.[9]

Moša Pijade praised the peasants for their great sacrifices in the National Liberation Struggle. In return for its support, Pijade asserted that "the new state's greatest obligation must be toward the middle and the poor peasants."[10]

In its portrayal of the peasantry during the NOB, the CPY leadership, represented by Tito, Djilas, and Pijade, did not appear as dogmatic Stalinists in their attitudes. The CPY did not have to wage a class struggle in the countryside or wage a war against the peasants to forge a socialist state. For them, the poor and middle peasants, through the partisan experience, had achieved consciousness, and were now ready to participate in the CPY's state-building enterprise. In a debate over the agrarian reform in August 1945, Pijade explained the peasants' journey to consciousness:

Our people through four years of fighting realized that only by
communal work and only by united effort could we achieve success.
They will follow behind our interests; they will cherish those habits
which they acquired during the fighting; and they will associate and
communally farm the land as was the case during the war. Just as it
worked during the fighting, so it will be now, without any goading
from the authorities. Through the efforts of the colonists and the
agrarian interests as well as through the efforts of the poor and
middle peasants, cooperatives will appear with the aim of
communal farming of the land.[11]

How easy the transformation of the countryside would be with this
mythical, loyal Yugoslav peasantry, undifferentiated, unwavering,
following the interests of the Communists, and willingly surrendering
their local and parochial interests to those of the new state? The CPY
really wanted to believe that this was true, and to a great extent they
did believe it. They also knew that in order to keep the poor and
middle peasants with them, they would have to honor their promises.
This meant enacting an agrarian reform which would give land to the
peasants. But, the Communists also had to honor the ideology which
had brought them this far, and this meant socializing the countryside.

The Theory: Agrarian Reform and Colonization

Moša Pijade became the CPY's point man for articulating how the
"Law on Agrarian Reform and Colonization" would address the peasants' role in the new state and the transformation of the countryside.
According to Pijade and the CPY leadership, this law would accomplish
three goals: 1) give land to the poor and middle peasants; 2) lay the
foundation for socialist forms of agriculture; and 3) continue the process
of changing the class and national consciousness of the peasants. Pijade
laid out these goals in the debates surrounding the adoption of the law
in August 1945.[12]

In the eyes of the CPY leadership, the agrarian reform had to pay
tribute to the peasants as well as bind the poor and middle peasantry
firmly to the new state. Pijade stated: "the new state, among its basic
tasks, must create an agrarian reform and colonization, that is, the
question of land for peasants who do not have land or who do not have
enough."[13] Pijade proposed using the land fund created by the
expropriations from collaborators, foreigners, war criminals, and
persons of German nationality as the basis of any reform. In theory, this
land was to be divided among those who needed land.[14] However,
land from this fund would not fall exclusively to the small and middle
peasants. The land fund was also to serve as a basis for the creation of
socialist holdings.

In Pijade's view, the loss of many eligible workers through death and injury justified and encouraged the creation of such enterprises. Families who had lost workers and suffered great damage to their working stock during the war could join these collectives.[15] Such communal institutions would provide an example of the advantages of large communal holdings to a skeptical peasantry, as well as helping to mold the peasants themselves into ideal agricultural workers. Thus, the CPY's program would not only reward the Yugoslav peasant but also lay the foundations for future socialist holdings and for institutions such as state farms, machine tractor stations, breeding, seed, and seedling stations, and cooperatives. The ideas expressed in Pijade's program were put into practice on August 23, 1945 when the provisional parliament (Skupština) passed the "Law on Agrarian Reform and Colonization".

This piece of legislation was the crux of the Yugoslav Communists' agrarian policy. Its basic tenet was "the land belongs to those who till it."[16] This meant that the agricultural land which had been confiscated and placed into the state's care was not to be nationalized, rather it was distributed to peasants who did not have any land or had less than 1.2 hectares.[17] The law ordered the complete expropriation without compensation, of land held by banks, enterprises, churches, monasteries, and other religious institutions.[18]

How to distribute the holdings of the land fund became more a matter of politics than economics. Theoretically, the reform was to benefit the poorest of peasants, those possessing no land or land less than 1.5 hectares. In practice, only fifty-one percent of the land distributed went to individual peasants. The total amount of land distributed to individual peasants was a little more than half of the land available in the land fund. The Ministry of Agrarian Reform and Colonization distributed only 797,000 hectares out of 1,500,000 to over 316,415 peasants and their families. This meant a little over 2.5 hectares per family. Of the 316,415 peasants, 136,454 were either landless or colonists. On Pijade's recommendation, the Skupština also used the reform to lay the foundations for large socialist holdings and the fund also supplied land for institutions such as state farms, machine tractor stations, breeding, seed, and seedling stations, and cooperatives.[19] In addition, the majority of the land abandoned after the war was in Vojvodina.[20] It was the intention of the Communists to distribute this land, some of the richest in Yugoslavia, to war veterans, to poor peasants from the soil poor and impoverished regions of Macedonia, Bosnia, Hercegovina, and Montenegro, and to "colonists."[21]

"The Law on Agrarian Reform and Colonization" altered the structure of land ownership. The majority of agricultural land was now in private hands, in parcels no more than 25-35 hectares of arable land, not in large state agricultural holdings. The land reform had given the peasantry the land, but it had not solved one of the most severe problems of pre-war Yugoslavia, the prevalence of small agricultural holdings. Vaso Čubrilović, the Minister of Agriculture and member of the left wing of the Union of Agrarian Workers, worried about the efficiency of small holdings and expressed concern about finding a solution to this problem:

> When the land reform is achieved, Yugoslavia will become a land of small and middle peasants. These small and middle farms will not have the possibility to procure or produce the necessary machines, quality seed and stock which are vital [for agricultural production]. Therefore, they must obtain all from the state.[22]

By obtaining all from the state, Čubrilović meant that the state should provide the means to improve the peasants' technical and material base.[23] In this sense, Čubrilović remained true to the Agrarian Union's idea that the state should concentrate on developing a strong network of credit, technical, and producer organizations for the peasantry. To the Communists, obtaining all from the state meant bringing about the socialist transformation of agriculture by encouraging, and sometimes intimidating, the peasants to link their production and marketing to the state. In time, they hoped this linkage would bring the peasantry's economic life, as well as its political life under the CPY's control. Such links had begun during the war, and the CPY lost no time in establishing them in peacetime.

Socializing the Countryside

The Yugoslav Communists' most pressing concern beginning in 1945 was how to supply the urban population, the army, and its veterans, and those peasants who lived in regions incapable of growing enough food for their survival, with basic foodstuffs and necessities. This meant consolidating scarce capital goods and services, as well as requisitioning basic agricultural products. Early in spring 1945, the CPY began to initiate practices and legislation which would bring scarce agricultural resources under their management and control. In addition, the CPY and their agrarian experts began to debate the merits and possible consequences of the Yugoslav version of the Soviet collective farm, the peasant work cooperative.

In the 1945 spring planting campaign, the Party placed great emphasis upon the consolidation of labor, machinery, and draught animals. The provisional government created local and regional sowing boards to oversee the planting and to "undertake a series of measures for the preparation and directing of spring planting."[24] In order to rationalize the available resources, those who still had tools, machinery, stock, and draught animals had to register them and lend them to the regional boards.[25] The government codified this practice several months later. In July, the Skupština issued the "Law on the Organization of Agricultural Machine Stations"[26] which introduced the creation of agricultural machine stations.[27] The agricultural machine stations would give the CPY firm control over the scarce commodities necessary for production and over the peasants who depended on these goods. Throughout 1945, the Skupština issued numerous laws and decrees which created communal agricultural organizations and regulated the agricultural sector.[28]

Concomitant with these measures, the CPY initiated a system of compulsory deliveries or collections (*otkup*) of certain agricultural products to be transported to state agencies. Borrowing from the Soviets, the Yugoslav Communists demanded that each region and locality deliver a fixed amount of certain agricultural goods to regional warehouses. These obligatory collections challenged the peasants' right to dispose of his/her goods at market prices. In August 1945, Andrija Hebrang, while still the chairman of the Economic Council, justified the introduction of this system with a comment on the current situation. He focused primarily upon the consequences of the 1945 drought and the war on grain yields. He stated:

> Without a doubt, the most important problem facing us is at the present time. While we succeeded in planting 90% of the available land, a drought occurred and this will cut the return of the grain harvest in half. The drought partially or entirely wiped out the crops in Macedonia, Montenegro, Bosnia and Hercegovina, and Slovenia. We, therefore, must depend upon last year's reserves and the harvest from Serbia and Vojvodina.[29]

In order to tap into the harvest yields, Hebrang recommended a plan for the collection of corn, wheat, and grain. The state, acting through the state agricultural agency, Poljopromet, would direct the collection of grain, set the price of grain, and the quotas for each region, a policy loathsome to the peasantry because of the way in which quotas and prices were set by inefficient, ignorant, and sometimes corrupt officials.[30] In a September 2, 1945 *Borba* article, Hebrang noted the already existing hostility to the collection policy. Calling those who refused to recognize the validity of the law enemies of the people and speculators, he admonished them for withholding their grain until higher prices were set and for not wishing to give up their surplus to those in the drought- stricken and war-torn regions.[31]

Borba, as well as local Communist officials, closely followed the activities and mood of the peasantry as it was confronted with the new laws regulating the production, procurement, and distribution of agricultural goods and services. As early as June 1945, there had already been complaints from various committees that the peasants were not bringing their produce to market because of depressed and inadequate prices for agricultural goods. The regional committee of the Communist Party of Croatia (CPC) for Dalmatia complained to the Central Committee of the Communist party of Croatia:

> Our greatest weakness was exposed when the order for the gradual maximizing of agricultural goods was passed. The Party organizations as well as the Yugoslav National Front did almost nothing to explain to the people and to the peasants the aims of our government. [They need to explain] that by passing this order, the peasants are helping the entire nation by being both consumers and producers. Because of their confusion about the current inadequacies of the pricing policy, the peasants have stopped carrying their produce to market, except those products which are not for consumption.[32]

In order to combat the peasants' noncompliance, the government used pricing to discriminate against the individual, independent peasants who sold their surplus in the marketplace, and favored those peasants who sold their produce to state agencies.[33] The government did this either by setting higher prices at the state procurement centers, or heavily taxing the peasant who sold on the free market. Despite these economic ploys and pressures, the peasants continued to circumvent the state agencies. An example of this obvious disregard for a directive, *Borba* reported a case in Novi Sad where local authorities rationed bread, but the peasants found a way to sell grain. "Enabling," as the local officials complained, "private sellers to sell bread everywhere."[34]

The reaction and resistance of the peasantry to the encroachment of the state on its ability to market agricultural surplus and control its own production precipitated the Skupština decision to define the peasants' activity as criminal. This is illustrated by the passage of a law on speculation, black marketing, and sabotage.[35] While covering all aspects of economic life, this law singled out peasants' activity in the realm of damaging, destroying, and slaughtering animate and inanimate inventory as well as stating that any willful action against decrees or written instructions from the federal government would be punished. The state intended to punish offenders with a fine, forced labor from one month to ten years, confiscation of property and livestock, or the death penalty. In spite of such harsh sentences, the peasantry continued to fight against the state's interference in its agricultural production, marketing, and consumption.

The CPY knew that it would not effect a fundamental change in peasant attitudes and practices through the appropriation of agricultural surpluses and regulation of scarce resources. These were measures designed to deal with the country's immediate supply problems. In order to transform the countryside, the Yugoslav Communists needed to establish forms of communal work and organization, and to discourage the emergence of a self interested, independent peasantry. They looked to the state farms and peasant work cooperatives as the institutions which would transform the countryside. However, the CPY and its advisors did not always agree on their function, form, or pace of development.

In several articles in *Borba*, the Yugoslav Communists focused on the formal organization of both land and peasant into more cohesive units. *Borba* lauded both the Soviet collective farm (kolkhoz) and the Soviet state agricultural farm (sovkhoz). Although, both types of farms attracted the attention of the CPY in 1945, it was the state farm on which the Party would concentrate. In an article reprinted in *Borba* in January 1945, the President of the Central Committee of the Syndicated Workers of the Soviet State Farms, Alexander Petruchin, described the advantages and superiority of the state farms and how they acted as "hotbeds of technical and cultural innovations which will demonstrate to the peasants the advantage of larger forms of organization."[36]

Moša Pijade, in March 1945, expressed his deep seated belief in the necessity of establishing farms under state direction. He saw the creation of state directed farms as a continuation of wartime polices as well as a viable economic unit for those who had suffered during the war. He emphasized the need for the state to set aside land specifically for promoting technical advances and communal work in the agrarian sector.[37] These "state directed" farms with staff sympathetic to the Communists and their ideals would be the perfect institution for the promotion of modern agricultural techniques and machinery. He insisted, "Today, we can help them through united efforts and ensure security and a future to those who suffered, and this will be possible simply through association in production cooperatives and mechanical farming."[38] Four months later, under Pijade's direction as the chairman of the Legislative Committee for the Democratic Federation of Yugoslavia, the committee pushed through the Law on State Agriculture Farms.[39] However, the function and purpose of these state farms were disputed.

Čubrilović argued that the primary responsibility of the state farm was to develop systematic, scientific methods for farming, and develop new types of seeds, breeding stock, and seedlings which could then be passed onto the poor and middle peasantry. He asserted, "The reason that the state needs to have such large holdings is so that they can produce materials [seed, fodder, seedlings, breeding stock, etc.] necessary for agriculture."[40] Čubrilović concluded, "We will not be able to advance agriculture quickly without a systematic means of work, if the state does not intervene through these holdings."[41]

Pijade saw the state farm as the model for socialist agriculture, using the most faithful of the partisans as participants. He believed that these farms would be ideal for the returning war veterans, their families, or displaced persons. He proposed that 200,000 hectares (500,000 acres) of land be separated from the land fund for the colonization of the war veterans into state farms."[42] He judged the war veterans as being more sympathetic toward communal work and Communist ideology than the poor and middle peasants who would gain land from the agrarian reform. Pijade advocated not only placing veterans in farms established and directed by the state; he wanted the veterans themselves to form cooperatives on their own initiative.[43] The veterans of the NOB were to be the party's vanguard in this process.

In 1945, the Yugoslav Communists also took the first step toward the adoption of collective forms of agriculture, but were skeptical about the possibilities for their immediate establishment and success. Vlajko Begović[44] examined the attributes of collective agriculture in a *Borba* article, "Concerning Collective Farms" ("O kolkhezima"). The Yugoslav version would be named the peasant work cooperative, and Begović considered them "nothing other than a well organized peasant production cooperative."[45] He saw the peasant work cooperative as "the way to the transition from individual peasant ownership to collective, societal ownership in agriculture. The peasant will learn communal work and organization in the cooperative. At first, a small number will be founded in order to serve as an example."[46]

Indeed, only a small number of collectives were established in the first year of the CPY's rule. At the end of 1945, only thirty-one work cooperatives had been formed; all were in Vojvodina and all members were either veterans, Communists, or their relatives.[47] Pijade was dismayed that only the colonists and the veterans chose to be members of the work cooperative. Absent from its rosters were the much more needy poor and middle peasants.[48] He recognized that the current trend was not toward "a mass movement for the creation of working cooperatives in the villages, and that to conclude otherwise would be more harmful than useful."[49] For the CPY, at this point, the road to the socialist transformation of agriculture was through a different institution, the cooperative.

The CPY decided that in order to pursue the establishment of the peasant work cooperatives, it would have to do it gradually and through a transitional institution, the agricultural cooperative (*zemljoradnicka zadruga*). The organizational framework of the cooperative and its strong link to the peasantry attracted Edward Kardelj, the CPY's leading theoretician. Kardelj targeted the cooperative's importance, not only in agriculture but in all economic activity. He stated:

> First of all, the cooperative's task consists of mobilizing the masses in order that the masses can overcome their great economic difficulties. And that the cooperative will unavoidably become and has already become the stimulus for social advancement in our

country, and that it becomes a strong defender of the basic
proletarian masses against exploitative tendencies.[50]

Kardelj saw that the cooperative could be useful, but he had not yet
figured out a way to blend Communist principles, pre-war conceptions,
and Lenin's views on cooperation into a clear definition of the
agricultural cooperative and its function in the transformation of the
countryside.

Taking into account the frail alliance between Party and peasant,
the CPY, in 1945, focused on developing this cooperative with the intent
of creating an institution which would strengthen the link between
peasant and state and convince the peasant of the advantages of
communal work and cooperation. Combined with the CPY's other plans
and policies in the countryside, the CPY intended to tie the private,
individual landholder to the state, and then through transitional
institutions socialize the countryside. In order for this gradual approach
to work, the poor and middle peasants had to reach a new level of
consciousness. Theory and the practice, as seen in the reform and
colonization of the Vojvodina, remained far apart.

The Practice: Colonization of Vojvodina

In Vojvodina, the Ministry of Agrarian Reform and Colonization
reserved 300,000 hectares for colonization and distribution to the
peasants.[51] In addition, the majority of land reserved for state
agricultural farms was also here. These facts make Vojvodina the perfect
place to observe how the CPY pursued its goals set out by their
discussions surrounding agrarian reform and colonization: giving land
to those who till it; transforming the countryside through various
socialist institutions and practices; and effecting a change in peasant
attitudes and consciousness. In addition, Vojvodina is also the perfect
place to see how the peasantry responded to the CPY's policies.

The CPY hoped that by giving land to the peasants, especially war
veterans, displaced people, and colonists, Vojvodina, its new settlers,
and its individual, state, and collective farms would serve as the first
examples of socialized agriculture. In addition, the peasants, as
members of the state farms, would learn the advantages of large-scale
mechanized farming, and spread the word to others. Pijade had said as
much when the CPY was first theorizing about the state farms. The
leadership obviously had thought this was a good idea; instead of
setting aside the requested 200,000 hectares (500,000 acres), 288,000
hectares were allotted for the state farms.[52]

Vojvodina was also the ideal place to effect a change in the peasants'
national consciousness or at least give a particular national group a new
address. The CPY planned to move Serbs from areas within Croatia,
Macedonia, and Bosnia-Hercegovina, reducing their numbers in these

territories and increasing their numbers in Vojvodina. The CPY hoped to reduce ethnic tensions in these areas by moving Serbs. Between 1940 and 1948, the number of Serbs in Vojvodina increased from 593,735 to 841,246.[53] In addition, the proposed movement of other groups would widen the ethnic mosaic already in existence in Vojvodina, primarily with the hope of cultivating a Yugoslav identity.[54]

The selection and the moving of colonists into Vojvodina became an immediate problem for the CPY because the Ministry of Colonization was inundated with requests, often from peasants who were not first priority. The law had intended that those peasants who had fought in the NOB were to be rewarded first.[55] However, in the early months of the colonization drive, requests for colonization far outpaced the quotas set by the Agrarian Council and the capacity of the Ministry of Agrarian Reform and Colonization to deal efficiently with them. The ministry received 10,749 requests from Bosnia-Hercegovina; 24,000 from Croatia; 15,108 from Serbia proper; 10,000 from Montenegro; 2,000 from Macedonia; and 1,776 from Slovenia.[56] The Agrarian Council also noted that the majority of requests from Bosnia-Hercegovina and Croatia came from Serbian peasants. "There are very few Muslims or Croats. They neither pick up requests or send them."[57] This trend also characterized the requests from Croatia and Macedonia. In the case of Croatia, Serbs from Dalmatia, Gorski Kotar, Lika, and Kordun submitted requests. These were regions where the Serbs had suffered considerably under the policies of the Ustaša. In the case of Macedonia, the vast majority of requests were from Serbs, who had moved into the region during the interwar period and who had been displaced by the new law on "Revision of Land Allotments to Colonists and Agrarian Interests in Macedonia and Kosovo-Methohija." By the end of the colonization drive in 1948, Serbs made up seventy-two percent of the new settlers. Montenegrins were the second largest group of settlers with eighteen percent.[58]

As the colonists moved into Vojvodina, Pijade and the CPY hoped that they would be infused with enthusiasm and the pioneer spirit which would make Vojvodina into the hothouse for socialist agriculture.[59] However, problems arose during the process of colonization which quickly convinced the new settlers that Vojvodina was not the land of milk and honey. Transportation, supply, and housing problems immediately sprang up as the CPY attempted to transport, feed, clothe, and shelter 150,000 people in the winter and spring 1946.[60] The pioneer spirit, after four years of war, had largely been spent by most of the colonists and they were not prepared for the disorder, difficulties, and discomforts they encountered.

Delegates representing the various republics met in mid-December 1945 to discuss the progress of the agrarian reform and colonization.[61] The delegates enumerated the problems facing their republic or region during the implementation of colonization. Each republican representative complained of the difficulties of transporting the colonists from their village of origin to their village of destination in the dead of winter. A delegate from Bosnia described how a courageous batch of peasant families from Hercegovina braved the snow and disregarded the weather conditions to board the train for Vojvodina. Upon arriving in Vojvodina, the authorities treated them with little regard and dispatched them to a village where they did not have a roof over their heads and no supplies.[62] The Macedonian representative complained about the inadequate transportation from the village of origin to the train station. "The transportation difficulties have been great and up to this point we have not been sent a single transport. The villages are far from the train station. There have not been enough trucks for transport. It has been necessary to use horse drawn carts."[63] The Macedonian delegate confirmed the Bosnian's report about the severity of the weather and claimed that Macedonia was not transporting young children because of the cold, winter weather. The Commission for Settling Veterans in Vojvodina, in a report dated October 18, had drawn attention to poor transportation for the colonists when it noted that the arriving colonists, exhausted from three days to two weeks of travel, were disappointed in their new homes and lands.[64] Two months later, the Center had done little to solve the problem of transport and left the local and regional agencies to smooth over the frustrations and tensions of the newly arriving settlers.

Dissatisfaction and disgruntlement with the available housing, food supplies, household wares, farm implements, and finally the actual parcels of land peppered reports coming from Vojvodina. The Commission for the Settlement of Veterans complained to the Ministry of Colonization in October that "in each village there are groups around ten who are discontented with their houses".[65] The Commission reported the disgust with which the colonists rejected the houses, usually because the houses offered very little protection from the elements. The complaint of one colonist that, "We did not come here to die [like animals] of exposure" was commonly heard.[66] Some individuals did not even enter into the houses and blackmailed the Commission's representatives by threatening to return to their villages, which would be a logistical nightmare, or by complaining to higher authorities.[67] The Commission stood by helplessly as colonists abandoned their assigned houses and looked for decent shelter, sometimes in structures reserved for public use. A report described how the colonists "entered into the houses during the night", and then refused to leave when confronted by the authorities.[68] The Commission remarked how in the village of Secanj, three to four families occupied houses not assigned to them, and how the local authorities found "it very difficult to turn them [the colonists] out of houses which do not belong to them."[69]

The willfulness of the colonists, especially those officers and veterans with partisan honors who adamantly refused to move into inadequate housing, presented the Commission with a real dilemma. They had prescriptions from the central ministry but no way to fill them. Faced with a large body of militant and intractable colonists, the Commission seemed ill at ease with the task before them. In its strongly worded conclusion to the October 1945 report to the Ministry of Colonization, the Commission for the Resettlement of Veterans argued that it did not have a strong enough authoritative position and this held true for the local boards which oversaw the settlement process.[70] These local boards felt that the colonization had been undertaken rather hastily with little regard for the deficiencies in the housing stock. One report stated, "Empty and half broken windows are waiting for them without fuel, poor food, no livestock. They are entering houses which have been abandoned for more than a year and have been buffeted by different elements."[71] The Commission declared uncategorically that houses had to be repaired, floors fixed, and new houses built with the help of the ministry.

Next to housing, feeding the colonists became the biggest worry of the Commission.[72] The Commission was dismayed at the story going around that there was enough food in Vojvodina for all; in fact, it reported information to the contrary. By December 1945, all that remained for the newcomers was some wheat and corn.[73] Lard was not plentiful, and salt, spices, and oil were not available at all. In addition, the Main Board for Supply had no idea how to divide and transport the food. Once the food actually arrived, the colonists had little means to prepare it. The grandiose idea of feeding the colonists from communal kitchens was thwarted because of the lack of facilities, damaged stoves without burners, and little fuel. Exasperation and frustration showed in the Commission's request for such simple and basic items as forks, spoons, dishes, pots, stoves, fuel for heating and cooking, and clothing.[74] Those supplies which actually were in the warehouses, not having been stolen or plundered, often were not enough for the colonists' demands.

Local cadres struck out at the colonists and their attitudes. One delegate remarked about some colonists from Bosnia, "People think that colonization is an opportunity to rest, to winter. Some think that this is their reward for having survived the difficulties of the war."[75] Delegates discussed the mood and attitude of some colonists from Hercegovina. The report argued that these colonists did not come to Vojvodina to work. It stated, "They will not load wheat onto the trains in order for it to be milled. They look for camp inmates to work for them. They simply look to be supplied with food, and will not pay for it."[76] The delegates chastised both the Party and the colonists for being such polyannas and suggested ways to prepare the colonists for settlement into the Vojvodina. They complained:

The colonists need to be prepared politically by the boards [reviewing applications for colonization], by anti-fascist organizations preparing the people for colonization. It must be clearly shown all those factors which have been introduced today. It must be said to them that the land has been ravished and that Vojvodina is not a land flowing with milk and honey. Vojvodina also has great problems.[77]

More exasperating to officials in Vojvodina were the accusations leveled at them for failing to meet the collection quotas amidst this chaos. *Borba* blamed the local people's committees for failure to propagandize the virtuous aims and goals of the collection.[78] The CPY was particularly disturbed by the shortfalls in Vojvodina, supposedly the laboratory for cooperative and collectivist attitudes toward socialist forms of production and distribution. *Borba* reported:

Even individual people's boards disrupted the carrying out of the collections . . . of the ones mentioned, they responded to local riots. For example, in the Vojvodina, they [local boards] maintained that they did not deliver to Poljopromet because they held on [to the grain] for local consumption. These harmful directives were given by the people's board in Bačka Palanika, and by individual committee members in Pančevo, Novi Bećej, and some other areas.[79]

This article also chastised those boards which refused to clamp down on smuggling by the peasants and their selling of grain on the black-market. Another report out of Vojvodina discussed the case of one peasant, Slavko Rakić, who was sentenced to five years of forced labor for stealing, pilfering from the common forest, and speculating.[80]

The colonization of Vojvodina, and the problems encountered by colonists and local and republican cadres alike, illustrate the limits of theories, hopes, and dreams. The CPY in its presentation and discussion of the "Law on Agrarian Reform and Colonization" expected to reward those peasants who had fought for the Partisans and to relieve pressure from those areas which still had potential conflicts due to policies undertaken by the interwar government or the occupiers.[81] The CPY leadership also believed that land redistribution would bring into its sphere those peasants who had their loyalties elsewhere. Moving through the process, the peasants would see the good intentions of the Communists to create cooperative forms of agriculture and wish to participate in the socialist experiment.[82]

The peasants on the other hand expected their resettlement to bring them independence, affluence, and a better life. Peasants moving in from all republics of Yugoslavia had certain expectations concerning the type of land they would receive and what other "perks" would come with the settlement. They wished to be left alone and to settle in Vojvodina on their own terms with the land and capital promised to them by the Communists. In between these two positions were the local cadres who expected the government and the party to support them materially, administratively, and psychologically in their tasks. Each group was soundly disappointed.

What each group expected is not what eventually occurred in Vojvodina. The peasantry of Communist Yugoslavia was already hearing and processing the rumors about colonization and land distribution. Promises made by the CPY were already being broken and the party-state was beginning to throw up restrictions about where and how the peasants could live. In response, the colonists began to ignore posted notices and local cadres' warnings about which structures and homes they could live in. Squatting became one way to resist the state's intentions. When the colonists could not settle on a piece of land reserved for state purposes, they threatened to return to their villages or to protest to higher authorities. Threats and slogans directed, not at the state, but at the local cadres voiced the peasants' anger at the actions of the state, which the peasant expected to benefit and aid them in the resettlement process.

Caught in between were the local cadres who were being squeezed from above and below. When they acted in the state's interest, they were the focus of most of the peasantry's discontent. As the "point persons" in the villages, the local representatives of the party and government sought to inform the CPY leadership of the peasant's displeasure and disappointment and of their own frustrations in attempting to implement policies.[83] In reporting this information, the local cadres had to take into account the peasants' demands, essentially creating a political discourse between the peasants and the Party.

The local cadres diligently noted the "glitches" in the settlement process. They hoped by sending the information back to the center that they would receive more help from the state, or at least receive orders relaxing previous directives. The local cadres had a vested interest in making sure both the colonists and the party were satisfied. The center would hold the local authorities responsible for any failures, and the peasants would target the cadres if their expectations were not met. This position in between peasant and Party made the local cadres, at times, a sympathetic ally of the peasants, and at other times, the hard-nosed representatives of the state. As a result, the leadership of the CPY could not always count on the local officials to do their bidding.

Throughout 1945 and into 1946, the CPY observed how the colonists and recipients of the redistributed land, many of them veterans of the NOB, fared with the colonization process and the land reform. What they saw was that the colonists, as well as other beneficiaries of the reform, were not about to join voluntarily or associate freely with organizations and groups which would limit their choice of home, neighbor, and work. This experience demonstrated to the CPY how far they still had to go in order to understand peasant psyche and moods.

As the actions of the peasantry had clearly revealed the problems associated with the implementation of its policies in the village, the CPY, in summer 1946, yielded to the peasant's reluctance and resistance to a procurement regime with the adoption of the "Law concerning a General Amnesty to the Violators of the Orders concerning the Obligatory Collections of Agricultural Produce."[84] This law pardoned those peasants who had not yet completed or had not yet begun their sentences for violating the collection orders. A delegate from Serbia, Mustafa Hodža, stated that this law confirmed the generosity and the care of the national government for the "little guy, for those poor workers and peasants who willfully and consciously, or perhaps unconsciously, committed a mistake concerning their legal responsibilities."[85] Another delegate, Miloš Carević, argued that "this amnesty was a necessary and appropriate measure because it showed that the Federal Government took care of its people and had deep connections with the national masses."[86] With the passage of this federal law, the government demonstrated its dependency on the good will of the peasantry to carry out policies and reforms in the countryside.

Faced with resistance, the Yugoslav Communists vacillated between their debt to the peasantry, and their conviction that socialist transformation of the rural world was necessary. The leadership had shared the horrors and violence of wartime with the peasantry and it hesitated to adopt coercive and violent measures to transform the countryside. Though generally convinced that the best form of agriculture was collective, centralized, and mechanized, the leadership did not always agree on how to accomplish this transformation. The CPY never doubted that its policies in the countryside were the correct ones. However, in the face of strong opposition from both cadres and the peasants, the CPY acknowledged societal resistance and discontent. The CPY's recognition of the peasants' resistance, however big or small, expanded the margins of permissible behavior and possible action, and forced the reconfiguration of ideology, state structures, and policies. This process began when the Yugoslav Communists entered the countryside in 1941, and they found it difficult to reign in when they came to power. The peasants, through everyday acts of resistance, chipped away at the CPY's power and legitimacy, and posed the first serious challenge to the new Yugoslav state.

Notes

1. This chapter has had the benefit of several drafts. The first draft was presented at the conference "The Establishment of Communist Regimes in Eastern Europe, 1945-1950:A Reassessment," Moscow, Russia. March 1994. The second

draft was presented at "Partisans to Patriots: State-Society Relations in Yugoslavia, 1945-1992," Albuquerque, NM. May 1994.

2. Works of this nature appeared not only in Western language literature but within Yugoslavia as well. For example of this work see: Steven L. Burg, *Conflict and Cohesion in Socialist Yugoslavia* (Princeton: Princeton University Press, 1983); April Carter, *Democratic Reform in Yugoslavia* (Princeton: Princeton University Press, 1982); Pedro Ramet, *Nationalism and Federalism in Yugoslavia, 1963-1983* (Bloomington, IN: Indiana University Press, 1984); Ivo Banac, *With Stalin against Tito* (Ithaca, NY: Cornell University Press, 1988); and Vojislav Koštunica and Kosta Čavoški, *Stranački pluralizam ili monizam: Društveni pokreti i politički sistem u Jugoslaviji, 1944-1949* (Beograd, 1983). Recent work has focused on the relationship between nation and state. See Jill Irvine, *The Croat Question: Partisan Politics in the Formation of the Yugoslav Socialist State* (Boulder, CO: Westview Press, 1993).

3. Yugoslav scholarship on this subject has focused primarily on the theoretical underpinnings of the CPY's relationship with the peasantry or on the CPY's policies concerning colonization and land reform immediately after the war. See Čedo Grbić, *Seljačko pitanje* (Zagreb: Porodica i domaćinstvo, 1988); Žarko Jovanović *KPJ prema seljaštvu, 1919-1941* (Beograd: Narodna knjiga, 1984); Edvard Kardelj, *O poljoprivredi, selu i zadrugarstvu* (Beograd: Srbija, 1983); Nikola Gačeša, *Agrarna reforma i kolonizicija u Jugoslavija, 1945-1948* (Novi Sad: Matice srpske, 1984); and Jelena Popov, *Narodni front u Jugoslaviji* (Zagreb, 1990). Western literature has focused primarily on agriculture as a sector of the Yugoslav economy. See Joseph Bombelles, *Economic Development of Communist Yugoslavia, 1947-1964* (Stanford: The Hoover Institution on War, Revolution, and Peace, 1968), and Ranko Brashich, *Land Reform and Ownership in Yugoslavia, 1919-1953* (New York: Mid-European Studies Center, 1954). For discussion of the ideological transformation of the CPY's thinking on the agrarian question see A. Ross Johnson, *The Transformation of Communist Ideology: The Yugoslav Case, 1945-1953* (Cambridge: MIT Press, 1972).

4. Much work has been done in recent years examining peasant resistance to state elites and structures. See James Scott, *Weapons of the Weak: Everyday Forms of Peasant Resistance* (New Haven: Yale University Press, 1985); and Forrest D. Colburn, ed, *Everyday Forms of Peasant Resistance* (New York: M.E. Sharpe, Inc., 1989).

5. Dennison Rusinow, *The Yugoslav Experiment, 1948-1974* (Berkeley: University of California Press, 1978), 13.

6. Rusinow, *The Yugoslav Experiment, 1948-1974* , 13.

7. Rusinow, *The Yugoslav Experiment, 1948-1974* , p. 13. Also see Johnson, *The Transformation of Communist Ideology,* 71-73.

8. AJ-Komisija za agrarnu reformu i kolonizaciju, F97/K2/F18, "Osnovi princip agrarne reforme u DFJ [1945]," 1.

9. Milovan Djilas, *Conversations with Stalin* (San Diego, Harcourt Brace Jovanovich, 1962), 30.

10. Moša Pijade, "Pred agrarnom reformom," in *Izabrani spisi*, vol. 1, pt. 3 (Belgrade: Institut za izučavanje radničkog pokreta, 1965), 228.

11. Pijade, "Pred agrarnom reformom," 261-262.

12. Pijade, "Pred agrarnom reformom," 229.

13. Pijade, "Pred agrarnom reformom," 229.

14. Pijade, "Pred agrarnom reformom," 229.

15. Pijade, "Pred agrarnom reformom," 230.

16. AJ-Komisija za kolonizaciju i agrarnu reformu, F97/K2/F18, "Osnovni princip agrarne reforme u DFJ, [1945]."

17. AJ-Komisija za kolonizaciju i agrarnu reformu, F97/K2/F18, "Osnovni princip agrarne reforme u DFJ, [1945]."

18. Savezni zavod za statistiku, *Jugoslavija, 1945-1964: Statisticki pregled* (Belgrade, 1965), 109.

19. AJ-Komisija za kolonizaciju i agrarnu reformu, F97/K2/F18, "Osnovni princip agrarne reforme u DFJ, [1945]."

20. For the definitive word on the colonization of the Vojvodina see, Nikola L. Gačeša, *Agrarna reforma i kolonizacija u Jugoslaviji, 1945-1948* (Novi Sad: Matica Srpska, 1984); *Agrarna reforma i kolonizacija u Bačkoj, 1918-1941* (Novi Sad: Matica Srpska, 1968); *Agrarna reforma i kolonizacija u Banatu, 1919-1941* (Novi Sad: Matica Srpska, 1968); *Agrarna reforma i kolonizacija u Sremu* (Novi Sad: Institut za izučavanje istorije Vojvodine, 1975).

21. The Law of Revision of Land Allotments to Colonists and Agrarian Interests in Macedonia and Kosovo-Metohija confiscated land from Serbs and Montenegrins who, at the invitation of the government of the Kingdom of Serbs, Croats, and Slovenes in 1920, settled the abandoned Turkish holdings.

22. Ministar poljoprivrede dr. Vaso Čubrilović, "Pretres o Zakonu o agrarnom reformi i kolonozaciji, 22 augusta 1945," Rad zakonodavnih odbora Pretsednistva AVNOJ i Privremene narodne Skupštine DFJ (3 aprila-25 octobra 1945). Po stenografskim beleskama i drugim izvora (Belgrade: Prezidium Narodne skupstine FNRJ, n.d), 454.

23. Ministar poljoprivrede DFJ, Vaso Čubrilović, "Pretres zakona o državnim poljoprivredim dobrima, 31 jula 1945," *Rad Zakonodavnih odbora*, 212.

24. "Zadaci setvenih odbora u prolećnoj setvi Srbije," *Borba*, March 15, 1945, 1.

25. "Mobilisimo sve snage za prolećnu sektoru u Vojvodini," *Borba*, April 2, 1945, 2.

26. "Zakon o organizaciji državne poljoprivredne mašinske sluzbe," *Službeni list DFJ*, no. 53 (July 27, 1945), 466-467.

27. "Naredba o organizaciji poljoprivrednih mašinskih stanica," *Službeni list DFJ*, no. 19 (April 6, 1945), 163-164.

28. See "Rešenje o ustanovljenju Komisije za zadrugarstvo," *Službeni list DFJ*, no. 63, (August 24, 1945), 611; "Rešenje o osnivanju Glavne poljoprivredne komisije za Vojvodinu," *Službeni list DFJ*, no. 53 (July 27, 1945), 471-473; "Naredba o obrazovanju odbora za setvu," *Službeni list DFJ*, no. 19 (April 6, 1945), 163; "Uredba o Agrarnom Savetu DFJ," *Službeni list DFJ*, no. 67 September 4, 1945), 657-658; "Rešenje o organizaciji poljoprivredne izveštajne sluzbe," *Službeni list DFJ*, no. 19 (April 6, 1945), 162; "Naredba o obaveznoj prijavi i gradjanskoj mobilizaciji poljoprivrednih stručnjaka," *Službeni list DFJ*, no. 32 (May 15, 1945), 257; "Uredba o plaćanju za ljudski rad i rad sa stokom u poljoprivredi," *Službeni list DFJ*, no. 43 (June 22, 1945), 373.

29. "Izjava pretsednika Privrednog saveta Andrije Hebrang o planu za prehranu stanovništva u postradalim i pasivnim krajevima," *Borba*, September 2, 1945, 2.

30. "Izjava pretsednika Privrednog saveta," 2.

31. "Izjava pretsednika Privrednog saveta," 2.

32. Arhiv Instituta za historiju radničkog pokreta Hrvatske, Zagreb-Centralni komitet, Savez kommunista Hrvatske (Hereafter cited as AIHRPH), box 3, "Politička izveštaj drugskim CK KPH," Oblasni komitet KPH za Dalmaciju," April 11, 1945, 3.

33. Brashich, *Land Reform and Ownership*, 56.

34. "Odluke Privrednog saveta o otkupa žita treba sprovesti brzo i odlaganja," *Borba*, September 6, 1945, 5.

35. "Zakon o suzbijanju nedopušten spekulacije i privredne sabotaže,"*Službeni list DFJ*, no. 28 (April 23, 1945), 213.

36. "Organizicija i rad sindikata radnika sovkheza za vreme rata," *Borba*, January 2, 1945, 3.

37. "Organizicija i rad sindikata radnika sovkheza za vreme rata," *Borba*, January 2, 1945, 3.

38. "Organizicija i rad sindikata radnika sovkheza za vreme rata," *Borba*, January 2, 1945, 3.

39. "Pregled Zakona o državnim poljoprivrednim dobrima," *Zakonodavni rad Pretsedništva AVNOJ i Pretsedništva Privremene narodne skupštine DFJ*. See "Zakon o državnim poljoprivrednim dobrima" *Borba*, August 6, 1945, 7.

40. Ministar poljoprivrede DFJ, Vaso Čubrilović, "Pretres zakona o državnim poljoprivredim dobrima, 31 jula 1945," *Rad Zakonodavnih odbora*, 212.

41. *Rad Zakonodavnih odbora*, 212

42. *Rad Zakonodavnih odbora*, 252.

43. *Rad Zakonodavnih odbora*, 252.

44. Vlajko Begović had been in Moscow working for the Communist Youth International during the 1930s and had been a principal organizer for the Union of Socialist Youth of Yugoslavia (Savez socijalističke omladine Jugoslavije, SSOJ).

45. Seldom would the Soviet term, kolkhoz, be used to describe a farm founded on the basis of communal land and work. Instead, the KPJ chose a deliberately familiar term in the name for its version of a collective--the peasant work cooperative (**seljačka radna zadruga, SRZ**). Zadruga was a term familiar to all the peasantry of Yugoslavia because prior to the nineteenth century, peasants had organized themselves around an extended family commune, the zadruga. Vlajko Begović, "O kolkhezima," *Borba*, March 17, 1945, 3.

46. Vlajko Begović, "O kolkhezima," 3.

47. Branko Horvat, *The Yugoslav Economic System* (New York: M.E. Sharpe, 1976), 111. Also see Branko Horvat, "Jugoslavenska agrarna teorija i politika u poslijeratnom razdoblju," *Pregled*, 7 (July 1975), 778. These accounted for 96,000 hectares of the total arable land in Yugoslavia at the end of 1945. Savezni zavod za statistiku, *Jugoslavija*, 111.

48. Branko Horvat, *The Yugoslav Economic System* , 173.

49. Branko Horvat, *The Yugoslav Economic System* , 173.

50. Edvard Kardelj, "O današnjem glavnom zadatku pozadine," in *Put nove Jugoslavije* (Belgrade: Kultura, 1949), 15.

51. Brashich, *Land Reform and Ownership in Yugoslavia, 1919-1953,* 50.

52. *Rad Zakonodavnih odbora*, 252, and Savezni zavod za statistiku, *Jugoslavija*, 109.

53. Gačeša, *Agrarna reforma i kolonizacija u Jugoslaviji, 1945-1948,* 374.

54. Gačeša, 286. Petrović and Andrei Simić, ed., "Montenegrin Colonists in Vojvodina: Objective and Subjective Measures of Ethnicity," in *Serbian Studies* 5:4 (Fall 1990), 5-21.

55. AJ-Komisija za kolonizaciju i agrarnu reformu, F97/K2/F18, "Osnovi princip agrarne reforme u DFJ, [1945]."

56. AJ-Savet za poljoprivredu i šumarstvo, F97/K2/F18, "Zapisnik ca sastanka delegata, December 15, 1945."

57. "Zapisnik ca sastanka delegata, December 15, 1945." 5.

58. Gačeša, *Agrarna reforma i kolonizacija u Jugoslaviji, 1945-1948,* 347.

59. Pijade, "Pred agrarnom reformom," 228.

60. The problems encountered by the colonists were documented in two reports. See AJ-Savet za poljoprivredu i šumarstvo, F97/K2/F18, "Zapisnik ca sastanka delegata, December 15, 1945," 9; and "Izvestaj, October 18, 1945", Glavna Komisija za naseljavanje boraca u Vojvodini, 3.

61. AJ-Savet za poljoprivredu i šumarstvo, F97/K2/F18, "Zapisnik ca sastanka delegata, December 15, 1945."

62. "Zapisnik ca sastanka delegata, December 15, 1945." 5.

63. "Zapisnik ca sastanka delegata, December 15, 1945." 5.

64. "Izveštaj, October 18, 1945," Glavna Komisija za naseljavanje boraca u Vojvodini, 1.

65. "Izveštaj, October 18, 1945,". 1.

66. "Izveštaj, October 18, 1945," 1. The disgust of this colonist is all the more poignant because of the use of the verb skapati to describe the possibility of death. Skapati is used for animals and is used colloquially for people.

67. "Izveštaj, October 18, 1945," 1.

68. "Izveštaj, October 18, 1945," 1.

69. "Izveštaj, October 18, 1945," 2.

70. "Izveštaj, October 18, 1945," 3.

71. "Izveštaj, October 18, 1945," 3.

72. "Izveštaj, October 18, 1945," 2.

73. AJ-Savet za poljoprivredu i šumarstvo, F97/K2/F18, "Zapisnik ca sastanka delegata, December 15, 1945," 6.

74. "Zapisnik ca sastanka delegata, December 15, 1945," 7.

75. "Zapisnik ca sastanka delegata, December 15, 1945," 7.

76. "Zapisnik ca sastanka delegata, December 15, 1945," 7.

77. "Zapisnik ca sastanka delegata, December 15, 1945," 7.

78. "Odluke Privrednog saveta o otkupa žita treba sprovesti brzo i odlaganja," *Borba*, September 6, 1945, 5.

79. "Iskustva i pouke iz kampanje otkupa žita," *Borba*, January 2, 1946.

80. "Agrarna rasprava u sremskom selu Dobanovicima," *Borba*, January 26, 1946, 3.

81. This is especially true for those Serbs who had moved into Macedonia and Kosovo in 1920. See previous discussion and the "Law of Revision of Land Allotments to Colonists and Agrarian Interests in Macedonia and Kosovo-Metohija."

82. Pijade, "Pretres Predloga o zakonu o agrarnoj reformi i kolonozaciji, August 11, 1945," *Zakondavni rad Pretsedništva AVNOJ*, 261-265.

83. The views of the local and regional cadres are seen in AJ-Savet za poljoprivredu i šumarstvo, F97/K2/F18, "Izveštaj, October 18, 1945," Glavna Komisija za naseljavanje boraca u Vojvodini, and "Zapisnik ca sastanka delegata, December 15, 1945."

84. "Zakon o opštem pomilovanju krivica iz uredaba o otkupu poljoprivrednih proizvoda," *Prvo redovno zasedanje Saveznog veća i Veća naroda: Stenografske beleške 15 maj-20 jula 1946* (Belgrade: Narodna Skupština, n.d), 342-343.

85. "Zakon o opštem pomilovanju," 343.
86. "Zakon o opštem pomilovanju," 344.

10

Communist Higher Education Policies in Czechoslovakia, Poland, and East Germany[1]

John Connelly

Stalinist theory demanded uniformity, yet East European societies produced various Stalinist practices. The origins of diverse practice stretch far back into the political traditions of each society, but World War II and its immediate aftermath had decisive influence in shaping this diversity. The war shattered polities and societies. After the rubble had been cleared, newly constituted societies had to build new foundations upon wartime ruin. The stability of the Stalinist edifice would depend upon the role taken by Communists in establishing these foundations.[2]

Given Stalinism's ambitions, this principle applied to all aspects of societal life throughout the emerging Soviet Bloc. The study of beginnings of diversity is promising ground for the comparative social historian, since the political logic that applied in these societies was nearly identical. If the outcomes of the Stalinist experiment varied, that was because the societies varied. Hardly any area of societal life figured as prominently in the Stalinist ambition to transform society as higher education. This was the tool for creating new elites.

The three most northern countries of the Soviet Bloc pursued very similar agendas in education, but achieved strikingly different outcomes. This became most evident after the fall of Communism. Academia in the former German Democratic Republic (GDR) has been massively purged. In the Czech Republic there have also been purges, but they have been far less severe. Poland has witnessed relatively little purging. These differences are partly reflective of the different governments now in power, but they also mirror the success with which the Stalinist regime was realized in each society. In no place, perhaps in all of Soviet-dominated Europe, was higher education better adapted to the needs of the ruling Party than in East Germany. This fact is exemplified by the singular failure of higher education in East Germany to contribute to the destablization of the regime. No doubt, much of this East German "peculiarity" derives from the Socialist Unity Party of Germany's (SED) peculiar challenges of legitimation; but the following chapter will argue that in higher education at least, events and processes of the 1940's prefigured later, post-Stalinist diversity.

The war had very different meanings for the academic communities in Germany, Poland, and the Czech lands. Only in Germany did universities remain open. Professors and students proved one of the groups in German society most loyal to the goals of the Nazi regime; consistent support of National Socialism robbed German universities of moral capital in the postwar era. During the war, instruction was curtailed and numbers of students sank dramatically. A tiny anti-Nazi student opposition "White Rose" emerged half way through the war, but was easily crushed. Despite damage from aerial bombing, instruction in support of Nazi ideology continued until war's end at German universities, almost up to the final shots of liberation.[3]

In 1939 universities were closed in both Poland and the Protectorate of Bohemia and Moravia. On November 6, the Gestapo summoned the professors of Jagiellonian University to a lecture on the "Policies of the Third Reich and National Socialism toward Questions of Science and Higher Education." Instead of hearing a lecture, the professors were arrested and deported to Sachsenhausen.[4] Polish higher and secondary education were disabled for the duration of the occupation; Nazi – and, in the East, Soviet – authorities brutalized the Polish intelligentsia to the extent that more than one-quarter of all Polish academics failed to survive the war.[5] Polish universities fought back, however, by organizing conspiratorial education. As of 1942, most faculties of the universities of Kraków, Warsaw, Poznań, Wilno, and Lwów were holding classes and giving examinations in private dwellings.[6] That same month, universities in the Czech lands were closed as a result of student-led anti-Nazi demonstrations. On November 19, 1939, 1,185 Czechoslovak students joined the almost 200 Polish professors in Sachsenhausen.[7] The Nazi occupiers made both of these cases of mass arrest very public, and so they left deep impressions upon the Polish and Czech national psyches. Despite – or perhaps because of – a more lenient occupation, there was no attempt in the Czech lands to carry out conspiratorial education. In fact, the occupiers permitted Czech professors to continue their research, and for a time even publish. They were not driven into camps and the underground in the way their

Polish colleagues were.

At the conclusion of war, the small parts of German professoriate that were not tainted by association with the Nazi regime assembled and attempted their own denazification. The Soviet occupiers observed their activities for some time, but unsatisfied with the results, kept universities closed. They then imposed a rigorous denazification. Except for the university in Jena, which reopened in October 1945, the six universities of the Soviet zone and East Berlin would reopen only in January/February 1946, completely purged of Nazi Party members. This meant a reduction of teachers active in the 1944/45 winter semester by over two-thirds. It meant cutting back the number of full professors from 615 to 279.[8] Even professors who had opposed the Nazis thought this was going too far, and that such a radical denazification must make university operation impossible. But they discovered it was possible. Because they suspected universities of harboring fascist sentiments, the Soviet occupation authorities preferred to keep universities running below capacity. Student bodies were thus reduced in size by about two-thirds, meaning that the depleted faculties had fewer students to teach. Only after 1948 would former NSDAP members be readmitted to teaching in significant numbers. By that time student bodies had been transformed by the addition of "workers and peasants." This experience taught the lasting lesson that political considerations *could* have precedence over academic considerations. During National Socialism, universities in what became the Soviet zone had forfeited the right to make independent judgments about academic matters. Henceforth, they could determine neither their own shape nor the shape of the elites they produced. Alone in Eastern Europe, East German universities were forced from 1945 onward to create a new academic elite; continuities in faculty were largely shattered, and the universities' ability to resist Soviet and German Communist incursions weakened severely.[9]

Though decimated, the Polish professoriate actually emerged strengthened from the war. Their leading and well-known role in opposition gave them moral capital; self-assuredly and without waiting for ministerial orders, they reopened universities shortly after the evacuation of Nazi occupiers. The remaining faculty (10 of 24) of the Catholic University in Lublin gathered in late August 1944, and the university reopened on November 12. A skillful Soviet maneuver had saved the city of Kraków from anticipated Nazi vengeance, and the university there could reopen in January 1945. As the only completely intact Polish university, it attracted scholars from the former Polish universities of Wilno and Lwów, as well as the destroyed universities of Poznań and Warsaw. Here, beyond state interference, the Polish academic community reconstituted itself; in the years after liberation Kraków served as a veritable "market" for academic talent, as the academic senates of new and old universities in Warsaw, Toruń, or Wrocław came and sought new colleagues. By integrating assistant professors, Polish university communities could quickly rebuild. Even Warsaw was back to full strength by 1947/48.[10]

In the Czech lands it was students who derived moral capital from wartime suffering and resistance. A "Students National Council" coordinated communications during the brief Prague uprising of May 1945. Student "legions" secured the buildings of Prague's higher schools. Scarcely a week after liberation, the Council's leader, Communist Jan Kazimour, declared that "our Czech universities will open shortly. They are not opening on the basis of any decree, rather Czech students are opening them, by their own strength, with their own weapons."[11] An extraordinary semester began at Charles University in June. In May and June the revolutionary trade union's (ROH) Central Council selected Charles University's rector, prorector, and deans. These choices were confirmed by the Minister of Education (Communist Prof. Zdeněk Nejedlý). The professoriate only gradually emerged from enforced passivity to assert traditional prerogatives. In the fall the university faculties themselves finally voted, endorsing the ROH's choices with one exception.[12] Now university life in the Czech lands, like societal life in general, would return to normal. But the early postwar "revolutionary" days had left precedents of extra-legal student activity and student activism.

After the uncertainties of the early postwar months, universities settled down to operating procedures that were inherited from the pre-war period. These procedures bore striking resemblances, because they were derived from common central European notions about the functions of a university. In important areas of student admissions, faculty promotion, and the drafting of curricula, university faculties retained great if not absolute sovereignty. Representatives of university faculties (the deans: Dekane, Dziekany, děkany) gathered in each case to elect the rector, who represented university interests to the outside. In each case universities served partly as transmitters of liberal education and centers of research, and partly as places of elite reproduction. People of working class or peasant background were heavily underrepresented.[13] Universities in Poland, the Czech lands, and Germany, remained by and large conservative institutions, with at best fringes of leftist opposition. They regarded Communism with hostility and suspicion.

For all these similarities, Polish, Czech, and East German universities existed in very different societies and political cultures. One reflection of these differences were the entirely different systems of governance that obtained in these three national contexts, which with the exception of East Germany, were largely reestablished in 1945. These were the final years of structural diversity for many decades, however; by the early 1950's both the internal and external organization of East Central European universities were nearly identical. It was based upon models imported from the Soviet Union.

East German higher education went through the most complex transition to that Soviet style system. East Germany was the only place with strong traditions of federalism and locally regulated culture and education, yet at the same time it was the only place where from 1945 onward Soviet advisors took strong roles in building the new educational system. From October 1945, local *Land* administrations could release decrees with the force of law, provided they did not contradict Soviet orders.[14] This arrangement might have spawned confusion if not for the fact that the five *Land* education ministries, as well as a nascent German Education Administration (DVV) in Berlin, were from the start entirely in Communist hands. They worked closely with local Soviet agencies. The Soviet administration more or less duplicated the German, so that each zonal capital also had its Soviet culture and education officers.

At first the Soviets took close interest in every move universities made, examining carefully not only proposals for hiring new faculty – which made their way from university rector offices through the *Land* ministries to Soviet agencies – but also each application to admit new students. Gradually Soviet authorities withdrew from day-to-day supervision, leaving ever more competences in the hands of German authorities.[15] But these authorities themselves were undergoing gradual transformation. Administration in the Zone was centralized, as by slow steps an East German government emerged. The process of centralization was driven forward by the increasingly centralized SED. In late 1946, it created two institutions to coordinate educational and cultural policies throughout the Zone: "minister conferences" directed by DVV President Paul Wandel; and "Central SED higher education council" meetings. The former took place monthly, the latter several times a year.

The DVV had been created by Soviet order in 1945, and technically speaking possessed competences only in Berlin, where it carefully supervised the development of the university. As its staff grew, it gradually extended control functions outward into the provinces. It spoke with particular authority, since it helped supervise the implementation of Soviet orders. DVV President Wandel had taught at the Comintern School during Soviet exile.[16] His deputy for higher educational affairs was Prof. Robert Rompe, a Communist and physicist who had been born of German parents in St. Petersburg in 1905.[17] They had intimate contact with the education department of the central offices of the Soviet Military Administration in Karlshorst (SVAG), directed by former rector of Leningrad University, P. V. Zolotukhin.[18] Because of the pervasive presence of SED cadres at all levels of administration, there were no serious disputes over competences between DVV and *Land* ministries. In 1949 the DVV became the Ministry of Education of the GDR, but centralization of educational affairs would be complete only with the 1952 abolishment of *Länder*.[19]

In both the Czech Lands and in Poland educational administration was traditionally centralized. In both places, Communists held the education ministry for only part of the pre-Stalinist period. The Education Minister in Poland from July 1944 to June 1945 was Stanisław Skrzeszewski, a pedagogue with a doctorate in logic from Jagiellonian University. He had joined the Polish Communist Party in 1924. Taking his place in the second provisional government was the teacher and historian Czesław Wycech. Wycech belonged to the left wing of the Polish Peasant Party (PSL) and later held high positions in "People's Poland." Until fall 1946, the Ministry's higher educational department was directed by the Communist Władysław Bieńkowski, and thereafter by fellow traveler Eugenia Krassowska (Democratic Party (SD), who retained that position until 1965. Skrzeszewski reassumed the post of Minister after the January 1947 elections.[19]

Communist musicologist and historian Prof. Zdeněk Nejedlý served as Education Minister in the first postwar Czechoslovak government. After their impressive victory in 1946, Czech Communists exchanged the education for the domestic trade portfolio, however. In June National Socialist deputy and professor of law Jaroslav Stránský was sworn in as Minister of Education. The Communist Party of Czechoslovakia (KSČ) showed little interest in educational matters before the February 1948 seizure of power.[21] Communist higher educational policy was left in the hands of Communist students. Students in the Czech lands had more powers than counterparts to the north; they controlled dispersal of stipend money, and cleansed their own ranks of Nazi collaborators. Using a precedent set in the early postwar days, in February 1948 Communist students staffed "action committees" that purged universities. For a time their domination appeared so complete as to give rise to the term "studentocracy."

Only in Poland did legal changes of the pre-Stalinist period affect the way universities were run. Because these changes were adopted before the onset of strict uniformization, they proved to be a compromise, however. The decree on higher education of October 28, 1947 accorded universities room for maneuver, and therefore acted to hinder change until a new law could be adopted in 1951.[22] In the East German case age-old laws remained on the books until 1949; but far more important than formal law was the factual ability of German Communists to interfere in university affairs by making use of Soviet patronage. As such the new higher educational ordinance of 1949 only confirmed existing practice; even before that point SVAG and the SED assured positive outcomes in nominally sovereign university organs of governance.[23] In the early postwar years Czech universities were governed by ordinances dating back to the nineteenth century. The faculties of Czech universities fully maintained traditional prerogatives until the 1948 student seizure of power.

The transformation of inherited structures of higher educational governance, as well as of universities themselves, depended to a great degree upon the strength of Communist parties in the Czech, Polish, and East German societies. The strength of these Parties was in turn heavily influenced by legacies of the pre-war and war years. Even in East Germany, Soviet advisors could have achieved little without dozens of committed German Communist Party (KPD) cadres who emerged from concentration camps and exile. The KPD may have been decimated by Stalin and Hitler, but it was still large enough to staff pervasively new organs of power. Two factors significantly enhanced its cadre pool in the early postwar years. On the one hand, Communists and Communist sympathizers increasingly left the western zones in order to take up positions in the East.[24] More importantly, in April 1946 the KPD was combined in the Soviet zone with the Social Democratic Party – the earliest such merger in Eastern Europe – and could thenceforth make use of the larger Social Democratic membership, which shared the Communists' visions of higher educational reform.

The presence of Soviet occupation forces gave SED functionaries drive and confidence. The SVAG did not, of course, openly pursue policies of socialization in its zone. It claimed to be establishing an "anti-fascist, democratic order." But the Soviets' particular understanding of "democracy" greatly constricted the range of political options. The "anti-fascist, democratic order" would not be a "parliamentary" democracy. How could it be? Soviet advisors had neither knowledge nor practice of such a system. The Soviets understood "democratic" student elections as those which guaranteed majority representation of the party of the majority of the people, i.e. the SED. Students that voted against the SED were by definition undemocratic. A "democratic" student admissions policy was one that favored worker and peasant children; a "democratic" curriculum was one that included Marxist-Leninist approaches to scholarship. The "antifascist-democratic" order the Soviets helped shape in East Germany would prove a solid foundation for Stalinism.

The Czech Party was even stronger in relative terms, with a large and well-disciplined apparatus and broad popular support. The war had done much to strengthen its position. On the one hand, the Western democracies bore the stigma of Munich. On the other, Communists benefitted from close popular association with the Soviet Army of liberation. The KSČ grew at the quickest pace of any East European Communist party in 1945; that growth continued after Soviet forces departed in November. One place in Czech society notoriously unreceptive to Communist advances was the university, however. Though they could establish strong footholds, Communist students could not win majorities in student councils, even with the help of Social Democrats. Words of leading KSČ functionaries reveal deep resentment at their failure to capture universities with persuasion; exploiting the rift that had grown between workers and intellectuals during the war, they unleashed an unparalleled campaign of vituperation against universities.[25] From the early postwar years, KSČ higher education policy was one of conscious neglect. The KSČ had freely abandoned the education ministry after its 1946 election *victory*, and despite its unrivalled power after the February 1948 coup, preferred to gut universities in severe purges, rather than carefully reconstruct them as centers of societal transformation. The Communist revolution in Czechoslovakia by-passed universities, but universities would revenge themselves for the neglect shown them. In the late 1980s they became centers of a new sort of revolution.

The Polish Communists had the most difficult starting point: they were smallest in number, most heavily decimated by war and, unlike their Czech comrades, by Stalinist purges. Also unlike Czech comrades, they *suffered* from close association with the Soviet Union. That country, with its doctrine of militant atheism and imperial dimensions, was widely viewed among the Polish populace as a threat to Polish nationhood. To make matters worse still, in the first postwar years the Polish Party was embroiled in a civil war with underground insurgents, and could not devote scarce cadres to the "educational front." After the insurgency had been quelled, the perception of confrontation with a hostile society on several fronts persisted, and Polish Communist policy toward universities was marked by a tendency to avoid direct clashes.

The positions of the three parties in their respective societies translated into varying conditions for action at universities themselves. This was especially true of Poland. Communist higher education functionaries in all three countries desired radical changes, including replacement of the old professorate, but Communists at universities in Poland were hesitant to come out into the open with their demands. In great contrast to East Germany or the Czech lands, there were even cases in which Polish Worker Party (PPR) members at the university would not admit to their membership![26] Two years after the war's conclusion, leading PPR ideologues complained that Communists had failed to emerge from the underground.[27] In the Czech lands the situation was almost the opposite. Despite their minority position in higher education, Czech Communists manifested their identity with great pride. Arnošt Kolman, the head of the KSČ propaganda section and professor of Soviet philosophy at Charles University recalled the atmosphere of the early postwar years:

> I had to scuffle with the most resolute and skilled polemicists, with the journalist Slavík of the National Socialists, with my colleague, the philosophy professor Kozák, with Pavel Tigrid and the right Social Democrat Bělehrádek. I will not pretend to be modest: I emerged victorious from all these battles of words and felt like a matador.[28]

Even his opponents recognized this aura. Josef Král, a neo-Thomist and colleague in the philosophy faculty of Charles University had voted freely for the addition of Kolman to the faculty as full professor, though Král knew that Kolman did not possess the proper academic qualifications. "He was supposedly a professor at Moscow University, but I believe he was really only a candidate of science." The gleam of Soviet power obscured inner doubts:

> Still in the glow of the Soviet contribution to our liberation, we wanted to have an expert in Soviet philosophy. I hesitated, I pointed out that according to his scientific qualifications he belonged in the natural science faculty... but since I was of the opinion that Marxism-Leninism had further developed in the Soviet Union and I felt a need to add the foreign philosophical influences to our thinking... I suggested his specialty be called exact sciences and Soviet philosophy.

But Král soon regretted his step, for it would prove the first in his own undoing. Kolman acted to pull apart the philosophical faculty along ideological lines, and then in February 1948, helped purge it of undesired staff, including Král.

> the enemy of the fortress was let inside, and supported by the Party, he worked at the faculty in an unprofessional [nevěcně] way, purely propagandistically, self-confident to the point of arrogance... at the faculty he demanded excessive influence in all things and was soon surrounded by numerous student adherents of communism.[29]

Not only did Kolman practically burst with self-confidence; professors of philosophy who "wavered" between Communism and anti-Communism behaved toward him "with complete lack of self-respect, even servility."[30] This self-confidence trickled down to Communist students, who carried out the purges of 1948/49 at universities, which were the severest in the region. For a time the word "studentocracy" gained currency.[31]

East Germany fit somewhere in between. On the one hand, an anti-Communist student movement emerged which was led by liberal and Social Democratic students, many of whom were officially recognized "victims of fascism."[32] On the other hand, Communist saturation of the education administration permitted the rapid introduction of supporters into the student bodies, so that for a while student meetings were marked by fierce partisan debate. The last free elections of any sort held in East Germany were the student council elections of late 1947. The Communists lost decisively. This loss caught the attention of top Party leaders, and waves of arrests and purges ensued. In self-defense, anti-Communist student leaders created the Free University in West Berlin in the fall of 1948.[33]

The relative strength of the three parties would have a direct effect on how quickly they could establish footholds in university professoriates. In all three places, universities were considered bastions of "reaction." Nowhere did Communists, or even Social Democrats, make up more than a handful of the professors. A report of early 1946 on the teaching staff of Berlin University gives some idea of the dimensions the problem. Of 102 full and associate professors who were permitted to teach after the severe denazification, only eight were described as "dependable." Of these none were Communists.[34] Yet the strong Soviet and SED influence on hiring, combined with a brain-drain of non-Communist professors westward, would cause numbers of SED members to rise steadily upward, reaching 28 percent by 1954.[35] At first, numbers in the Czech Lands were quite low as well. Of teachers active in 1949 – that is after the 1948 purges – four of thirty were pre-1948 KSČ members in Prague's law faculty (7.5 percent), twenty-two of 118 in the medical faculty (5.4 percent), and at the Prague's Higher Technical School fifty-nine of 229 (26.0 percent). The Party experienced a massive influx of sudden converts to Communism after the February 1948 purges, however.[36] In Poland, recruitment of professors into the Party proved far more difficult. In May 1948, 3.7 percent of the professors belonged to the PPR; five years later, the number of Polish United Workers Party (PZPR) members among Poland's teachers was 7.5 percent.[37]

Given the time required to select and train Communist cadres to become professors, the East German and Polish parties decided at first to concentrate their attention upon student admissions. Students would help convert "reactionary" higher schools to places the Party could use to train its elites. Władysław Gomułka explained the policy at the First Congress of the PPR in late 1945:

> It is true that professors are reactionary, but we cannot train professors at courses overnight. Professors spend years gaining qualifications, long years, and we have only been in power a few months. We still have to educate our professors and educate them we will, yet this will take years – as many as one needs to educate a professor. We have to work to help the professors that have now, since we will not shut the schools down.
>
> There are hundreds and thousands of ways to exert our influence and to hinder reactionary activity. One of the main and most important ways is the development of our work among youth at school and university. If we have strong support among them, then they will exert influence upon professors.[38]

Yet this task was itself extremely difficult. With the exception of the Czech lands, Communist support among students was exiguous. Worse, the social strata from which Communists claimed to draw support were grievously underrepresented at university. Before Communist seizures of power, these "worker and peasant children" attended university in numbers far beneath their classes' proportions of the general population.[39] The lower classes had not had the means to afford higher education, and indeed lacked the means even to afford the secondary education that prepared for university. To increase numbers of "workers and peasants" and "democratize" universities meant not only making college affordable through stipends, it meant rapidly training chosen "workers and peasants" for college. In 1945 both the East German and Polish Parties supported the creation of courses that would prepare worker and peasant children for university study. In the former case the courses were called "pre-study institutes", (*Vorstudienanstalten*) in the latter "introductory year" (*rok wstępny*).

The East German courses scored early successes because grass-roots Communist and trade union organizations became involved from the start, and were far stronger than in Poland. The Polish academic community demonstrated far more suspicion of these courses, seeing in them Red Trojan horses, and gave only limited help. The German universities had less opportunity for this sort of resistance, since the admissions process was no longer completely a university domain. Commissions with only partial university representation decided who would be accepted for studies; the SVAG then approved these candidates. Moreover, the East German pre-study institutes were set up outside university premises, so that local Communist or Social Democratic pedagogues were able to educate the worker students beyond the influence of conservative university milieus. These worker students were then introduced to the university in yearly waves like fresh shock troops to the front.

The most active and successful of all East German regions was Saxony, home to strong Party and trade union organizations. The major innovations in worker studies came from there. Saxony had the highest concentration of industry and of KPD/SED members of any *Land* in the Soviet zone, and it quickly had the largest number of worker preparation courses.[40] By mid-1946 the regional KPD/SED along with the trade union had set up courses in the industrial towns of Chemnitz, Görlitz, Plauen, Zwickau, Dresden, Freiberg, and Leipzig. KPD *Kreis* organizations were instructed to control carefully the selection of the 1,000 people scheduled for these courses. They must above all come from the working class [*Arbeiterschaft*] and possess no more than grammar school education, and 40 percent should be KPD members to guarantee that the university become a "true people's university."[41] The first contingents from the pre-study courses were enrolled as normal students in the winter semester of 1946/47. From figures of the University of Leipzig one sees that at first, success was greater in admitting "politically correct" rather than "socially correct" students:

Table 1[42] : University of Leipzig

	Total	Workers		SED Members	
WS 45/46	1,267	126,	10.0%	192,	15.1%
WS 46/47	1,330	363,	27.3%	689,	51.8%
SS 47	2,411	663,	27.5%	921,	38.2%
WS 47/48	3,483	1,062,	30.5%	1,549,	44.5%
SS 48	3,270	1,002,	30.6%	1,475,	45.1%
WS 48/49	4,082	1,444,	35.4%	1,859,	45.5%

From: "Soziale Struktur der Studierenden an den wissenschaftlichen Hochschulen des Landes Sachsen seit dem Wintersemester 1946/47," 3 November 1948, in SAPMO-BA, ZPA, IV2/9.04/465 (unnumbered).

In the first postwar semesters, the Communists' desire simply to get a foot in the door favored organizational membership as a criterion for university acceptance. In addition, some Soviet advisors encouraged high organizational membership among students because they took it to signify willingness to break with the past. But since demand for studies was great, often with three candidates for one spot, prospective students joined parties in great numbers, regardless of deeper political convictions. In the summer of 1947, Leipzig Rector Hans-Georg Gadamer sarcastically remarked that most applicants for university study could present proof that they were "Party functionaries."[43]

In first meetings with professors in Kraków in January 1945, Minister Skrzeszewski had demanded that greater numbers of workers' and peasants' children be introduced to university. That spring, universities were already drawing up plans of study for a first course of "introductory year." Yet neither the Minister nor his Ministry's decree made the goal of these courses sufficiently clear. Unlike the East German directives creating pre-study institutes, the Polish decree did not state clearly at which social groups the measure would be directed. It merely mentioned a "catastrophic decrease in the influx of candidates who possess full preparation for higher education" on account of German occupation.[44] Not surprisingly, most of the participants in the courses were neither of worker/peasant background nor politically organized.

But the problem was not only with the decree. The "qualifying commissions" set up by the Ministry in each university town to screen candidates were not under proper control of Party or Ministry. They interpreted Ministry guidelines in widely varying ways. Only in two of the courses (Łódź and Gliwice) did commissions consciously and successfully aim at workers or peasants. A further weakness of the Polish system was that it left courses in university hands. This was particularly true in Kraków. Professors there objected that courses for filling in gaps in high school education should be conducted at high schools; they never viewed such courses as more than a dubious method of skirting normal admissions requirements.[45] Communist higher education functionaries in East Germany were not so dependent on the good will of the academic community. With Soviet help they could simply requisition building space and draw upon relatively larger numbers of Social Democratic and Communist teachers.[46]

Not surprisingly, the first year of "introductory year" in Poland was a disaster. In some places only handfuls of students signed up (Kraków); in others, large percentages of those who signed up dropped out. Even in the best places social composition was unfavorable.[47] At this point an organization intervened which would take a leading role in pressing for social transformation at Polish universities: the leftist youth organization AZWM "Życie." At its second congress of January 1946, "Życie" decided to search for new organizational forms to prepare worker/peasant youths for studies. In March it helped form a Society for the Advancement of Worker/Peasant Studies (TPKU).[48] By April the TPKU had set up "preparatory courses for the introductory year" with 4,000 carefully selected participants in nine towns. The social composition of "introductory year" improved dramatically. Now the way was open for a gradual change of the social composition of Poland's student body as a whole.

By 1948 both the SED and the PPR had noticeably changed the social character of student bodies. Yet because of its closer control of the admissions process, and the ease with which denazification concerns permitted politicization of educational life, it had already begun tying students down to a web of organizational loyalties. Far more than was the case in Poland, students belonged to the youth organization, trade unions, and to the Party itself. In 1948 numbers of PPR members among the students of Polish universities did not exceed 4 percent.

Table 2: PPR Members in the Freshman Class, Academic Year 1947/48

	Freshmen	PPR Members	
Jagellonian Univ.	2,988	46	(1.5%)
Warsaw Polytechnic	936	28	(3%)
Univ. Poznań	1,440	32	(2.2%)
Univ. Toruń	620	35	(5.6%)
Univ. Polytechnic			
Wrocław	709	56	(7.9%)

From: AAN KCPPR/295/XVII/61 passim.

The total numbers of Polish freshmen in any sort of political organization did not exceed 10 percent.[49] By the 1946/47 academic year, the East German totals for students belonging to the SED alone were far higher: Berlin 9.8 percent, Jena 30.7 percent, Leipzig 41.4 percent, Halle 34.8 percent, Greifswald 17.8 percent, Rostock 21.0 percent.[50] By 1950, the number of Czech students belonging to the KSČ exceeded one-half the total. Even as late as 1953 only 8.9% of the entire Polish student body belonged to the PPR's successor party, the PZPR, however.[51] Polish Communist student admissions policy was not a complete failure, however; early on remarkable successes were achieved in socially recasting student bodies:

Table 3: Social Origin of Freshmen in Polish universities[52]

	1935/36	1947/48
Workers	9.9%	22%
Peasants	11.7%	19.7%
Intellectual		
Workers	38.2%	45.6%
Free Professions		
Craftsmen	40.2%	12.7%

From: "Skład społeczny studentów I roku szkół wyższych w/g wydziałow w porównaniu ze stanem przedwojennym 1935/36." AAN MO/2879 (unnumbered).

Table 4:
Worker/Peasant students as a percentage of total (SS = Summer Semester, WS=Winter Semester) in the Soviet Zone of Occupation of Germany[53]

	1945/46	1946/47	1947/48
Berlin	14.2% SS	9.7% WS	17.0% WS
Jena	12.9% WS	30.2% WS	33.5% WS
Leipzig	13.3% WS	24.4% WS	40.3% WS
Halle	7.5% WS	10.7% WS	31.6% WS
Greifswald	8.5% WS	14.6% WS	26.6% WS
Rostock	13.8% SS	13.9% WS	27.0% WS

From: BAAP R2-865/7, 35-37; 1060/23-26, 32-34; Kasper, "Der Kampf der SED," 273-275.

The need to increase the representation of worker-peasant students was almost never mentioned in Czech Communist discourse on higher education. This is odd, since worker-peasant students constituted a small fraction of Czech student bodies, and the KSČ possessed the political leverage to take first steps at ameliorating this situation.[54] Instead, after abandoning the Ministry of Higher Education, the Party left higher educational policy in the hands of students. Thus, student life in the Czech lands was far more politicized than in either of its northern neighbors. The smallest issues could become subjects of intense partisan rivalry. In the first "revolutionary" days of 1945 proportional representation, combined with superior organization, gave Communist students control of student clubs in separate faculties, and of city-wide institutions, like the "honor courts" that pronounced judgments about students suspected of wartime collaboration. Just as in society as a whole, with time Communist machinations aroused distrust and mobilized opposition. In student council elections of October 1947 Communists lost decisively. As in East Germany these were the last freely contested elections of any kind, and they caught the attention of the Party leadership.[55] The year 1948 would witness arrests of students in Prague and Brno – as well as Leipzig, Jena, Berlin, and Rostock.

Beyond student admissions none of the three Parties undertook major policy offensives in the pre-Stalinist era. There were minor structural changes. In all three countries pedagogical faculties were appended to institutions of higher learning, and their faculty as well as students tended to be left-leaning. In East Germany, "social-science" faculties were added to the universities in Rostock, Jena, and Leipzig. Their faculty and students also tended to be left-leaning.[56] At Charles University in Prague three new chairs were created: in Soviet Law, Soviet Philosophy, and Soviet Literature. They were staffed by men without proper academic credentials.[57] In East Germany and Poland fledgling courses of ideological training were set up, but several years would pass before students would have compulsory examinations in Marxism-Leninism.[58]

Conclusion

By early 1948, Czechoslovakia, East Germany, and Poland had reached turning points in their developments; the path beyond that point was supposed to be the same. The fact that they approached it from different directions at different velocities would influence how long they stayed on this path, which later became known as Stalinism. The crucial issue in higher education for the Communist parties was to achieve a decisive breakthrough and separate themselves clearly from the past. The major prerequisite for this was putting an end to the power of existing elites.[59]

The SED could claim the greatest success. The war had served to delegitimize existing university elites, and the SVAG could insist upon their replacement. By 1946 German Communists had a prerogative that the PPR/PZPR would never have: they could choose each teacher and each student who would enter the university community. The question of cadres was settled from the start, and the SED thus possessed a very solid foundation upon which to construct *its* higher educational system. Moreover, with the SVAG's backing, it operated in an atmosphere of enormous self-confidence.

The Polish Party failed to achieve a decisive breakthrough in higher education, either in the 1945-48 period or later. From the start, its higher education policy was a series of half-measures, which taken together did not amount to domination. With one third the number of Party members per capita, the PPR/PZPR faced more internal enemies than either of its fraternal Parties. It could not afford to launch an offensive against several "fronts" of Polish society at once: the Church, the peasantry, the industrial proletariat, the intelligentsia - not to mention the truly military fronts of domestic insurgency. Education could not become a priority before the population had been pacified, and basic questions of power settled.

PPR/PZPR higher education policy was therefore premised upon the necessity of compromise. The strategy adopted in 1945 inhibited incursions into the old elite, and that strategy accumulated inertia. No new revolutionary moment was encountered or manufactured after 1945 that might break it. In 1945 Poland's new leaders had permitted professors to reconstitute universities according to pre-war norms. These professors possessed great self-assurance owing to leading roles in wartime conspiracy. Far from being able to reconstitute the old, the PPR could hardly determine the shape of the new. For example, PPR leaders felt helpless to hinder the largely anti-Soviet professoriates of Lwów and Wilno from organizing new Polish universities in Wrocław and Toruń. The tasks of reconstruction appeared so daunting that even these professors could not be alienated; as Gomułka had said, one could not simply close down universities. Once dependent on the old professoriate, the Party would find it impossible to free itself.

The Polish Party's strategy of "exploiting" the old intelligentsia in order to train younger generations could not succeed. Polish Communists indeed managed to bring large numbers of worker-peasant students to university. But once they entered the university milieu, these students were mostly lost to the Party. That milieu had not been transformed; its standards and norms continued behind any new facades that might be constructed. Even in an examination of Marxism-Leninism-Stalinism, one could still tell what was proper Polish.[60]

Adverse circumstances hence prevented the Polish Party from exploiting the rare postwar conjuncture, when suddenly age-old assumptions seemed amenable to reconsideration, and from constructing *its* system of higher education. Enjoying broad support in Czech society, the KSČ was able to exploit two such conjunctures, however. The first came in May 1945 and the second in February 1948. In each case "normal" legality was suspended, and institutions of long-standing were restructured if not simply erased. The activities of "action" committees in 1945 produced a momentary rupture in consciousness. Buoyed by popular perception of wartime suffering and conspiratorial activity, students eased into decisive positions in university affairs. Professors, who for the most part had spent the war in contemplation, drawing their regular salaries though universities were closed, found themselves temporarily paralyzed.

Professors and universities recovered, and enjoyed several years of relative freedom as the KSČ apparatus concerned itself with other things. In both rectoral and student council elections, universities exhibited themselves as decided enemies of "people's democracy" in this period, and thus attracted special attention after the February 1948 seizure of power. "Action" committees were set up, and they quickly reasserted the power over universities their forerunners had lost in the normalization of 1945. Largely run by students, they were the longest lasting action committees in all Czech society. They effected the decisive break with the past that the East German Communists achieved with other means in 1945, and that would elude Poland's Communists throughout the postwar period.

In many ways the trajectories of Communist higher educational policy had thus been established at the moment Polish, East German, and Czech societies entered the Stalinist period. The SED controlled the higher educational terrain, and as ever more "bourgeois" professors fled westward, universities became increasingly effective instruments for making the East German elite.[61] In Poland, the professoriate maintained its hold on universities, and frustrated the PZPR's attempts to make workers into Communists. The outcome in the Czech Lands was more ambiguous. The KSČ did indeed sweep away the "reactionary" professoriate, but due to neglect and a late start, would never socially transform the Czech student bodies. The student of 1968 or 1989 was drawn more or less from the same socio-cultural milieus as the student of 1939 or 1948. He or she carried on the Czech student tradition: students had protested the crushing of democracy most loudly in 1939 and 1948; in 1967 and 1989 they would inaugurate return to democratic norms.

Notes

1. An amended version of this chapter is appearing in *East European Politics and Societies*, vol. 10, no. 3, Fall 1996.

2. For discussion of the meaning of the war for postwar experience, see Jan Gross's chapter in this book, "War as Revolution."

3. Berlin's university held a series of lectures on "Proving One's Worth at Historical Turning Points" [weltgeschichtliche Bewährungsstunden] until shortly before the city was stormed by Soviet troops. Siegward Lönnendonker, *Freie Universität Berlin: Gründung einer politischen Universität* (Berlin: Duncker & Humblot, 1988), 50.

4. Stanisław Gawęda, *Uniwersytet Jagielloński w okresie II wojny światowej 1939-1945* (Kraków, Wrocław: Wydawnictwo Literackie, 1986), 40-41.

5. 29.5 percent of Poland's academics were lost in the war, which is more than half the average wartime loss of the Polish population. Tomasz Szarota, "Upowszechnienie Kultury" in Hanna Jędruszczak et al., eds., *Polska Ludowa 1944-1950, przemiany społeczne* (Wrocław: Zakład Narodowy im. Ossolińskich, 1974), 411.

6. These spectacular activities have attracted several scholars' attention, but precisely how much they offset the effects of Nazi anti-cultural policies remains unknown. Cf. Gawęda, *Uniwersytet Jagielloński w okresie II wojny światowej,* Gabriele Lesser, *Leben als ob: die Untergrunduniversität Krakau im Zweiten Weltkrieg* (Freiburg im Breisgau: Treff-Punkt, 1988), Marian Walczak, *Szkolnictwo wyższe i nauka polska w latach wojny i okupacji 1939-1945* (Wrocław: Zakład Narodowy im. Ossolińskich, 1978).

7. František Burianek et al., eds., *17. listopad Odboj československého studentstva* (Prague: Orbis, 1945), 140.

8. Bundesarchiv, Abteilungen Potsdam (BAAP), R2/1060/21. Denazification in the American zone was at times rigorous, reducing the law faculty in Erlangen for example to one professor in 1947. Yet on the whole practice was uneven, and never removed every former NSDAP member from the teaching staffs. After a visit to Berlin in late 1945, the leading American higher educational officer wrote that the purges in the Soviet Zone "more extreme than in our Zone." James F. Tent, *Mission on the Rhine: Reeducation and Denazification in American-Occupied Germany* (Chicago: University of Chicago Press, 1982), 66, 98.

9. The Soviets could intervene in university matters when they desired, and often did so in response to denunciations. The SVAG in Thuringia by Order no. 36 of March 5, 1948, dismissed the elected rector of Jena University Zucker and ordered a re-examination of the student body, which led to many expulsions; the issue had been supposedly fascistic remarks made in the student council. Staatsarchiv Weimar, Ministerium für Volksbildung Land Thüringen 3123/6ff. In early 1947 the SVAG ordered the removal of the dean of Berlin's medical faculty, Prof. Else Knake, since she had supported anti-Communist students in the student council. BAAP R2/1142.

10. Bolesław Krasiewicz, *Odbudowa szkolnictwa wyższego w Polsce Ludowej w latach 1944-1948* (Wrocław: Zakład Narodowy im. Ossolińskich, 1976), 82-85, 138, 154, 228.

11. Jan Havránek, "Studenti University Karlovy na jaře a v létě roku pětačtyřicátého," in *Zprávy Archivu Karlovy* 7 (1985): 80.

12. Jan Havránek, "Studenti University Karlovy," 85.

13. See below, ft. 38.

14. On October 22, 1945, the Supreme Commander of the SVAG, Marshall Zhukov, issued Order no. 110, which conferred upon the *Land* governments the right to issue "laws and decrees with the force of law," as long as they did not contradict the orders of the Allied Control Council or the SVAG. Furthermore, the existing laws and ordinances that had been enacted by the *Land* governments to that date were declared valid, as long as they did not contradict Soviet injunctions. Gottfried Handel and Roland Köhler, eds., *Dokumente der Sowjetischen Militäradministration in Deutschland zum Hoch- und Fachschulwesen 1945-1949* (Berlin: Institut für Hochschulbildung, 1975), 26-27.

15. Occasionally, German hesitance to become more directly involved in decision-making provoked Soviet impatience. In a regular meeting of March 29, 1946, SVAG representative Nomofinov complained to DVV representatives that "Since October not a single representative of the DVV has been seen in the Province [sic] Mecklenburg-Westpommern, [sic] with one exception, and that gentleman was merely picking up his personal possessions. Such an old-fashioned attitude and bureaucratic understanding of the tasks of leadership is not compatible with today's realities and will not lead to the ideas of the new Germany." BAAP, R2/1332/107. SVAG education department director Zolotukhin told SED functionaries in April 1947 that the German administration was to concentrate upon "large tasks" and not get caught up in details. "The SVAG offices should not replace the German administration, they should help them." BAAP, R2/52/51.

16. Former pupil Wolfgang Leonhard described Wandel as the "perfected prototype of the intelligent Stalinist": "He kept himself under control at all times; he was incapable of ill-considered or inexact formulations. He chose his words precisely, and one could be sure that they coincided with the official line in the smallest detail... when the line changed he was prepared to change his opinion from one day to the next and with crystal clear logic to argue precisely the opposite of that which he had said the day before." Wolfgang Leonhard, *Die Revolution entlässt ihre Kinder*, vol. 1, (Leipzig: Reklam, 1990), 217-218.

17. BAAP, R2/934/137. The DVV was created by SVAG Order no. 17 of July 27, 1945 and was given responsibility for the "administration of schools, kindergartens, educational establishments, and of artistic, scientific, cultural institutions." Handel and Köhler, eds., *Dokumente der Sowjetischen Militäradministration*, 14-15. Several drafts of statutes were made in 1946 and 1947, but the SVAG never approved of them. See the undated drafts in BAAP, R2/1033/21-26 and Staatsarchiv Weimar, Ministerium für Volksbildung Land Thüringen 3115/292-297. The latter, probably from 1947, says that "the higher education department supervises, examines, and steers all universities." Concerned about repercussions for German policy as a whole the SVAG refused to formalize the DVV's role until 1948, with Order no. 32 of February 12, which

granted the German Economic Commission (DWK) "legal authority to issue ordinances and instructions binding upon 'all German organs within the territory of the Soviet occupation zone.'" The DVV could share this new authority. David Pike, *The Politics of Culture in Soviet-Occupied Germany 1945-1949* (Stanford, Calif.: Stanford University Press, 1992), 440.

18. He had a higher educational office beneath him, which until late 1947 was directed by chemist N. M. Voronov, and thereafter by his deputy, the physicist P I. Nikitin. Helmut Klein, ed. *Humboldt-Universität zu Berlin, Überblick 1810-1985* (Berlin: VEB Deutscher Verlag der Wissenschaften, 1985), 94, 96.

19. Many of the *Land* staffs then moved to Berlin.

20. Tadeusz Mołdawa, *Ludzie Władzy 1944-1991* (Warszawa: Wydaw. Naukowe PWN, 1991), 337, 379, 422, 443-444. Bieńkowski was a close associate of Gomułka and later a dissident. Krassowska, graduate of Wilno University, had taught in Wilno schools from 1939-41, and was thereafter involved in conspiratorial education in Białystok.

21. Nejedlý was a prominent interwar leftist intellectual, who taught at Moscow University during the war; his victim of the 1948 purges, Prof. Václav Černý, described the Nejedlý of 1945 as "a person long since creatively powerless and of weakened character." *Paměti, 1945-1972*, vol. 3 (Brno: Atlantis, 1992), 146-147. On Stránský: *Československý biografický slovník* (Prague, Encyklopedický institut ČSAV: Academia, 1992), 663-664.

22. Premature and distorted versions of the decree's content had mobilized the resistance of Polish professors. In the end, it did not seriously contest two of the university's most important powers: granting of *venia legendi,* and deciding student admissions. The decree created an advisory council called the Main Council for Science and Higher Education, which became a competitor for power with the Ministry of Education, thus in fact reducing its direct influence over university affairs. Krasiewicz, *Odbudowa*, 332-334.

23 . On May 23, 1949, the "Vorläufige Arbeitsordnung der Universitäten und wissenschaftlichen Hochschulen der sowjetischen Besatzungszone Deutschlands" (VAO) went into effect. The VAO placed universities under direct "supervision" of the DVV, and stripped them of their powers to determine students admissions. For details see Marianne and Egon Erwin Müller, *"...stürmt die Festung Wissenschaft!" Die Sowjetisierung der mitteldeutschen Universitäten seit 1945* (Berlin: Colloquium-Verlag, 1953), 141-145.

24. Much of the staff of the Social Science Faculty (*Gewifa*) created in 1947 in Leipzig – including Walter Markov, Hans Mayer, Werner Krauss, Gerhard Harig, Friedrich Behrens, Arthur Baumgarten – had been educated or had taught at West German and Swiss universities. The *Gewifa* was the earliest cadre training institute in East Central Europe. J. Connelly, "Creating the Socialist Elite:

Communist Higher Education Policies in the Czech Lands, East Germany, and Poland; 1945-1954," (Unpublished Ph.D. Dissertation, Harvard University, 1994), ch. 7.

25. Public statements of Trade Union Chief Antonín Zápotocký in particular were consistently hostile toward the academic community. He announced a cultural war against students in a 1947 student newpaper: "This caste upbringing was perhaps not as noticeable in schools as it was in social education. Student dance hours, student soirees, student balls, etc. All of this neatly limited to the caste, only for the invited, and for their guests 'coming out' into society. All of this so that venerable bourgeois matrons would have a guaranteed selection of the men who in the future were supposed to inseminate their ripening seedlings. And for that reason this selection, before its own ripening to real life, had to receive its own registered trade marks: JUC, PhC, MUG, IngC, etc." *Studentské Noviny*, January 21, 1947. Information Minister Václav Kopecký proclaimed that "*Rudé Právo* [the KSČ daily] is our university!" Cited in Antonín Kratochvil, *Žaluji: Cesta k Sionu*, vol. 3 (Prague: Dolmen, 1990), 9. The Czech working class was conspicous by its absence from anti-Nazi resistance. Vojtech Mastny, *The Czechs under Nazi Rule* (New York: Columbia University Press, 1971), 37, 77, 80, 85. In February 1946 a lecturer at Brno's Technical University told students: "you students were not simple-minded workers (during wartime - JC), who saved up Reichsmark after Reichsmark, voluntarily worked overtime, and discerned life's very meaning in black market trading... the intelligentsia is the center of the atom, everything else must keep an honest distance." Rioting broke out between students and Brno armaments plant workers after that lecturer was dismissed. Among other things, the Communist-inspired workers had chanted "professors to the mines." *Čin* (Brno) February 10, May 23, 1946; *Práce* (Olomouc) February 8, 1946; Hana Kráčmarova, *Vysokoškoláci v revolučních letech 1945-48*, (Prague: Oddělení vysokoškolských organizací ÚV SSM v nakl. Mladá fronta, 1976), 151; František Jordan, ed., *Dějiny University v Brně* (Brno: Universita J. E. Purkyně, 1969), 271.

26. In November 1947 the PPR delegate for university admissions in Warsaw wrote to the Central Committee that he could not tell them precisely how many candidates for admission were Party members, because "many members have not revealed their affiliation." Rather, if they belonged to another "democratic organization," they often listed it alone, and did not mention their membership in the PPR. Fear of discrimination by professors weighed heavier than the PPR's promise of preferential treatment. Archiwum Akt Nowych, Warsaw (AAN) KCPPR/295/XVII/61/429, 429a.

27. Stefan Jędrychowski, director of the Economics Department of the PPR Central Committee, told a meeting of PPR academics on June 5, 1947, that "a few Marxists are even ashamed of their Marxism." Adam Schaff seconded this view

saying that "we often feel embarrassed because we represent such an unpopular view... Party circles at universities must feel that they have full rights." AAN KCPPR/295/XVII/57/11,20. A meeting of PPR and PPS professors was told in September 1947 that "The atmosphere of the underground still prevails at universities, and democrats are as if smothered by the sheer quantity of non-Party members." AAN KCPPR 295/XVII/58/79. See also AAN KCPPR 295/XVII/38,46 for mention of "the inability to divest oneself of an atmosphere of illegal work" and "the persistence of an atmosphere of illegality in (Communist) activity."

28. Arnošt Kolman, *Die verirrte Generation. So hätten wir nicht leben sollen. Eine Biographie* (Frankfurt am Main: S. Fischer, 1979), 180. In Kraków non-Communists stood on more even footing with Communist opponents. For a relation of 1946 debates between Father Jan Piwowarczyk and Bolesław Drobner and Władysław Bieńkowski see Robert Jarocki, *Czterdzieści pięc lat w opozycji* (Kraków: Wydawnictwo Literackie, 1990), 125-128.

29. From: "Vysoké školy - universita," a handwritten memoir of Prof. Josef Král in Král Papers, Czech Academy of Sciences, Prague.

30. Král papers. Immediately in 1945 certain professors "feeling that they have the strongest political party behind them acted self-confidently." Servile behavior toward them began in 1945, but intensified after February 1948. Prof. F. Weyr wrote his friend ,deposed Prague rector K. Engliš, of the servile behavior of professors in Brno after the coup: "Every decent person at our age has, it seems to me, primary concern for the memory he leaves behind after death and this he will not jeopardize recklessly (*beze všeho*) for the sake of some financial advantage (merit bonus, etc). But it seems that there are not many such people among us and that people don't give a damn what will be written about them in history books fifty years from now. But it matters to me and I suspect it does to you too." Letter of Weyr to Engliš, April 10, 1948 in National Museum Archive, Prague, Engliš Papers, Carton 399.

31. Communist student leader Jiří Pelikán wrote on March 3, 1948: "progressive students have assumed the leadership of universities and progressive organizations." *Svobodné Noviny* (Prague), March 5, 1948.

32. J. Connelly, "East German Higher Education Policies and Student Resistance, 1945-1948," *Central European History*, 28:3 (1995).

33. James F. Tent, *The Free University of Berlin: A Political History* (Bloomington: Indiana University Press, 1988), Bernd Rabehl, *Am Ende der Utopie: die politische Geschichte der Freien Universität Berlin* (Berlin: Argon, 1988), Lönnendonker, *Freie Universität Berlin*.

34. Ralph Jessen, "Professoren im Sozialismus. Aspekte des Strukturwandels der Hochschullehrerschaft in der Ulbricht-Ära," in Hartmut Kaelble, Jürgen Kocka, Hartmut Zwahr, eds., *Sozialgeschichte der DDR* (Stuttgart: Klett-Cotta,

1994), 225.

35. Jessen, "Professoren," 241. In Leipzig 18.9 percent of the professors belonged to the SED in early 1948. Stiftung Archiv der Parteien und Massenorganisationen im Bundesarchiv (SAPMO-BA), ZPA IV2/9.04/458/107-110. In early 1948 the SED Party leadership (*Vorstand*) was told that 18 percent of the professors were "socialist," but that one could not believe that "all are Marxists and socialists in the true sense of the word." Dietrich Staritz, "Partei, Intellektuelle, Parteiintellektuelle: Die Intellektuellen im Kalkül der frühen SED," in Klaus Schönhoven/Dietrich Staritz eds., *Sozialismus und Kommunismus im Wandel, Hermann Weber zum 65. Geburtstag* (Cologne: Bund Verlag, 1993), 390.

36. By January 1950, the percentage of university faculty belonging to the KSČ had exceeded half the total at the four most important higher educational institutions in Bohemia and Moravia (Charles University in Prague, Masaryk University in Brno, and the Technical Universities of Prague and Brno). Statní ústřední archiv (Archiv ústředního výboru Komunistické strany Československa), SÚA (AÚV KSČ), F. 19/7 313/373, 314/17, 311/214, 328/14. An additional reason for the high number of KSČ members among teachers in the post-1948 era were the purges of non-Communist faculty in 1948/49. In Brno's Law Faculty, for example, seven of thirteen professors had been dismissed for political reasons. Jordan, ed., *Dějiny University v Brně,* 274.

37. *Partia w cyfrach od I do II zjazdu 1945-1948* (Warsaw, 1948), 149; cited in B. Fijalkowska, *Polityka i twórcy (1948-1959)* (Warsaw: PWN, 1985), 67. Piotr Hübner, *Nauka polska po II wojnie światowej - idee i instytucje* (Warsaw: Centralny Ósrodek Metodyczny Studiów Nauk Politycznych, 1987), 174.

38. Władysław Gomułka, *Ku nowej Polsce: sprawozdanie polityczne i przemówienia wygłoszone na I Zjezdzie PPR* (Łódź: Spółdzielnia wydawn. "Książka," 1946), 139.

39. In 1935/36, 9.9 percent of freshmen at Polish universities were of worker background, and 11.7 percent of peasant background. "Skład społeczny studentów I roku szkół wyższych w/g wydziałów w porównaniu ze stanem przedwojennym 1935/36." AAN MO/2879 (unnumbered). Only 7 percent of Czech University students before 1948 were of working class origin. In 1948, manual laborers constituted 40 percent of society; in 1947, 3 percent of Brno's students were of working class, 11 percent agricultural background. Jordan, ed., *Dějiny University v Brně,* 269. In 1932, 3.0 percent of Germany's students were of worker, 2.2 percent of peasant background. "Zehn-Jahresstatistik des Hochschulbesuchs 1943." Zentralarchiv des FDGB, Bundesvorstand, 11/-/785, cited in Hans-Hendrik Kasper, "Der Kampf der SED um die Heranbildung einer Intelligenz aus der Arbeiterklasse und der werktätigen Bauernschaft über die Vorstudienanstalten an den Universitäten und Hochschulen der sowjetischen Besatzungszone Deutschlands (1945/46 bis 1949)," (unpublished Ph.D.

dissertation, Bergbauakademie, Freiberg in Sachsen, 1979), 269.

40. Saxony had 32 percent of the Soviet zone's population but 40-48 percent of its industry, 60 percent of its working class population and the highest concentrations of SED members. In June 1947, 10.3 percent of its population belonged to the SED, compared to 10.0 percent in Saxony-Anhalt, 9.3 percent in Thuringia and Mecklenburg, and 8.3 percent in Brandenburg. Martin Broszat and Hermann Weber, eds., *SBZ-Handbuch: Staatliche Verwaltungen, Parteien, gesellschaftliche Organisationen und ihre Führungskräfte in der Sowjetischen Besatzungszone Deutschlands 1945-1949* (Munich: R. Oldenbourg, 1990), 126-128, 510, 1070.

41. Letter from KPD Betriebsgruppe, Sächsische Landesverwaltung to KPD Bezirksleitung Sachsen of 8 February 1946. SAPMO-BA, ZPA IV2/9.04/697 (unnumbered).

42. "Soziale Struktur der Studierenden an den wissenschaftlichen Hochschulen des Landes Sachsen seit dem Wintersemester 1946/47," 3 November 1948, in SAPMO-BA, ZPA, IV2/9.04/465 (unnumbered).

43 . Membership in an "anti-fascist-democratic" party was considered proof of "democratic basic convicitions." [Gesinnung] The Academic Senate voted to condemn "this method of proving basic democratic convictions." It unanimously approved a motion to recognize party membership as proof of anti-fascist conviction, but only if it began before February 1946, since "only after the opening of the university did people begin joining parties." Protocol of University Senate meeting, August 16, 1947, Universitätsarchiv Leipzig, Rektorat 1/136ff.

44. "Dekret z dnia 24 maja 1945 o utworzeniu wstępnego roku studiów w szkołach wyższych," *Dziennik Ustaw* Nr. 21, poz. 122 (1945).

45. This attitude worsened with the growing competitiveness for entrance to Polish university, and increasing signs of widespread corruption. Professors and other interested parties often used informal connections – and sometimes payoffs – to get young people into university. Rector Czarnocki of the Medical Academy in Gdańsk complained in August 1947 that every one of the entrance places to his school (120) had been "protected". AAN KC PPR 295/XVII/61/162-163. The Academic Senate of Warsaw University expressed fears that turning the selection process over to boards outside the university would only worsen this problem. See the statement of Warsaw University Senate of February 24, 1947 in Archiwum Uniwersytetu Jagiellońskiego (AUJ) SIII/18.

46. For example, in mid-1947 the SVAG Land administration in Saxony received received reports that workers preparation courses there were not staffed with the most competent teachers available. Soviet Commandandant Dubrovskii thereupon took a personal interest in this issue until it was rectified. Kasper, "Der Kampf der SED," 77.

47. In Łódź, 91 of 347 (26.2 percent) introductory year students at the

polytechnic and university were of worker/peasant origin. Not only were "bourgeois" students overrepresented; some worker/peasant youths were actually refused admission. J. Baculewski, "Z doswiadczeń kursów wstępnych do szkół wyższych" *Kuźnica*, no. 16, April 23, 1947. Those who successfully completed introductory year could be admitted to university without the normal entrance examinations; this fact led many to sign up who already had high school education, which in turn contributed to the demoralization of true worker/peasant candidates without high school education.

48. The TPKU's members were recruited chiefly from four leftist youth organizations. Jan Lewandowski, *Rodowód społeczny powojennej inteligencji polskiej (1944-1949)* (Szczecin: Wydawnictwo naukowe Uniwersytetu Szczecinskiego, 1991), 74.

49. AAN KCPPR/295/XVII/61 passim.

50. BAAP, R2/1060/46. Kasper, "Der Kampf der SED," 272.

51. Hübner, *Nauka polska*, 134, 173.

52. The total number of students increased by 75.1 percent from 1935/36 to 1947/48. "Skład społeczny studentów I roku szkół wyższych w/g wydzialow w porównaniu ze stanem przedwojennym 1935/36." AAN MO/2879 (unnumbered).

53. BAAP R2-865/7, 35-37; 1060/23-26, 32-34; Kasper, "Der Kampf der SED," 273-275.

54. Communists were fully aware that low numbers of working-class students at university spelled political weakness. For example the newspaper *Pochodeň* of Hradec Králové wrote on February 15, 1946 that a reason for anti-Communist student demonstrations in Brno was the weak position of students from "worker and petty rural families" especially in law faculties. The complete failure of Communist Party organizations to become engaged in recruiting workers for university suggests the low esteem higher education held both within the Party and in working class circles. The contrast to Poland and East Germany is remarkable. Neither in the correspondence of the Central Committee's Cultural Section, or of Minister Zdeněk Nejedlý is a single letter preserved that requests assistance getting a pupil into high school. The same is true of the records of the KSČ *Kraj* cultural sections. Archiv ÚV KSČ; fond 19/7; a.j. 1-30.

55. In Prague, Communists won 28.07 percent of the votes, the Social Democrats 9.56 percent, National Socialists 38.12 percent, and Popular Democrats 22.08 percent. In Brno the non-Communist "democrats" fared even better, winning over 40 percent of the seats. Kráčmarová, *Vysokoškoláci*, 134, 193.

56. After taken by the National Socialists, the Czechoslovak Ministry of Education took steps to frustrate the development of pedagogical faculties.

Otakar Chlup, "O pedagogickou fakultu" in *Tvorba*, no. 23 (June 4, 1947), 419.

57. These were Vladimír Procházka, Arnošt Kolman, and Bohumil Mathesius. Their addition to Charles University had been agreed to by Czechoslovakia's new leadership at Košice in spring 1945. Interview with Prof. Jan Havránek, July 7, 1993. Procházka's supporter Prof. Hobza sought to finesse Procházka's lack of academic qualifications by citing his broad knowledge of "public administration in Soviet Russia." See the letter of Dean Jan Matejka to Zdeněk Nejedlý of November 14, 1945 in Archiv ČSAV, Nejedlý Papers, Carton 31. Procházka was member of the KSČ Central Committee from 1949-54, and Czechoslovak ambassador to the U.S.A. in 1951-52. *Československý biografický slovník*, 572. In 1925 Mathesius had co-founded the "Society for Cultural and Economic Rapprochement with the New Russia." *Československý biografický slovník*, 445.

58. In East Germany the courses were called "social and political problems of the present,"and were to begin in the winter semester 1946/47. By mid-1947 lectures were taking place only in Greifswald, Halle, and Berlin, however. Leipzig claimed to have insufficient space. BAAP, R2/1489/81. Polish Ministry of Education Order MO IV SH-10527/47 of October 6, 1947, created "studies on Poland and the contemporary world," but instruction in Marxism-Leninism was not required of all Polish students until 1950.

59. In a general discussion of nation building, Kenneth Jowitt defines "breaking through" as "decisive alteration or destruction of values, structures, and behaviors which are perceived by a revolutionary elite as comprising or contributing to the actual or potential existence of alternative centers of political power." *Revolutionary Breakthroughs and National Development: The Case of Romania, 1944-1965* (Berkeley: University of California Press, 1971), 7. In the context of higher education policy, one might posit that the East German leadership had both the most acute perception of the conditions necessary for "breaking through," as well as the greatest institutional resources for achieving this.

60. In Kraków, for example, examiners judged entrance examination essays on topics like "The Role of Youth in Building the Foundations of Socialism in Poland" on the basis of grammar, style, and coherence of thought. See the examinations from 1951 for admission to the law faculty in AUJ WPIV 45.

61. The open border to the West strengthened the SED's command over the university community, because potential opponents simply took positions in West Germany. The SED's most outspoken opponents in Leipzig, Profs. Gadamer and Litt, had left by 1948. Many hundreds more would follow until 1961. See J. Connelly, "Zur 'Republikflucht' von DDR-Wissenschaftlern in den fünfziger Jahren," *Zeitschrift für Geschichtswissenschaft*, 4 (1994), 331-352.

11

Censorship in Soviet-Occupied Germany

David Pike

Propaganda was the most overt, censorship one of the most covert instruments in the manipulation of political, intellectual, and cultural developments by the Soviets and their allies in Soviet-occupied Germany.[1] Both propaganda and censorship were informed by political ideology, which itself underwent a complex evolution in the postwar years. When the public rhetoric of the time is reviewed at face value, it would seem to provide a chronicle very similar to the "official" history of the Soviet zone. A critical reading of the propaganda, however, yields a representation of Soviet-occupied Germany that significantly diverges from the "official portrayal."

Ideology and propaganda accompanied the Communists' consolidation of power in Soviet-occupied Germany every step of the way, often anticipating political twists and turns before these manifested themselves in concrete actions, and at times revealing far more about German Communists' (acting in concert with their Soviet counterparts) objectives than it was probably wise to divulge. The present discussion is limited, however, to some general comments about the Soviet censorship of the Germans (rather than Soviet self-censorship) in accordance with the prevailing ideology, as well as the role of propaganda in relation to censorship. Establishing a system to police and control German expression was the challenge that faced the Soviet occupation administration (SVAG) in summer 1945.

Because its internal workings were veiled in secrecy, there is still a great deal that we do not know about censorship in the Soviet zone. Prior to the opening of the archives in the former German Democratic Republic (GDR), next to nothing was known about the work of the German censorship organizations set up by the Soviets. The only information about the activities of those SVAG offices in Berlin-Karlshorst and its outlying branches that were charged with the task of censorship was limited to the occasional U.S. Army intelligence report.[2] Even now, the files of German organizations like the Deutsche Verwaltung für Volksbildung (DVV), established in the fall of 1945 to oversee all educational and many cultural policies in the zone, are too fragmentary to allow for a reconstruction of all aspects of their internal operations. Although it has been possible since 1990 to elucidate the regulation of publishing, as well as to trace the gradual evolution of central control over theaters in East Germany, many questions about the institutions and procedures of censorship remain.

Some of the best information currently available on early censorship in the Soviet-occupied zone exists in the form of specific SVAG policy objectives formulated as orders and published at the time. These were usually binding instructions or directives issued to the appropriate agencies of German "self-administration."[3] Most of these original orders governed the administration of censorship for the duration of the occupation and for a few months after it, even though the German agencies established on the basis of these instructions changed considerably over the same period of time. Given the Soviets' penchant for secrecy, it seems remarkable that these orders were published in the first place; many others were not. But early censorship in Soviet-occupied Germany seems to have been regarded as purely military censorship, and in 1945 neither the Soviets nor their wartime allies felt any need to apologize for instituting such controls.

In the beginning, the biggest problem facing the Soviets was the absence of an apparatus with which to censor the Germans systematically, and it was far too early to transfer these responsibilities to fledgling German agencies. In September 1945, for instance, the deputy foreign minister Andrei Vyshinsky sent Central Committee secretary Georgii Malenkov the draft of a resolution calling for more censors to be attached to the "censoring apparatus" of SVAG.[4] At the time, the "sector for propaganda and censorship," which several weeks later became the propaganda directorate or *Upravleniia propagandy* run by Sergei Tiul'panov, had existed for barely a month, and Soviet censorship was more piece-meal than it was methodical.[5]

The creation of the sector, as its full name attests, was said to serve the purpose of establishing "control over propaganda in the area of press, radio, theaters, movie houses" — specifically, over the four newspapers sponsored by the sector's political parties, but also over radio broadcasts originating in Berlin. The primacy which the Soviets accorded the task of censorship is evident from the fact that the head of the sector, I. F. Filippov, was the deputy director of SVAG's important political division. But censorship needed censors. It was premature to trust Germans (even the Communists) to police themselves. Vyshinsky complained that in spite of several attempts to staff the "censoring apparatus" fully, doing so without the help of the Red Army's political directorate, GlavPURKKA, was impossible. The relevant department of the Central Committee approved only half the requested number of censors before sending the request on to I. V. Shikin, the head of GlavPURKKA.[6]

Of course, it would have been easy to censor without battalions of qualified censors if the Soviets had been interested in simply banning everything. Occupation law certainly provided for the possibility, at any time, of such strict enforcement. Right after the war, the regulations in the Soviet zone were hardly more prohibitive than those in place in the American zone. In fact, the earliest U.S. directives on the control of German "information services" revealed underlying intentions that differed little in principle from Soviet orders and instructions. Consider Directive no. 1 for Propaganda Policy of Overt Allied Information Services (May, 1945). It noted that the "first step of re-education" was to be "limited strictly to the presentation to the Germans," by the Americans, "of irrefutable facts which will stimulate a sense of Germany's war guilt and of the collective guilt for such crimes as the concentration camps."

Nevertheless, the Americans were clearly aware that this information should be skillfully packaged and disseminated in order to avoid alienating the Germans with "overt" allied propaganda. This was all the more important considering that re-education at this juncture aimed at little more than awakening "a sense of collective responsibility for Germany's crimes." This purpose was best served by increasing the "sense of objectivity" by reporting in radio bulletins and newspapers in such a way as to remove "the last vestiges of 'propaganda.'" Therefore, "obvious propaganda cliches, and particularly obvious propaganda headlines will be eliminated." If the information provided by the Americans was tainted by the brush of obvious propaganda, the Germans were thought likely to "transfer their critical attitude from the [Nazi] Propaganda Ministry entirely upon us." It was clearly understood that the first stage of re-education would have the "opposite effect to that intended, if it is permitted even to look like a propaganda campaign." [7]

Directive no. 2 for Information and Control Services was issued a few weeks later. It initiated the process by which "information services" were to be placed in the hands of the Germans themselves. "Genuinely democratic elements" were to be encouraged to "assist in urgent tasks required by the Military Government," and re-education would continue by "differentiating clearly between the active guilt of the criminal [Nazi] . . . and the passive guilt of the people as a whole, which can be atoned for by hard work, national restitution and a change of heart."[8] Directive no. 3, issued on June 28, 1945, set forth "the policy that would enable acceptable non-Nazi Germans to secure licenses for the publication of German-language newspapers." Directive no. 3 "commenced the shifting of emphasis" that was then formulated in the post-Potsdam Directive no. 4 for Control of German Information Services first drafted on August 16, 1945. This directive, "a large step forward from Directive no. 3," expanded the freedom provided German information services by ending the blanket ban on the dissemination of "information" by Germans and accelerating the conversion of overtly American information services to German services that operated under the supervision of the Americans.[9]

The first three directives were issued by the U.S. Army's Psychological Warfare Division (PWD), which "functioned as a special staff division" of SHAEF — Supreme Headquarters Allied Expeditionary Force. When SHAEF was dissolved on July 13, 1945, PWD then became the Information Control Division (ICD), U.S. Forces, European Theater (USFET), before ICD "entered a new stage of its operations," when it was discontinued as a separate staff division of USFET. ICD's responsibilities were transferred to the Office of Military Government (OMGUS) on December 11, 1945. This development marked "the beginning of the long term policy for Germany when the functions of Military Government would be separated from those of the security forces, and information media gradually would be turned over to the Germans." The Information Control Division, both of USFET and OMGUS, was broken into two groups — staff (Plans and Directives, Intelligence Branch, Administrative and Personnel) and operations. Operations was comprised of four branches: press control, publications control, radio control, and film, theater, and music control. In its earliest stage, mid summer of 1945, the "immediate purpose" of licensing Germans to publish newspapers under "Allied supervision" was seen as the "first step in the establishment of what should subsequently become a free, independent, and democratically inclined press."[10]

The Americans' Information Control Division was the closest approximation of the Russian's incipient propaganda directorate, and they had similar origins in the war against the Germans. The Americans referred to their operations as "psychological warfare," whereas the Soviets used the less belligerent, more politically nuanced term "counterpropaganda." The latter was the charge of the 7th Division of the Red Army's political department, GlavPURKKA, and it was largely out of GlavPURKKA that SVAG's propaganda directorate developed.

Throughout occupied Germany, then, "information control" began as strict military censorship. But for the Soviets, censorship existed from the outset as the precondition of Soviet propaganda, and this never changed. The later renaming of SVAG's propaganda directorate to "information directorate" reflected nothing more than a belated Soviet awareness of the importance of public relations. In late December 1946 or early January 1947, a draft report prepared for Stalin by a Central Committee commission that had "examined" the work of the directorate the previous fall recommended that the name be changed to "information" because "propaganda" was discredited in the eyes of the German population due to the use of the word by the fascists.[11] This was something that the Americans had understood from the beginning. The Soviets, by contrast, rarely appreciated how unpopular they were – much less why – and changing the name of an agency treated only a symptom, rather than the root cause of their bad image. Indeed, in searching for the cause of chronic problems with their own policies, the Soviets routinely looked to an improvement of "our Soviet propaganda" – *nasha sovetskaia propaganda* – for answers. The head of the Soviet zone "information bureau" worried in summer 1946 that

> our propaganda exhibits extraordinarily blunt qualities, hits you right over the head. Just as at the front, where to win the war we had to switch from the practice of grouping all our forces along a line at the front and learn techniques of maneuvering in our military conduct, in the area of propaganda, too, we must reject dogmatic assertions and the primitive practice of boasting. We must develop more subtle and intelligent propaganda – acquainting the reader without his noticing it with the superior qualities of our social system.[12]

The advice was never followed. At any rate, by early 1947 the die was cast. Indeed, the year brought a marked increase in the pitch of Soviet propaganda produced by both Soviets and German Communists. A full-blown propaganda war with the Allies, the Americans especially, then erupted in fall 1947 and never subsided. In the meantime, a draft report evaluating SVAG's propaganda directorate which was prepared for Stalin in early 1947 criticized it for shortcomings all subsumed under the heading of "propaganda.." According to the report, the directorate had no "general plan of propaganda based on long-term thinking." It had poorly organized the popularization of the "politics of the Soviet government toward Germany," failed to engage in "propagandistic work exposing the imperialist essence of English and American policies toward Germany," and did not organize "systematic and effective counter-propaganda." Although SVAG's propaganda directorate "controlled" (censored) thirty-seven newspapers, five radio stations, and fifty-two journals, it had made "insufficient" use of them for an "active struggle with anti-democratic and anti-Soviet propaganda," and paid inadequate attention to operative methods of work (*neoperativno*).[13]

Eighteen months after the war's end, with the disappointing elections of fall 1946 behind them, the Soviets' concern with the results of their own policy is understandable enough. But they habitually dealt with such disappointments by looking to "improve" the general methods of censorship and propaganda that they were accustomed to using back home. The fact is that the Soviets had been hamstrung from the beginning. They knew they needed to sell themselves, the occupation, their policies, and in a broad sense, even their system of government to the local population — even while, using the German Communists as their mouthpiece, they publicly eschewed the "imposition" of a Soviet system upon Germany. Accordingly, the Soviets and their local allies needed to stifle many of their customary inclinations and play at being democrats. But democracy precluded the necessary consolidation of power in Soviet-occupied Germany, and without a consolidation of power by the German Communist and Socialist Unity Party (KPD; SED), the Soviets probably felt that they had no German policy — whatever their broader objectives may have been. Robert Murphy, the American political advisor, summed up this contradiction in early 1946:

> The record of the German communist Party is not particularly attractive. Yet under our policy in this and other areas we classify Communist parties as democratic parties. When the Allied decision to allow the Red Army to capture Berlin was made I am not sure that the Combined Chiefs of Staff paid much attention to the political implications of such a course. We arrived in Berlin to set up shop as participants in the Military Government of the Greater Berlin area over two months after the capture of the city. In the interval, Soviet military authorities had laid a substantial foundation of a city administration along lines which they described as democratic. German exiles who had been trained in Moscow, German Communists released from concentration camps, and others of Soviet preference were placed in public office. It was obvious that this would happen. We discussed this when you were at Potsdam. It may be due to natural lethargy but I cannot work myself up into a lather about it. The Red Army used strong-armed methods placing its chosen people in public office and in operating Military Government generally. . . . However, that does not mean necessarily that in so doing the Soviets endeared themselves to the hearts of the population and carved out a permanent political situation favorable to them. The actions of the Red Army in the area created more intense hatred for the Soviet Union on the part of the Germans if such a thing is possible. You know that [the imposition of public officials] on a people by a foreign occupying power . . . eventually seems to have repercussions. The Soviet technique in all these things seems to me exceedingly primitive, and in their obvious determination to

impose a single party structure I think they will meet with failure and I believe that their efforts delude but few.[14]

The Soviets had every reason to worry about the sullied image of the KPD-SED. The connection between the SED and SVAG, read one internal Soviet report, was too "conspicuous"; the Party often presented itself to the "masses" as some kind of an intermediary between ordinary Germans and the occupation forces, an intermediary able to advance German interests through supplication to the proper Soviet authorities. "This lowers the authority of the SED as a national Party and nourishes reactionary elements in their efforts to spread every conceivable kind of slander about the SED as if it were an 'agent (*agentura*) of Moscow,' etc." The Soviets understood that the SED's liaison with them was deleterious both to the Party and Soviet policy, although they could not dispense with this liaison without reducing their policy to shambles. The Soviets attempted to solve this dilemma by calling for an increase in the propaganda used to bolster the myth that the SED was a German national Party. "It is necessary to emphasize the national character of the Party to a far greater extent."[15]

Later American analyses, by the way, were less sanguine about the future than Murphy's. True enough, as Murphy had conjectured, few were "deluded" by the show of democracy. But Soviet tactics contributed to the Allies' doubts that they could arrive at a *modus vivendi* with Stalin. American intelligence put the case succinctly in late 1947:

> The totalitarian principles that begin to penetrate into the last corners of every-day life in the Soviet zone are even more evident when the so-called "democratic" or "non-political organizations" are considered. Their real functions form a sharp contrast to the terms by which they are officially described, because these organizations are anything but democratic, they are highly political. . . . The entire structure is reminiscent of the Nazi Party with its affiliated organizations for special fields, such as charity, youth, women, etc. (Actually, the Nazis imitated to a large degree patterns invented by the Soviets.) One of the main differences is that the Nazis had a much heavier hand; they boasted about the controls they were exercising over all ways of life, while the Communists seek to hide the power which they actually wield.[16]

Referring to the "Sovietization of the eastern zone," which had been achieved to "a considerable degree" and which "Soviets and Communists are doing everything within their power to make . . . irrevokable and final," this report concluded: "In the last analysis, all the problems dealt with in this report boil down to these fundamental questions: Whether cooperation is possible with the Soviets, and to what degree; and, if cooperation is possible, what safeguards are required in order to obtain true Russian cooperation instead of Communist sabotage under the cover of pretended cooperation."[17]

The Soviets went about the establishment of censorship in Soviet-occupied Germany in ways designed to sustain the facade of democracy while ensuring their control of German public life. The earliest known SVAG order involving regulations that fit the description of censorship actually predated formation of the sector for propaganda and censorship. The order was numbered 19, dated August 2, 1945, and linked the "improvement of the work of publishing houses and print shops" to the "establishment of controls governing their activity." Order no. 19 required the registration of all printing presses by their owners or operators with the appropriate Soviet commanders at all levels of local administration by August 10, and allowed for the publication of every imaginable kind of printed matter — newspapers, books, journals, posters, leaflets, appeals, and Party literature — only by publishers and printers in possession of SVAG's approval.[18]

Several days later, on August 18, 1945, the occupation administration drew up Order no. 29, which provided for the creation of the "sector for propaganda and censorship within the political division of the Soviet Military Administration in Germany." Though the sector assumed responsibility for a broad range of activities that conformed more or less to the sweeping Soviet definition of propaganda, the order itself spoke only of its duties as an office of censorship. Nothing was said about the extensive supervisory responsibilities that the soon-to-be directorate would perform in virtually every area of German political and cultural life. The order began by reassigning all existing SVAG activities related to central censorship to the new sector and, in the provinces and states, to the political divisions of SVAG's regional headquarters. Censors were to be appointed and assigned to the Berlin city and district commanders by August 25, and "chief censors and censors" were to be attached to the SVA administrations at the provincial level and in larger cities. Their duties were defined as the "censoring in advance" (*Vorzensur* or *predvaritel'naia tsensura*), as opposed to the post-publication censorship practiced by the Americans, of all printed matter zone-wide and in Berlin and the regulation of all printing shops. The new organization's further tasks included the establishment of complete control over the work of radio stations; the complete regulation of cinema; and censorship prior to release of all news issued by German agencies. Finally, the repertoires of all theaters and cabarets had to pass "the censors."[19]

It bears repeating that Order no. 29 said nothing about the assignment of any of these responsibilities to German agencies or offices. Indeed, the order that established central administrations of German self-government in Soviet-occupied Germany, no. 17, had been drawn up only a short time before, on July 27, 1945. This order provided for creation of the DVV or education administration, headed by Paul Wandel, and formally charged Wandel with supervising the public school system, "artistic activity," museums, theatres and cinemas, as well as exercising authority over other "performances" and over all "scientific and cultural educational institutions [*Aufklärungs-institutionen*]."[20] Unlike SVAG Order no. 29, Order no. 17 was published. It did not identify the SVAG division to which Wandel reported nor indicate that the DVV's supervisory responsibilities would be supervised, in turn, by the Soviets. In any event, the sector for propaganda and censorship had a short life, and was reincarnated in the propaganda directorate on October 5, 1945 in accordance with a "decision," No. 2534-679-C, of the Council of People's Commissars. The decision was formalized by secret Order no. 074 issued on October 23, 1945 by Georgii Zhukov, SVAG commander-in-chief and head of Soviet occupation forces in Germany. Sergei Tiul'panov was placed in charge of the adminstration at about the same time.

Orders were one thing, however, implementation was quite another, and it took considerable time to establish systematic control over publishing in Soviet-occupied Germany. The earliest references to the future work of a central office overseeing publishing date back to internal administrative memoranda of October-November 1945. One of the earliest extant reports indicated that, with few exceptions, publishing firms had permission neither to have books printed nor to engage in any other kind of activity. [21] A memorandum circulated in mid-October 1945 by the the head of the DVV's office of press and publishing, Lothar von Balluseck, noted that there was not yet any "central control of press and publishing within the Soviet zone of operations" and that some kind of "central solution" was "urgently necessary." Problems were arising due to the fact that certain publishers in outlying areas had apparently received some kind of authorization to begin work.[22] Though Balluseck's memorandum is not explicit, the memorandum seems to suggest that these "authorizations" had been issued by Soviet authorities in the provincial or state offices of SVAG who had yet to receive any specific instructions from their central headquarters in Berlin-Karlshorst and were improvising in accordance with the local authority granted them by Order no. 29.

On December 13, 1945, Balluseck outlined a course of action for the commencement of the publication of books and journals in Soviet-occupied Germany, and sent his proposals to Karlshorst. The DVV would first request from the provincial and state administrations a list of those publishing firms whose reactivization should be undertaken in a "politically and culturally favorable way." These firms would then be organized in an official group overseen by an executive board that would require the approval of both DVV and SVAG. This group would then screen all new applications for publishing licenses as well as coordinate and limit the publishing proposals of the individual firms that comprised the group. This would ensure the publication of the "most important literature," though the result of all preliminary screening was to be submitted to the DVV, which would make final decisions in consultation with SVAG. The DVV would then distribute paper and other raw material based on the overriding criteria of need. Balluseck proceeded to enumerate the "top" publishing priorities, broken down according to "fictional and anti-fascist literature," scientific writing, specialized literature, pedagogical material, and journals; and he asked SVAG to set aside a certain percentage of paper available to all publishing houses, including newspaper publishers, for books and journals that fulfilled cultural needs. "In terms of propaganda," he said, "books, journals, and brochures exercise a more lasting influence on the transformation of the German people toward democratic thinking than the daily press alone."[23]

But soon enough, a crisis ensued. In the interim, the Soviets had still been unable to settle on a policy governing the work of publishing houses. Reluctant to license private publishers at all, they first explored alternative approaches such as the group set-up proposed by Balluseck. In January 1946, it appeared as if the Soviets would license only five private publishers and that remaining firms were to be somehow "fused" into one collective enterprise. At the time, this "fusion" seems to have been the only proposal under consideration, although the Soviets deemed it important to maintain businesses with long publishing traditions on the territory of Soviet-occupied Germany and to put "them to use in the reconstruction of cultural life" in the zone.[24]

It seems reasonable to assume that these months of hesitation reflected Soviet uncertainty about how to reconcile the occasionally conflicting needs of "propaganda" and "censorship." The nature of this conflict, by the way, was alluded to in a report on "Soviet propaganda" prepared by SVAG's deputy political advisor, Filippov, for the then deputy foreign minister Solomon Lozovskii. Filippov pointed out that Tiul' panov's propaganda directorate concerned itself with everything imaginable (parties, unions, women's and youth organizations, etc.), just not with propaganda in the customary sense of the word. Although the directorate had a division in charge of the German press, it did not engage in the preparation of "propaganda directives" and was linked to press and radio only by way of censors "who, as is well-known, carry out a different function and do not concern themselves with propaganda."[25] By licensing private publishers, the Soviets probably feared that they risked losing control, and yet propaganda presupposed the existence of firms whose publications could then be influenced positively.

Even after discussions that finally initiated the process of issuing a small number of licenses took place in mid February 1946 between SVAG's Major Davidenko and German officials like Paul Wandel and Wilhelm Girnus (who ran the DVV's overall division of cultural enlightenment),[26] the situation remained precarious. The problem was certainly exacerbated by SVAG's self-defeating habit of assigning administrative responsibility for major regulatory oversight to the DVV and its individual divisions without providing either the necessary resources or policy guidelines. Girnus lamented these impediments and related woes in a letter to Walter Ulbricht written about this time. The DVV's draft statutes spoke of its responsibility for the Soviet-zone press, he said, but SVAG had not gotten around to approving the personnel lists submitted, and the exact nature of the duties remained unclear. But Girnus was especially upset at SVAG's procrastination in the matter of Soviet-zone publishing. There was a real risk of a full-blown catastrophe because the availability of licenses in the Western zones had led to the flight of a number of businesses already. All the while, SVAG continued to insist that private publishers would *not* be given operating licenses, whereas Girnus emphasized that some private initiative ought to be permitted as a means of keeping "an instrument in hand for use in exerting influence throughout the other zones."[27]

SVAG finally issued licenses to over a dozen publishing firms between mid-March and early April 1946,[28] and the first German censorship offices came into existence to supervise them. The Kultureller Beirat (KB) began meeting in early summer of 1946 and operated under that name until spring 1951, when the organization's regulatory responsibilities were bequeathed to a "new" agency, the Amt für Literatur und Verlagswesen (AfL or Office of Literature and Publishing).[29] From the beginning, the shortage of raw materials combined with a determination to publish only those books and journals that made obvious contributions to "reconstruction" in Soviet-occupied Germany tended to generate one-sided notions of "necessity" and "urgency." The concept of a "*Dringlichkeitsstufung*," an "urgency" or priority ranking, was considered early on to be a better method of censorship than what seems to have been the only alternative approach, what Balluseck called the "difficult formalism of lists of prohibited authors."[30] A policy of urgency classification which was dictated by a dire paper shortage enabled Soviet authorities to suppress undesirable books without imposing a categorical ban. The "propaganda" advantages of this more subtle approach are clear.

Books were regarded as a way of inculcating into ordinary Germans a "consistently democratic world view, based upon a scientific foundation," and meeting the need for such books presupposed the complete reorganization of the publishing trade with respect to its "new, educational responsibility." Publishing licenses had to be closely examined, therefore, and themselves ranked according to the "degree of urgency," as part of the process of "unifying the publishing trade." "Influencing" the publishing trade and "control of its development" was next on the agenda, and was to be achieved by "consultation" and the careful scrutiny of all publication plans.[31]

References to a Kultureller Beirat, a cultural advisory council, first appear in memoranda drawn up in April and May 1946. According to these, Balluseck would remain as overall head of the DVV's office of publishing, but be otherwise involved mostly in the operation of the new agency. A man by the name of Alfred Frommhold remained in charge of the prescreening of publishing house licenses and the preparation of recommendations for issuance sent for final dispensation to SVAG. But it is important to remember that neither the DVV nor any other German agency had the right to make final decisions and actually license publishing firms until after the formation of the German Democratic Republic. Much the same was true of the early prerogatives, or lack of them, granted the Kultureller Beirat. Even with a favorable recommendation from the KB, books still required an individual SVAG license before they could be published. The organization's powers were therefore severely limited; and for quite some time, it did little more than prescreen for SVAG and prepare tentative recommendations based on determinations of "urgency."[32] Positive recommendations were then sent to SVAG, which issued permission for the publisher to begin work. Even then, the Soviets required that additional final permission be secured prior to the actual job of printing. Such were the "advisory" duties of the new German censors, whose office was approved by the SVAG on or about May 24, 1946 (no SVAG order officially authorizing formation of the KB was located among DVV files).

The Kultureller Beirat held its first meeting on June 3, 1946.[33] Six months later, it was on the verge of disintegration. The crisis had its origins in a collusion of unfavorable factors: SVAG's continuing reluctance to license firms in the first place; the bureaucratic ineptitude of the Kultureller Beirat in dealing with proposals and plans submitted by approved presses; the interminable additional delays encountered in waiting for SVAG to render a final decision on those recommendations passed along to Karlshorst; and the crippling effects of paper shortages in the case of those books that managed to surmount the aforementioned obstacles. Ironically, the resolution of one problem – an increase in the numbers of operating licenses issued by SVAG – exacerbated the others because the Kultureller Beirat was then even less able to keep up with the influx of manuscripts due to the licensing of more firms. The number of submissions to the KB doubled between December 1946 and the end of the first half of 1947.[34]

This general crisis led to a major reevaluation of the activity of the Kultureller Beirat in early 1947. In December of the previous year, the KB had actually suspended its activities altogether.[35] Ironically, the Soviets responded to the crisis by agreeing to an expansion of the KB's responsibilities, only to withhold again the support necessary to do the job "right." SVAG Order no. 25, dated January 25, 1947, was issued to govern the expanded role of the Kultureller Beirat in matters of publishing in Soviet-occupied Germany. The order itself referred to the

KB by a name that actually characterized its purpose more accurately than the old designation. Although the agency was always known as the cultural advisory council, the order spoke of a "council for ideological questions connected with publishing in the Soviet occupation zone of Germany" and described its purpose as the "control of the ideological content of literature published in the Soviet zone of occupation as well as all publishing activity."[36] This description was misleading only in the sense that the KB did *not* receive from SVAG the authority to issue new licenses to publishing houses; its new responsibilities went no further than the authority to evaluate and approve for publication those books and lists of projects submitted to it by publishers. Order no. 25 thus required that the previous SVAG controls over publishing, Order no. 19 of August 2, 1945, be replaced by new ones; and this occurred in Order no. 90, which eliminated most SVAG "censorship in advance" by the SVAG on April 17, 1947.[37] Soviet censorship in advance, however, was merely replaced by German censorship in advance on the basis of "urgency."

Order no. 25 also provided for a larger office of permanent employees funded with a budget adequate to the job. But the actual implementation of the order again conflicted with its original provisions, and the Kultureller Beirat ended up in no better a position to do its job following the expansion of its authority than before. By mid-1947, inadequate paper supplies had reduced the agency's operations to an absurdly low level. During the second quarter of 1947, the KB screened 900 publishers' plans or proposals and distributed 300 tons of available paper. The problem was that 300 tons satisfied no more than 30% of the raw material requirement of *approved* proposals.[38] Still, the Kultureller Beirat limped along, with private discussions about its internal mandate taking place that (at least in part) welcomed the opportunity to make a political virtue out of the scarcity of paper supplies. In November 1947, Frommhold told an assembly of Party people and administrators that the publication of books and periodicals was "a means of ideologically influencing the people," and refering to the contradictory presence of private publishing houses doing business in Soviet-occupied Germany with valid licenses, he explained that the Kultureller Beirat existed to oversee their operations and prevent them from publishing according to their own whims. Because the KB made decisions that were influenced by the availability of paper, Frommhold said, the organization had made "a virtue out of the vice of insufficient raw materials" and subjected all Soviet-zone publishing houses to what he called "sensible planning that takes our special circumstances into account."[39]

Three months later, in March 1948, the Kultureller Beirat suffered yet another crippling blow — a planned reduction in the size of its main office staff that would have made an impossible situation still worse.[40] At roughly the same time, new discussions began about the future of the Kultureller Beirat that apparently developed out of a preliminary decision by SVAG to issue yet another set of guidelines concerning the activities of publishers and printing presses. The only noteworthy aspect of these internal discussions about an "office of censorship," the proposed Deutsche Kommission für das Verlagswesen, was the connection made between the success of the two-year plan passed in summer 1948 and the publication of literature that met both the needs of economic reconstruction and cultural progress while furthering the process of ideological consolidation. The references to "censorship" here, combined with the emphasis upon literature, in particular, as a means of "propaganda," underscore the linkage between the two objectives.

These goals, however, presupposed the existence of a "central ideological planning and regulatory apparatus" capable of transforming the publishing trade into a "usable instrument."[41] But no measures were taken to facilitate this transformation, apparently because the Soviets still objected. According to Wandel, "a representative of SVAG's office of culture and education" vigorously opposed the proposed "new arrangement," which called for attaching the publishing commission to the DVV, and insisted that "an office of censorship modeled after GLAVLIT" — the Soviet censorship bureaucracy — be set up instead, either independently or "within the ministry of the interior." This move would have made censorship a responsibility of the police. According to the Soviet officer, the DVV would be neither sufficiently "independent" nor "strict enough in its censorship activity." As late as November 17, 1949, more than a month after formation of the GDR, SVAG representatives still made it clear to the Germans that Order no. 90 had not been rescinded, and this seems to have remained the case until February 1950, when the head of the Soviet Control Commission, General Chuikov, lifted it.[42]

Theatre censorship in Soviet-occupied Germany evolved along parallel lines, albeit much more slowly, because several indirect approaches were tried first in an effort to avoid the appearance of outright censorship. As in publishing, the Soviets initially were intent on finding German administrative solutions to the problem of what came to be called, euphemistically, "repertory management" (*Spielplangestaltung*) and later manifested reluctance to relinquish fully their right to censor under occupation law. Much like SVAG Orders 19 and 29, an early SVAG instruction, Order no. 51 of September 4, 1945, placed tight restrictions on all undertakings associated with the "reopening and activity of artistic institutions in the Soviet occupation zone of Germany."[43] While Order no. 29, which had established the sector for propaganda and censorship, limited the description of its authority to censor all publishing and stage activity to a simple statement,[44] Order no. 51 addressed specific issues of implementation, set forth the various levels of both German administrative and Soviet occupation authority, and delegated explicit responsibilities to the local administrative or regulatory apparatus.

Order no. 51 embodied much of the thinking which linked propaganda and censorship when it called for the liberation of art from Nazi, racist, military, and "other reactionary ideas and tendencies," but promptly added that artistic means should be utilized actively "in the struggle against fascism and for the reeducation of the German people in the sense of a consequent democracy." Blanket prescriptions then followed that required the registration of all types of theaters and musical ensembles in the Soviet sector of Berlin with SVAG's educational division (not the sector for propaganda and censorship), following recommendation by the DVV. The same theaters, along with varieté and popular music stages, cabarets and their repertoires, had to be registered by SVAG in the provinces, states, and counties, and by the Soviet military commander in cities and localities. Administrative and artistic directors were also required to register personally with SVAG at all administrative levels of the zone, as were acting troupes and musical groups, all following "recommendation by the organs of the local German administrative offices." Moreover, all art societies and associations that had existed prior to the end of the war were considered dissolved as of May 9,1945, and permission for any new organizations would be granted by SVAG's educational division, again, "upon recommendation by the Zentralverwaltung für Volksbildung or its local offices."

Likewise, tight restrictions were placed on art exhibits throughout Soviet-occupied Germany and in the Soviet sector of Berlin. These were under a blanket ban unless the DVV or its local offices approved them in advance. Paul Wandel, as head of the DVV, was ordered to prepare a list of all persons active in theater, music, dance, film, and the graphic arts, and to supply SVAG's educational division with the names of appropriate, presumably pre-screened candidates for the administrative and artistic directorships of all theaters and musical groups active in the Soviet sector of Berlin. Finally, Wandel was expected to submit the repertory plans of all theaters for approval, though these instructions were scarcely feasible at the time. The man in charge of SVAG's educational division, Zolotukhin, remained responsible for the overall implementation of Order no. 51, and city and county military commanders were instructed to supervise all stage activity and exhibitions. No performance was allowed without approval by the relevant SVAG authorities.[45]

Actual implementation was a different matter. The German agencies were overwhelmed by the immensity of the task, and the DVV itself seems to have been hobbled by its lack of authority to issue central mandates governing the policies and procedures to be followed by its ministerial counterparts at the state and provincial level. Stage censorship during the first year and a half after the war's end seems to have occurred largely on an ad hoc basis. Discussions probably took place when the need arose between local or regional Soviet zone censors and their German counterparts; and these discussions may very well have been limited to the scheduled performance of a specific play. No evidence has surfaced of what soon became the primary objective — the "management" or "planning" of any given theater's seasonal repertory.

Thus, prospects were not very good for the rapid realization of centralized control of repertoires. True, inspired by the crackdown on "foreign" plays being performed on Soviet stages, which began in August 1946 with the issuance of a Central Committee edict that demanded a greater number of contemporary, topical Soviet plays, the SED tried to pressure Soviet zone stage producers and directors into a more "voluntary" form of compliance by publishing countless articles criticizing both foreign plays and those considered insufficiently "topical" in a narrow political sense. But without censorship to back it up, this kind of propaganda was limited in its ability to influence repertoires.

Not until late 1946 were major initiatives first planned by the Party, the DVV, and SVAG in hopes of developing a more coherent system of control over performing theaters. These internal discussions fell into two general categories. The first was the question of licensing theaters altogether, or, far more likely, a future relicensing of those presumably operating on the basis of early SVAG approval or registration. The second category of discussion was the entire range of organizational questions and political intentions associated with formation of so-called people's theaters, *Volksbühnen*, in Berlin and throughout Soviet-occupied Germany. Licensing itself must have occurred up through late 1946 more or less in conformity with the general registration provisions of SVAG Order no. 51. But in December 1946, there was talk internally of an impending new SVAG "Theater Order" apparently intended to cover the approval of stage repertories as well as the naming of theater directors, and may also have included licensing provisions. It is possible that the Soviets ultimately intended to transfer their authority to license theater operations centrally to an appropriate German agency. When the subject of a new order was first broached, however, the man in charge of these matters within the DVV, Herbert Volkmann, concluded that the Soviets had already changed their minds about releasing it and would probably not do so in the current draft version known to Volkmann.[46]

Nothing more is known about this "Theater Order." Volkmann's remarks allow only for the inference that the order would have centralized broad authority in the offices of the DVV and viewed centralization as a necessary step in securing more effective control. But no SVAG order was issued, although discussions took place within the DVV during the first several months of 1947 about a new "theater law" to govern the licensing of theaters. These talks used regulations apparently passed in Saxony, as well as a "version" of a similar Thuringian draft, as the basis for discussion of a document containing provisions that the DVV presumably planned to recommend to the newly elected state and provincial governments for final enactment as legislation.[47] The draft under discussion in the Berlin offices of the DVV in the spring of 1947 proposed that all professional theater and stage organizations would be licensed by the state or provincial ministries of culture and education. Such licenses would be granted according to the following criteria: 1) "recognition of public need"; 2) "personal and political reliability, suitability, and economic efficiency of the applicant and his deputy"; 3) "composition of the ensemble and all other personnel from elements supportive of reconstruction in terms of a democratic view of the state"; and 4) "shaping of the repertory in accordance with democratic renewal, the elimination of kitsch, as well as anything politically and artistically questionable."[48]

None of the provisions allowed for "repertory planning" as such. However, if enacted by all state or provincial parliaments, the new law may have been intended to replace the previous requirement that all theaters be "registered" with SVAG. The automatic expiration of old licenses three months after the passage of the new law, thereby obliging the theaters to reapply and be reassessed according to the new criteria, implied that politically problematical theaters would fall in line when threatened with the cancellation of their licenses. The draft law was accepted in its final version by the state and provincial ministers during their meeting in the offices of the DVV on June 3-4, 1947.[49] Its actual fate is not certain, however; acceptance by the state and provincial ministers meant only that the "law" would have been slated for formal introduction as draft legislation in the local parliaments. Whatever became of the proposed legislation, there are no indications that a systematic examination of Soviet-zone theaters in accordance with the criteria set forth in the "theater law" took place during the next few years.

The discussions that led to acceptance of a draft theater law at ministerial meetings held in the offices of the DVV paralleled efforts through late spring 1947 to create a much different kind of system with the potential for influencing repertory plans throughout the zone. *Volksbühnen*, "people's theaters," never approached in actuality the original idea — the creation of a centralized organization, the League of People's Theaters, to coordinate the activities of corresponding smaller outfits set up within all theaters as distinct ensembles with a separate repertory or as something akin to "repertory" advocacy groups within these otherwise independent theaters. The idea was so slow in development, and such a League was so cumbersome in practice, that it died a natural death well before *Volksbühnen* offered themselves as a viable substitute for some form of central censorship. The modestly successful establishment in various cities of *Volksbühnen* with their own acting troupes, management, and stages was a separate development because, whatever political purpose they served, it was limited to their own repertories and activities.

The early history of the *Volksbühne* illustrates the improvisational nature of certain cultural-political processes in Soviet-occupied Germany. In this case, SVAG and the SED, working in tandem and together with the DVV, tried to arrange for a solution that avoided the thorny issue of a more direct intervention in the affairs of Soviet-zone theaters. This approach failed. Suffice it to say that the Soviets were behind the idea of a "people's theater movement" from its inception, in December 1946 and January 1947; that the idea probably resulted from a growing awareness that the mere approval or disapproval of individual plays by local SVAG censors and their German administrative counterparts did not allow for centralized planning; and that the entire undertaking probably fizzled because such indirect forms of censorship lacked the effectiveness of direct administrative intervention.[50]

Scarcely had the people's theater "movement" gotten underway in the spring of 1947 when other suggestions began to appear in internal memoranda. These proposals more accurately fit the description of centralized oversight. Even then, they fell short of outright censorship by Germans themselves and would not have altered the fact that banning or sanctioning a play remained a SVAG prerogative for almost three more years. Under the circumstances, some kind of hybrid system of oversight was probably the most that could have emerged from these particular discussions in 1947 and early 1948, and the introduction of real "repertory planning," using SVAG or German censorship organs not merely to obstruct certain performances, but to promote others, remained as yet unrealized. Censorship was always more effective in prohibiting then promoting. Banning a performance could not guarantee its replacement with a politically more desirable production. Simple censorship offered no possibility for long-range, strategic planning in the design of a theater's entire repertory and could not speak to the related issue of the centralized coordination of repertories throughout *all* of Soviet-occupied Germany. Nothing like that existed, though tentative proposals for something more akin to centralized oversight were drawn up in early 1948 in connection with the suggested formation of "artistic advisory boards." Set up within the state ministries of culture and education, these would have reported directly to a central "artistic council" or *Kunstbeirat* attached to the DVV.[51] The establishment of these boards, especially the top-tier committee within the DVV, would have required the issuance of a specific SVAG Order; and the matter was indeed discussed with the Soviets.[52] The board proposed was not referred to as an office of censorship, but rather was considered an approach necessary to "improve" the quality of stage performances.

The job of "improving" theaters in Soviet-occupied Germany would fall, then, to the main artistic board set up within the DVV. It was to be charged with "enhancing the artistic niveau of the theaters in the sense of making them progressive in a way appropriate to the times and of putting them more directly into the service of democratic renewal." The board would function therefore as an "advisory and regulatory institution in all matters pertaining to repertorial issues" and pay close attention to the development of "artistically and ideologically usable young talent." The new group would screen performances for possible "militaristic or Nazistic tendencies"; evaluate "foreign and domestic amateur theater productions"; give all such evaluations to SVAG "censors"; and prepare something called "certificates of acceptability" for use by all Berlin road companies traveling throughout the zone. These evaluations, along with the necessarily positive opinion of what this document called the "central office of military censorship," meant that once a SVAG order activated plans for the new board, no regional or local Soviet office of censorship, nor any German agency, would be authorized to interfere by requiring yet another evaluation.[53]

There is no evidence that these boards were ever established. Certainly, no such committee ever came into existence within the DVV. In fact, by the spring of 1948 indications are that new initiatives were under discussion, possibly in connection with the preparation of the Party's two-year plan. But these initiatives never materialized. As a consequence, the establishment of a central system of repertory control receded still further into the future. But discussions addressing the problem of "program planning and improving the artistic niveau of theaters in the Eastern zone," did occur after the Party released its two-year plan on July 16, 1948. At a large-scale conference of some sixty stage managers on July 29, 1948, with SVAG's chief cultural officer Alexander Dymschitz in attendance, it was decided to form an entirely new organization called the *Büro für Theaterfragen* or Office of Theater Affairs. This office may have been a reincarnation of the earlier idea of an artistic board designed to set repertory policy. Many of the documents generated by the organization cite as its responsibilities the oversight of theaters throughout the zone. There was also talk of a "repertory commission" to be set up within the new office. A representative of the SED's division of culture and education attended one meeting, for example, and suggested that such a commission be established within the new office in order "to coordinate" the repertoires of theatres in the Soviet sector of Berlin.[54] But for the time being, any such repertory commission would, strictly speaking, have remained advisory because no German organization had yet received the authority from the Soviets to go any further. The commission would offer only "help and advice" to stage managers in the development of their repertories.[55] As usual, SVAG most likely remained reluctant to place "censorship in German hands";[56] and for the time being, according to these documents, censorship appears to have occurred as before. The managers of theaters throughout the zone discussed matters directly with the local offices of Soviet military government.[57]

Discussions continued throughout 1949 and right up to the formation of the German Democratic Republic in October 1949. In a DVV planning document dated February 21, 1949, "creation of a German office of theater censorship (consultation with the information division of the SVAG)" was listed as a top priority.[58] But as late as November 1949, no decision had been reached as to whether the *Volksbühne* or the office of theater affairs would assume responsibility for "repertory management" — this in spite of periodic talk of what the Germans should do in the event that the job of "theater censorship" was indeed assigned to them.[59] That the Soviets finally relinquished the authority to supervise the repertories of all East-German theaters in connection with the formation of the GDR,[60] giving up their legal right to approve or ban the performance of individual plays, did not necessarily solve the problem because a specific agency or organization still had to be duly constituted and authorized. This process again took time. The original idea was to create a "repertory commission" comprised of representatives of the Ministerium für Volksbildung (or MfV, the former DVV), the SED, the union, and the office of theater affairs.[61] This is basically what happened, too, though centralized censorship, even as a mere organizational possibility, was still many months away. Plans for the first quarter of 1950 called for "taking over control of theater programming with the goal of improving theater programs"; and the MfV intended to propose formally to the new government that it create a specific commission to operate as a "regulatory organ for dramatic literature performed on stage."[62] Still nothing had happened as late as September 1950; a decision had yet to be made whether the commission should be "anchored" in the MfV or be independent.[63]

The repertory commission finally began its existence around November 1950, when the MfV sent out a circular informing theaters throughout East Germany that the new commission was responsible for "advising all theaters in terms of planning a progressive repertory."[64] "Advising" then became central control and censorship with the issuance of "directive no. 99," dated April 2, 1951, which provided all East German theaters with binding instructions. All repertories, including changes contemplated at any time during the season, required the approval of the MfV ("repertory commission"). No play could be accepted, rehearsed, or performed without prior ministerial approval, and programs for the entire new season were to be submitted to the repertory commission of the MfV in Berlin by May 31, 1951.[65]

Notes

1. For detailed discussions of a range of issues pertaining to Soviet-occupied Germany, see Norman Naimark, *The Russians in Germany. A History of the Soviet Zone of Occupation, 1945-1949 (Cambridge: Harvard University Press, 1995), and my book, The Politics of Culture in Soviet-Occupied Germany, 1945-1949 (Stanford: Stanford University Press).*

2. A good example is the 12-page report on the operations of Radio Leipzig, OI-VA/76, 25 August 1947. See National Archives (NA), Record Group (RG) 260/7/52/20/3-6/715, 1-12.

3. See Jan Foitzik's discussion of SVAG orders *Inventar der Befehle des Obersten Chefs der Sowjetischen Militäradministration in Deutschland (SVAG) 1945-1949. Offene Serie.* (Munich: K.G. Sauer, 1995).

4. Vyshinsky to Malenkov, early September 1945. Russkii Tsentr Khraneniia i Izucheniia Dokumentov Noveishei Istorii (RTsKhIDNI), Fond 17, opis' 125, delo 354, l. 51.

5. See the report, signed by Vladimir Semenov and Filippov, "Otchet o rabote sektora propagandy i tsenzury Politicheskogo otdela SVAG s 15 iiulia po 15 oktiabria 1945 g.," in *SVAG. Upravlenie propagandy (informatsii) i S.I. Tiulpanov 1945-1949. Sbornik dokumentov* [cited hereafter as *SVAG*]. ed. Bernd Bonewitsch, Gennadii Bordiugov, Norman Naimark (Moscow: "Rossiia Molodaia," 1994), 137.

6. Vyshinsky to Malenkov, early September 1945, RTsKhIDNI, Fond 17, opis' 125, delo 354, l. 51.

7. SHAEF. Psychological Warfare Division. May, 1945. Directive No. 1 For Propaganda Policy of Overt Allied Information Services." NA, RG 260/7/52/30/6/454.

8. SHAEF. Psychological Warfare Division. May 28, 1945. Directive no. 2 For Information and Control Services. In ibid.

9. For Directive no. 3, see History. Information Control Division. Office of Military Government (U.S.). May 8, 1945 – June 30, 1946; and SHAEF. Information Control Division. Directive no. 4 for Control of German Information Services. In ibid.

10. History. Information Control Division, in ibid.

11. See "Proekt zapiski komissii TsK VKP(b) I.V. Stalinu o rabote Upravleniia propagandy SVAG [no later than December 25, 1946]." In *SVAG*, 197.

12. Bespalov, "O nashei propagande v Germanii," July 15, 1946, RTsKhIDNI, f. 17, o. 125, d. 392, l. 123.

13. "Proekt zapiski komissii TsK VKP(b) I.V. Stalinu o rabote Upravleniia propagandy SVAG," *SVAG*, 194-95.

14. Murphy to H. Freeman Matthews, 28 March 1946, NA, RG 84/4/61/32/5.

15. See "Nedostatki v rabote Upravleniia Propagandy SVA po rukovodstvu partiiami, zhenskimi, molodezh-nami i dr. organizatsiiami," RTsKhIDNI, Fond 17, opis' 128, delo 153, ll. 62-66.

16. "Special Intelligence Summary. The Other Zones of Germany. Part II. Political Developments in the British, French and Russian zones," November 22, 1947. NA, RG 260/52/28/4-5/b. 156, S32-33.

17. Ibid., S37

18. "Zur Verbesserung der Arbeit der Verlage und Druckereien und der Regelung der Kontrolle ihrer Tätigkeit," *Befehle der Sowjetischen Militärverwaltung in Deutschland. Aus dem Stab der Sowjetischen Militärverwaltung in Deutschland.* Sammelheft 1. 1945 (Berlin: SWA-Verlag, 1946), 16-17.

19. Befehl des Obersten Chefs der Sowjetischen Militärischen Administration in Deutschland. Stadt Berlin. 18. August 1945. no. 29. Inhalt: Über die Tätigkeit der Sektion für Propaganda und Zensur der Politischen Abteilung der Sow. Mil. Admn. in Deutschland, Bundesarchiv, Abt. Potsdam, X-1.

20. "Errichtung von deutschen Verwaltungen in der sowjetischen Okkupationszone," *Befehle der Sowjetischen Militärverwaltung in Deutschland,* 34-5; and "Befehl no. 17 der SVAG über die Bildung von deutschen Zentralverwaltungen in der sowjetischen Besatzungszone Deutschlands (Auszug)," *Geschichte des Staates und des Rechts der DDR. Dokumente 1945-1949* (Berlin: Staatsverlag der Deutschen Demokratischen Republik, 1984), 69-70.

21. "Tätigkeitsbericht für September 1945," October 11, 1945, Bundesarchiv, Abt. Potsdam., R-2/896/198.

22. See "Die allgemeine Lage im Presse- und Verlagswesen," October 18, 1945, ibid., R-2/896/196-7.

23. An die Sowjetische Militärverwaltung. Betr. Das Deutsche Verlagswesen in der sowjetischen Besatzungszone, December 13, 1945, ibid., R-2/893-4/9-11.

24. Verlagsabteilung. Aktennotiz. Betr.: Fusionierung nicht zugelassener Verlage mit dem Verlag Volk und Wissen. January 14, 1946, ibid., R-2/896/155.

25. "Zapiska zamestitelia nachal'nika politotdela politsovetnika v Germanii I. Filippova zamestiteliu ministra inostrannykh del S. Lozovskomu o perestroike sovetskoi propagandy v Germanii," May 25, 1946, in *SVAG,* 149.

26. Verlagswesen. Aktennotiz, February 19, 1945, Bundesarchiv, Potsdam, R-2/896/114.

27. Girnus to Ulbricht, "Bericht über die Abt. Kulturelle Aufklärung," February 26, 1946, ibid., R-2/629-30/35-42.

28. See Bericht. Gez. Girnus, undated, ibid., R-2/629-30/44-45.

29. Most of what can be reconstructed on the basis of extant DVV files can be found in Pike, *The Politics of Culture in Soviet-Occupied Germany*, 134-35, 356-75, 512-20, 648-54

30. See Balluseck, Aufgaben der Abteilung "Presse- und Verlagswesen," Bundesarchiv, Abt. Potsdam, R-2/896/190.

31. Abt. Allgemeine Volksbildung. Bericht, November 17, 1945, ibid., R-2/629-30/106.

32. See Verlagswesen. Arbeitsplan, April 4, 1946; and Aufgaben des Kulturellen Beirats. Entwurf!, April 12, 1946, ibid., R-2/896/65-68 and 59-61.

33. Verlagswesen. Aktennotiz. Betr.: Kultureller Beirat, May 24, 1946; Verlagswesen. Arbeitsplan für Juni 1946, 4 June 1946, ibid., R-2/896/45-46.

34. Verlagswesen. Tätigkeitsbericht über das 2. Vierteljahr 1947, June 27, 1947, gez. Frommhold, ibid., R-2/1090/258.

35. Aktenvermerk. Betr.: Arbeitsbedingungen, June 27, 1947, ibid., R-2/1132/109.

36. Befehl des Obersten Chefs der sowjetischen Militäradministration in Deutschland. no. 25. Z 164/47. Inhalt: Über die Einrichtung eines "Rates für ideologische Fragen des Verlagswesens in der sowjetischen Besatzungszone Deutschlands. Zur Sicherung der Kontrolle über den ideologischen Inhalt der in der sowjetischen Besatzungszone Deutschlands erscheinenden Literatur, sowie über die gesamte Verlagstätigkeit," January 25, 1947, ibid., R-2/1055/35-36.

37. See "Über die Tätigkeit von Verlagen und Druckereien/Befehl 90," *Börsenblatt für den deutschen Buchhandel* 30 (1947): 306-7.

38. "Tätigkeitsbericht über das 2. Quartal 1947," June 27, 1947, Bundesarchiv, Abt. Potsdam, R-2/1090/258.

39. "Protokoll der internen Besprechung über Verlags- und Buchhandelsfragen," November 13, 1947, ibid., R-2/1149/67-9.

40. See the vivid description of the situation in Volkmann to Personalbestandskommission bei der Deutschen Zentralfinanzverwaltung, 3 March 1948, ibid., R-2/1007/147-56; Personalbestandskommission bei der Deutschen Zentralfinanzverwaltung an die Deutsche Verwaltung für Volksbildung, March 15, 1948, ibid., R-2/1007/202.

41. "Begründung für die Notwendigkeit zur Errichtung einer deutschen Verlagskommission," ibid., R-2/741/31-32.

42. See Hauptabteilung Kunst und Literatur. Arbeitsbericht Monat Februar 1950, March 3, 1950, ibid., R-2/4775/102.

43. "Über die Wiedererrichtung und die Tätigkeit der Kunstinstitutionen in der sowjetischen Besatzungszone Deutschlands," *Tägliche Rundschau*, September 25, 1945.

44. The relevant provisions in the area of stage censorship read simply that the SVAG sector for propaganda and censorship was to "assume control over the

work of theaters and cabaretts, whose productions are to be scrutinized by censors." See Befehl no. 29, Bundesarchiv, Abt. Potsdam, X-1.

45. See "Über die Wiedererrichtung und die Tätigkeit der Kunstinstitutionen in der sowjetischen Besatzungs-zone Deutschlands," *Tägliche Rundschau*, September 25, 1945.

46. Volkmann to Paul Wandel and Erich Weinert, December 17, 1946, ibid., R-2/51/7.

47. See Konferenz der Minister für Volksbildung aus den Ländern und Provinzen der Sowjetischen Besatzungszone Deutschlands am 18. und 19. Dezember 1946. Beschluß-Protokoll vom 18. Dezember 1946. 5. Lizenzierung von Theatern, ibid., R-2/51/9-10.

48. "Entwurf eines Theatergesetzes der Länder und Provinzen der sowjetischen Besatzungszone Deutsch-lands," Fassumg vom 27.5.47, ibid., R-2/1035/39.

49. "Beschlußprotokoll der Ministerkonferenz," June 3-4, 1947, ibid., R-2/55/10.

50. I tell the story in detail in *The Politics of Culture in Soviet-Occupied Germany*, 333-56, passim.

51. See "Betr.: Volksbühne," January 24, 1948, Bundesarchiv, Abt. Potsdam, R-2/72/43.

52. "Betrifft: Künstlerischen Rat für das Theaterwesen," January 24, 1948, ibid., R-2/72/44.

53. Ibid.

54. See "Protokoll über die Sitzung des 'Berliner Ausschusses,'" July 9, 1949, R-100/900/89.

55. Ibid.

56. See the vague references in "Protokoll über die Kommissionssitzung des Berliner Ausschusses," March 6, 1949 and April 26, 1949, ibid.

57. See "Protokoll der zweiten Tagung des 'Büro für Theaterfragen,'" November 13 and 14, 1948, ibid., R-100/900/89.

58. "Übersicht über den Arbeitsplan für 1949," February 21, 1949, ibid., R-2/1155/77a-77h.

59. "Zur Situation der Volksbühnen-Organisation," November 14, 1949, ibid., R-2/1095/34-9.

60. See "Protokoll über die Tagung des Arbeitsausschusses der Mitglieder des 'Büro für Theaterfragen,'" October 14 and 15, 1949, ibid., R-100/900/3 and 101.

61. Ibid.

62. Hauptabteilung Kunst und Literatur. Arbeitsplan für das 1. Quartal 1950, December 15, 1949; Ministerium für Volksbildung. Arbeitsplan 1. Quartal 1950; Hauptabteilung Kunst und Literatur. Arbeitsbericht Monat März;

Hauptabteilung Kunst und Literatur. Arbeitsbericht April 1950, May 6, 1950, ibid., R-2/4775/41, 46, 83, 91.

63. Sekretariat des Ministers. Protokoll über die Sitzung der Abteilungsleiter am 28.8.50, September 4, 1950, ibid., R-2/2146/62.

64. Ministerium für Volksbildung. HA Kunst und Literatur. Anweisung no. 72, November 13, 1950, ibid., R-2/3994/119.

65. Mfv. HA Kunst. Spielplankommission. Betr.: Spielpläne. Anweisung no. 99, April 2, 1951, ibid., R-2/3994/56/7.

12

The Czech Road to Communism

Igor Lukes

The history of Czechoslovakia spans only three quarters of a century. Its intermittent crises have captured the world's attention, while its decades of humiliation and melancholy have slipped by unnoticed. Thus far, historians specializing in Czechoslovak affairs have tended focus primarily on events that invite attention: President Masaryk's triumphant return to Prague from exile in 1918; the Munich capitulation on September 30, 1938; the Heydrich era in 1941-1942; the Communist terror of the 1950s; and the "Velvet revolution" of 1989. Each of these can be described in rather clear-cut terms. The period from May 1945 to February 1948 is different. It defies any simplistic categorization, for it embodies joy and hope, as well as frustration and failure.[1]

Between May 1945 and February 1948, Czechoslovakia plummeted from the heights of postwar euphoria to the pit of a Kafkaesque totalitarian regime. Some writers have characterized the postwar Czechoslovak crisis as the victorious march of progressive forces to Communism. For them, the Communist coup of 1948 was a domestic affair – the triumph of the Communist Party of Czechoslovakia (CPC) over its bourgeois rivals. Others have viewed the crisis of 1948 and the Communist take-over in February as the rape of Czechoslovak democracy by the Kremlin. Documents obtained from newly opened archives in Prague show that neither approach adequately explains the developments between 1945 and 1948.

I propose to argue the following three points. First, Czechoslovak Communists did much of the dirty work that they typically ascribed to the Kremlin. From April 1945, they controlled the Ministry of Interior, and that alone made them more powerful than all of their democratic rivals put together. Stalin would hardly have hesitated to resort to naked force. But he could afford to limit his involvement to intermittent corrections of Czechoslovakia's direction. Two, Czechoslovakia entered the postwar period prepared for some kind of socialism. Even the most Western-oriented among Prague politicians accepted the primacy of Czechoslovakia's alliance with the Soviet Union. The electoral victory of the CPC in 1946 was neither a coincidence nor a conspiracy. It resulted from circumstances which culminated in the Munich agreement of 1938. Three, the West played a most confusing role in the Czechoslovak crisis of 1948. In March 1946, Winston Churchill's "Iron Curtain" speech incomprehensibly placed sovereign Czechoslovakia, a multi-party democracy, in the same bag as occupied Prussia, Hungary, Bulgaria, Romania, Yugoslavia, as well as with NKVD-brutalized Poland. Later, when the threat of unilateral Communist action in Prague became real, the West illogically expressed the view that Czechoslovakia's democratic tradition would make it impossible for Communists to prevail. When the crisis reached its peak in early 1948, although the battle was still far from over, Western powers began to operate on the assumption that a Communist victory in Prague was a fait accompli.

Causes of Czechoslovakia's Move to the Left

Before World War II, Czechoslovakia had been one of the few countries in Europe which seemed immune to Communist ideology.[2] Yet, in May 1946, the CPC won a stunning electoral victory. In the Czech lands (Bohemia and Moravia), it gained 40.2 percent of the vote (93 seats). The results were no less impressive in Slovakia. Given that the Hlinka fascist party, headed by Jozef Tiso, had lost power only about a year ago, the 30.37 percent (21 seats) won by the Communist Party of Slovakia had to be considered more than adequate.[3]

Overall, the Communist Party won some 38 percent. How did this come about? The Communist Party of Czechoslovakia (CPC) emerged as a revolutionary, internationalist, and Moscow-oriented branch of the Social Democratic Party in May 1921. It was formed officially on October 30, 1921.[4] After the victory of the Bolshevik faction under the leadership of Klement Gottwald in February 1929,[5] the CPC had become a tool of power in the hands of the Kremlin leaders.[6] By the time the Czechoslovak-German crisis culminated in the spring of 1938, the CPC was an integral component of the international strategy of the Stalinist Executive of the Communist International (EKI). On the domestic scene, however, the Party was advancing only slowly toward its revolutionary goals. The Czech egalitarian tradition and the social-mindedness of Czechoslovakia's founders, Tomas G. Masaryk and Edvard Beneš, had deprived the Party of a well-defined political platform.[7] The CPC, according to a confidential police report of November 1936, could boast only some 60,000 registered members, of whom just one sixth paid dues. Of these 10,000, the majority merely paid dues without devoting much time to revolutionary plotting. Despite embracing politically popular measures – such as across-the-board salary increases for various employees and drafted soldiers – the CPC had to rely for its continued existence on regular injections of hard cash from the EKI coffers. According to an intelligence source in Prague, in 1936 the Party received around $5,000 per month from Moscow in order to maintain its apparatus.[8] Considering the EKI's overall financial commitments to revolutionary movements abroad, this was a considerable portion – almost ten percent.[9] The CPC would have been unable to operate without it.

As the threat of Adolf Hitler's Third Reich became more ominous in the 1930s, the CPC increased its visibility on the Czechoslovak political scene by posturing as the only determined anti-fascist force. The Party's membership grew to some 90,000 dues-paying members by the end of June 1937. The CPC attempted to adapt to the ever-changing line established by the Comintern. But the percentage of voters who had cast their ballots for the Party changed little between 1929 (10.2 percent) and 1935 (10.3 percent).[10] It was to remain around 10 percent until the CPC was driven underground shortly after the Munich defeat.

In order to isolate the Prague government and to weaken the value of its alliance with Moscow, based on the Czechoslovak-Soviet treaty of 1935, Josef Goebbels initiated a campaign designed to show that Czechoslovakia was a *Flugzeugmutterschiff* [aircraft carrier] of the Red Air Force. In reality, the country was at the time perfectly free from any danger of becoming a corridor for the advancement of Soviet troops into Europe. It was the Third Reich and its propaganda which changed the situation. Goebbels's campaign painting Czechoslovakia as a haven for various Red conspiracies against European civilization started to legitimize both the idea of Communism and the country which represented it: the Soviet Union. Hitler's policy toward Czechoslovakia was the first virus which attacked the country's immune system protecting it from Communism.

The second factor which weakened Czechoslovakia's defenses was directly linked to the behavior of the Western democracies – especially France and Great Britain – during the Munich crisis. In explicit violation of the terms of the Franco-Czechoslovak Treaty of Mutual Assistance of October 1925, French diplomats pushed president Edvard Beneš toward capitulation to Adolf Hitler. Great Britain had no binding commitments toward Czechoslovakia during the 1930s. Nevertheless, British politicians pursued what turned out to be a policy of retreat and, ultimately, failure. Moreover, Basil Newton, the British envoy in Prague during the crisis of 1938, his predecessor Sir Joseph Addison, and other British diplomats treated president Beneš arrogantly and contemptuously. He never forgot it.

The Franco-British deal with Hitler and Mussolini at Munich horrified most Czechoslovaks. An hour and a half after the Prague Government had accepted the Munich *Diktat,* Beneš met with a group of politicians who came to plead with him against capitulation. The president looked very tired and his eyes were red. The Allies, he said, were "cowards." "Out of fear of Communism, the French and the English will join up with the Germans." Just look at it, said Beneš to his guests, the Munich agreement was signed by four powers – and two of them were Czechoslovakia's "friends."[11]

Conversely, Soviet diplomacy had engaged in a variety of maneuvers in order to create the impression that Moscow stood ready to fight for its Czechoslovak ally come what may. Rudolf Beran of the Republican Party, Beneš's frequent critic from the right side of the political spectrum, pointed out that, in contrast to the rude behavior of the French and British envoys in Prague, the Soviets acted in a sophisticated, enigmatic manner.[12] As it happened, Stalin was not prepared to provide Czechoslovakia with any military assistance during the crisis of 1938.[13] Nevertheless, his behavior toward Czechoslovakia and his courteous treatment of Beneš stood in stark contrast to the policy of appeasement practiced by France and Great Britain. This made a lasting impression on millions of Czechoslovakia's citizens. The same people who had been immunized against Communism by the Masaryk-style philosophy of democracy and equality in social affairs were shocked by the sight of French and British statesmen, whom they had esteemed as the pillars of the Western world, shaking hands with Adolf Hitler at Munich. Unlike the Poles and Hungarians, the Czechs had never been directly involved with Russia. It was, therefore, easy for them to sympathize with the country which brought an end to the string of German victories for which they held France and Great Britain at least partially responsible.

The Munich affair proved to be a godsend for the Communist Party of Czechoslovakia. Klement Gottwald spoke about the Czechoslovak-German crisis on December 26, 1938 before the EKI's Presidium in Moscow. He noted that the CPC had succeeded in drilling into the minds of Czechoslovak citizens that there was a link between the security of their country and the security of the Soviet Union. During the crisis, Gottwald observed, anti-Communism had for the first time become unfashionable and unpatriotic. Party propaganda had managed to persuade the public that hostility towards the CPC meant endangering Czechoslovakia's national security, and that hostility towards the Soviet Union also meant, in the final analysis, endangering Czechoslovakia.[14] As a result of the West's abandonment of Czechoslovakia in the fall of 1938, Beneš and many Czechoslovak citizens started thinking about their country's position in Europe from a new angle. The Munich agreement legitimized the view that "old Europe" was unable to deal with "dynamic" political ideologies, such as Nazism.

It allowed a link between Czechoslovak patriotism and sympathy for Stalin. It set in motion processes which slowly gained momentum and culminated in the electoral victory of the CPC in 1946.

Most Western Europeans – horrified by the prospect of war – were overjoyed by the promise of peace in the fall of 1938. In contrast, Beneš watched with barely concealed delight as the world slid closer and closer to the abyss of war. He believed that the European community was responsible for the rise of Hitler between 1933 and 1939, and that only war would wash away its sins.[15] Even the Franco-British declaration of war on Germany in September 1939 did not satisfy the exiled president. He was convinced that the anti-Hitlerite alliance would have to include the Soviet Union to be complete. Beneš needed to wait until the day Germany attacked Stalin's Soviet Union to see his dream fulfilled. A day later he explained to his staff:

> The events of yesterday gave me great satisfaction, also personal, for everything I had to suffer. This constituted a reparation for Munich. Now a situation exists which I wanted at the time when we should have gone to war . . . It [Hitler's attack on Stalin] is an outstanding satisfaction for our policy; our path was correct. It was not our mistake that others did not understand what needed to be done in September 1938 . . . Now we are all on one side: Russia, England, France . . . and also ourselves as well as Poles and Yugo-slavia.[16]

From the beginning, Beneš was convinced that Hitler was going to fail in his campaign against Russia. The president's colleagues asked whether there was a danger that the Soviet Union would disintegrate. "Russia will hold," replied Beneš. The GPU would be deployed throughout the country and "it will kill anyone who would attempt to carry out a coup d'état."[17] In 1938, Beneš had tried in vain to help forge a broad anti-Hitler alliance of France, Great Britain, the Soviet Union, possibly the United States, and several smaller European countries, including Czechoslovakia. He was delighted that it was coming into existence at last three years later. The experience in June 1941 served to reaffirm his old conviction that he was endowed with the ability to see farther ahead than others.

Barely a month after Hitler's attack on the Soviet Union, Beneš was convinced that after the war Russia would play a decisive role in Central Europe. France had shown itself incapable of leadership, and it would take years before it could recapture its standing among other European states. And Great Britain? The course of the present war would eventually drive it closer and closer to the United States. In five years, Beneš predicted, Great Britain would pull out of Europe. Only two foci of power would be left on the continent: Germany and Russia. Of the two, Germany would be wiped out by allied armies. Ergo,

Russia would be the only European power.[18] In June 1943, Beneš heard from a Soviet diplomat in London that the Soviet Union "will never give up its influence over Central Europe." It is in the Kremlin's interest to keep the German threat at bay, the diplomat said, "and therefore we will stay permanently in Central Europe."[19] It is unclear whether Beneš was pleased to hear this line of thinking but it confirmed his analysis of the future balance of power. In his view, Russia needed Europe and Europe needed Russia.[20]

Beneš's trip to the Soviet Union in 1943 presented an opportunity for a meeting between the president and the leadership of the CPC in Moscow: Klement Gottwald, Jan Šverma, Václav Kopecký, and Rudolf Slansky. In a series of five meetings in December, Beneš predicted that the CPC was going to be "the strongest [party] in the left bloc, and therefore you'll lead. If you play it well," he said, "you'll win."[21] This must have taken the hard-core Bolshevik leaders by surprise. But Beneš went on to say the next day that he had "always conducted propaganda for the Soviet Union and followed the line of friendship with the Soviet Union. Also, he always had a friendlier attitude toward the CPC than toward the [governing] coalition. However, he could not have conducted politics exclusively for 10 percent of [Czechoslovak] citizens, i.e., Communists." This was strong stuff and one can easily imagine that Gottwald and his colleagues were listening with growing disbelief.

During the last meeting, Beneš seemed to have lost perspective. He told Stalin's Czechoslovak Communist allies: "You Communists are doing the best [among Czechoslovak politicians in exile] . . . You've got to be careful not to exaggerate things so that people would not be able to say that everything is being 'bolshevized' in Czechoslovakia too quickly." Gottwald proved to be the more cautious party in this discussion. He responded: "If our agreement is sincere and honorable then Communists and Beneš represent together a force which no one will be able to withstand." The president nodded approvingly.[22]

Some three months after his return from the Soviet Union, on March 23, 1944, the president displayed a great deal of confidence during his conversation with Philip Nichols, the British envoy and future ambassador in Prague, about Czechoslovakia's role in postwar Europe. He stated that thanks to the support he was getting from Moscow, his country's international position had been fully secured. The Foreign Office should take it into consideration since he, Beneš, was no longer willing to get involved in further debates with the British. "The Soviets will definitely support us in everything."[23] This is what the Munich experience had done to Edvard Beneš.[24]

The Czechoslovak Postbellum

In May 1945, Czechoslovakia tried to resume self-government after a six year interruption. On the surface, it appeared that its political life would simply pick up where it had stopped at noon on September 30, 1938. But the circumstances under which the Czechoslovak republic was to return to normal political life were far from normal. Beneš explained his policy in the spring of 1946 to a *New York Times* correspondent. He denied that Russia was driven by a lust for more territory in Central Europe. After all, Stalin had withdrawn his troops from Czechoslovakia. In Czechoslovakia, Austria, and Hungary, said Beneš, conveniently omitting Poland, Russia's aim was "to assure herself that elements hostile to her do not again get the upper hand. I am convinced," Beneš continued, "that when she is satisfied of this she will be ready to retire." And what about Beneš's policy? "Above all we want no trouble between the East and West... we shall do everything in our power to try to interpret them to each other."[25] This was a public formulation of the policy Beneš had in mind when he suggested to Czechoslovak Communists in Moscow during their meetings in late 1943 that he was ready to work with them once the war was over.

Initially, it seemed that this strategy was working. A quick look at Poland, Hungary, Romania, Bulgaria, and the Soviet zone in Germany showed that, for all its imperfections, Czechoslovakia was the only democratic country in the region – at least for the time being. To keep it that way, the reasoning went, the CPC had to be kept satisfied. As long as the CPC felt contented, Stalin would have no reason to interfere in Czechoslovak domestic affairs. True, some democratic politicians, such as Hubert Ripka, Petr Zenkl, Vladimír Krajina, Ota Hora, and Prokop Drtina, would on occasion challenge Klement Gottwald when the Communists openly violated democratic procedures. However, it never occurred to them to try to expel the Communists from power. That would have been perceived as an unwise invitation for an allout Soviet intervention.[26]

It should also be borne in mind that in the spring of 1945, many in Czechoslovakia had come to believe that capitalism – both as a style of economic production and a *Weltanschauung* – had become obsolete. Influential intellectuals saw the world emerging from the ashes of the war in black and white terms: here was Auschwitz and there was Stalingrad. The former was a by-product of a crisis in capitalist Europe of the 1930s; the latter stood for the superiority of socialism. For instance, Václav Černý, whose democratic credentials and dislike of Stalinism could not be doubted by anybody, stated in the fall of 1945 that it was impossible to imagine the world reconstituting itself after the war in any other way but the socialist one. Similarly, Ferdinand Peroutka, another intellectual star of pre-war democratic Czechoslovakia and a concentration camp survivor, saw the laying down of the foundations for Czechoslovakia's socialist development as the main objective of the years ahead.[27] Many among the Czechoslovak political class shared the view expressed by the People's Party (Catholic) leading newspaper: "As we renew our economic and social life it is impossible to return to the capitalist system which prevailed here during the first twenty years of our republic. This war put a period at the end of the capitalist era. We stand on the threshold of a new economic and social order."[28]

Seen from this perspective, the CPC's electoral victory on May 26, 1946 – the Party won 114 out of 300 contested seats – is not surprising. Gottwald responded by pledging on behalf of the Party that in the next elections, scheduled for May 1948, the Communists would win 51 percent of parliamentary seats. But this was easier said than done. In the spring of 1947, Communists were forced to leave governments in France and Italy, and now Czechoslovakia was becoming the central battlefield of the Cold War. The Beneš administration found it more and more uncomfortable to sit astride the fence between East and West. But even in May 1947, Beneš found reason enough to be optimistic. He explained to Bruce Lockhart that Stalin and Gottwald had intended to establish Communism in Czechoslovakia right after the war. However, two years later, the democratic side was in a favorable position. "There were still difficulties, but the Communists were now losing ground, and today he could say that Czechoslovakia was out of the woods." Beneš went on to praise the realism of Czechoslovak Communists. Even Gottwald, the president thought, had his share of Czech patriotism and common sense.[29] And just a few days later, Beneš asked Lockhart to tell the British Foreign Office: "Give us a fair chance in the international field, and we'll pull through."[30] It turned out to be the last meeting of the two old-fashioned diplomats.

It remains unclear whether there ever was ground for this kind of optimism. But if there was, it disappeared with the Marshall Plan affair. In July 1947, Czechoslovakia received an invitation to attend the Paris conference. The attendees were to discuss the so-called Marshall plan for European recovery, announced by Secretary of State George C. Marshall in June 1947. From the Kremlin's perspective, the Marshall plan meant two kinds of danger. First, that the United States was not going to leave Europe as it had done after World War I; second, that the rivalry between East and West would acquire a new, and from the Soviet perspective distinctly unwelcome, dimension: economic competition. The Soviets had made clear on July 2, 1947, that they would take part neither in the conference nor in the Marshall plan itself. But the Czechoslovaks, as late as July 7, 1947, were prepared to go.

Two days later, the delegation from Prague sat in the Kremlin and listened to Stalin's tirades against the West and the Marshall plan. It is a matter of greatest importance, said Stalin, it is a *"vopros druzhby"* (a question of friendship). The Americans, under the cover of offering credits, "are trying to form a Western bloc and to isolate the Soviet Union." Foreign Minister Jan Masaryk attempted to propose a compromise, but Stalin remained firm. There was no one in the Soviet government, he said pointedly, who would doubt Czechoslovakia's friendly feelings toward Moscow. But going to Paris would be "intolerable."[31] Even Gottwald seemed embarrassed by the tone which the Kremlin team had adopted towards their Czechoslovak guests. Others were left speechless.[32] Masaryk summed up his feelings famously: "I went to Moscow as the Foreign Minister of an independent sovereign state; I returned as a lackey of the Soviet Government."[33]

After a dramatic meeting of the Prague government on July 10, 1947, Czechoslovakia announced the next day that it would not be represented in Paris. The British Ambassador Philip Nichols reported to London on July 12, 1947, that there was "disillusionment and resignation" in Czechoslovakia. "Many speak of a second Munich."[34] That sentiment was not without foundation. On July 9, 1947, just as the Czechoslovak delegation was receiving Stalin's stern lecture, George C. Marshall wrote quite matter-of-factly to the United States Embassy in France: "[The] Czechs are eager to participate in Paris talks; their participation or absence will depend almost entirely on degree of Moscow pressure."[35] At that time, a firm statement on behalf of Czechoslovakia's sovereign right to take part (or not to take part) in international conferences would have strengthened its resolve to remain a master in its own house. The absence of any such signal from the West was well understood in Prague on both sides of the ideological divide. Why was it that Secretary Marshall was so fatalistic when it came to the centrallylocated Czechoslovakia, and so proactive in Greece and Turkey, both in the underbelly of Europe? There seems to be but one explanation: because he accepted the Stalinist maxim that whoever liberated a given country in 1944-45 would determine its political allegiance. Europe was to return to a version of the principle *cuius regio, eius religio*. Secretary Marshall's premature fatalism would have tragic consequences for Czechoslovakia some seven months later.

Popular opinion in Prague was critical of Stalin's heavy-handed treatment of his democratic ally, Central Europe. In November 1947, the university students' elections resulted in a stunning victory of democratic candidates (74 percent) and a defeat of the Communists (20 percent). In the same month, a congress of the Social Democratic Party dismissed Zdeněk Fierlinger, a *de facto* Communist, from its leadership.[36] It had become likely that in the next elections, scheduled for May 1948, the CPC would not only fail to achieve its declared objective (51 percent). It could even lose ground. It seemed that many Czechoslovaks had had second thoughts regarding the value of their country's Soviet alliance. There was also an economic dimension to the shift from East to West: the former was poor and backward while the latter seemed opulently rich and exciting. To the leaders of the CPC this merely indicated that they could not afford to rely exclusively on the ballot-box. They would have to resort to naked power. It so happened that – when it came to pure power-politics – the Communist Party was in a better position that any of its rivals.

The CPC and Czechoslovak Security

From April 4, 1945, to September 14, 1953, the Ministry of Interior was under the command of Václav Nosek.[37] Unlike his colleague, Defense Minister General Ludvík Svoboda, Nosek never hid his affiliation with the Communist Party of Czechoslovakia.[38] He spent the war in Great Britain, far from most of his comrades who had gone to Moscow. Nosek was therefore well known to the politicians and soldiers who rallied around Beneš and formed the London-based Czechoslovak government-in-exile. It is noteworthy that even his adversaries, such as František Moravec, the war-time chief of Czechoslovak Military Intelligence (Second Bureau), confirmed that Nosek had a good reputation in emigré circles in London.[39] He was considered one of the "decent" Communists; he displayed joviality and always appeared ready for a compromise.[40] As late as 1947, Beneš believed in Nosek's "decency and loyalty,"[41] and also his "realism," "rationalism," and "common sense," although the minister was at that time fully engaged in preparations for the Communist coup d'état.[42] This seemingly convivial and sociable man managed to preside over the centrally important Ministry of Interior with Communist firmness, but without giving enough provocation to the democratic parties for them to demand, let alone obtain, his dismissal.

In addition to the top post in the Ministry of Interior, the Communist Party was gradually able to fill various other positions in the security apparat with its own candidates. When the democratic parties tried to criticize some of the most obvious Communist attempts to manipulate appointments, they were met with denials and threats. In many cases, democratic politicians simply retreated. They were unprepared for the kind of rough politics practiced by the Party boss and Prime Minister Gottwald, and his Moscow-trained colleagues. Party members working in the security apparat were well coordinated by the Security Department of the Central Committee (CC CPC). In 1946, the Central Committee established the so-called *bezpečnostní pětka*, (security five), a group consisting of Minister Václav Nosek, Karel Šváb (Chief of the Security Department of the CC CPC), Jindřich Veselý, Josef Pavel, and Rudolf Slánský. This group met once a month and coordinated the activities of Party members in the security apparatus. Most importantly, it determined and coordinated Party policy with regard to the crucially important issues of recruitment and appointments.[43] As early as 1945 the Security Department of the Central Committee was in a position to issue concrete orders to Party members employed by the Ministry of Interior. The department's chief, Karel Šváb, had his own networks of secret informers in the StB and ZS; their reports gave him the necessary feedback and means of control over officers-Communists who might otherwise have been reluctant to work exclusively (or even primarily) for the benefit of the Communist Party.[44] The struggle for control over the Ministry of Interior manifested itself in various different forms in the summer of 1945. Minister Nosek's decree of June 30, 1945, abolished the uniformed state police, state troopers and local police. All were replaced by the State Security Guard *(Sbor národní bezpečností,* SNB).[45] The new police was to recruit primarily among former political prisoners, former concentration camp inmates, and members of war-time underground resistance organizations. Throughout 1945, the following branches of the SNB were formed:

- *Pořádková služba SNB,* a network of uniformed security personnel which covered the whole country;
- *Pohotovostní pluk SNB* Rapid deployment force which gradually transformed itself into border police units;
- *Kriminální služba,* Criminal Police;
- *Státní bezpečnost,* State Security (StB);
- *Zpravodajská služba,* Intelligence service (ZS).

From the beginning, the StB and ZS had a privileged and mostly independent position within the SNB. In fact, many employees of the two services originally were not even members of the SNB; this was changed with law no. 149 of 1947, which put all security personnel in Czechoslovakia – from a rookie policeman to the top spy-master – under one unified command of the SNB and the Minister of Interior.[46] A subsequent law (no. 286 of December 21, 1948), passed after the Communist coup d'état, stipulated that the StB and ZS were "militarily organized" units which belonged "indivisibly" to the SNB. Finally, in 1949, the ZS became part of the StB.[47] (This situation had lasted until January 1990, when the StB was abolished and offensive intelligence reorganized under a succession of different labels.)

The State security *(Státní bezpečnost,* StB)[48] received its first postwar legal framework by a decree of Minister Nosek dated October 23, 1946.[49] The Intelligence service *(Zpravodajská služba, ZS),* originally designated as "Department Z" and later "Department VII" of the Ministry of Interior, had its mission legally defined by a decree of January 8, 1947. An examination of the two decrees shows a marked shift toward the growth of a police state in Czechoslovakia. In 1946 the StB was still constructed as a security organization with a zone of operation delimited by law. Its mission was to safeguard the democratic and republican form of government, protect elected representatives as well as foreign dignitaries visiting Czechoslovakia, and guard against economic espionage. The ZS, on the other hand, was endowed with a virtually unlimited field for its activities just two and a half months later. The language of the decree reflected the Soviet approach to state security. The Intelligence service was charged with two main missions. One was "to observe *preventively* (my italics) persons who for political, ethnic, or class reasons could be considered covert or overt enemies of People's Democracy." The second mission was "to observe developments on both sides of State borders because it is where one finds links between external enemies and domestic resisters." The basic method of the operations to be run by the ZS was described in the decree as "direct [agent] penetration of hostile centers." In order to carry out its tasks in such a manner, the ZS was ordered to build up a network of three kinds of collaborators: informers, trustees, and agents. Finally, the ZS was charged with operating in three related areas:

•Politické zpravodajství (PZ), Political Intelligence was to gather information relevant to Czechoslovak national security.

•Obranné zpravodajství (OZ), Counter Intelligence was to compile information needed for an effective struggle against wrecking and hostile intelligence activities by foreign agents. (The OZ is not to be confused with the OBZ, Vth Department of the Ministry of Defense, i.e., Military counter-intelligence.)

•Hospodářské zpravodajství (HZ), Economic Intelligence was to protect various nationalization projects and to guard against attempts at economic wrecking and sabotage.

The ZS had a mandate to work abroad as well as at home. On the home front, it created a network of intelligence centrals. Each unit was called *Zemský odbor bezpečnosti* (Land security section), ZOB; the latter was renamed in 1947 *Zemská ústředna zpravodajska* (Land intelligence central), ZUZ, with various sub-sections in important locations, known as OZO and their sub-departments, OZPO. From the beginning, this intelligence apparatus was under the control of the Communist Party. Not surprisingly, the ZOB, and its successor the ZUZ, targeted the Party's political opponents: democratic parties and politicians, the Church, and various youth organizations. ZS reports on Czechoslovak nonCommunist parties went regularly to top CPC political strategists.[50] Information which the ZS obtained abroad was used for analytical position papers, and those were regularly delivered by a courier to Communists who occupied responsible positions in various ministries, e.g., foreign affairs, industry, and commerce.

A number of democratic politicians repeatedly demanded an end to this blatant violation of the basic principles of free political life. In July 1946, the Social Democratic Party presented its proposal to remove the Intelligence service from the jurisdiction of the Ministry of Interior and place it under the Presidium of the Government. The proposal also stipulated that chiefs of various intelligence centrals should belong to a party other than the one to which the Interior Minister belonged. The Communist Party responded with a verbal barrages, *ad hominem* attacks, and delaying tactics. The greatest conflicts between the Party and the democrats were related to the Law on National Security, no.

149, which passed (after much and bitter debate) on July 11, 1947. The law stipulated the dissolution of the ZUZ (formerly ZOB) network and the merging of the State security (StB) and Intelligence service (ZS). It was too little, too late. In desperation, a democratic politician pointed out that no matter who would win the next election, scheduled to take place in May 1948, there would be a Communist security apparatus.[51] By 1947, the Communist Party was in almost absolute control over the Ministry of Interior and all its branches. In the spring, Lockhart heard in Prague that the Communists made up for what they had lost with the electorate by filling "all the internal key-posts in the Government and [they] controlled the secret police." The democratic parties were in no position to counter such maneuvers. "The physical power," Lockhart was told at the time, "was already in the hands of the Communists."[52] It was true. On Wednesday, September 10, 1947, three democratic ministers, Petr Zenkl, Jan Masaryk, and Prokop Drtina, received package-bombs in the mail. As it happened, nobody was hurt. But when the culprits were identified as members of the Communist Party apparat who possibly acted on instructions of Alexej Cepička, Gottwald's son-in-law, the investigators ran into a wall. This case of political terrorism was to come before the court in early March 1948, but the coup d'état in February stood the course of justice on its head. The terrorists were released from prison and the investigators were arrested. At least one, Zdeněk Marjanko, was tortured to death.[53]

The Communist Party had prepared for the political crisis of 1948 better than any of its democratic rivals. But it must not be overlooked that the events in Prague were evolving within the framework of a larger East-West conflict. The ups and downs of the democratic cause in the global context were, necessarily, reflected in the ups and downs of the democratic parties in Czechoslovakia. In the spring of 1947, Beneš and Jan Masaryk expressed the view that the cause of democracy in Czechoslovakia still warranted optimism – provided that Stalin would not get directly involved in the political crisis in Prague. "Of course," said Masaryk to Lockhart in December 1947, "if the Russians interfere, we are finished."[54] The second assumption was that the Western powers would wake up to the Stalinist threat and signal that they drew the line at Kremlin intervention in Czechoslovakia. Despite their bitter experience a decade ago, neither the realistic Beneš nor Masaryk believed that the democracies would stand by quite so passively while Czechoslovakia was about to fall to Stalin.

What Beneš and Masaryk did not know was clear to the Communist Party leadership: that the Western powers had no plans whatsoever to act, politically or otherwise, on behalf of the democratic cause in Prague. By late 1947, the Intelligence service (ZS) was reporting exclusively for the benefit of the Party central apparatus and certain Party members in the Czechoslovak government. Thus, in the Foreign Ministry the ZS reported to Vladimir Clementis,[55] the Deputy Foreign Ministry, but not to his boss, Minister Masaryk. An examination of the ZS reports found in the Clementis archive of the Ministry for Foreign Affairs reveal a new dimension of the Czechoslovak political crisis of 1948.

The ZS wrote on December 29, 1947, that, according to British politicians, Czechoslovakia was in a unique position. Its parliamentary democracy had remained virtually intact, its industry, albeit nationalized, had preserved its contacts with the outside world, and its technical standard had not been diminished. The view in Britain, stated the report, was that "Czechoslovakia has today a key position in Europe in the struggle between East and West." It also indicated that the "cultural sophistication" of Czechoslovaks will make them resist any further growth of Communist power. However, political circles in Great Britain

> express doubts that under the present circumstances the anti-Communist elements [in Czechoslovakia] will prove strong enough to resist outside pressures, pressures which are, in the opinion of the aforementioned circles, likely to increase.[56]

The report made no reference to any kind of British action, or even a propaganda campaign, on behalf of the struggling democratic cause in Czechoslovakia. Other ZS reports analyzed the British political scene.[57] Considerable attention was paid to a speech by Ernest Bevin before the House of Commons on January 22, 1948. He had stated that British foreign policy was guided, *inter alia*, by the principle of the balance of power. This, Bevin observed, had "led to all kinds of difficulties, particularly for the smaller states, which often became the instruments of the great powers." This was unfortunate, but one had to be realistic. It had become clear that "Eastern Europe had been cut off and turned into a bloc of police states. The free nations of Western Europe had to draw together." "I believe," said Bevin, "the time is ripe for a consolidation of Western Europe."[58] The ZS implied that, as far as the British were concerned, Czechoslovakia had already been overrun by the Russians. Now the task was to keep them out of Western Europe.

And France, Czechoslovakia's traditional ally? The ZS reported in late January 1948 that influential circles in France had become convinced that, if there was another war, its brunt would be carried by the United States. Both the British and the French were said to believe that the next conflict would have to be fought by American troops and at American tax-payers' expense.[59] But how eager were the Americans to play that kind of role? On January 22, 1948, the ZS reported on a top secret briefing in Paris of United States military attachés posted to various Western European capitals. The participants noted that British policy was based on the assumption that in the next conflict, the United States would have to do the fighting. General Lucius D. Clay[60] was said to believe that, in case of conflict with the Soviet Union, a defense of

Europe was conceivable only if a strong Germany had been built up. Otherwise, "it would be necessary to retreat from Europe at the beginning of military operations." The assembled military attachés expressed the sentiment that present-day Europe was not worth fighting for.[61]

From the perspective of Joseph Stalin in Moscow and Klement Gottwald in Prague, the Czechoslovak crisis offered no great puzzle and there seemed to be little risk involved. British national security concerns were focused on efforts to secure the Empire and not Central Europe. The United States would have to move swiftly to fill the vacuum the British were leaving behind in Greece and Turkey, and Stalin was not inclined to take France seriously. Therefore, the lands between Germany and Russia were open to Soviet domination. The ZS reports seemed completely plausible: no one in the West was prepared to challenge the imposition of totalitarian rule over Czechoslovakia. In fact, it had been accepted as a fait accompli well before it actually took place. Some three weeks prior to the Communist takeover, Pierson John Dixon, the new British Ambassador in Prague, came to see Minister Prokop Drtina. The Ambassador told him that according to his sources, the Communist Party was likely to take action in the near future in order to impose a Communist dictatorship, as had already happened in Poland, Hungary and elsewhere. He gave no indication that the British government had a particular view or even preference regarding this foreseeable event. Minister Drtina was grateful that Ambassador Dixon did not offer any false hope.[62] One day before the Prague coup d'état, Secretary of State George Marshall notified the U.S. Embassy in France that a seizure of power by the Communists "would merely crystallize and confirm for the future previous Czech policy." Since Czechoslovakia had behaved as a *de facto* ally of the Soviet Union in the UN, Marshall was saying, there was really nothing new to fear should the Communists wrest power in Prague. The only reason for concern was that a successful Communist action in Prague might encourage Communist action in Western Europe.[63]

The ZS reports made clear that the Western alliance had written off President Beneš and the democratic cause in Czechoslovakia, and had started building trenches against a further Soviet advance on Czechoslovakia's Western borders. Nobody in the West was going to intervene – even politically – on behalf of the anti-Communist majority in Prague. From the perspective of the Communist Party's strategists the foreign scene seemed secure. Moreover, there was a strong domestic reason for the Party to take action, and soon. When the war ended, the popularity of the CPC was genuine. It was demonstrated in the elections of May 1946 when it won 38 percent of the vote. But by late January 1948, the U.S. Embassy estimated that "80 percent of Czech people favor Western style democracy over Communism . . ."[64] The democrats in Prague believed that after the next elections they were going to have a majority even if the Social Democrats decided to side with the CPC.[65] Given this, the Communist leadership had a choice: to do nothing, and preside over the decline of the Party's popularity and ultimate defeat in future elections, or to resort to a kind of *Machtergreifung.* Under these circumstances, it seems obvious why Gottwald and his colleagues began in the fall of 1947 deliberately inciting and escalating conflicts with the democratic parties.[66]

Democratic politicians in Prague decided to challenge Gottwald and Nosek on the Communists' domination of the police force and Nosek's habit of dismissing without proper cause police officials who did not belong to his Party. On February 13, 1948, the majority of the government passed a resolution instructing Nosek to stop treating the police as an instrument of the Party and to reverse the recent illegal dismissal of eight police officials whose only discernable fault was that they had not joined the CPC. Only the Communists opposed the resolution. Gottwald and Nosek decided to ignore it. Conveniently, Nosek got a case of political influenza and stopped attending governmental meetings, and Prime Minister Gottwald refused to put the resolution back on the agenda for as long as the responsible minister, i.e., Nosek, was absent. The last meeting of the government on February 17, 1948, nearly degenerated into fisticuffs. The democrats, in desperation, resigned three days later from the government, claiming that the Communists were preparing a dictatorship.[67] They hoped that the government would fall and new elections would reveal the decline of Communist popularity. It did not happen. Contrary to a previous understanding, the Social Democratic ministers did not resign, and Masaryk also chose to keep his post as foreign minister. Out of twenty-six ministers, fourteen stayed and only twelve resigned. Gottwald's government did not fall.

During the crisis, President Beneš stated on two occasions that if Gottwald tried to force him to accept a government in which the democrats were replaced by Communists or their puppets, he would decline. He would rather resign his presidency.[68] But when Gottwald aggressively confronted Beneš (whose health had once again severely declined) with his scheme to replace democratic ministers with Communists, the president accepted the new, Communist government on Wednesday, February 25, 1948. Beneš was probably hoping to be in a position to make deals with the victorious party, but it established a complete monopoly on power within just three months, and it had neither interest in nor need for deals with the president. Prodded mercilessly by arriving Soviet advisors, Gottwald, Nosek, and their colleagues launched a massive purge of all democratic politicians and state employees and unleashed the first wave of mass persecution. Beneš realized there was nothing he could do about it. After he refused to sign the new, "Gottwald" Constitution, he had the presidential banner pulled down from the Prague Castle, and moved to his country villa in Sezimovo Usti in southern Bohemia. He resigned in June and died, alone and broken, in September 1948. The crisis was over and the terror could now start in the open.

The Prague affair contributed significantly to the growth of a viable Western bloc. Finally, an alliance of the United States, Great Britain, and France emerged to protest the Communist take-over in Czechoslovakia. The common declaration of the three powers would have an impact on the future of Western Europe, but it had no influence on the course of events in Czechoslovakia. The ZS analyzed Western responses to the coup d'état in Prague in its report of March 5, 1948. It summed up the situation simply: "Informed observers are convinced," the ZS stated, "that, unless seriously provoked, [Secretary George] Marshall and the State Department will not resort to any precipitous measures."[69] Since he had just acquired in Czechoslovakia the last outstanding Central European country, Stalin had naturally no reason to further provoke Secretary Marshall.[70] He could now sit and await the other side's next move. Stalin's job was done.

Notes

1. Even a partial list of works dealing with the Czechoslovak crisis of 1948 would be too long. Let us mention only Karel Kaplan, *Poslední rok prezidenta: Edvard Beneš v roce 1948* (Prague: Ústav pro soudobé dějiny AV ČR, 1993); Karel Kaplan, *Nekrvavá revoluce* (Toronto: Sixty-Eight Publishers, 1985); Karel Kaplan, *Mocní a bezmocní* (Toronto: Sixty Eight Publishers, 1989); Karel Kaplan, *The Short March: The Communist Takeover in Czechoslovakia, 1945-1948* (London: Hurst, 1987); Karel Kaplan, "Czechoslovakia's February 1948," in Norman Stone and Eduard Strouhal, eds., *Czechoslovakia: Crossroads and Crises, 1918-88* (London: Macmillan, 1989); Edward Taborsky, *President Edvard Beneš between East and West, 1938-1948* (Stanford: Hoover Institution, 1981); Edward Taborsky, "President Edvard Beneš and the Czechoslovak Crises of 1938 and 1948," in Norman Stone and Eduard Strouhal, eds., *Czechoslovakia: Crossroads and Crises, 1918-88* (London: Macmillan, 1989); Jaromír Smutný, *Únorový převrat 1948* (London: Ústav Edvarda Beneše, 1953); Hubert Ripka, *Le coup de Prague: une révolution préabriquée* (Paris: Librairie Plon, 1949)

2. Beneš and Jan Masaryk held this view even as late as May 1947. Bruce Lockhart, the well-informed British diplomat, was to write that "what perturbed me most was the conviction of both Beneš and Jan Masaryk, and doubtless many others, that of all peoples the Czechs were the least likely to accept Communism

and that Czech Communists were not as other Communists." *My Europe* (London: Putnam, 1952), 120.

3. Klement Gottwald, the Czechoslovak Communist boss, did not share this view. He and his Slovak colleagues (Husák, Siroky, Bacilek et al.) were disturbed by the situation in Slovakia and determined to improve it dramatically it before the next elections. For a discussion of this, see Karel Kaplan, *Nekrvavá revoluce,* 63-64.

4. A useful introduction to the origins of the Communist Party of Czechoslovakia can be found in the Archives of the Central Committee of the Communist party of Czechoslovakia [ACC CPC], Fond 19, inventory number 5.

5. The Klement Gottwald faction won over the so-called opportunists at the Party's 5th Congress in Prague, February 18-23, 1929. Thereafter, the CPC attempted – with minor exceptions – to follow Moscow's instructions.

6. This is described in Jacquest Rupnik, *Historie du parti communiste tchécoslovaque* (Paris: Presses de la fondation nationale des sciences politiques, 1981), and Igor Lukes, *Czechoslovakia Between Stalin and Hitler: The Diplomacy of Edvard Beneš* (New York: Oxford University Press, 1996); see also Jacques Rupnik, "Czechoslovak Communists and the State (1928-48)," in Norman Stone and Eduard Strouhal, eds.,*Czechoslovakia: Crossroads and Crises, 1918-88* (London: Macmillan, 1989), 169-82.

7. Before World War II, Lockhart wrote that "Czechoslovakia had been the European democracy with the least contrast between wealth and poverty." See, *My Europe,* 123. 8ACC CPC, Fond 19, inventory no. 5, signature 123.

8. ACC CPC, Fond 19, inventory no. 5, signature 123.; the intelligence report is dated November 13, 1936.

9. According to the official EKI publication, *Thesen und Beschlüße* (Basel: Prometheus, December 1933), 24, the organization spent $650,000 per annum in support of Communist movements world-wide.

10. ACC CPC, Fond 19, inventory no. 5, signature 1223. The report of the Intelligence Central of the Presidium of the Police Directorate is dated July 2, 1937.

11. ACC CPC, Fond 100, inventory number 24, file 172, archival unit 1524. The meeting took place on September 30, 1938 and started at 2 p.m.

12. The State Central Archives, Prague, The Ministry of National Security, 109-4-227.

13. These themes are explored in Igor Lukes, "Stalin and Beneš in the Final Days of September 1938: New Evidence from the Prague Archives," *Slavic Review,* 52/1 (Spring 1993): 28-48, and in Igor Lukes, "Did Stalin Desire War in 1938? A New Look at Soviet Behavior during the May and September Crises," *Diplomacy & Statecraft,* 2/1 (March 1991): 3-53.

14. ACC CPC, fond KI 20, file 85. A Czech translation from the German original has been deposited in the archives. The copy is marked "Presidium of the Executive, Communist International," 9516/4. This seems to be a transcript of Gottwald's speech, not the full text. There are several places in the transcript where Dimitrov and Manuilskii interrupted Gottwald with various observations or questions.

15. Beneš to J. Smutný, Aston Abbots, June 23, 1941; Libuše Otahálová and Milada Červinková, eds., *Dokumenty z historie československe republiky, 1939-1945*, vol. 1 (Prague: Academia, 1966), 235.

16. Beneš to J. Smutný, Aston Abbots, June 23, 1941; Otahálová and Červinková, eds., *Dokumenty z historie*, 234.

17. Beneš to J. Smutný, Aston Abbots, June 23, 1941; Otahálová and Červinková, eds., *Dokumenty z historie*, 234.

18. Beneš to J. Smutný, Aston Abbots, June 23, 1941; Otahálová and Červinková, eds., *Dokumenty z historie*, 241-242.

19. Beneš to J. Smutný, Aston Abbots, June 23, 1941; Otahálová and Červinková, eds., *Dokumenty z historie*, 336.

20. Beneš wrote on this topic often. See, for instance, *Prager Presse*, December 25, 1921

21. According to an official publication, M. Klimeš et al., eds., *Cesta ke květnu: Dokumenty o vzniku a vývoj lidove demokracie v Československu do února 1948* (Prague: Academia, 1965), 40-68, there were in fact six meetings. But the archival source quoted in this text, based on hand-written notes of Václav Kopecky, lists only five meetings. I will follow the archival source.

22. ACC CPC, fond 100/24, file 172, Archival unit 1526. The first meeting took place on December 13, the last on December 16, 1943

23. The Beneš Archives, Invalidovna, fond World War II, box 278a.

24. It was not the Munich experience alone. Beneš felt mistreated by the British even during his exile in England. The Czechoslovak government had remained unrecognized by the British until July 18, 1941, and Beneš considered it an outrage. As far as he was concerned, it was a sign that the appeasers had remained influential in various pockets of the government in London. For them, naturally, Beneš was unacceptable since he reminded them of the failure of their policy. Furthermore, in the words of U.S. Ambassador to Prague Lawrence Steinhardt, "President Beneš received a polite but non-committal reception in Washington early in 1943." In contrast, Stalin, whom Beneš saw after his visit to Washington, D.C., gave President Beneš the red-carpet treatment. Steinhardt to the Secretary of State, Prague, April 30, 1948, no. 309, *Foreign Relations of the United States, 1948*, vol. IV [FRUS] (Washington, D.C.: Government Printing Office, 1974), 748.

25. John MacCormac, "Beneš Sees no War but Notes Spheres," *The New York Times,* March 10, 1946.

26. On February 18, 1948, a day after the last meeting of the government before the coup d'état, the Communist press accused the democratic ministers of having tried to expel Communists from the government. "It was a pure fabrication," comments Prokop Drtina. See his *Československo: můj osud* (Toronto: Sixty-Eight Publishers), 499.

27. The opinions of Černý and Peroutka are reported in Kaplan's *Nekrvavá revoluce,* 381.

28. *Lidova demokracie,* May 23, 1945.

29. Lockhart, My *Europe,* 95-96. The view that Gottwald had a share of patriotism and common sense may now seem grotesque. But Prokop Drtina describes how in early June 1947, Gottwald stood in a brotherly manner between two democratic politicians, greeting (and being greeted by) participants of a congress of one of the democratic parties. Even Rudolf Slansky was briefly present. Drtina, *Československo,* 293.

30. Lockhart, *My Europe,* 113.

31. Drtina, *Československo,* Appendix IV, 683-690.

32. ACC CP, Fond 100/24, a recording of the meeting of the Czechoslovak governmental delegation with Stalin and Molotov on July 9, 1947.

33. Lockhart, *My Europe,* 125.

34. Philip Nichols to Ernest Bevin, July 12, 1947. Public Record Office, FO 371/v. 65785-115754. As quoted by John O. Crane and Sylvia E. Crane, *Czechoslovakia: Anvil of the Cold War* (New York: Praeger, 1991), 297.

35. As quoted by Crane, *Czechoslovakia,* 297.

36. Information on students elections in November 1947 and the ousting of Fierlinger is based on Josef Korbel, *Twentieth-Century Czechoslovakia: The Meaning of Its History* (New York: Columbia University Press, 1977), 244.

37. Before World War II, Nosek (b. September 26, 1892) had been briefly a coal-miner in Kladno; he later became a full-time Communist apparatchik and, subsequently, one of the Party's parliamentary deputies. During the war, his wife and son stayed in occupied Czechoslovakia and were murdered by the Nazis. Nosek died in 1955.

38. Svoboda (b. November 25, 1895) was an officer of the Czechoslovak army. After the German occupation in 1939, he went to Poland and assumed command of a unit of Czechoslovak volunteers who later saw action on the Eastern front. Although he was technically not a party member, Svoboda acted in accordance with Gottwald's instructions. He joined the Communist Party openly in October 1948. Svoboda was president of Czechoslovakia from 1968 to 1975; he died four years later.

39. After extensive service in World War I, Moravec (b. July 23, 1895) became a career officer of the Czechoslovak army. In 1930, he was ordered to the Second Bureau of the General Staff, i.e., military intelligence. At the height of the crisis of the 1930s, Moravec was in charge of the offensive and counterintelligence section and a deputy commander of the whole service. On March 14, 1939, he escaped with ten of his colleagues and their files to Great Britain. Moravec died in the United States in 1966.

40. František Moravec, *Špion, jemuž nevěrili* (Prague: Rozmluvy, 1990), 340.

41. Moravec, *Špion, jemuž nevěreli* , 352.

42. Lockheart, *My Europe, 96.*

43. Information on the structure and history of the StB is derived from "Organizace statobezpečnostni a zpravodajské služby v ČSR v letech 1919-1938, 1945-1948," (The organization of state security and intelligence service in Czechoslovakia, 1919-38 and 1945-48). I will refer to this as "Organization." The document was prepared by a special commission of experts in the Ministry of Interior, headed by Colonel Zdeněk Zikmundovský, March 1990. Information on CPC's control mechanisms in the Ministry of Interior is in "Organization," 37-8.

44. "Organization," 38.

45. "Organization," 17.

46. "Organization," 19.

47. "Organization," 34.

48. It is not generally known that the StB had been formed already before World War II. It emerged for the first time on January 1, 1938. At that time, its mission was to protect the security of the state, its representatives, and state property. It was also to guard defense installations, oversee local and foreign press, and maintain personal files on individuals active in subversive political causes. The StB was also one of several pre-war Czechoslovak institutions involved in foreign espionage. The primary organizational unit of the StB network was *Zpravodajská ústředna (ZUS)*, the intelligence central.

49. "Organization," 20.

50. See, for instance, ZS report of December 30, 1947, no. VII/B-22.588/taj.-47, signed by Dr. Zdeněk Toman (on the Minister's behalf), dealing with the situation in the Social Democratic party. Analytical papers prepared by the ZS can be found in the Archives of the Ministry of Foreign Affairs, [AMFA], Section A, The Cabinet of State Secretary and Minister [Vlado] Clementis, 1945-50.

51. "Organization," 28.

52. Lockhart, *My Europe,* 108.

53. Drtina, *Československo můj osud,* 369-408. Gottwald's direct threat to Drtina, one of the three victims of this act of terrorism, was revealing: "I'm telling you, you'll end up like van der Lubbe!"

54. Lockhart, *My Europe,* 127.

55. JUDr. Vladimír (Vlado) Clementis (b. September 1902) was a Slovak attorney who joined the Communist Party of Czechoslovakia in 1925. He had left the country on Party business before the Munich crisis in September 1938, and he spent the next six years together with Nosek and other Czechoslovak Communists in London. From April 4, 1945, Clementis was the State Secretary in the Foreign Ministry, i.e., the Deputy Minister. After Masaryk's death, Clementis became the Foreign Minister (on March 18, 1948). In February 1951, he was arrested and later tried on charges of high treason, sabotage and espionage with the so-called Slansky group. Clementis was executed on December 3, 1952.

56. ZS report of December 29, 1947, no. VII-B-22597/taj. -47, signed Dr. Zdeněk Toman (for the minister).

57. ZS report of February 5, 1948, no. 04606/48, signed Dr. Zdeněk Toman (for the minister) and ZS report of February 10, 1948, no. 04306/48, signed Dr. Zdeněk Toman (for the minister).

58. Bevin's speech is quoted from John D. Campbell, *The United States in World Affairs, 1947-1948* (New York and London: Published for the Council on Foreign Relations by Harper & Brothers, 1948), 495-96.

59. ZS report of January 28, 1948, no. 05123/48, signed Dr. Zdeněk Toman (for the minister).

60. General Clay was Commanding General of U.S. forces in Europe and Military Governor for Germany.

61. ZS report of January 22, 1948, no. 04132/48, signed Dr. Zdeněk Toman (for the minister).

62. Drtina, *Československo,* 470-72.

63. Marshall to Jefferson Caffery, U.S. Ambassador in Paris, Washington, D.C., February 24, 1948, *Foreign Relations of the United States, 1948,* vol. 4 (Washington, D.C.: United States Government Printing Office, 1974), [FRUS] 736.

64. John H. Bruins, U.S. Charge in Prague, to the Secretary of State, January 28, 1948, FRUS, 733.

65. Drtina, *Československo,* 467-68.

66. Drtina, *Československo,* 438.

67. In retrospect, many have criticized the tactics of Czechoslovak democrats during the crisis. But, as Drtina points out, when Gottwald and the Communist minority began openly establishing their kind of dictatorship, the choice was clear. "Either collaboration, or resignation... *Tertium non datur." Československo,* 495.

68. Drtina, *Československo,* 543.

69. ZS report of March 5, 1948, no. 0511/1948, signed Dr. J. Wehle (for the minister).

70. Reacting to the coup in Prague, Secretary Marshall stated on March 10, 1948, that the situation in Europe was "very, very serious." Nine days later, he compared the Soviets to the Nazis and, on March 20, 1948, he called for an "urgent and resolute action" if the United States was to defend western civilization. Campbell, *The United States*, 506-507.

13

The Marshall Plan, Soviet-American Relations, and the Division of Europe

Scott Parrish

On June 5, 1947, Secretary of State George C. Marshall delivered a speech to the graduating class at Harvard University. In the speech, Marshall made a dramatic offer of large-scale American economic aid to help in the reconstruction of war-ravaged Europe, which more than two years after the end of hostilities, had not yet landed solidly on the road to recovery. Despite increasing tensions between the United States and the Soviet Union over the postwar European order, the offer of aid was not restricted to any particular set of countries; Marshall welcomed the participation of "any country that is willing to assist in the task of recovery." After some initial hesitation, however, the Soviet Union rejected the American proposal, and coerced its Eastern European neighbors into following suit. The division of Europe into two competing blocs, each led by one of the emergent superpowers, soon followed. In Eastern Europe, the region's states – Poland, Czechoslovakia, Hungary, Bulgaria, and Rumania – were fully sovietized. The Marshall Plan thus seems to have been a watershed in the development of the Cold War.

While this general point has been clear for some time, debate has long raged over what sort of watershed the Marshall Plan represented. Did the division of the continent and the sovietization of Eastern Europe represent the inevitable development of Stalin's expansionist designs on the region? Or did the American offer and the conditions attached to it prompt a reappraisal of foreign policy priorities in Moscow, leading to a fundamental shift in Soviet policy? To put this question in another way, was the imposition of Communist regimes in Eastern Europe foreordained by the military division of the continent in 1945, or might Stalin have tolerated more political pluralism in the area under less stringent international conditions? Although we are still far from having enough information to put together a definitive picture, with new documentation from former Soviet archives, we can begin to address these questions in a more informed manner.

This new documentation, incomplete though it may be, suggests that Soviet policy shifted in 1947 because of Stalin's fear of the offensive potential of American economic power expressed in the Marshall Plan. Before the Marshall Plan was announced, Stalin had pursued a relatively moderate policy in some of the Eastern European states, in order to avoid antagonizing the United States, with whom he still hoped to compromise on contentious issues like the future of Germany. So long as the possibility of limited cooperation with the United States remained open, Stalin was willing to moderate his policies in Eastern Europe. After the details of the Marshall Plan became clear, however, the Soviet leadership came to view it as an attempt to use economic aid not only to consolidate a West European bloc, but also to undermine recently-won, and still somewhat tenuous, Soviet gains in Eastern Europe. Stalin feared that the American economic aid program aimed to transform his new chain of Soviet-oriented buffer states into a revised version of the "cordon sanitaire" of the interwar years. Faced with this apparent threat, Stalin concluded that only total control over Eastern Europe would suffice to repel it, and he acted accordingly.

But while the Marshall Plan may have provided the immediate impetus for the division of Europe, in a broader sense, the unstable international conditions in Europe foreordained this outcome. These conditions impelled both the United States and the Soviet Union to adopt policies which were strategically defensive in their intent, but which appeared offensive to the other. Both countries confronted what international relations theorists term a "security dilemma," in which international conditions made it all but impossible for either to increase its security without decreasing that of the other.[1]As a result, the Marshall Plan, conceived by American policy-makers primarily as a defensive measure to stave off economic collapse in Western Europe, appeared to the Soviet leadership as an offensive attempt to subvert the security interests of the Soviet Union. While Stalin had not previously been seeking confrontation, in the situation created by the Marshall Plan he apparently felt he had no other choice. The upshot was the Soviet-American conflict known as the Cold War, and its concomitant, the imposition of Communist regimes across Eastern Europe, which would persist for over 40 years.

The Security Dilemma and Postwar Europe

Scholars in international relations have long recognized that the structural condition of anarchy in which states operate often makes it difficult for states to insure their own security without threatening the security of other states. Only a few years into the Cold War, John Herz wrote that organized groups coexisting under conditions of anarchy must seek to achieve their security through unilateral action. But their efforts to do so, he argued, might lead to a paradoxical outcome:

> Striving to attain security from such attack, they are driven to acquire more and more power in order to escape the impact of the power of others. This, in turn, renders the others more insecure and compels them to prepare for the worst. Since none can ever feel entirely secure in such a world of competing units, power competition ensues, and the vicious circle of security and power accumulation is on.[2]

Cooperation among sovereign states may therefore be very difficult to achieve when anarchy prevails. This analysis has been the foundation of many interpretations of the Soviet-American Cold War confrontation.

Certain international conditions, however, make such security conflicts more likely. While somtimes states may increase their own security without decreasing that of others, under different international conditions, that may prove impossible. Robert Jervis's theory of the security dilemma identifies two variables which influence the possibility of states adopting compatible security policies: first, the balance between offense and defense; and second, the distinguishability of offensive and defensive policies. If offense has the advantage over defense (which is to say that overturning the status quo is relatively easier than defending it), then even status quo states may be forced into adopting offensive strategies and tactics. Under these conditions it will be difficult for any state to increase its own security without decreasing the security of others. On the other hand, when defense is strong, relative to offense, there is no incentive for status quo powers to attack. A state can then defend its position without using offensive means which threaten others.[3]

The second variable which influences the security dilemma is the degree to which offensive and defensive policies and weapons are distinguishable from one another. If defensive policies are clearly distinguishable from offensive policies, then a state which desires only to uphold the status quo can do so without appearing to threaten others. Without such clarity, however, a policy which is intended to bolster the status quo may appear to other states as an offensive threat. Thus, for example, tanks can be used to implement a blitzkrieg strategy of attack and conquest. Yet the same tanks are also perhaps the most effective weapon with which to repel just such an attack. A state might then procure tanks as a defensive measure, yet nevertheless appear to threaten its neighbors. According to Jervis's theory, then, under conditions where the offense has the advantage, and when it is difficult to distinguish offensive from defensive policies, it will be very difficult for states to protect themselves without simultaneously menacing other states.[4] Under such conditions it should be extremely difficult for great powers to adopt compatible security policies, and highly likely that each state's attempt to insure its own security would provoke the other. The expected outcome of interaction between two states under such conditions is a conflict spiral, in which each state would become increasingly convinced that the other had aggressive intentions.[5]

The literature on the security dilemma largely deals with the implications for state behavior of a world in which offense is dominant in a strictly military-technical sense. There is no logical reason, however, why the same implications would not follow from a broader definition of the balance between offense and defense. Unstable political and economic conditions, for example, could create an offense advantage similar to that created by certain innovations in military technology. Such instability might also make it difficult for states to design clearly defensive policies which would protect their interests without menacing others. Postwar Europe represents such a case of unstable political and economic conditions creating an offensive advantage, confronting both the Soviet Union and the United States with an intense security dilemma.

In the chaotic conditions of Europe after 1945, in which a vacuum of power had encompassed the entire continent after the elimination of Germany, it appeared that whichever side intervened first in a given area could consolidate political and economic control over it. The resources of such areas could then be used to make further gains. Consequently, both the Soviet Union and the United States feared that the other would unilaterally attempt to fill the void. And since each viewed resources in Europe as vital to its security, these fears were magnified.

At first glance, this argument seems counter-intuitive. The situation in 1945 appeared to provide the basis for arriving at a stable modus vivendi. The continent was divided, and those dividing lines subsequently remained stable for over 40 years. From the outset, both sides appeared willing to grant the other predominant control over a part of Europe – the U.S., despite some noisy protests, acquiesced in Soviet dominance in East Central Europe, and Stalin seemed willing to concede Western Europe, at least for the medium-term future, to the American "sphere."

However, while that division of Europe may have become stable, it was not formally codified until many years after 1945. Instead, it emerged *de facto* only after a series of intense crises in 1947-1949, which were triggered by the effects of the security dilemma. The problem was twofold: 1) the two sides could not agree on the disposition of Germany, the economic resources of which presented a significant long-term threat to each, if the other managed to consolidate control over them; and 2) the means which each side used to consolidate control over its "sphere" were not clear cut defensive measures, but rather ambiguous, and difficult to distinguish from offensive attempts to undermine the other's "sphere."

Both of these problems resulted from the conditions identified in Jervis's theory of the security dilemma. European instability made it seem plausible to both the major powers that the whole continent might align itself with the other. The United States feared the political clout of the large Communist parties in France and Italy, suspecting that it would be expoited to align these countries and their resources with the Soviet Union. In 1947, Truman administration officials felt that the alignment of these states was very tenuous indeed. And if these two countries aligned themselves with Moscow, the economic resources of the entire continent might well follow. On the other hand, the picture from Moscow looked equally threatening. The Communists in France and Italy were not quite strong enough to have a decisive influence over government policy there. In Eastern Europe, Moscow wielded much greater influence, but remained constrained. The coalition governments which ruled in several of the East European states were not fully controlled by Communists, and the non-Communist members still hoped to keep their autonomy. Under the right conditions, some would wish to align themselves with the West against the USSR, as they had done in the 1930s. As a result, the Soviet sphere appeared no more stable than the American. Both Soviet and American leaders had plausible fears that the other could undermine its still tenuous control and put the whole continent in its pocket.

In addition, Moscow and Washington also feared that the offensive instruments with which the other could undermine its "sphere" were more potent than the defensive measures with which it could hope to retain control. In this sense, each thought that "offense" was dominant. And as the policy instruments which the Soviets and the Americans had at their disposal were very different, they had difficulty distinguishing offensive from defensive policies and tactics. Policies which each country adopted for strategically defensive ends were often ambiguous or included tactically offensive maneuvers, which signalled to the other that its objectives were not limited and defensive, but rather offensive and unlimited. The result, in the summer and fall of 1947, was a conflict spiral which transformed the character of Europe.

Moscow's Grand Strategy Before the Marshall Plan

Since 1945, relations between the Soviet Union and its erstwhile partners in the anti-Hitler alliance had been deteriorating. By early 1947, the United States and the Soviet Union were no longer allies in any real sense; they had too many disagreements over too many major issues. But neither did they yet view one another as antagonists in a zero-sum confrontation. Rather, each side in the nascent Cold War had come to view the other in two roles: as a partner in the ongoing negotiations to solve such questions of common interest as the future of Germany; and as an adversary because each had the capability to present a significant threat to important security interests of the other.[6] From the viewpoint of Moscow, this situation created incentives to pursue a mixed strategy of selective cooperation and competition with the West.

The threat of a resurgent Germany for example, could be dealt with most effectively through multilateral action. Since the Western powers occupied about two-thirds of Germany (including the lion's share of its industrial resources), Stalin could not hope to unilaterally achieve a satisfactory long-term solution to the "German question." Only a mutually acceptable compromise with the Western Allies would make it possible to forestall future German aggression. Without such a compromise German settlement, the Soviet Union could lose all influence over future developments in the Western sectors of Germany. Whatever security gains the Soviet Union could make through unilateral action – such as the construction of a politically subservient "buffer zone" in Eastern Europe – had to be weighed against the potential benefits of such selective cooperation with the West.

As long as the benefits from such cooperation with the West appeared potentially significant and achievable, Stalin was willing to act with some degree of restraint in other areas. In Eastern Europe, for example, between 1945 and 1947, Stalin settled for less than total control. During this time, coalition governments with non-Communist participation held power in several of the East European states. While these governments were not paragons of liberal democratic values, neither were they yet Soviet-style police states. And while Moscow had considerable influence, especially over questions of foreign policy, it did not yet aim at total domination.

In large measure Stalin's strategy from 1945 to mid-1947 stemmed from uncertainty about the future of Germany and its enormous economic potential. While peace treaties were signed with Germany's former wartime allies – Italy, Hungary, Rumania, and Bulgaria and Finland – in February 1947, little progress had been made on a permanent peace settlement with Germany. Even the provisional agreements reached at the Potsdam Conference in July 1945 had not been fully implemented by early 1947. The wartime allies turned their full attention to concluding a formal agreement with Germany at the New York meeting of the Council of Foreign Ministers: New York (CFM) in November and December of 1946, and then continued at the Moscow CFM meeting (March-April 1947), which was devoted primarily to this question. The significance and urgency of the issues involved varied for each side. For the West, the solution of the German question was a matter of great economic and political significance. German industry had been the "motor" of economic growth in prewar Western Europe. While Germany remained divided into occupation zones with no common economic policy, the economic recovery of the other Western European nations would remain stagnant. Reflecting this reality, after some gains in the first year after the war, the economic recovery of Western Europe had begun to slow drastically in 1947. Only increased economic aid from the United States and/or the reintegration of German resources into the European economy offered the possibility of stemming the economic hemorrhaging in Western Europe. And if the economic collapse of Europe could not be constrained, American officials feared that hunger and deprivation might make socialist economic planning attractive to Western European populaces, and that the entire region might gradually gravitate towards the Soviet Union and away from the United States. The potential of such a combination of Russian and European resources represented a serious security threat to the United States.[7]

For the Soviet Union, too, the German question had great significance. On the economic side, the USSR wanted reparations from Germany in the sum of $20 billion. The Soviet leaders wanted these reparations partly as shipments of dismantled German factories to the USSR, but also in payments from current German production. Given the devastation caused by the war, the Soviet leaders viewed these reparations as a major source of capital for reconstruction. On the political side, the Soviets were concerned to prevent a possible resurgence of German power. To achieve this goal Soviet Foreign Minister Vyacheslav Molotov argued for demilitarization and the creation of a German political system that assured a significant role for German Communists.

The Moscow conference, however, proved unable to bridge the gap between Western and Soviet concerns. The Western powers refused to grant Moscow the reparations that were so crucial to the Soviet leaders.[8] Without a deal on reparations, Molotov and Stalin remained unwilling to compromise on the question of Germany's political structure, nor would they agree to Western proposals on the formation of an interim unified economic policy for all the occupation zones. The conference dragged on in deadlock for over three weeks, with each side tediously repeating its arguments to apparently deaf counterparts.

It was in this atmosphere that American Secretary of State Marshall went to speak with Stalin on April 15. Marshall was deeply concerned with the failure of the conference to reach any agreement on German economic unity, a failure which he felt had wide-ranging implications. His advisor, Charles Bohlen, reports that Marshall asked for the interview to tell Stalin "how dangerous it was to leave Germany in a chaotic and divided state."[9] After lamenting the failure of the conference and the breakdown of cooperation in Soviet-American relations, Marshall told Stalin that the United States hoped to aid "those countries that are suffering from economic deterioration which, if unchecked, might lead to economic collapse and the consequent elimination of any chance of democratic survival." At the end, Marshall stated that he hoped to "rebuild the basis of cooperation which had existed during the war and that he had come to Generalissimo Stalin with that hope, feeling that if they cleared away some of the suspicion it would be a good beginning for the restoration of that understanding."[10]

In his reply, Stalin showed that he did not share either Marshall's pessimism or his sense of urgency. He first lodged a protest that the British and the Americans did not take the issue of reparations seriously enough. "The United States and England might be willing to give up reparations," he declared, "but the Soviet Union could not." Despite the failure to achieve agreement, however, Stalin took a more optimistic view of the longer-term prospects for reaching a mutually acceptable compromise solution. He described the conference as

> only the first skirmishes and brushes of reconnaissance forces on this question. Differences had occurred before on other questions, and as a rule after people had exhausted themselves in dispute they then recognized the necessity of compromise. It is possible that no great success would be achieved at this session, but that should not cause anyone to be desperate. Stalin added his belief that compromises were possible on all the main questions including demilitarization, political structure of Germany, reparations and economic unity. It was necessary to have patience and not become depressed.[11]

Stalin's remarks gave the impression that he remained unswayed by Marshall's concern over the rapidly deteriorating situation in Europe. Stalin's indifferent attitude toward the economic implications of the deadlock over Germany convinced Marshall that Stalin was merely stalling, hoping that economic collapse in Western Europe would create conditions favorable to the further expansion of Soviet influence in the region. As another member of the American delegation, John Foster Dulles, put it: "the Moscow conference was, to those who were there, like a streak of lightning that illuminated a dark and stormy scene. We saw as never before the magnitude of the task of saving Europe for Western civilization."[12] Marshall shared this view, and he returned to Washington from Moscow determined to take some action that could arrest Europe's precipitous economic decline, to prevent a crisis that the USSR could exploit for political advantage. Marshall and other American officials had thus come to view Stalin's inaction on Germany as an offensive move designed to undermine American influence in Europe, with potentially disastrous implications. And in the fluid political and economic conditions of Europe in the spring of 1947, they feared the consequences of such a Soviet "offensive."

Initial Soviet Reaction to the Marshall Plan: Opportunity or Threat?

Given Marshall's remarks to Stalin during their conversation in April, it cannot have come as a surprise to the Soviet leader when Marshall gave his famous speech at Harvard University on June 5, declaring that the United States was prepared to give economic aid to Europe in order to forestall economic catastrophe there.[13] Initial Soviet reaction to the speech itself was cautious, but far from categorical, in keeping with Stalin's overall strategy. The ambiguity of Marshall's speech made definitive interpretation difficult. Did the new American initiative represent a threat or an opportunity? Ultimately Stalin would reach the conclusion that this new American policy represented a very real threat to the Soviet Union, but at the outset the situation was not nearly so clear.

Reflecting this uncertainty, the Soviet ambassador in Washington, Nikolai V. Novikov, cabled Moscow on June 9 that although Marshall had relied on generalities in his speech, the American initiative appeared to lend support to the "Monet Plan," put forward earlier in France. In his analysis, based on a close reading of the American press, Novikov suggested that the purpose of Marshall's speech was to inspire the British to join the French in creating an economic plan for European recovery. But voicing some suspicion about American objectives, Novikov concluded that this plan would have more than simply economic objectives:

> in this proposal of the Americans, the outlines of a Western
> European bloc directed against [the USSR] are patently visible. The
> State Department is now working furiously on this plan.[14]

To the extent that one can judge from available documentation, Soviet Foreign Minister Molotov was also cautious in his initial assessment, but not as pessimistic as his ambassador. The original translation of Marshall's speech into Russian that Molotov read is heavily underlined, suggesting the interpretation he placed on it. Molotov underlined the sections that emphasized the seriousness of the economic situation in Europe. He marked not only the sentence: "Thus a very serious situation is rapidly developing which bodes no good for the world," but also later Marshall's remark that "It should be clear to everyone what effects this could have on the economy of the United States." Molotov then underlined the conclusion: "the United States must do everything within its power so as to assist in the return of normal economic conditions in the world."

Secondly, as one would expect from the suspicious Molotov, he marked the following two sentences: "Our policy is directed not against any country or doctrine, but against hunger, poverty, desperation, and chaos," as well as the phrase, "governments, political parties or groups which seek to perpetuate human misery in order to profit therefrom politically or otherwise will encounter the opposition of the United States." Molotov also noted in the margin three main points of the plan's structure that Marshall alluded to in the closing paragraphs of his speech 1) that the European countries must come to an agreement about their economic requirements; 2) that the initiative must come from the Europeans themselves; and 3) that the American role should be limited to aid and support of such an economic program.[15]

What can one conclude from Molotov's underlining of the speech? First, it seems that he concentrated on the self-interested motives of the Americans in putting forward the proposal, by highlighting Marshall's warning about the effects on the United States of an economic collapse in Europe. He seems to have viewed the proposal as motivated by economic necessity. Other evidence presented later also supports this conclusion. Second, Molotov appears to have suspected that the plan was directed against the Soviet Union in that he circled the same passage about American opposition to states which seek to profit politically from economic misery. But Molotov's marking of the three points at the end of the speech suggests that despite these difficulties, he may have hoped that the proposal might be turned to Soviet advantage; perhaps the Soviet Union could gain some much-needed reconstruction credits. That Marshall suggested the Europeans themselves draw up such a plan made this interpretation plausible. In this respect it is quite possible that Novikov was deliberately more pessimistic than his boss to protect himself from charges that he was insufficiently vigilant.[16]

In retrospect, Molotov and Novikov had a good foundation for their suspicions about American intentions. Most of the available evidence indicates that the Western powers never intended to allow Moscow to participate in the aid program. The Americans, British, and French agreed that Soviet participation would lead to protracted bargaining and delays in implementing any plan. The suspicious and opportunistic Soviet leaders would certainly attach demanding conditions to their participation. The West Europeans and the Americans, however, felt quick action necessary. If, as Marshall put it, "the patient is sinking while the doctors deliberate," then endless haggling with the Soviets had to be avoided. Such haste to intervene with economic aid again shows the strength of the political-economic offense. Hesitation could be fatal, for once the economic situation worsened further, potential Soviet gains could become irreversible.

Reflecting these fears, in the days following Marshall's speech both the British and French governments scrambled to put together a rapid response to Marshall's offer. They found themselves on the horns of a difficult political dilemma, however. On the one hand, they did not want to include the USSR in their plans. But on the other, domestic political conditions in the United States compelled them to propose some sort of all-European plan. By the summer of 1947, it had become clear that the U.S. Congress would not approve any further piecemeal aid to individual European countries. American legislators felt that too much aid had already been sent into the "black hole" of the European economies. As a result, any response to Marshall's plan – if it was to pass muster in the American legislature – had to take the form of an all-European plan which held out the prospect of re-creating a self-sustaining European economy within the near future.

The domestic political situation in Western Europe aggravated these contradictions. The politically weighty Communist parties in France and Italy constrained the British, French, and Americans, and compelled them to make a visible, if not entirely sincere effort to include the Soviet Union in any recovery program. For France and Italy, two countries whose participation was absolutely necessary to any successful recovery program, participation in an economic plan which deliberately excluded the Soviet Union would be all but politically impossible. In both countries, socialist-led governments had only just that past spring excluded the Communists from the governing coalition and were hanging on to bare majorities in their respective Parliaments. Any further action which would antagonize the Left – as the deliberate exclusion of the USSR would do – might throw these countries into a political crisis. Consequently, even though British Foreign Minister Ernest Bevin and his French counterpart Georges Bidault did not desire Soviet participation in the American aid program, they felt constrained to invite the USSR to participate in the initial planning.[17]

This basically tactical decision had far-reaching implications. Because the plan could not be restricted to Western Europe alone, it became a more sweeping enterprise, holding out the promise of aid for the Eastern half of the continent as well. But precisely because the proposed aid program became so far-reaching, it also became potentially more threatening, potentially more "offensive" from the perspective of Moscow. As a result, the Western powers were forced by the fluid political conditions within their own states to adopt an economic aid plan which was not strictly limited and defensive in character, but much more ambiguous. In essence, the circumstances forced the West to take actions resembling a political-economic offensive, even though Bevin and those of like mind in Washington probably did not hold out much hope of breaking Moscow's grip over Eastern Europe. In order to protect their own security, the Western states, under these conditions, could hardly have avoided threatening the Soviet Union, as Jervis's theory of the security dilemma would predict.

Taking into account all these overlapping political demands, Bevin and Bidault met in Paris a few days after Marshall's speech, and carefully transmitted to Moscow their desire to enter into consultations with the Soviet government about a joint European response to the American initiative. As Bevin reported to London "the main concern of the French government was to disarm domestic criticism to the effect that Russia had not been given in good faith a full and cordial opportunity to join in the discussions at the outset." Thus, following their discussions, Bevin and Bidault extended an invitation to Molotov to join them in a discussion of the American aid offer at a meeting in Paris to be held the week of June 23. Both Bevin and Bidault assured the American ambassador in Paris, Jefferson Caffery, however, that the invitation was little more than window dressing to defuse domestic criticism from the Left. Both told Caffery that "they hope the Soviets will refuse to cooperate and that in any event they will be prepared to 'go ahead full steam even if the Soviets refuse to do so.'"[18]

At the same time, aware of the British-French consultations, the Soviet foreign ministry attempted to clarify both the intent of Marshall's speech and the nature of the Anglo-French discussions regarding a response. In a series of early June meetings with the French chargé and the British Ambassador, Deputy Foreign Minister Yakov Malik attempted to discover more details about American intentions. He was especially interested in how much aid the United States might offer and what conditions might be attached. His French and British interlocutors claimed to know nothing beyond what Marshall had said in his speech, however.[19] Despite these assurances, the Soviet leaders must have suspected, (and as we have seen, not without reason), that the British, French, and Americans were already planning a unified approach to the question. Even the invitation to the Paris conference probably failed to quell such apprehensions.

In order to supplement reports from the field, sometime in early June Molotov requested that Yevgenii Varga, the economist mentioned above, draft a report assessing the motivations behind the American initiative. In response, Varga submitted a report to Molotov on June 26. In a hand-written note on its cover of the report, Molotov noted that copies had been sent to Stalin and other senior Soviet leaders.[20] Predictably, Varga put forward an economic explanation of Marshall's proposal, contending:

> The economic situation in the United States was the decisive factor in the putting forward of the Marshall Plan proposal.The Marshall Plan is intended in the first instance to serve as a means of softening the expected economic crisis, the approach of which already no one in the United States denies.

Varga then went on to outline the dimensions of the economic crisis which he expected would soon overtake the United States. He anticipated a 20% drop in production during this crisis, throwing 10-

million out of work, and wreaking havoc on the American banking system. As to the political effects of these economic difficulties, he concluded: "the explosion of the economic and financial crisis will result in a significant drop in the foreign policy prestige of the United States, which hopes to play the role of stabilizer of international capitalism."[21]

The Marshall Plan, wrote Varga, represented an attempt to forestall this crisis. He argued that the United States was now compelled to increase exports in order to avoid the onset of a serious economic depression. To accomplish such an increase in exports, the United States would grant credits to the European countries, even if they could not repay them. Varga observed that this expedient would prove especially beneficial to "monopoly capital." He then concluded:

> Seen against this background, the ideal behind the Marshall Plan is the following. If it is in the interest of the United States itself to sell abroad American goods worth several billion dollars on credit to bankrupt borrowers, than it is necessary to attempt to gain from these credits the maximum political benefits.[22]

In Varga's analysis, economic self-interest required the United States to extend credits to Europe in order to avoid economic catastrophe. Naturally, however, the American capitalists would attempt to extract the maximum political advantages out of this situation.

In the final section of his report, Varga explained why Marshall insisted that the European countries put together a single, all-European plan for American aid. He listed five reasons: 1) to show American superiority over Europe, since all the European countries together must make the request, rather than on a more equal bilateral basis; 2) the possibility "within the framework of a unified plan of aid to Europe to put forward a demand for the economic unification of Germany on a bourgeois basis. In this way, the United States is striving for the creation of a unified front of the bourgeois states of Europe against the USSR on the German question"; 3) "the possibility of putting forward the demand of removing the 'iron curtain' as a precondition for the ostensible economic reconstruction of Europe"; 4) To create pressure to form an anti-Soviet bloc in Europe if the USSR refuses to participate; and 5) to blame the USSR if the plan fails.[23]

Varga's analysis, like that of Molotov and Novikov, reflected a strong degree of caution and suspicion, but it did not explicitly recommend outright rejection of the American initiative. The report, while pointing out the "imperialist" motivations behind the proposal, did not seem to exclude the possibility of Soviet participation, provided, of course, that any conditions which the Americans might attach to the aid were acceptable. In fact, since Varga contended that the United States must grant credits or face economic catastrophe, his analysis implicitly assumes that the USSR might be able to obtain some of these credits without agreeing to unacceptable political conditions. The final section outlined possible American strategies for imposing such conditions, but stopped short of asserting that the Soviet Union would be forced to accept them; Varga simply argued that the Americans would propose them. One could infer from this analysis that with astute bargaining, the Soviet Union could possibly gain from participation in a plan largely driven by economic necessity.

Interestingly, the report dovetails with Varga's well-known controversial arguments in his 1945 book, *Changes in the Economy of Capitalism as a Result of the Second World War*. In that volume, he discussed the possibility of capitalist states sucessfully regulating their economies.[24] Were the Marshall Plan to succeed, the impending economic crisis in the United States would be averted, at least temporarily. Indirectly, here too, Varga seems to counsel moderation. For if this sort of government intervention could forestall economic crisis in the West, then the Western powers could prove more stable and less agressive than traditional Soviet thinking would suggest. If the United States could avert collapse from such economic "crises," then it would prove necessary to deal with the Western powers for a considerable interval of time. Strictly speaking, Varga's analysis left the door open for Soviet participation.[25]

When Bevin and Bidault issued their reluctant invitation then, Molotov accepted. The conference was set to open on June 26 in Paris. The decision to participate in the talks was fully consistent with both Molotov's reading of Marshall's speech and Varga's analysis. To the extent one can judge from available evidence, the Soviet leadership viewed attendance at the conference as necessary in order to clarify the details of the American proposal and learn what conditions the Americans might attach to their aid. Significantly, the Soviet leadership not only decided to participate, but it encouraged those East European states that had fought against Germany to take part as well. On June 22, even before he read Varga's report, Molotov cabled the Soviet embassies in Poland, Czechoslovakia, and Yugoslavia. He ordered the ambassadors there to inform their host governments that Moscow

> thought it desirable that the friendly allied countries, from their side, take the initiative in arranging their participation in the drawing up of such an economic program, and announce their desire to participate, keeping in mind that several European countries (i.e. Holland, Belgium) have already made such requests.[26]

Within a few days, the Czech and Polish governments told Molotov they would ask to participate in the proposed American aid program, in which both expressed a strong interest.[27]

As the conference in Paris approached, Soviet apprehensions about American intentions appear to have increased. Mocow's fears centered on the idea that Marshall's proposal, far from being a simple plan of economic aid, actually represented the first step in the formation of a Western European alliance, led by the United States, and directed against Soviet interests, especially in Eastern Europe. Ambassador Novikov sent a cable to Moscow on June 24 in which he explicitly articulated such fears. This cable was notably more pessimistic in its appraisal of the situation than the one he had sent earlier in the month. Novikov's new analysis started by observing that the "Truman

Doctrine," initiated in March, had proven a political failure. Its "crude" methods and clear anti-Soviet orientation had proven unpopular both in the United States and Europe. Marshall's speech at Harvard represented an attempt to devise more subtle tactics which would prove more politically acceptable to the Western European countries. The Europeans, argued Novikov, did not want to get caught up in a conflict between the USSR and the United States; they had therefore until now remained aloof from the "openly anti-Soviet program of Truman."[28]

Novikov characterized the underlying goal of the American initiative as "the hindering of the democratization [code for the establishment of pro-Soviet regimes] of the countries of Europe, the stimulation of forces opposing the Soviet Union, and the establishment of conditions for the strengthening of the position of American capital in Europe and Asia." He thus interpreted the Marshall Plan as an attempt to roll back Soviet influence in Europe. This impression is strengthened by his later comments on the form in which Marshall put forward his proposal:

> Externally, the "Marshall Plan" appears as if the United States has decided to give the European states themselves the initiative in establishing a program of economic reconstruction for Europe... But it cannot be doubted, however, that matters here will not be decided without some prompting [from the U.S.]. This task, apparently is already being carried out by American representatives in the appropriate countries. It is to this end that the talks of [Undersecretary of State] Clayton in London are directed.[29]

Novikov was not far off the mark in his reporting here. In fact, Clayton, who was Undersecretary of State for Economic Affairs, did travel to London shortly before the opening of the Paris conference, and he held several meetings with Bevin. The subject of these talks was a matter of speculation in the Western press, which Soviet diplomats duly noted in dispatches to Moscow.[30] As Novikov suspected, Bevin and Clayton did indeed discuss ways of precluding Soviet participation in the American aid program without incurring the political costs of openly excluding the USSR. In the discussion, Bevin also expressed the hope that some East European states might be lured away from Soviet tutelage with American economic aid.[31] The suspicious Novikov was right on target, then, when he inferred that Clayton and Bevin were working out a plan of action for the Paris conference, a plan which envisioned the use of American economic power not only to defend Western Europe, but also if possible to undermine Soviet influence in Eastern Europe.

Novikov concluded that the new American initiative should be regarded as the first stage of a coordinated plan to create an anti-Soviet alliance in Europe:

> In this way, the "Marshall Plan" in place of the previous disorganized actions, directed at the economic and political subordination of the European countries to American capital and the

creation of anti-Soviet groupings, envisions a broader frame of action, aiming to solve this problem more effectively.

As a result, Novikov concluded that Soviet participation in the program was not desired by Washington, and he cited Marshall's statement in the speech that "governments, political parties or groups which seek to perpetuate human misery in order to profit therefrom politically or otherwise will encounter the opposition of the United States," as evidence for this view. This statement, he argued, was "clearly directed against the USSR."[32] Formal Soviet participation in the Paris conference remained possible because it would be politically costly to exclude the USSR explicitly. But this formal opportunity was really only illusory, contended Novikov.

On the other hand, perhaps not wanting to commit himself fully to a pessimistic analysis, Novikov also noted the role economic pressures had played in shaping American policies. Like Varga, he observed that to some extent, economic necessity drove the American proposal. Truman's economic policies, wrote Novikov, had come under harsh criticism from his political opponents in Congress. He also noted the huge export-import imbalance between Europe and the United States. These factors in combination had forced a new turn in American policy, designed to enable the United States to strengthen its economy and achieve its foreign policy goals. Furthermore, the United States was not well-prepared to implement a European aid plan. The Truman administration would face "significant opposition from various circles" to its proposal for large-scale aid for Western Europe. While the economic interests of the country seemed to require such an aid program, said Novikov, no one could be certain that such a plan would receive the necessary support in the U.S. Congress.

Putting all these considerations together, Novikov prudently avoided reaching sweeping conclusions in the absence of definitive instructions from Moscow. Despite his suspicions, he asserted that American intentions remained unclear. As a result, he recommended that the Soviet Union attend the Paris conference in order to clarify the terms of Marshall's proposal. "It will be possible to further develop our position on the question of American aid after the concrete plans of the Americans, their conditions, and so on become clear," Novikov suggested.[33] He added that participating in the aid program would give Moscow the opportunity to shape the American aid program to its advantage, thus possibly "hindering the realization of the American plans for the subordination of Europe and the creation of an anti-Soviet bloc."[34]

On a related topic Novikov remarked that since German resources would play an important role in any plan for European recovery, the discussion of Marshall's proposal would serve as a opportunity to again raise the issue of reparations. This comment implied that by participating in the process of drawing up the plan, the USSR might receive not only American aid, but also further reparations from Germany.[35] So while Novikov suspected that this latest initiative by the United States was designed to build-up a West European bloc in opposition to the Soviet Union, he too did not rule out Soviet participation.

Moscow and the Paris Conference on the Marshall Plan

All of these threads of advice and information were tied together in the instructions for the Soviet delegation to the Paris conference, written by Molotov himself, and presumably approved by Stalin. In his cover letter to Stalin, Molotov noted that the instructions were "insufficiently worked out," but did not elaborate on what he meant exactly. Perhaps further changes were made after Stalin read them, and before the Soviet delegation departed for Paris.[36] As one would expect from Molotov's reading of Marshall's speech, Varga's analysis, and Novikov's reporting, the instructions did not call for outright rejection of Marshall's proposal. Rather, they broadly outlined the terms under which Moscow would be willing to participate in an American aid program.

The primary objective of the Soviet delegation, according to the instructions, was to determine the details of the American aid offer, since Marshall's speech had been rather vague. This goal also followed from Novikov's speculation that Marshall's initiative might not be supported in the American Congress. In addition, the Soviet delegation was instructed to call for the economic recovery plan to be implemented on a country-by-country basis, rather than through an all-European framework.[37] Such a sweeping all-European framework, the Soviet leaders feared, could form the basis for an anti-Soviet alliance. It might also be used to undermine Soviet influence in East Central Europe, by allowing the West to influence the economic development and policies of the states in the region. Such intrusive multilateral intervention had to be avoided.

The instructions also directed the delegation to oppose the imposition of certain conditions on any aid which might be offered. In particular, the delegation received instructions that

> In the discussion of any concrete proposals dealing with American aid to Europe, the Soviet delegation should object to any conditions of such aid which would carry with them the infringement of the sovereignty of the European countries or their economic enslavement. In the process of discussion this question, the Soviet delegation should make clear the negative attitude of the Soviet Union to such conditions of aid as were put into place in Greece and Turkey.[38]

Underlining the exact focus of this concern about economic "enslavement," the instructions further directed that "the Soviet delegation should object to possible proposals about the formation of a unified European aid plan which would obstruct the industrial development of Eastern Europe and would reinforce the pre-war relationships between the economies of individual European countries."[39]

On the question of German participation in any plan of American aid, the delegation was instructed to take a hard bargaining stance, following Novikov's suggestions. It was to object to any use of German resources unless agreement could be reached on the now long-standing Soviet demands for reparations and the establishment of four-power control over the Ruhr. If such an agreement could not be reached, then the Soviet delegation received instructions to object to any use of German resources in such a plan on a zonal basis.[40]

Overall, then, the Soviet position coming into the Paris conference remained cautious, but still moderate. The delegation's instructions were generally negative, in the sense that they outlined potential Western proposals to which the Soviet delegation must object. They devoted little space to the issue of the terms of a potential agreement. But acceptance of an American offer of aid under certain conditions was not precluded; the possibility of Soviet participation remained open. In order to achieve Soviet agreement, however, the Western powers would probably have had to accept a package deal which included concessions on German reparations. In addition, any aid program which the Soviet Union agreed to would have to be based on the aid requests of individual countries, only loosely coordinated.

The behavior of the Soviet delegation during the meeting itself reinforces the impression that Soviet leaders remained undecided about how to respond to the American proposal until after the Paris Conference. When Molotov arrived in Paris, his delegation numbered nearly 100, many more than necessary if he had come simply to delay the proceedings or to deliver a ceremonial refusal to participate. The size of the delegation itself suggested a willingness to engage in serious discussion.[41] The tone of Molotov's speech on the first day was quite moderate, and his main thrust consisted of getting the Americans, who were not at the conference, to outline the proposed aid program more clearly. In this context, a French diplomat noted after the first day of the conference that Molotov "has been extremely mild," and that "the Soviets wish at all costs to avoid giving the French or British a valid pretext to break with them."[42]

Despite this promising beginning, the conference ultimately foundered on the issue of what sort of aid request to forward to the Americans. The French and British wanted to set up a multi-national committee which would examine the aid requests of all European states and then coordinate them, so as to make most efficient use of the aid. The Soviets, on the other hand, simply wanted to aggregate all the individual requests and forward them to Washington. They did not want to create any multinational institutions, which they argued would infringe upon the "sovereignty" of individual states. In addition, the issue of Germany – with its huge economic potential casting a long shadow – again proved divisive. Molotov wanted assurances that any German participation in the aid program would not jeopardize possible reparations payments or lead to an increase in German industrial capacity. The British and the French would not directly address the issue, but refused to agree to these terms. When it became clear that the French and British would not agree with the Soviet proposal, Molotov delivered a harsh denunciation of the Western states and stormed out of the conference. Essentially, the Western states had attempted to impose exactly those conditions which the Soviet leaders had defined as unacceptable in their pre-conference analyses.[43]

In his closing speech, on July 3, Molotov accused the Western powers of seeking to divide Europe into two hostile camps. He rhetorically asked what the adoption of the Anglo-French plan would result in:

> This [plan] would lead England, France and a group of countries following them to separate themselves from the other states of Europe, which would split Europe into two groups of states and would create new difficulties in the relations between them.[44]

The Soviet leaders clearly feared that if they accepted the Anglo-French proposal, it would mean allowing Western penetration into the economies of East Central Europe. Before the war, the region had traded extensively with Western Europe. Regional trade patterns had then been directed towards the Soviet Union by a series of bilateral agreements signed after 1945. Acceptance by the region of the British-French-American economic aid plan would reorient the trade of the region in accordance with an all-European plan, perhaps revitalizing trade links between Western and Eastern Europe. Economic reintegration with Western Europe would have political effects too; it might reinforce the resistance of those elements in the East European states which hoped to avoid the imposition of Soviet hegemony. All these developments would greatly dilute Soviet influence in Eastern Europe. The Marshall Plan, then, once the details were filled in, appeared as an attempt to use American economic power to undermine the newly established buffer zone in Eastern Europe. And once Soviet influence in East Central Europe weakened, Western gains in the region might prove irreversible.

The Soviet Response to the Marshall Plan

Very quickly after Molotov's withdrawal from the talks in Paris, the Soviet Union began pressuring its East European neighbors to refuse to participate in the American aid plan as well. Where earlier Moscow had offered encouragement, it now engaged in heavy-handed political coercion. Moscow sought to counter the lure of American dollars by exploiting its considerable, if yet incomplete political influence in the region. Both Poland and Czechoslovakia had earlier communicated to the Western powers their desire to participate in the American program, following Molotov's suggestion. For a time, documents in the Moscow archives show, Molotov and Stalin even toyed with the idea of using Poland and Czechoslovakia as foils to obstruct the American aid program and thus prevent it from serving as the basis of a unified anti-Soviet bloc in Europe. But rather quickly they appear to have concluded that the participation of the East European "New Democracies," even for purposes of disrupting the American program, would be too dangerous.

The "New Democracies," after all, were led by coalition governments over which local Communist – and hence Soviet – control was incomplete. They might not prove able to resist the temptation of American economic aid, unless the Soviet Union moved quickly to consolidate its political control over them. Previously, such governments had seemed sufficient for the realization of Soviet interests in the region, at least for the near-term future. The Marshall Plan – once the details were filled in – resembled an offensive attempt to undermine Soviet influence in Eastern Europe. This development created a much more threatening international environment. Fairly loose control over the region had been satisfactory when the Western powers did not seem immediately threatening, and when selective cooperation with the West could deliver significant benefits.

The Marshall Plan drastically changed Soviet calculations in this respect. Under the political-economic assault which the plan appeared to represent, Stalin concluded that the indirect and somewhat circumscribed control over Eastern Europe that could be exercised through the participation of local Communist parties in coalition governments was no longer adequate. Had the Marshall Plan been proposed in such a way as to limit its focus to Western Europe, it would have been less threatening to the Soviet Union, and might not have had such sweeping repercussions. Then the plan would only have presented Stalin with the threat of a unified West European economic bloc, linked closely with the United States. This type of aid program would have been a threatening development, but not nearly so threatening as the version put forward by the French and British at Paris, which apparently aimed to lure away East European states to join this bloc. By trying to make the plan more inclusive in the initial phase, then, the Western powers simply created a plan that was even more threatening to the Soviet Union.

In the wake of the Marshall Plan, Stalin moved quickly to consolidate more effective means of control over the countries of Eastern Europe, to counter the threat presented by American economic power. First, of course, as detailed documentation from the archives in Prague shows, Stalin forced the Czechoslovak coalition government to withdraw its initial request to participate in the American aid program.[45] Similar pressure was exerted on Poland. Once this short-term objective had been achieved, Stalin and his colleagues began to search for an appropriate means to counter the Marshall Plan in the longer-term. The offensive threat which the Marshall Plan appeared to represent seems to have convince the Soviet leader that the West, led by the United States, was intent on encircling the Soviet Union with a hostile alliance. Since the West has shown itself as intrinsically hostile to the Soviet Union, Stalin seems to have reasoned, there was no longer any benefit to be gained from attempting to work out compromise solutions to common problems. From the summer of 1947 until his death, Stalin would rely principally on confron-tational unilateralism to ensure the security of the USSR.

This shift in strategy received its clearest expression in the Soviet decision to form a new coordinating center for European Communist parties, the Cominform. Documents from the personal archive of Stalin's lieutenant, Andrei Zhdanov, who at the time held responsibility within the Central Committee of the Soviet Communist Party for relations with other Communist parties, show that the Cominform was designed as a response to the Marshall Plan. The new organization would be used both to mobilize resistance to the Marshall Plan in Western Europe, and to consolidate Soviet control over the countries of Eastern Europe. Zhdanov's correspondence with Stalin about the agenda of the founding conference of the Cominform, as well as early drafts of Zhdanov's famous speech to the conference, titled, "On the International Situation," strongly confirm this analysis. Interestingly, the drafts of Zhdanov's speech show that it was only at the last minute that Zhdanov decided to introduce the concept which has become known as its central theme: the "two camp" thesis. Its introduction at the last minute underlines the essentially reactive nature of Soviet foreign policy in the wake of the Marshall Plan, and suggests that it was only following the Marshall Plan that Soviet strategy called for the division of Europe into two rigid spheres of influence.[46]

The Marshall Plan and the Division of Europe

The result of the Cominform meeting was a dramatic turn in the strategy of Communist parties across Europe. Where before broad-based coalition tactics and legal means were the order of the day, now the course was reversed. At the meeting Zhdanov instructed the European Communists to eschew cooperation with non-Communists, and to use all means – not excluding violence – to oppose the implementation of the Marshall Plan. The practical result of Zhdanov's instructions was two-fold. First, in the course of the next several months, the remaining elements of political pluralism were purged from the regimes in Eastern Europe. In countries like Hungary and Czechoslovakia, coalition governments were replaced by single-party Communist regimes, which immediately embarked on a process of forced Stalinization. In Western Europe, France and Italy were soon plunged into a series of violent Communist-led strikes, which temporarily damaged the economic recovery of the region, but ultimately served only to push these countries more firmly into the arms of the United States. Earlier misgivings in the West about Soviet intentions began to solidify and find more strident political expression, leading to the diplomatic isolation of the USSR and its now increasingly servile East European allies.

What the new Soviet archival evidence allows us to see more clearly then, is the importance of the Marshall Plan in precipitating the division of Europe which was so characteristic of the Cold War. Once its content became clear, the Marshall Plan appeared to Stalin and Molotov as an offensive move, designed not only to unify Western Europe into an anti-Soviet bloc, but also to undermine Soviet influence in East Europe. Where prior to the Marshall Plan, Stalin had held out some hope for selective cooperation with the Western powers, afterwards, he concluded that such cooperation was impossible, and that only through confrontational unilateral action could the offensive threat presented by American economic power be successfully thwarted and Soviet security guaranteed. This conclusion led directly to the sovietization of Eastern Europe, and the harshly confrontational foreign policy line which Stalin pursued until his death in 1953.

None of this should be taken to suggest, of course, that the Marshall Plan itself "caused" the division of Europe. The unstable international conditions in Europe which presented both the Western powers and the Soviet Union with a security dilemma were the underlying cause of this division, while the Marshall Plan itself was simply the event that triggered it. It was those conditions which constrained the Truman administration and its British and French counterparts to design the Marshall Plan as they did – making it appear open to Soviet and East European participation when in fact this appearance hardly had any substance behind it. And it was this ambiguity that led Stalin to draw the conclusion that the plan was an offensive move against Soviet interests, making the Soviet response more intense and aggressive than it might otherwise have been. The Marshall Plan, then, crucially affected the timing and the form of the division of Europe and served as the trigger for the intensification of the nascent Soviet-American conflict that would become known as the Cold War.

Notes

1. Robert Jervis, "Cooperation Under the Security Dilemma," *World Politics* 30 (January 1978), 167-214.

2. John Herz, "Idealist Internationalism and the Security Dilemma," *World Politics* 2 (January 1950), 157-180.

3. Jervis, "Cooperation under the Security Dilemma," 38.

4. Jervis, "Cooperation under the Security Dilemma," 49-50.

5. Jervis, "Cooperation under the Security Dilemma," 60-61. For further elaboration of the implications of offense-dominance for state behavior, see Stephen Van Evera, "Causes of War," (PhD Dissertation, University of California at Berkeley, 1984), 80-105, Tom Christensen and Jack Snyder, "Chain Gangs and Passed Bucks: Predicting Alliance Patterns in Multipolarity," *International Organization* 44 (Spring 1990), 137-168, and Scott Parrish, "The USSR and the Security Dilemma: Explaining Soviet Self-Encirclement, 1945-1985," (PhD Dissertation, Columbia University, 1993), ch. 2.

6. See William Taubman, *Stalin's American Policy: From Entente to Detente, to Cold War* (New York: Norton & Norton, 1982), ch. 6.

7. Melvyn Leffler, "The United States and the Strategic Dimensions of the Marshall Plan," *Diplomatic History* 12 (Summer 1988), 279. See also Melvyn Leffler, *A Preponderance of Power: National Security, the Truman Administration, and the Cold War* (Stanford University Press, 1992), 190-92.

8. German reparations were offered to the Soviet leaders, but only under extremely restrictive conditions which made it unlikely the USSR would actually receive any substantial payments. See *Foreign Relations of the United States: Diplomatic Papers, 1947*, vol. 2, (Washington, DC: USGPO, 1979), 298-99; 301-03. Volumes from this series will hereafter be referred to as FRUS, followed by the year and volume number.

9. Quoted in Taubman, *Stalin's American Policy*, 157.

10. *FRUS:1947*, vol. 2, (Washington, DC: USGPO, 1979), 340-41.

11. *FRUS:1947*, vol. 2, 343-44.

12. John Foster Dulles, *War or Peace* (New York: Macmillan, 1950), 105.

13. For the text of Marshall's speech, see *FRUS, 1947*, vol. 2, 237-39.

14. "Novikov to Molotov," June 9, 1947, AVP RF, 059/18/ 39/250/207-209, also printed in *Mezhdunarodnaia Zhizn* , no. 5 (May 1992), 118-119.

15. "Translation of Secretary of State Marshall's speech of June 5, 1947," AVP RF, f. 06, op. 9, d. 209, p. 18, l. 2-5.

16. This sort of caution in reporting would hardly have been an irrational strategy for Novikov at the time, given the fate of many Soviet diplomats in the purges of the 1930s.

17. William C. Cromwell, "The Marshall Plan, Britain, and the Cold War," *Review of International Studies* 8 (October 1982), 240.

18. "Caffery to Marshall," June 20, 1947, *FRUS: 1947*, vol. 3, 260.

19. "Memorandum of Conversation between Soviet Deputy Foreign Minister Malik and British Ambassador Peterson," June 10, 1947, and "Memorandum of Conversation between Soviet Deputy Foreign Minster Malik and French Chargé Charpantier," June 11, 1947, AVP RF, 06/9/217/19/12-25.

20. "Report of Academician Varga to Foreign Minister Molotov," June 24, 1947, AVP RF, 06/9/213/18/2. The complete distribution list included Stalin, Beria (head of State Security), Zhdanov, Mikoyan, Malenkov, Voznesenskii (all Politburo members), Vyshinskii (Deputy Foreign Minister), and Malik. Unfortunately, the author had no way to verify whether these individuals, especially Stalin, actually read this report. Nor have any materials documenting Politburo deliberations on this subject been released. Despite the considerable material which is available on this topic, this gap at the highest level of decision-making imposes serious limitations on any analysis of the decision to send Molotov to the Paris meeting. These limitations could perhaps be addressed if scholars were allowed access to the historical sections of the "Presidential" or Kremlin archive.

21. "Report of Academician Varga to Foreign Minister Molotov," l. 3.

22. "Report of Academician Varga to Foreign Minister Molotov," l. 4.

23. "Report of Academician Varga to Foreign Minister Molotov," l. 5.

24. Eugene Varga, *Izmeneniia v ekonomike kapitalizma v itoge vtoroi mirovoi voiny* (Moscow, 1946). For an English summary, see Leo Gruilow, trans., *Soviet Views on the Post-War Economy* (Washington, DC: Public Affairs Press, 1948).

25. Varga's caution and his circumspection in laying out the implications of his analysis, like Novikov's, can be attributed in part to his desire to protect himself against future accusations of insufficient vigilance. Varga had already come under attack at this time for his views on the possibility of planning in the West, and although he had refused to recant his views, he may well have felt the need to adopt a more "vigilant" stance toward the Western powers in this assessment for Molotov. He may have been more optimistic about the possibility of cooperation with the West than this report suggests. It becomes rather difficult,

under such circumstances, to determine what Varga was trying to convey in the report. This is one of many difficult issues of interpretation which scholars face in dealing with primary documents from the late Stalin era.

26. "Molotov to Soviet Embassies in Eastern Europe," June 22, 1947, AVP RF, 06/9/214/18/19. Printed in *Mezhdunarodnaia Zhizn'* no. 5 (May 1992), 125.

27. "Polish Ambassador M. Nashkovskii to Molotov," June 24, 1947, and "Czechoslovak Government to Soviet Government," July 1, 1947, AVP RF, 06/9/212/18/1, 11.

28. "Novikov to Molotov," June 24, 1947 AVP RF, 059/18/39/250/314-320. Printed in *Mezhdunarodnaia Zhizn''* no. 5 (May 1992), 121.

29. "Novikov to Molotov," 121.

30. For Soviet press coverage of Clayton's visit, see *Pravda*, June 29, 1947. This article suggested that Clayton had travelled to Paris in order to "lay out for the British government the viewpoint of the American government about what Bevin should do at Paris." For an internal Foreign Ministry analysis of speculation in the Western press about the purpose of Clayton's visit to London, which also notes the possibility that the Americans are acting behind the scenes to influence the outcome of the Paris meeting, see "Survey of the Press for June 27, 1947, Soviet Embassy in Paris," AVP RF, 06/9/18/ 220/125.

31. For information on the Clayton-Bevin meeting, see *Leffler, Preponderance of Power*, 183. For an American summary of the discussion, see, *FRUS: 1947*, vol. 3, 268-69.

32. "Novikov to Molotov," June 24, 1947, AVP RF, 059/18/39/250/314-320. Printed in *Mezhdunarodnaia Zhizn* no. 5 (May 1992), 121-22.

33. "Novikov to Molotov," 123

34. "Novikov to Molotov," 122.

35. "Novikov to Molotov," 122.

36. "Instructions for the Soviet Delegation to the Foreign Ministers Meeting in Paris," June 25, 1947, AVP RF, 06/9/214/18/2. From the cover letter one can assume that Stalin was sent a copy of the instructions, but nothing in the files to which the author had access indicated that Stalin actually read the report, or shed any light on what changes, if any, the Soviet leader may have made to these instructions. (Again, this gap in documentation underscores the need to gain access to the "Presidential" or Kremlin archive). These instructions have been published in *Mezhdunarodnaia Zhizn* no. 5 (May 1992), 123-125.

37. "Instructions for the Soviet Delegation to the Foreign Ministers Meeting in Paris," l. 1-3.

38. "Instructions for the Soviet Delegation to the Foreign Ministers Meeting in Paris," l. 9.

39. "Instructions for the Soviet Delegation to the Foreign Ministers Meeting in Paris," l. 10.

40. "Instructions for the Soviet Delegation to the Foreign Ministers Meeting in Paris," l. 11-13.

41. *FRUS: 1947*, vol. 3, 310.

42. "Instructions for the Soviet Delegation to the Foreign Ministers Meeting in Paris," 300.

43. For another view of Soviet motives and actions during the Paris Conference, including telegraphic communications between Molotov in Paris and Stalin in Moscow, see Mikhail Narinsky's article in Mikhail Narinsky and Scott Parrish, "New Evidence on the Soviet Rejection of the Marshall Plan, 1947: Two Reports," Working Paper #9, Cold War International History Project, Woodrow Wilson Center, Washington DC, March, 1994.

44. "Stenographic Record of the Paris Conference of Foreign Ministers," July 3, 1947, AVP RF, 06/9/215/18/96.

45. Karel Krátky, "Czechoslovakia, The Soviet Union and The Marshall Plan," in O. A. Westad et al., eds., *The Soviet Union in Eastern Europe, 1945-1989* (London: Macmillan, 1993), 35.

46. For a discussions of the formation of the Cominform which use newly-available archival evidence, see Leonid Gibianskii, "Kak voznik Kominform," *Novaia i Noveishaia Istoriia,* no. 4 (July-August 1993), and Vladislav Zubok and Constantine Pleshakov, *Inside the Kremlin's Cold War* (Harvard: Harvard University Press, 1996), ch. 4.

14

The Soviet-Yugoslav Split and the Cominform

Leonid Gibianskii

In the first years following World War II, Yugoslavia was one of the most important components of the Soviet Bloc ("the socialist camp"). The country was distinguished by the fact that a Communist regime had come to power earlier than in the other Eastern European nations, and was the outgrowth of an indigenous Communist movement, rather than one propped up and prodded by Moscow. Both within the Communist movement and among the movement's adversaries, Yugoslavia was considered the USSR's number one ally, the country which was most advanced in creating a socialist order. In matters of foreign policy, Yugoslavia stood unwaveringly at the USSR's side during increasing confrontations with the West.[1] Moscow deeply appreciated the domestic and foreign policy of the Yugoslav Communist regime and consistently expressed its positive appraisal in analytical and instructive materials. Moreover, in their public pronouncements, Soviet leaders invariably mentioned Yugoslavia first among the countries of Eastern Europe.[2]

Moscow supported Belgrade in the international arena and rendered large-scale aid to the nascent Yugoslav Army. The USSR was also Yugoslavia's principal foreign-trade partner and offered extensive aid in the country's industrialization. Yugoslav leaders viewed close cooperation between Moscow and Belgrade as essential in consolidating Yugoslavia's position in the international arena, as well as in building socialism.[3] Despite this mutual aid and admiration, there were bound to be conflicts of interest between the Yugoslavs and their mentors. For example, the Yugoslavs were disenchanted with the Soviets' inclination to compromise with the West over the question of Trieste. While the Yugoslavs vigorously asserted their claim to Trieste, the Soviets, though trying so far as possible to support the Yugoslav cause, considered it inadvisable to risk a clash with the West over Trieste.

Tito's speech in Ljubljana at the end of May 1945 caused the Soviets considerable consternation. Referring to the anti-Yugoslav campaign which was being launched by the West in response to the Trieste crisis, Tito protested that Yugoslavia did not wish to be used as "small change" or as an object of exchange "in a policy of spheres of interest."[4] Moscow interpreted Tito's comments as a reproach aimed not only at the Western allies, but also at the USSR, and warned the Yugoslav leadership that such statements were inadmissible. In this case, the Yugoslavs humbly accepted the criticism and offered the requisite apologies.[5]

On other occasions when the Yugoslavs expressed their dissatisfaction with the Soviet position on the Trieste question, Moscow responded with displeasure, asserting that the Yugoslavs' criticisms were unfounded. In July 1946, at the Council of Foreign Ministers meeting in Paris, France proposed that Trieste be designated a special zone under U.N. control. When Tito learned that the Soviet delegation had expressed its willingness to consider the French plan as a basis of discussion, and had put forward a proposal of its own regarding the status of such a zone, he sent Stalin a coded telegram in which he castigated Soviet representatives in Paris for not giving Yugoslavia sufficient support. In his reply to Tito, Stalin refuted the charges, and declared that the Soviet delegation consistently defended Yugoslav interests, but was obliged to compromise because it was obvious that the Western Powers "will in no case agree to hand Trieste over to Yugoslavia."[6]

Complications arose in economic relations, as well, especially in the creation of Soviet-Yugoslav joint-stock companies in various branches of Yugoslavia's economy. Although the companies were provided for in an agreement concluded on June 8, 1946, the partners did not see eye to eye on the amount to be invested by each side, especially in the mining sector. Belgrade insisted that the estimated value of the mineral deposits be considered in calculating its investment, while the Soviets objected that the deposits could not, in fact, constitute an investment value.[7] At the session of the Politburo of the CPY Central Committee in September 1946, participants expressed their discontent with the Soviet attitude, likening it to capitalist countries' exploitation of Yugoslav mineral deposits before the war. The Soviet ambassador in Belgrade got wind of the Yugoslavs' disgruntlement, and relayed it to Moscow.[8] Stalin, however, preferred not to exacerbate the problem. In a conversation with Kardelj, who was visiting Moscow on April 19, 1947, Stalin proposed that the joint-stock companies be abandoned altogether, and that Soviet aid be rendered in the form of equipment and technical assistance.[9] An agreement to this effect was signed on July 25, 1946.

Thus, the Yugoslav leadership, which had come to power without outside intervention, was sufficiently confident to oppose Soviet decisions if they conflicted with Belgrade's interests. Nevertheless, the Yugoslavs continued to observe the established Communist hierarchy, and regarded the USSR as the center of the "socialist camp." For its part, Moscow sought to avoid conflict with its number one ally, and instead made every attempt to strengthen its ties with Yugoslavia.

Although the Kremlin was relatively tolerant of disagreements in the sphere of bilateral relations, Stalin reacted very sharply in August 1947, when Yugoslavia and Bulgaria concluded a treaty of friendship, cooperation, and mutual aid without Moscow's sanction. In a coded telegram sent to Tito and Dimitrov, Stalin censured the Yugoslav and Bulgarian governments for having, in "their haste," "made a mistake" which could be exploited by "reactionary Anglo-American elements." As is clear from the telegram, the fact that this had been done "without consulting the Soviet Government" particularly provoked Stalin's ire.[10]

Stalin's rebuke was accepted by both the Yugoslav and the Bulgarian governments in the spirit of the hierarchical discipline that prevailed within the Communist movement and the incipient "socialist camp." Like Sofia, Belgrade moved to conclude the treaty only after Tito and Dimitrov had received authorization from the appropriate quarter in mid-September. Moreover, a month before signing the treaty, the Yugoslavs sent the draft treaty to Moscow for approval. They followed the same procedure in concluding treaties with Romania and Hungary in December 1947.[11]

The Bulgarian-Yugoslav incident, which had been kept under tight wraps by all three parties, was apparently settled. Yugoslavia continued to enjoy the Soviets' approbation, and the CPY received favorable evaluations in instructive articles which appeared in Communist Party papers, and in Andrei Zhdanov's assessment of the Yugoslavs' representatives' attitudes and contribution at the September 1947 conference of the nine Communist parties.[12] Yet, almost immediately after the Cominform meeting, Belgrade and Moscow were at loggerheads over Yugoslav-Albanian relations.

During the first postwar years, the CPY continued to play the role of guardian in its relationship with the Communist Party of Albania, and Belgrade was as important to Tirana as Moscow was to Belgrade. The Yugoslav leadership was able to exercise considerable influence on the policy and activity of the leading Albanian organs through advisors and instructors it had sent to Albania, as well as through the representative of the Yugoslav Central Committee who was attached to the Albanian Central Committee. Albania and Yugoslavia concluded agreements which were to lead to the integration of the two economies, and Yugoslavia continued to push for political integration. Archival documents reveal that Yugoslavia's aspirations in Albania attracted Moscow's attention.[13]   When Stalin met with Tito during the latter's visit to Moscow in May 1946, he did not object to Albania's inclusion in a Yugoslav federation, but cautioned that steps toward federation would be premature until the question of Trieste was settled. Nevertheless, Stalin approved measures that would effectively tie Albania more closely to Yugoslavia, and confirmed that Soviet aid to Albania would continue to be rendered through the Yugoslavs, thereby giving his "blessing" to Yugoslavia's "guardianship."[14]

After the visit of Albanian leaders to Moscow in May-July 1947, however, direct communication between the Soviets and Albanians was established, and Soviet economic advisors were dispatched to Albania. The Yugoslavs did not look kindly upon the Soviet interlopers, and considered them potential competitors for influence in Albania.[15] When the Yugoslav leadership learned that one of the most influential members of the Albanian leadership, Nako Spiru, maintained special contacts with the Soviet representatives in Tirana, their fears seemed justified. In November 1947, Belgrade accused Spiru of deliberately sabotaging economic cooperation with Yugoslavia, but Spiru committed suicide before the charges were investigated by the Politburo of his own party. At this point, Tito instructed the Yugoslav ambassador in Moscow, Vladimir Popović, to present the Yugoslav case to Stalin.[16]

Zhdanov, rather than Stalin, received the ambassador at the beginning of December 1947. After setting forth the accusations against the deceased Spiru, and emphasizing that the latter had sought to use his contacts with the Soviet representatives to further his anti-Yugoslav aims, Popović tried to secure the Soviets' agreement to withdraw their specialists from Albania, and to yield the predominant role in Albania to Yugoslavia.[17] In reply, Stalin telegraphed Tito on December 23, 1947, asking the Yugoslavs to send to Moscow "a responsible comrade, perhaps Djilas, or someone else more familiar with the situation in Albania," as he, Stalin, was "ready to comply with all your wishes," but needed to know "precisely" what those were.[18]

After arriving in Moscow, Djilas received the Soviets' agreement that Albania's development should be completely tied to Yugoslavia's, even to the point of unification, and that the activity of Soviet military and economic advisers in Albania should be co-ordinated with the Yugoslavs. However, as at his meeting with Tito in May 1946, Stalin had urged the Yugoslavs not to rush towards formal unification with Albania, but to wait for a suitable moment.[19] From available archival materials, it is impossible to ascertain whether Stalin was expressing his real intentions, or if his compliance was merely a tactical maneuver. A few months earlier, in late summer/fall of 1947, the Foreign Policy Department of the Soviet Central Committee stated in a memorandum: "The leaders of the Yugoslav CP are very jealous because Albania is trying to forge direct links with the Soviet Union. In their view,

Albania ought to communicate with the Soviet Union only through the Yugoslav government."[20] This "jealousy" was cited as one of the Yugoslav leadership's negative qualities, and as evidence that "when deciding questions of foreign policy, certain leaders of the Yugoslav CP sometimes display national narrowness, failing to take account of the interests of other countries and of brother CP's."[21] Thus, even before Belgrade presented Moscow with its claims concerning Albania, these were regarded very critically.

This indictment of Yugoslavia's "national narrowness" in matters of foreign policy was part and parcel of the memorandum's more general criticism: "When speaking of the successes of the Yugoslav CP in strengthening the democratic regime... one cannot avoid mentioning certain tendencies among the Party's leaders to exaggerate their achievements, and endeavor to cast the Yugoslav CP as a sort of 'leading' party in the Balkans."[22] The Kremlin found such pretensions unacceptable, since it saw itself as the one and only center of the Communist movement and the Soviet bloc.

We have no evidence indicating how, and to what extent, the Soviet leadership took into account this criticism of Yugoslavia's ambitions in the Balkans when they were negotiating with the Yugoslavs regarding Albania. There is also no record of their reaction to reports sent by the Soviet embassy in Belgrade, which also charged the Yugoslavs, including Tito himself, with "local nationalism" and "national narrowness." As proof of this accusation, the ambassador's dispatches cite the Yugoslavs' exaggeration of their own role in the armed struggle of 1941-1945, and the minimization of the USSR's role in liberating Yugoslavia.

Reports from the Soviet embassy in Belgrade became even more disapproving between the autumn of 1947 and January 1948, when the ambassador, Anatolii I. Lavrentyev and the military attaché, Major-General G. S. Sidorovich, accused prominent Yugoslav leaders of failing to understand "the essence of Marxism-Leninism," of lacking a clear-cut ideological-political orientation, and of deliberately counterposing Tito's "leaderism" to the "legitimate" charisma of the sole great leader – Stalin. As early as autumn 1947, the ambassador suggested to Moscow that criticism of the Yugoslav leadership, and of Tito personally, be expressed to the representative of the CPY's Central Committee who was permanently attached to the Soviet Central Committee. Lavrentyev and Sidorovich proposed that the issue be raised with Djilas, who had been sent to see Stalin. The military attaché further recommended that "these mistakes be addressed in an 'exchange of experience' according to the procedure of the Information Bureau of certain Communist Parties."[23]

Sidorovich's suggestion regarding the Information Bureau seems strange, to say the least, since at that time the Cominform had not yet begun to function as a permanent organizational structure. Not only was there no established procedure for such "an exchange of experience," but the Cominform's only working body at the time was the editorial board of the newspaper *For a Lasting Peace – For a People's Democracy!*, which had been created after the Conference at Szklarska Poręba. In any case, at the second meeting of the Cominform on January 18, 1948, there was no hint of the complaints against the Yugoslavs, nor (despite Lavrentyev's and Sidorovich's recommendations) had there been any criticism at Djilas's meeting with Stalin, Molotov, and Zhdanov earlier that month, when the Soviet leaders declared their willingness to support the Yugoslavs' aspirations in Albania.

Within a few days, however, the Albanian issue resurfaced with a vengeance. After receiving Djilas's report from Moscow on the Soviet leadership's position, Tito sent the First Secretary of the Communist Party of Albania and the Albanian Chairman of the Council of Ministers, Enver Hoxha, a telegram in which he proposed the establishment of a Yugoslav military base in Southern Albania. In the telegram, Tito cited the threat of invasion by "Greek monarcho-fascists backed by the Anglo-Americans" as the raison d'être for a Yugoslav military presence. Hoxha agreed to Tito's proposal on January 20.[24] Djilas later asserted in his memoirs that Tito actually wanted to send in his troops so as to strengthen Yugoslavia's position in Albania.[25] Whether or not that was the case, Tito took action without consulting Moscow and did not inform them of his correspondence with Hoxha.

When the Soviets learned from other sources of Belgrade's intention to send a division to Albania, they reacted immediately. Molotov fired off a fusillade of telegrams to Tito at the end of January and the beginning of February 1948, declaring that "the USSR regards such a procedure as abnormal," and "cannot reconcile itself to being presented with a fait accompli." The telegrams grumbled about "serious differences" with the Yugoslav leadership "on foreign policy questions" and "in the conception of relations between our two countries." In the spirit of hierarchical discipline, Tito acknowledged his "mistake," refrained from sending troops to Albania, and assured the Soviet leadership of his intention to consult the USSR without fail in matters of foreign policy. In spite of this, a summons followed from Moscow for "two or three responsible representatives of the Yugoslav Government" to attend a meeting at which "differences" would be discussed.[26]

The Bulgarians were also invited to attend this meeting, since Dimitrov had crossed the line on January 17, 1948, when he indiscreetly told reporters about the future creation of a federation of East European countries, which would include all the "people's democracies," plus Greece, where the Communist Party was waging a war to establish a similar regime.[27] Evidently, the simultaneity of these "independent" initiatives in foreign policy, which not only ignored the hierarchical principle, but conflicted with the Kremlin's own plans, particularly provoked the Kremlin's concern.

On February 10, 1948, the Yugoslav and Bulgarian delegations, headed respectively by Kardelj and Dimitrov, met with Stalin, Molotov, Zhdanov, Malenkov and Suslov.[28] At the meeting, the Yugoslavs and Bulgarians were reprimanded for a series of transgressions including: "the premature" announcement in August 1947 of a Yugoslav-Bulgarian treaty (which had purportedly been forgotten); Dimitrov's announcement of a federation in Eastern Europe; and the Yugoslav attempt to send a division to Albania. The Soviets emphasized both the "incorrectness" of these steps and the inadmissibility of any action taken without informing the USSR. Predictably, the Yugoslav and Bulgarian delegations dutifully admitted their "mistakes." The upshot of this confrontation was the signing on February 11, 1948, of protocols in which the Yugoslavs and Bulgarians agreed to consult the Soviets on international questions. Stalin once again reiterated his opposition to the deployment of Yugoslav troops in Albania, clearly insinuating that "the Yugoslavs are afraid of the Russians in Albania and for that reason are hurrying to send their own troops into that country."

While warning against "haste" in unification with Albania, and sharply criticizing Dimitrov's idea for a future federation of all East European countries, Stalin unexpectedly suggested the creation of three federations in this region – a Polish-Czechoslovak federation, a Romano-Hungarian federation, and Yugoslav-Bulgaro-Albanian federation. Although Stalin did not come down definitively on a time-table for the establishment of these federations, he clearly indicated that only the Balkan federation was slated for the near future. In fact, he insisted upon the urgency of a Yugoslav-Bulgarian federation, which Albania would subsequently join.

The archival materials give no indication of Stalin's motives for presenting this plan. In practice, however, his scheme acted as a counterweight, first, to Dimitrov's notion of a general East-European federation, and second, to the unification of Albania with Yugoslavia, which Belgrade so ardently desired. That unification was not only deferred, but altogether altered – instead of swallowing Albania, Yugoslavia was demoted to a constituent unit of a federation proposed by Stalin.[29]

Judging from the documents currently available, the Yugoslav delegation made no definitive reply to Stalin's proposals, but at its February 19 meeting, the CPY Politburo rejected a federation with Bulgaria.[30] This decision was later confirmed at a general meeting of the Politburo on March 1, with the frank assessment that because of the Soviets' influence in Bulgaria, a federation with that country might become a means for Soviet control over Yugoslavia, as well. The Politburo also reiterated its intention to maintain Yugoslavia's predominance in Albania.[31] At the end of February and the beginning of March, Belgrade renewed its efforts to achieve this. First, as the result of Yugoslav influence, the Albanian leadership, which was unaware of the February 10 meeting in Moscow, once again raised the question of Yugoslav troops in Albania with Soviet representatives. Second, the Yugoslavs also began urging Tirana to propose the unification of Albania with Yugoslavia.[32]

Finally, the Yugoslav leadership ignored Stalin's instructions regarding Greece. At the February 10 meeting, when Kardelj had attempted to justify the introduction of Yugoslav troops into Albania by citing the need to defend Albania against the threat of invasion from Greece, the Soviet leader suggested curtailing support to the Greek CP. While Stalin justified his position by disparaging the Greek partisans' chances of victory in the civil war, he also mentioned that the aid the Yugoslavs were rendering the Greek movement constituted the only serious problem for the "Anglo-Americans," who would do everything possible to hold on to Greece.[33] Stalin's words can be interpreted in keeping with traditional Yugoslav and Western historiography; namely, the Soviet attitude was indicative of Moscow's fear of a military clash between the Soviet bloc and the West, as a result of the West's opposition to the establishment of a Communist regime in Greece. This version, which continues to be argued in recent works,[34] appears logical, but it is not supported by Soviet documents. We cannot exclude the possibility that the Soviets were also deeply influenced by a festering distrust of the Yugoslav leadership – the fear that the Yugoslav intervention in the Greek civil war would evolve beyond the Kremlin's control.

Whatever his reasons, Stalin expressed himself plainly enough at the February 10, 1948, meeting. However, on February 21, at a meeting arranged in Belgrade by Tito, Kardelj, and Djilas with the general secretary of the Greek CP, Nicholas Zachariades, and a member of its Political Bureau, I. Ioannides, the Yugoslavs agreed with the Greek Communist leaders on the necessity of continuing to support the partisan movement in Greece.[35] Their ready agreement, of course, was due to the fact that it furthered the Yugoslav leadership's own aspirations.

Thus, the Yugoslav leadership, which had hitherto submitted to the hierarchical discipline within the Communist movement and the "socialist camp," defied the Kremlin and acted according to its own interests. This defiance was legitimized by a session of the Politburo of the CPY on March 1, which concluded that the USSR was unwilling to take account of the interests of Yugoslavia or of the other "People's Democracies," and was exerting pressure in order to impose its own will upon them. The Politburo cited the Soviet side's delay in settling a number of pressing questions regarding the supply of arms to the Yugoslav Army, and the development of economic cooperation, as examples of the means employed by the Soviets to exert this pressure.[36]

Inevitably, Moscow learned of Belgrade's defiance through its informants: specifically, Sreten Žujović, a member of the Yugoslav Politburo, who frequently provided the Soviet ambassador with inside information about the proceedings of the Politburo.[37] Lavrentyev immediately forwarded Žujović's damning report on to Moscow.[38] Understandably, the Soviets construed the Yugoslav attitude as an inadmissible challenge to Soviet supremacy in the "socialist camp." In a coded telegram sent on March 7, 1948, to Lavrentyev, Molotov instructed the ambassador to thank Žujović, on behalf of the Soviet Central Committee, for exposing "the sham friends of the Soviet Union in the Yugoslav Central Committee."[39]

The icing on the cake was yet another "criminal offense" by Belgrade, which implicitly challenged Soviet domination. On March 9, Lavrentyev telegraphed Moscow with the news that the Yugoslavs, acting contrary to previous practice, had refused to provide information about the country's economy to the Soviet trade representative. In his dispatch, the ambassador concluded that this behavior "reflects changes" in the attitude of the Yugoslav leaders to the USSR.[40] On March 11, Lavrentyev left Belgrade in response to urgent summons to Moscow, where Soviet leaders were contemplating what tack to take in dealing with the "disobedient" Yugoslavs.[41] At the same time, the Soviets received a number of official complaints from the Yugoslavs regarding the Soviets' procrastination in settling questions of military and economic collaboration. In response to these, Molotov sent Tito a telegram on March 13 which seemed to declare the Soviet government's willingness to settle the questions, and in his March 18 response, Tito proposed that the negotiations be resumed as soon as possible.[42]

However, this letter had not yet left Tito's hands when the Soviet embassy forwarded another telegram from Molotov, dated March 18. This one took the Yugoslavs to task for their refusal to supply the Soviet representative with information they had requested about the Yugoslav economy, which the Soviet government interpreted as "an act of mistrust towards the Soviet officials in Yugoslavia and as a manifestation of unfriendliness towards the USSR." The Soviets therefore immediately recalled all Soviet citizens who had been working as civilian specialists in Yugoslavia, as well as all military instructors and advisors.[43]

Quite clearly, these measures were intended to "punish" Belgrade for its refusal to provide economic information to Soviet representatives, as well as for the Yugoslav breach of Stalin's directives regarding Balkan politics. On March 18, the same day that Moscow had announced the recall of Soviet military and civilian specialists from Yugoslavia, the Foreign Policy Department of the Soviet Central Committee presented to Suslov, one of its secretaries, a lengthy memorandum, evidently prepared by order of the leadership, "On the anti-Marxist positions of the leaders of the Communist Party of

Yugoslavia on questions of foreign and domestic policy." This document stated: "Intoxicated by their successes in consolidating the people's democratic state and creating the preconditions for socialist construction, the leaders of the Yugoslav CP overrate their achievements and allow elements of adventurism to enter into their estimation of their future prospects and foreign policy, laying claim to a leading role in the Balkan and Danubian countries."[44]

From the memorandum presented to Suslov on March 18, it is also clear that the apparatus of the Soviet Central Committee had been ordered to prepare extensive politico-ideological accusations of "anti-Marxist positions," which would be presented to the Yugoslav leadership in order to "cut short the sedition." The memorandum further alleged that in defining their practical tasks and prospects, the leaders of the CPY were "ignoring Marxist-Leninist theory and failing to use it as a guide to action"; displaying "an incorrect, malevolent attitude" to the USSR and the CPSU(b), "the tried and acknowledged leader of all the progressive, anti-imperialist forces in the world"; underestimating the difficulties of building socialism in Yugoslavia, especially the possibility of an increase in the kulak element, since they were permitting "opportunism in their policy towards the kulaks"; and pursuing an "essentially liquidationist policy" in the organization of the CPY, "dissolving the Party in the People's Front."[45]

Almost all of these charges were leveled at the Yugoslavs after Tito's March 20 reply to Molotov, in which he refuted the allegations concerning the Yugoslavs' purported hostility towards the USSR and their refusal to comply with the Soviet trade representative's routine request for information. While Tito asserted that economic information should only be dispersed through the Yugoslav Central Committee, he declared his desire to address all the issues which provoked discord between the two countries. But the Soviets would not be mollified. On March 27, a letter signed on behalf of the Soviet Central Committee by Stalin and Molotov charged the Yugoslav leadership with pursuing an anti-Soviet line, committing opportunist errors, and revising very important propositions of Marxism-Leninism.

When confronted with the choice of throwing themselves upon the dubious mercy of the Kremlin rulers, or resolutely defending their positions, the Yugoslavs chose to refute the charges, and present the Soviets with an account of acts directed against Yugoslavia in a letter to Stalin and Molotov on April 13. The letter provoked even more serious political and ideological charges in Soviet missives dated May 4 and 22. According to the Soviets, the Yugoslav leaders had clearly abandoned Marxism-Leninism and had embraced nationalism; their positions were compared with those of Bernstein, the Mensheviks, Bukharin, and the ultimate Soviet bogey, Trotsky.[46]

Tellingly, in this secret correspondence, the Soviet side omitted all mention of Belgrade's Balkan policy, which was the fundamental and immediate cause of the crisis in Soviet-Yugoslav relations, while the general political and ideological accusations (of opportunism and departure from Marxism-Leninism) had no basis in the Yugoslavs' foreign or domestic policy. The only truth to the Soviets' accusations was their criticism of anti-democratic procedures in the CPY and the semi-secret nature of its activity. But the Kremlin had little concern for democracy in the CPY, and merely threw in this charge to reinforce its general onslaught against the Yugoslav leadership.

When the Soviets began their campaign against the Yugoslavs, they counted on two factors which would ensure either the surrender of Tito and his closest associates, or else their forcible removal; in fact, they contemplated organizing an anti-Tito revolt in the CPY which would involve some of the leading cadres, as well as the Cominform. The Soviets considered the aforementioned Žujović as their first possible trump card. Žujović maintained secret contact with the USSR's embassy in Belgrade and had discussed with Soviet diplomats possible measures which might induce Tito and his coterie to recant. In the wake of these discussions, Žujović imprudently opted for open revolt at the CPY Central Committee plenum held on April 12-13, 1948. However, he remained isolated and was expelled from both the Central Committee and the Party.

Shortly thereafter, on May 7, Žujović was arrested. On the eve of the Cominform conference, the arrest of Žujović, as well as that of a second prominent member of the CPY, Andrija Hebrang, provoked yet another sharp exchange between the Soviet and Yugoslav leaderships. Moscow charged that the Yugoslavs intended to liquidate Žujović and Hebrang, and stated that if Belgrade "carries out this intention, the Central Committee of the CPSU(b) will consider the Politburo of the Central Committee of the CPY to be murderers." The Soviets demanded that the investigation of the case against Hebrang and Žujović "take place with the participation of representatives of the Central Committee of the CPSU(b)." The Yugoslav leadership rejected the Soviet demands,[47] and Moscow did not manage to organize any more uprisings within the CPY before the 1948 Cominform conference.

The June 1948 conference had hardly gotten off the ground before the Cominform itself was dragged into the mêlée. Without informing the Yugoslavs, the Soviets promptly circulated their March 27 letter to the CPY to the Central Committees of the East European Communist parties which were Cominform members. Both archival documents and some memoirs attest to the fact that a number of East European leaders – e.g. Władysław Gomułka, Georgi Dimitrov and Gheorghe Gheorghiu-Dej, among them – did not accept the Soviet allegations against the Yugoslavs at face value.[48] Nevertheless, the principle of hierarchical subordination to Moscow proved stronger than doubts as to the veracity of the Soviet claims. In April, the leading organs of all five parties (Hungary, Bulgaria, Poland, Czechoslovakia, Romania) had sent the

Soviet Central Committee their endorsements of the Soviet position, without having given the Yugoslavs the opportunity to present their case. The Politburo of the French Communist Party Central Committee and the Secretariat of the Italian Communist Party Central Committee obediently fell in line, as well.[49] By involving the other Cominform members, the Kremlin not only hoped to subdue the Yugoslavs, but to preempt such insubordination on the part of other Communist Parties.

Archival documents reveal that by the spring of 1948, Moscow had begun to prepare a similar "case" against Gomułka and the Polish leadership. On April 5, 1948, the Foreign Policy Department of the Soviet Central Committee presented Suslov with a long memorandum "On the anti-Marxist ideological positions of the leaders of the Polish Workers' Party." The memorandum had evidently been prepared upon the Soviet leadership's orders, like its March 18 forerunner indicting the Yugoslavs, and was remarkably similar to that document in tone and content. In fact, one of the drafts of the "Polish Memorandum" is dated March 24.[50]

Like the Yugoslav leaders, the Polish Communist leadership was accused of departing from Marxist-Leninist theory; ignoring the Stalinist stage of development as well as the importance of Soviet experience; and regressing to nationalist positions. In order to illustrate Poland's perfidy, the memorandum quoted some statements by Gomułka and other Polish Workers' Party leaders, as well as by the Party press, which suggested that Poland's path to socialism diverged somewhat from the Soviet Union's. After the war, Stalin himself had endorsed these divergences in a number of private conversations with Western statesmen and with East European Communist leaders, but such ideas were now not only deemed inimical to the foundations of Marxism-Leninism and interpreted as an attempt to reconcile the ideology of the Polish Workers' Party with that of the Polish Socialist Party, but as outright opposition to the Soviet Union, as well.

As in the Yugoslav case, the memorandum charged the Polish leadership with trying to minimize and even ignore the role of the USSR in the liberation of Poland from Nazi occupation. While the Yugoslavs were accused of harboring a negative attitude to Soviet military advisers, the Poles were charged with attempting to get rid of the Soviet generals and officers who had been in the Polish Army since it was formed in the USSR in 1943-44. Finally, as in the Yugoslav case, the memorandum particularly emphasized the unwillingness of the Polish Workers' Party in implementing collectivization in the countryside.

The Foreign Policy Department of the Soviet Central Committee had previously expressed its dissatisfaction with Gomułka,[51] and its abhorrence of nationalist manifestations in the PPR's policy. However, the ultimate tone and the conclusions of the "Polish Memorandum" were significantly harsher than they would otherwise have been due to the Kremlin's show-down with Belgrade. Moscow was determined to nip any insurgency in the bud. Poland evidently figured as a prime candidate for the Kremlin's prophylactic measures, not only because the Soviets were discomfited by Gomułka's attempts to depart, if only somewhat, from the Soviet model, but also because the Polish leader had wavered in endorsing the establishment of the Cominform at the conference of the nine CPs in 1947. Gomułka had also vacillated in the spring of 1948 on the Yugoslav question. According to scattered evidence, when Gomułka received the first Soviet letter addressed to the Yugoslavs (March 27, 1948) he expressed some doubt regarding the legitimacy of the accusations leveled at the Yugoslav leaders.[52]

The March 18 memorandum on the Yugoslav question became the basis for subsequent Soviet letters attacking the Yugoslavs, as well as for Zhdanov's report at the Cominform conference of 1948. The composition of a similar memorandum regarding the Polish leadership demonstrates that as early as spring, 1948, Moscow intended to take serious action against the Poles. The main propositions of the memorandum presented to Suslov in April formed the core of charges of "Right-nationalist deviation" which were brought against Gomułka six months later, at the August-September 1948 plenum of the Polish party's Central Committee. In Poland, however, the Poles themselves did the Soviets' dirty work and took action against the "the Right-nationalist deviation" and Gomułka.[53]

As the Poles were brought to heel, Moscow also turned its attention to the Czechoslovak Communist leadership. The Soviets proceeded methodically and predictably; on the same day, the Foreign Policy Department of the Soviet Central Committee presented Suslov with a memorandum which was entitled "On some mistakes by the Communist Party of Czechoslovakia."[54] In this case, the charges were reminiscent of those leveled at the Yugoslavs and Poles, but of a somewhat less serious nature: the Czechoslovak leaders were accused of holding "anti-Marxist" positions concerning a peaceful road to socialism for Czechoslovakia"; spreading parliamentary illusions; substituting a Social Democratic approach for Bolshevik principles of organization in the building of the Party; underestimating the Kulak element; and lacking a clear program for socialist reorganization of the countryside. The Soviets were less severe in reproaching the Czechoslovak leadership, which subsequently demonstrated considerable zeal in carrying out Soviet directives.

Having dispatched its March 27 letter (about the Yugoslavs) to the leaders of the East European members of the Cominform, Moscow required that they take a stand on the conflict. Stalin's calculations proved correct: no one dared to contradict the Soviet line, although some (especially the Hungarians) were more ardent in their expression of loyalty than others (the Poles and the Czechoslovaks). Nevertheless, all the East European Parties joined the Kremlin in its condemnation of

Yugoslavia, thereby increasing the pressure upon Yugoslavia to submit and underscoring their own submission.

After ensuring that the Cominform member parties would play their prescribed roles, the Soviet leadership announced in a letter to the Yugoslavsdated May 4, 1948, that "the Soviet-Yugoslav differences" would be examined "at the next meeting of the Information Bureau." A subsequent letter sent to Tito over Suslov's signature proposed that the Information Bureau meet "in the first half of June, around June 8-10... in one of the southern regions of the Ukraine."[55] The leaders of the other Cominform member parties received similar letters.[56]

In reply, Tito, who had previously invited Soviet representatives to Belgrade in order to resolve the conflict, fired off letters to Suslov, Stalin, and Molotov. In them, the Yugoslav leadership refused to discuss the problem at a meeting of the Cominform. They justified their refusal by asserting that the other Cominform member parties had already assumed anti-Yugoslav attitudes on the basis of Soviet charges.[57] But in a May 22 letter drafted by Zhdanov, Stalin, and Molotov, the Soviets informed the CPY Central Committee that "the Central Committee of the CPSU(b) insists on a discussion of the question of the situation in the Yugoslav CP at the next meeting of the Information Bureau," which would be postponed "to the second half of June." The letter plainly stated that the discussion would take place "regardless of whether or not representatives of the Central Committee of the CPY are present," and declared that "refusal to attend the Information Bureau signifies that the Central Committee of the CPY has broken away from the united socialist front of the people's democracies with the Soviet Union," and chosen to travel the road of "treason to the cause of international solidarity of the working people."[58]

The leaders of all the other Cominform parties agreed to the Soviet proposal to hold a conference to discuss the Yugoslav question. Gomułka's supposed attempt – often referred to in the historiography – to "mediate" between Moscow and Belgrade, consisted of his May 25 appeal to the CPY Central Committee, in which he argued that the Yugoslavs ought to take part in the forthcoming conference of the Cominform. Dutifully informing the Soviet Central Committee of his intentions, Gomułka impressed upon the Yugoslavs that their absence at the conference would "inevitably lead" to "breaking with the world revolutionary movement, with all the consequences this entailed." Gomułka expressed his readiness to travel to Belgrade in order to persuade the Yugoslavs of this, but Tito disliked the way in which Gomułka had posed the question, and the visit did not take place.[59]

As for Wilhelm Pieck's ostensible attempt at mediation, which is likewise mentioned in the historiography without further elaboration, the archives contain a June 8 letter to Tito in which Pieck proposed that they meet in Sofia, where the East German leader intended to celebrate Dimitrov's sixty-sixth birthday. Although the letter expressed Pieck's willingness to talk with Tito, it was strangely reticent on what they would in fact talk about.[60] Needless to say, Tito did not go to Sofia.

As it turns out, Gheorghiu-Dej had made the first attempt to sway the Yugoslavs, and in a May 16 conversation with the Yugoslav ambassador, had argued that the Yugoslavs' boycott of the Cominform conference would sow the seeds of dissent between the CPY and other CPs, and would thereby "help the enemy." He advised the Yugoslav leadership to placate Moscow by admitting to at least some of their "errors," and to dispatch to Moscow a Yugoslav delegation headed by Tito so as to regularize relations and end the conflict through direct talks with the Soviet Central Committee.[61] The documents at our disposal do not show whether Gheorghiu-Dej was acting upon his own initiative or by prior agreement with the Kremlin. A few days later, however, he said in a conversation with N. L. Norovkov, a functionary of the Foreign Policy Department of the Soviet Central Committee, that the Yugoslavs had made egregious mistakes, which had to be corrected as soon as possible.[62] According to some reports sent by Yugoslav representatives in Moscow to Belgrade, the Soviet side had intimated in late May-early June 1948 that the conflict could be settled if the Yugoslavs acknowledged that they had taken an incorrect stand on at least some points.[63]

But the Yugoslav leadership did not think it advisable to follow this course of action. On May 21, Tito said in his conversation with V. V. Moshetov, deputy head of the Foreign Policy Department of the Soviet Central Committee, that the Yugoslavs might be willing to discuss confidentially some possible mistakes with the Soviets. However, Tito stated, since Moscow had already taken it upon itself to inform other Cominform member parties of the issue, the Yugoslavs would not participate in any general discussion. According to Moshetov's report to Suslov, Tito suggested the issue be taken up again when things had "settled down."[64]

Judging from Soviet Central Committee documents, preparations were in full swing in Moscow for a Cominform conference on the Yugoslav issue. The Soviets were combing archival documents for compromising materials concerning the activities of the CPY in the 1930s.[65] Eventually, their efforts yielded some information which was appropriately doctored and included in Zhdanov's report to the Cominform.[66] In early June, draft documents for the future conference were being prepared. First, a draft resolution of the Cominform, *On the situation in the Communist Party of Yugoslavia,* was drawn up under Zhdanov's supervision. The first draft was presented to Stalin, and revised according to his instructions, so that the accusations against the Yugoslavs were even more vituperative.[67] The revision process was repeated several times.

A week before the Cominform conference, a dress-rehearsal of sorts took place, in the form of an editorial board meeting of *For a Lasting*

Peace – For a People's Democracy! It was held on June 12 in Belgrade, where the Cominform headquarters and the newspaper's editorial offices were still located. The meeting had been prompted by Ziherl's June 7 letter (written on the behest of the CPY Central Committee) to editor-in-chief Pavel Yudin, in which he protested the publication of materials which, without directly referring to the CPY, quite clearly supported the Soviet position on the Yugoslav question. Ziherl decried this as "a line of indirect attack on the Communist Party of Yugoslavia," and also protested the exclusion, or significant abridgment of Yugoslav views on the conflict. At the editorial meeting, all of the Cominform member parties repudiated Ziherl's position, and condemned the Yugoslavs. The editorial board then passed a resolution stating that "the anti-Soviet and anti-Marxist policy of the Central Committee of the CPY deserves to be criticized directly, not indirectly."[68]

Until recently, we have known virtually nothing about the June 19-23, 1948 Cominform conference, which was held in Romania, rather than in Ukraine. Its participants did not mention it in their memoirs, as Eugenio Reale, Kardelj, and Djilas had done in the case of the inaugural Cominform meeting.[69] However, recently available archival materials have shed some light on the second conference.[70] According to these documents, the Communist Party delegations toed Moscow's line from the outset. In contrast to the first conference, where Gomułka had made an attempt to oppose the Soviet leadership's proposal on the organization of the Cominform,[71] not the slightest attempt was made to challenge the Soviet stand.

At the opening session of the conference on June 19, Zhdanov's repeated his proposal – this time on behalf of the Cominform – to invite the CPY delegates to attend the conference.[72] This was merely a tactical maneuver, since the Soviet side had every reason to believe that Belgrade would decline, and thereby conveniently confirm the Soviets' accusations.[73] Belgrade's chance acceptance of the invitation would likewise suit Moscow, for it would provide the ideal opportunity to hold a trial of the Yugoslav Communists in person. Something along those lines had already occurred at the editorial board meeting of *For a Lasting Peace – For a People's Democracy!* Either way, the Soviets were assured of victory, and no doubt cognizant of this fact, the Yugoslavs refused to attend the Cominform conference.[74] While the conference breathlessly awaited the Yugoslavs' reply, Zhdanov, Malenkov, and Suslov made use of the caesura to "lobby" representatives of the other parties, ascertaining their positions and inducing them to accept Soviet guidelines. In the course of these conversations, the Soviet side insisted on the following version of events: the Yugoslav leadership had clearly been infiltrated by agents of Western special services![75] This version swiftly gained currency, thanks to the efforts of Traicho Kostov and Palmiro Togliatti.[76]

Zhdanov's report, delivered on June 21, largely reiterated the standard accusations against Belgrade, with the surprising inclusion of the immediate cause of the conflict – Yugoslavia's aspirations with respect to Albania.[77] The participants in the "discussion" parroted the main theses of Zhdanov's report. All of them took an irreconcilably anti-Yugoslav stand. Apart from the obvious desire to curry favor with Moscow (Rákosi outdid all the rest in this respect), almost all participants at the meeting manifested a desire to avenge themselves on Belgrade for its former privileged position in the Soviet bloc in the first postwar years, for its haughtiness and its criticism of the other CPs when it was the Soviet Union's number one ally. Party leaders in countries bordering Yugoslavia, especially the Bulgarians, had some old accounts to settle with Belgrade on border issues as well as on the controversial South Slav or Balkan federation.[78]

Curiously enough, in discussing the draft resolution, even Rákosi, who was supported by Jakob Berman, suggested formulating a more moderate version of the statement regarding collectivization in the East European countryside. Although they had exhibited considerable loyalty and zeal in their support of Soviet accusations against the Yugoslavs, the Communist leaders feared that they would be obliged to step up the collectivization campaign in compliance with the draft resolution. Since this would quite clearly be politically problematic, both Rákosi and Berman asserted that since the peasants in their countries abhorred the idea of collective farms, any mention of collectivization could be used by opponents of "People's Democracy." They produced a more moderate version, which replaced "collectivization" with "cooperation" and appended a phrase about the voluntary nature of cooperation, which was to be implemented in stages after "most of the toiling peasantry" had been convinced of the advantages of collective farming. Zhdanov rejected the initial part of the proposal and adopted, with some amendment, the second one. Neither Rákosi nor Berman dared to dispute the matter further.[79]

The final resolution was almost a carbon copy of the Soviet draft, and has been frequently analyzed in the historiography. However, apart from the resolution, the conference adopted several other decisions on the Yugoslav issue which were not publicized, including the relocation of the Cominform's headquarters – along with the editorial offices of its newspaper – from Belgrade to Bucharest.[80] The conference also moved to disband the Belgrade Trade-Union Convention and the Council of Balkan Youth, on the pretext that the two organizations interfered with concerted action by the World Federation of Trade Unions and the World Federation of Democratic Youth.[81]

Twelve days after the Cominform conference, on July 5, 1948, the Cominform Secretariat convened to adopt measures designed to implement the conference's decisions. It also discussed how Cominform member parties should respond to Yugoslav invitations to send delegations to the Fifth Congress of the CPY which was to commence on July 21, 1948. Rákosi had suggested that all the parties send delegations, and attempt to "influence the situation in Yugoslavia," – that is, denounce the Yugoslav leadership. At the Secretariat's meeting, however, Suslov stated that "the Central Committee of the CPSU(b) considers it inexpedient to send delegations to the Fifth Congress of the CPY."[82] As a result, not a single Party sent representatives to the Congress.

Thus, Moscow was effectively able to isolate and neutralize the intransigent Yugoslav leadership, and its actions were endorsed by the Cominform. Although the Cominform-member countries might have been somewhat gratified to see the Yugoslav leadership dislodged from its pedestal, they were quailed by its fate, and effectively dissuaded from diverging from the course charted by the Soviets. With the consent of all but the Yugoslavs, the Kremlin had forged an organizational weapon – the Cominform – with which to control the Communist movement and the Soviet Bloc.

Notes

1· On the Yugoslav social and political system see: V. Koštunica and K. Čavoški, *Stranački pluralizam ili monizam: Društveni pokreti i politički sistem u Jugoslaviji 1944-1949*, (Belgrade, 1983); B. Petranović, *Politička i ekonomska osnova narodne vlasti u Jugoslaviji za vreme obnove* (Belgrade, 1969); idem, *Istorija Jugoslavije 1918-1988*, vol. 3, (Belgrade, 1988) 29-119. On Yugoslav foreign policy see: B. Petranović, *Istorija*, vol. 3, 162-196; L. Ia. Gibianskii, *Sovietskii Soiuz i novaia Iugoslavia, 1941-1947 gg*, (Moscow, 1987), 140-192.

2. See, e.g., A. A. Zhdanov's report at the ceremonial meeting in Moscow on November 6, 1946, for the 29th anniversary of the October Revolution. *Pravda*, November 7, 1946; and V. M. Molotov's report at a similar meeting on November 6, 1947, for the 30th anniversary. *Pravda,* November 7, 1947.

3. See L. Ia. Gibianskii, *Sovietskii Soiuz i novaia Jugoslavia*, 140-192.

4. *Borba*, May 28, 1945.

5. *Arhiv Jugoslavije* (Belgrade), F.507, CK, SKJ (later, AJ-CK SKJ), l-I/22, l. 18, 52; M. Djilas,*Vlast i pobuna* (Belgrade, 1991) 81-82; Lj. Djurić, *Sećanja na ljude i dogadjaje,* (Belgrade, 1989), 285.

6. The ambassador also discussed the matter with Tito when he gave him the telegram. See: *Arhiv Josipa Broza Tita (Belgrade), F. Kabinet Maršala Jugoslavije* (henceforth, AJBT-KMJ), I-3-b/634; Arkhiv vneshnei politiki Rossiiskoi

Federatsii [Foreign Policy Archives of the Russian Federation, henceforth, AVPRF], f. 0144, op. 30, p. 118, d. 16, l. 28-30.

7. AVPRF, f. 0144, op. 30, p. 118, d. 16, l. 75, 109-110.

8. AJ-CK SKJ III/21; AVPRF, f. 0144, op. 30, p. 118, d. 16, l. 75-76.

9. Arhiva Saveznog sekretarijata za inostrane poslove. (Belgrade), Politička arhiva (henceforth, ASSIP-PA), 1947 god, F-IV, Str. Pov. 1234; AJBT-KMJ, I-3-b/639, 1.2-3.

10· AJBT-KMJ, I-2/17, I.70. AVPRF, f. 06, op. 9, p. 82, d. 1285, l. 79, 84, 119; Tsentralen durzhaven arkhiv, Sofia (henceforth, TsDA), TsDA, f. 146, op. 4, a. e. 639, l. 9, and op. 6, a. e. 1064, l. 1.

11. AJBT-KMJ, I-2/17. l. 69; ASSIP-PA, 1947 god, F-IV. Str. Pov. 1685.

12. RTsKhIDNI, f. 77, op. 3, d. 92, l. 46-47, 52-54.

13. AVPRF, f. 0144, op. 30, p. 118, d. 10, l. 1-3; d. 15, l. 38-39, 45, 76; "Poslednii visit I. Broza Tito k. I.V. Stalinu," *Istoricheskii Arkhiv*, no. 2, (1993), 23, 26.

14. "Poslednii visit," 23, 26.

15. AJBT-KMJ, I-3-b/651, l. 1-5; ASSIP-PA, 1947 god, F-IV. Str. Pov. 1765.

16. AJBT-KMJ, I-3-b/651, l. 1,2.

17. RTsKHIDNI, f. 77, op. 3, d. 99, l. 1-5, 8; AJBT-KMJ, I-3-b/651, l. 1-5; ASSIP-PA, 1947 god, F-IV. Str. Pov. 1765.

18. AJBT-KMJ, I-3-b/651, l. 6.

19. AJBT-KMJ, I-3-b/651, l. 10-11, M. Djilas, *Razgovori sa Staljinom*, (Belgrade, 1990), 93-95; idem, *Vlast i pobuna*, 127-128.

20. RTsKhIDNI, f. 575, op. 1, d. 41, l. 23.

21. Ibid., l. 22.

22. Ibid., l. 22.

23. For more details, see: I. V. Bukharkin and L. Ia. Gibianskii, "Pervie schagi konflikta," in *Rabochii klass i sovremennyi mir* no. 5, 1990 (Moscow), 159-163;

24. AJ-CK SKJ, IX, 1/I-154, l. 1-2; AJBT-KMJ, I-3-b/34; I-3-b/651, l. 24.

25. Djilas,*Vlast i pobuna*, 125.

26. For more details, see: Bukharkin and Gibianskii, "Pervie schagi konflikta," 152-159; Gibianskii, "Vyzov v Moskvu," in *Politicheskiie issledovaniia*, no. 1, 1991 (Moscow), 201.

27. See Gibianskii, "U nachala konflikta: balkanskii uzel," *Rabochii klass i sovremennyi mir*, no. 2, 1990: 181-185.

28. Until recently, only Dedijer's books, and the memoirs of Djilas and Kardelj provided information on the proceedings, but scholars have now unearthed relevant documents in the Yugoslav, Bulgarian, and Soviet archives. Tito's archives in Belgrade have yielded two important documents: a coded telegram with a brief report of the meeting, which the Yugoslav delegates sent on the following day to Belgrade; and a detailed hand-written account, prepared by

Djilas upon his return to Belgrade (see: AJBT-KMJ, I-3-b/65, l. 33-40). The Soviet minutes of the February 10 meeting were found in the archives of the Political Bureau of the Central Committee of the CPSU(b), which are now the archives of the President of the Russian Federation. The document has not yet been declassified.

29. The February 10, 1948 conference and its outcome are examined on the basis of new materials from the archives in: L. Ia. Gibianskii, "K istorii sovetsko-iugoslavskovo konflikta 1948-1953 gg.: sekretnaia sovietsko-iugoslavo-bolgarskaia strecha v Moskve 10 fevralia 1948 goda,"*Sovietskoie slavianovedenie* (since 1992 *Slavianovedenie*

30. AJ-CK SKJ, III/31a.

31. AJ-CK SKJ, III/32; Dedijer, *Novi prilozi za biografiju Josipa Broza Tita,* vol. 3 (Belgrade, 1984), 303-307.

32. AJ-CK SKJ, IX, 1/I-135, 1/I-166, 1/I-169; RTsKhIDNI, f. 17, op. 128, d. 472, l. 78-79, 84-86; AJBT-KMJ, I-3-b/35, l.l,3.

33. AJBT-KMJ, I-3-b/651, l. 37-38.

34. B. Heuser, *Western "Containment" Policies in the Cold War: The Yugoslav Case, 1948-1953,* (London and New York, 1989), 29, 31.

35. AJBT-KMJ, I-2/35. In a letter sent to the Soviet Central Committee on June 15, 1948, when he had just learned of the Soviet-Yugoslav conflict, Zachariades tried to justify himself in the eyes of the Soviet leadership by alleging that at the above-mentioned meeting in Belgrade (he mistakenly dates it March 1948). Tito himself proposed to furnish further aid to the partisans in Greece, despite Stalin's attitude. (RTsKhIDNI, f. 17, op. 128, d. 1160, l. 61).

36. AJ-CK SKJ, III/32; Dedijer, *Novi prilozi,* vol. 3, 304-307.

37. See, for example, AVPRF, f. 0144, op. 30, p. 118, d. 15, l. 112-113; d. 16, l. 75-76.

38. "Sekretnaia sovetsko-iugoslavskaia perepiska 1948 goda" *Voprosy Istorii,* no. 4/5 (1992), 122.

39. "Sekretnaia perepiska," 135.

40. "Konflikt, kotorovo ne dolzhno bylo byt' (iz istorii sovietsko-iugoslavskikh otnoshenii)," *Vestnik MID SSR* no. 6, 1990 (Moscow), 60.

41. AVPRF, f. 202, op. 5, p. 110, d. 1, l. 17.

42. "Sekretnaia perepiska," 124-125.

43. "Sekretnaia perepiska," 125-126.

44. RTsKhIDNI, f. 17, op. 128, d. 1163, l. 9; see also l. 16.

45. Ibid., l. 9-24.

46. See the publications *Pisma TsK KPJ i pisma TK SKP (b)* and "Sekretnaia perepiska," *Voprosy Istorii,* no. 4/5, 6/7, 10.

47. Zhdanov quoted this part of the correspondence in full in his report at the Cominform conference. See *The Cominform: Minutes of the Three Conferences, 1947/1948/1949* (Milan, Feltrinelli Foundation, 1994). 532-537.

48. RTsKhIDNI, f. 575, op. 1, d. 62, l. 31-32, 71-72; AJBT-KMJ, I-3-b/549; J. Ptasiński, *Pierwszy z trzech zwrotów czyli rzecz o Władysławie Gomułce,* (Warsaw, 1984), 111; A. Werblan, *Władysław Gomułka: Sekretarz Generalny PPR* (Warszawa, 1988), 520-521; Djilas, *Vlast i pobuna,* 155.

49. AJBT-KMJ, I-3-b/212;I-3-b/142, l. 1-4; I-3-b/184; I-3-b/328; RTsKHIDNI, f. 575, op. 1, d. 46, l. 52-53, 75.

50. RTsKhIDNI, f. 17, op. 128, d. 1161, l. 2-19; f. 575, op. 1, d. 375, l. 143.

51. See, for example, f. 575, op. 1, d. 32, l. 26-28.

52. J. Ptasiński, *Pierwszy,* 111; A. Werblan, *Władysław Gomułka,* 520-521.

53. It is interesting to note the editorial changes in the text of J. Berman's speech at the second Cominform conference when it was included in the minutes. Referring to the proliferation of petty-bourgeois nationalist sentiments among the members of the Polish Workers' Party, Berman stressed that the rank-and-file members were particularly affected. When editing the speech, Soviet representatives deleted "rank-and-file members" (RTsKhIDNI, f. 575, op. 1, d. 47, l.6). In light of the Soviets' plan to launch an attack against Gomułka, these words did not serve their interests.

54 RTsKhIDNI, f. 575, op. 1, d. 39, l. 164-193.

55. "Secretnaia perepiska," *Voprosy istorii,* no. 10, 151-152.

56. RTsKHIDNI, f. 77, op. 3, d. 103, l. 1-3.

57. "Sekretnaia perepiska," *Voprosy istorii,* no. 10, 152-153.

58. Ibid., 154-155.

59. AJBT-KMJ, I-3-b/514, l. 1,5,6;Archiwum Akt Nowych (Warsaw), 295/VII-73, k. 12-13a, 16-17.

60. AJBT-KMJ, I-3-b/443.

61. AJBT-KMJ, I-3-b/549, l. 2-3.

62. RTsKhIDNI, f. 17, op. 128, d. 1160, l. 146, 148.

63. AJ SKJ, CK SKJ IX, 1-I/24, l. 23-26; Dedijer, *Novi prilozi,* vol. 3, 354-357.

64. RTsKhIDNI, f. 17, op. 128, d. 1163, l. 73.

65. RTsKhIDNI.f. 17, op. 128, d. 1163, l. 52-68; f. 495, op. 277, d. 21, l. 330-337; f. 575, op.1, d. 411, l. 1-146.

66. RTsKhIDNI, f. 77, op. 3, d. 105, l. 49-50; f. 575, op. 1, d. 46, l. 33-34.

67. RTsKhIDNI, f. 77, op. 3, d. 104, l.1-26.

68. RTsKhIDNI, f. 575, op. 1, d. 52, l. 15-16, 18-24.

69. E. Reale, *Avec Jacques Duclos au Banc des Accuses a la Reunion Constitutive du Kominform a Szklarska Poręba, 22-27 September 1947* (Paris, 1958); E. Kardelj, *Borba za priznanje i nezavisnost nove Jugoslavije 1944-1957: Sećanja* (Belgrade and Ljubljana, 1980); Djilas, *Vlasti i pobuna.*

70. Archival documents currently available include the conference's minutes and texts of its participants; Zhdanov's notes, as well as the notes of L. S. Baranov, deputy head of the C.C. Foreign Policy Department; and the Soviet delegation's daily reports to Stalin. RTsKhIDNI, f. 575, op. 1, d. 46, 47, 48; f. 77, op. 3, d. 106, 107, 108. The minutes are published in *The Cominform...,* 506-623.

71. For further details, see: L. Ia. Gibianskii, "Kak voznik Kominform. Po novym arkhivnym materialam." *Novaia i noveishaia istoriia,* no. 4, (1993); Idem. "La costituzione del Cominform (alla luce di nuovi materiali d'archivio)," *Storia contemporanea,* no. 4, (1993).

72. *The Cominform,* 506-511.

73. RTsKhIDNI, f. 77, op. 3, d. 106, l. 21.

74. *The Cominform,* 512-515. The Yugoslavs published their refusal.

75. Stalin was informed of these conversations. RTsKhIDNI, f. 77, op. 3, d. 106, l. 5-18; d. 108, l. 6.

76. Ibid., d. 106, l. 6-7, 18.

77. *The Cominform,* 532-533. For the whole of the report, see *ibid.,* 522-541.

78. *Ibid.,* 556, 562-565, 574, 578; f. 77, op 3, d. 106, l. 5-6, 13, 15; d. 108, l. 18, 29, 30-31.

79. RTsKhIDNI, f. 575, op. 1, d. 48, l. 102-103.

80. *The Cominform,* 596-597.

81. *Ibid.,* 596-601.

82. RTsKhIDNI, f. 575, op. 1, d. 49, l. 2-5.

About the Contributors

Melissa Bokovoy is Assistant Professor of History, University of New Mexico.

Anna M. Cienciala is Professor of History, University of Kansas.

John Connelly is Assistant Professor of History, University of California, Berkeley.

Alexei Filitov is a Senior Researcher of the Institute of World History of the Russian Academy of Sciences (RAN).

Leonid Gibianskii is a Senior Researcher and a Group Head at the Institute of Slavonic and Balkan Studies of the Russian Academy of Sciences, ISBS-RAN.

Jan Gross is Professor of Political Science at N.Y.U. and editor, *East European Politics and Societies.*

Padraic Kenney is Assistant Professor of History, University of Colorado.

Igor Lukes is Associate Professor of International Relations, Boston University.

John Micgiel is Director of the Center for East Central Europe, Columbia University.

Norman Naimark is Robert and Florence McDonnell Professor of East European Studies and Chair of the History Department of Stanford University.

Scott Parrish is a researcher and writer at the Open Media Research Institute in Prague, the Czech Republic..

David Pike is Professor of German Studies at the University of North Carolina, Chapel Hill.

Yelena Valeva is a Senior Researcher of ISBS-RAN.

Vladimir Volkov is Director of ISBS-RAN.

Inessa Iazhborovskaia is a Senior Researcher at the Institute of Comparative Politology and Problems of Worker Movement-RAN.

Bela Zhelitski is a Senior Researcher at the Institute of Slavonic and Balkan Studies, Russian Academy of Sciences.

Index

About the Book and Editors

The collaborative effort of scholars from Russia and the United States, this book reevaluates the history of postwar Eastern Europe from 1944 to 1949, incorporating information gleaned from newly opened archives in Eastern Europe. For nearly five decades, the countries of Yugoslavia, Poland, Albania, Bulgaria, Romania, Hungary, Czechoslovakia, and the Soviet zone of Germany were forced to live behind the "iron curtain." Though their experiences under communism differed in sometimes fundamental ways and lasted no longer than a single generation, these nations were characterized by systematic assaults on individual rights and social institutions that profoundly shaped the character of Eastern Europe today. The emergence of the former People's Democracies from behind the iron curtain has been a wrenching process, but, as this book demonstrates, the beginning of the communist era was just as traumatic as its end.

With the opening of the archives in Russia and Eastern Europe, the contributors have been able to get a much firmer grasp on Soviet policies in the region and on East European responses and initiatives, which in turn has yielded more satisfying answers to vexing questions about Soviet intentions in the region and the origins of the Cold War. Exploring these events from a new, better-informed perspective, the contributors have made a valuable contribution to the historiography of postwar Europe.

Norman Naimark is Robert and Florence McDonnell Professor of East European Studies and chair of the history department of Stanford University. **Leonid Gibianskii** is a Senior Researcher of the Institute of Slavonic and Balkan Studies of the Russian Academy of the Sciences, ISBS-RAN.